ARCHITECTURE

FROM COMMISSION TO CONSTRUCTION

Jennifer Hudson

Published in 2012 by
Laurence King Publishing Ltd
361–373 City Road
London EC1V 1LR
Tel: +44 20 7841 6900
Fax: +44 20 7841 6910
e-mail: enquiries@laurenceking.com
www.laurenceking.com

A catalogue record for this book is available from the British Library

ISBN: 978 1 85669 823 8

Design: Draught Associates

Printed in China

Author's acknowledgements

The following pages are dedicated to Jon Vanner who kept me sane during the writing of this book.

I would like to offer my gratitude to the architects featured for their time and patience in answering my endless questions, and for their support in supplying me with the visual material, much of it not normally released for editorial use. I would also like to thank my editor, Susie May, for all her hard work and advice, the copy-editor, Tessa Clark, and the production, publicity and marketing departments here at Laurence King Publishing. In addition, I would like to acknowledge the expertise of Helen Cliffe of Draught Associates in producing such a clear graphic design from the mountain of images supplied to her and for putting up with my many additions and amendments throughout the various layout stages. Without all of the above, *Architecture From Commission to Construction* would not have been possible.

CONTENTS

Introduction

'A great building must begin with the unmeasurable, must go through the measurable means when it is being designed and in the end must be unmeasurable' – Louis Kahn

Generally speaking, architecture books fall into three categories. They are historical, theoretical or, most often, they concentrate on providing an analysis and criticism of completed buildings. In this selection of projects, however, I have sought to highlight the process involved in taking an architectural commission from concept through all the stages of design, development and construction to the end result.

The most obvious way to chart this progression was to consult the architects concerned, and the pages that follow are informed by direct interviews with lead architects as well as, in many cases, conversations with local architects and structural engineers. The selection was made on the basis of representing a rich background of practitioners and building genres. I have chosen individuals at different points in their careers, from published and lauded architects, who not only practise but also teach and theorize on their profession, to those who are less well known but whose work is nonetheless of a high quality. The content is international and the projects are diverse in scale, so the case studies express a variety of aspects of the built environment. Each one begins with an overview and is followed by extensively captioned illustrations that help the reader understand the methodologies adopted in each case: the project team's way of working together, be that collegiate or more hierarchical; how the brief was received and developed; presentation to the client (in some cases only one design was delivered while in others the architects opted to show alternatives for discussion); the development of the concept through sketching, physical model-making and computer-aided design (the last is still a hotbed of discussion – some architects use the computer in the design process itself, others see it only as a drawing and presentation tool and a minority consider the employment of renderings to be fraudulent); detailed design; collaboration with, and input from, architects of record, consultants, specialists and contractors; and, finally, the time spent on site.

The temptation when considering the design process is to simplify it to the key plan of work stages outlined by the Royal Institute of British Architects or equivalent international professional bodies of architects. Although the specifics may vary from country to country, they essentially comprise a 'prepare, design, construct and use' cycle that encompasses:

- Appraisal: The identification of the client's requirements and any possible constraints on development.
- Strategic brief: The preparation of the brief and a general outline of requirements, plus examination of the range of consultants and others to be employed on the project.
- First proposals: An outline of the proposals, and sketch plans to ensure they are functionally, technically and financially feasible.
- Schematic design: The development of the strategic brief into a project brief that includes the preparation of the concept design and the submission of planning applications and drawings.
- Final proposals: A detailed design of appearance and construction methods. This is the moment when building regulations have to be satisfied.
- Production information: Final decisions on every matter relating to the design, specification, construction and cost of the project.
- Tender documents and action: The identification of potential contractors and/or specialists for the construction of the project and the tender process.
- Mobilization: Handover of the site to the main contractor or project manager.
- Construction to practical completion: Operation on site to final construction.
- Completion: Final inspection to ensure the specifications have been met.
- Feedback: This allows for minor adjustments and for the final account to be settled.

However, to quantify the architect's role as a logical series of tasks in such a sequential order would be to do him/her a disservice. Although a cognitive procedure is necessary, it is interesting to observe (as the pages that follow attest) the extent to which the phases overlap and initial objectives are found to have more than one correct solution as the process advances. Problems that arise are understood through the attempts to solve them, and can become generative factors in the design. It is often the case that an architect makes refinements up to and during construction. Although from the outset he or she holds in his or her mind's eye an approximation of the outcome, each project is a journey that only the most inquisitive, creative and open of minds can navigate to address the issues, from technical to budgetary concerns, that are met along the way.

Above all, an architect can be likened to the conductor of an orchestra. Many of those published in this book are instantly recognizable names and it is all too easy to presume theirs is the sole signature on a building; but, of course, this is not so. Architecture is a joint venture both in-house (in the formation of a project team, how it is organized and the methods the principal and designers adopt to communicate with each other) and in collaboration with outside agents. Whether an architect is involved in a design-build or in a design-build bid contract where he/she hands over to another party (local architect or project manager) after detailed design for the tender and construction process to be completed, the success of a project is dependent on how well the architect can communicate and inspire confidence.

A mutually supportive relationship between architect and client – regardless of whether the latter is an individual or a committee representing an institution – is paramount. Some clients have very specific demands while others are less clear. It is the architect's role to outline possibilities based on his/her professional experience and aesthetic expression while delivering what clients think they want or, in many instances, what they can hope to expect. At its most rewarding, the liaison can be highly interactive and inventive, but in all cases it needs to be close and trusting. The best projects result from an open and communicative cooperation from first meeting to delivery. The more problematic schemes are those that are large-scale with extended schedules, when members of a client team may change with a concomitant loss in continuity, lack of personal commitment and little appreciation of the core concept. If the client is not going to occupy a building, the architect needs to assess the requirements of the user through observation-based evidence, participatory consultation with the third party or by imagining him/herself to be an occupant of the finished project and deciding what will make it appealing.

In his book *Design in Mind*, Bryan Lawson quotes the Austrian philosopher Ludwig Wittgenstein, who reportedly said: 'You think philosophy is difficult enough, but I tell you it is nothing to the difficulty of being a good architect.' Designing a building is one thing, but the responsibility it brings is immense. Architecture is not just the art and science of conceiving and erecting physical structures; it is not only the construction of space, form and ambience or the creative manipulation and coordination of material, technology, light and shadow. Architectural works can be perceived as cultural and political symbols and signifiers of an era but, more importantly, they are also where, day-to-day, we shelter, eat, sleep, work, raise our families, are entertained, educated and edified. More than fulfilling Vitruvius' three basic principles of *firmitas*, *utilitas* and *venustas*, or being limited to the Modern Movement's diktat that 'form follows function', a successful building today is not merely durable, practical and beautiful; it encompasses all criteria of use, perception and enjoyment, and psychologically stimulates and influences the way we live our lives and interact. Speaking as much for his profession as for himself, Sir Richard Rogers' words make a fitting conclusion: 'My passion and great enjoyment for architecture, and the reason the older I get the more I enjoy it, is because I believe we – architects – can affect the quality of life of the people.'

Villa Welpeloo

2012Architecten

Location: Enschede, The Netherlands
Principal use: Family residence
Client: T. J. Knol and I. E. C. Blans
Site area: 900 m² (9,687½ ft²)
Interior area: 250 m² (2,691 ft²)

Total build area: 310 m² (3,336¾ ft²)
Design period: May 2004 – May 2005
Construction period: November 2005 – November 2009
Budget: €900,000

Villa Welpeloo is a house made from 60 per cent recycled materials. It's the first building designed by 2012Architecten and acts as proof that the methodology the partners, Jan Jongert, Jeroen Bergsma and Césare Pereen, have been developing since the practice's foundation in 1997 can be applied to architecture. 2012 shot to prominence with a series of small projects, installations and exhibitions created to illustrate that the reuse of materials need not be confined to the DIY specialist but can result in highly original and innovative visual objects. In 2005 it launched the recyclicity.org website, an internet resource where demand and supply of recyclable, residual and scrap materials are brought together and where model projects are showcased.

2012's creativity lies in its awareness of the interaction between design and the availability of existing materials, and its motivation is the pursuit of minimal energy consumption by cutting down on processing and transport. In a leaflet produced by the practice to expound their philosophy a scenario is proposed. A chemical plant is demolished, and its tanks are driven to a scrapyard to be shredded and taken onwards to a steel factory a thousand miles away where the pieces are fed into a blast furnace and transformed into raw material. Rolled sheets of steel are then transported back to where the journey started to be welded into cylindrical shapes and used in a dance hall an architect has designed with curved walls. The text ends: 'Their [the walls'] dimensions are similar to the ones of the tanks they stem from. A lot of effort and energy could have been saved if the design of that cool dance hall had included Superuse.'

The Superuse Relevancy Factor is the means by which 2012 describes the amount of energy that has to be added to reuse a waste product. The architects have devised a standard procedure to source all the recyclable elements for their projects. They create what they refer to as a harvest map that shows available local material sources and indicates the geographical position, amounts, dimensions, availability and potential for each. In the case of Welpeloo a radius of 15 kilometres (9⅓ miles) was researched around Enschede where the villa was to be located.

The site is in the Roombeek district of Enschede, which was completely destroyed by a devastating explosion in a fireworks warehouse in 2000. The environmentally conscious clients are long-standing acquaintances of Jan Jongert and had earmarked the forward-looking studio to design their new home. As collectors of contemporary art, Knol and Blans' brief demanded a semi-public and private residence that could accommodate both living space and an area set aside to showcase their collection and mount exhibitions.

Most architects let their design dictate the materiality they choose, but 2010 used the harvest map to locate the fabric that informed the look and form of the villa. The main structure is made out of steel profiles that previously constituted a machine – the Paternoster – used for textile production, an industry once very important in the region. The façade is clad with wooden slats from redundant cable reels sourced at a local cable factory. The 1,000 reels provided enough material for the façade and interior walls. Wood for beams was taken from a demolished building nearby, as was the EPS, glass wool and reflective foil used for the insulation.

Jongert and Bergsma conducted a dynamic and ongoing dialogue with the clients through all stages of the design process. Two concepts were presented. The first was based on redundant railway sleepers that in the end couldn't be used because they were too toxic, but remained as inspiration for the form of the building, which was then developed with the steel structure. Presentations were made using renderings, 3-D and physical models, plans and the harvest map to give the clients the possibility of choosing from different materials.

The architects were pragmatic in using traditional products: steel, timber and polystyrene, albeit derived from unusual sources. The engineer, who is used to working with Superuse materials, was involved from schematic design to maximize their structural potential. The house was meticulously detailed and the architects collaborated closely with the contractors (the first was replaced by a second who was employed to complete the finishing work). To save resources 2012 would have preferred to work with pre-existing foundations but they were not extant. In the end, as the plot had three different soil depths and in order to make the newly built concrete foundation stable, a considerable amount of the budget and schedule was used in constructing supporting poles that had to be of a maximum length, measuring 40 centimetres by an incredible 22 metres (15¾ inches by 72 feet). Unforeseen circumstances, ironically associated with the use of new materials, delayed the build, which took almost four years to complete.

Jongert says, 'Saving money was of secondary importance: the objective was to save energy.' Welpeloo was completed for approximately €100,000 less than a standard construction, which seems a considerable saving but in percentage terms is minimal. The success of the project lies in the fact that 2012 has defined a new method of construction while meeting its energy objectives. With the façades emitting 5 per cent of the amount of CO_2 a cladding made from a new material would produce and the steel frame 12 per cent of the amount of a similar new structure, this modish villa demonstrates that 'green' need not mean a compromise on style.

1 / The Villa Welpeloo is made from 60% reclaimed materials. Its distinct form and materiality were determined by the availability of waste products surrounding the building site.

1

2

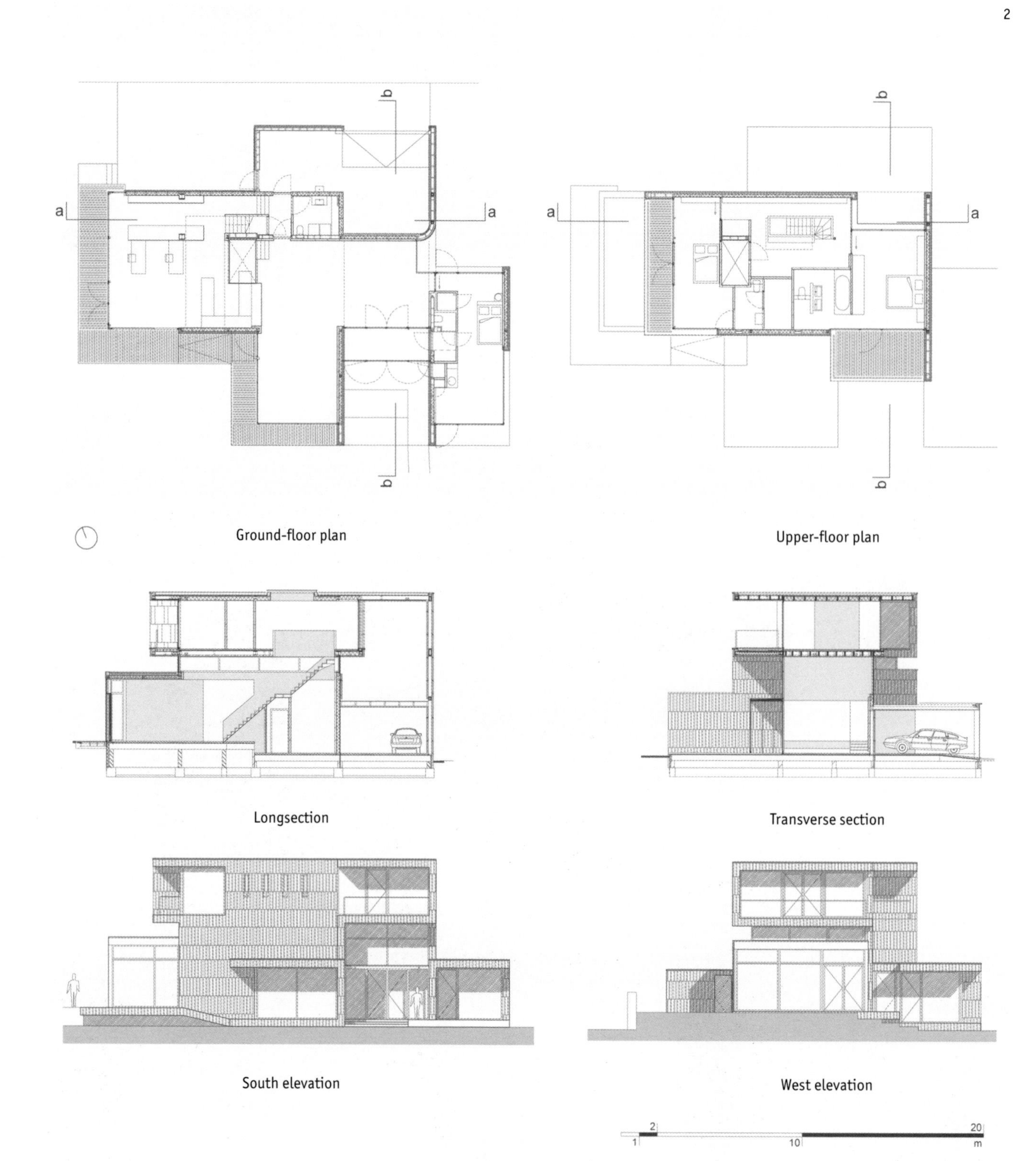

Ground-floor plan

Upper-floor plan

Longsection

Transverse section

South elevation

West elevation

3

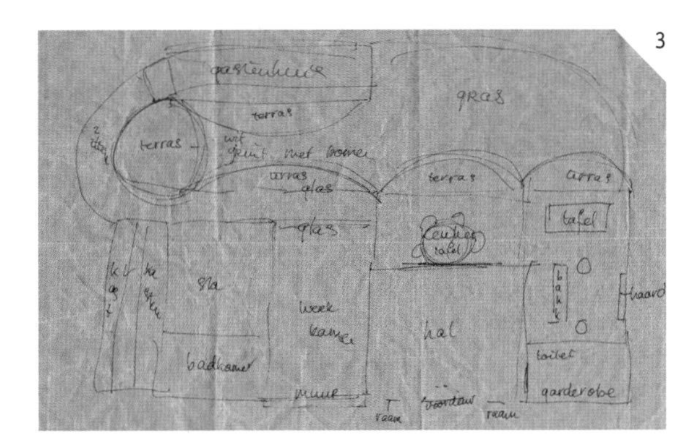

4

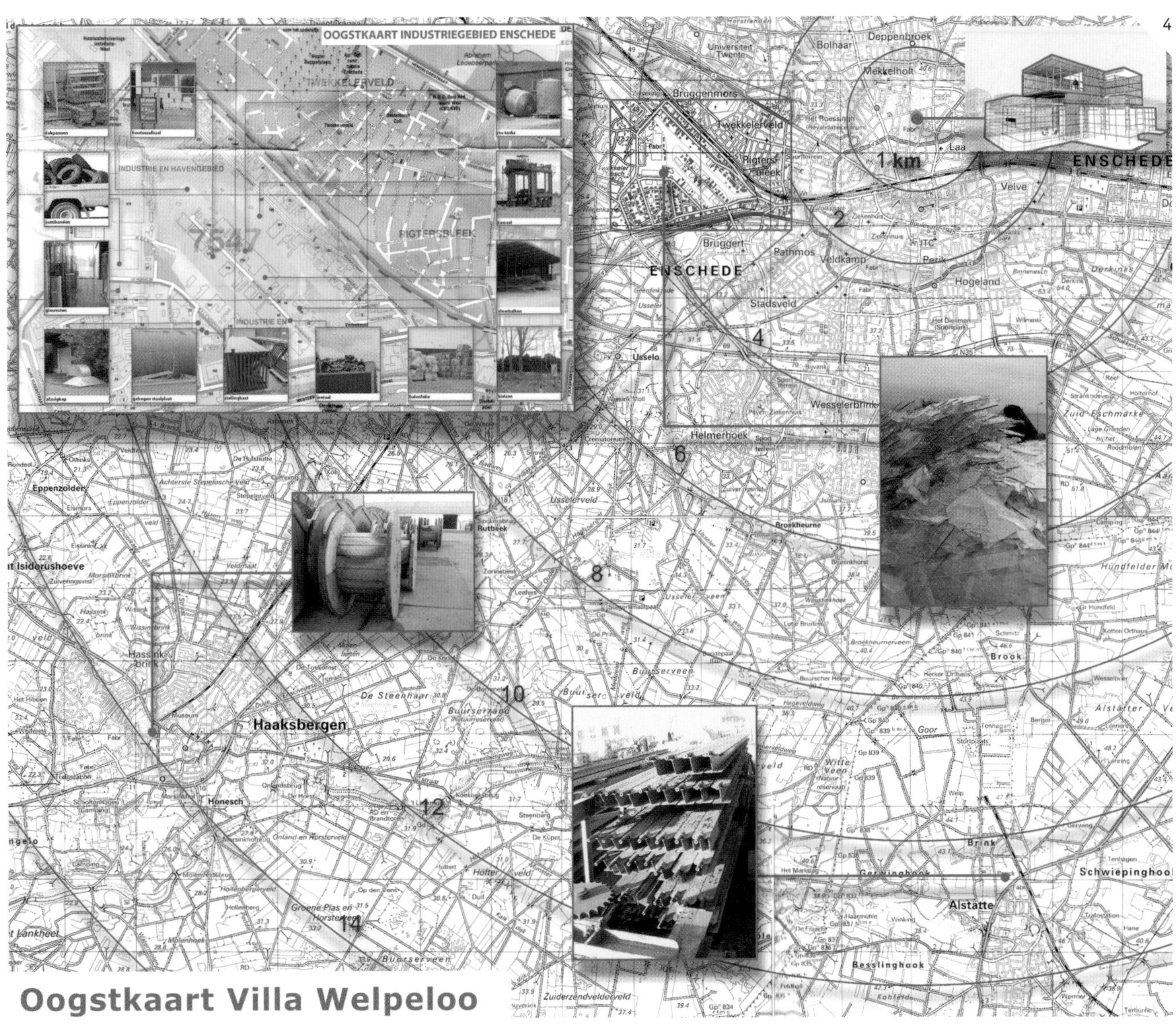

2/ Ground- and first-floor plans: The storage of artworks shapes the core of the building. The various spaces of the villa are formed by surfaces extending out of this central element that act as display walls for the clients' art collection.

3/ The clients' drawn programme.

4/ Harvest map of the area around Enschede: A harvest map typically reveals available material sources, derelict buildings, wastelands and infrastructures as well as potential energy sources. 2012 used to send out scouting teams but now has enough experience to rely on a list of industrial-waste sources produced by the Dutch Chamber of Commerce.

5

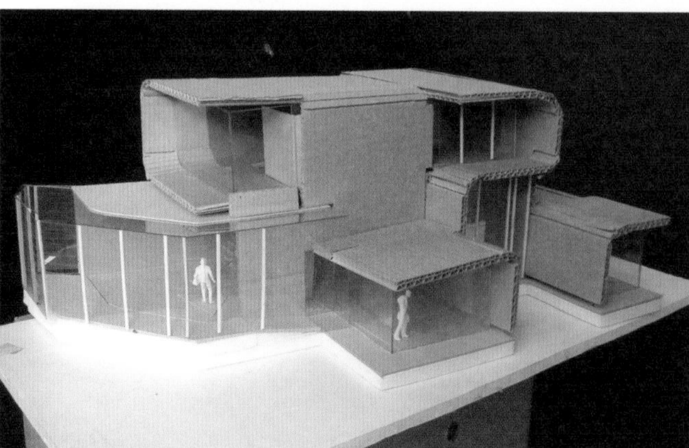

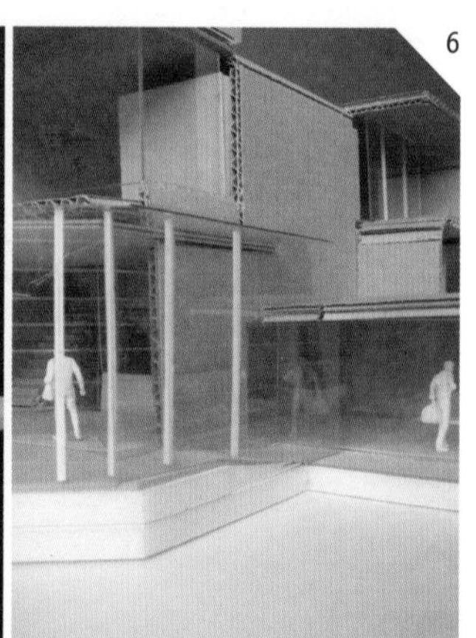

6

7

8

9

5 / Renderings: The architects held an ongoing dialogue with the clients throughout the design process. Ideas were presented using plans, renderings and physical models. These renderings for the concept were based on railway sleepers (left) and for the eventual building (right).

6 / Series of models made at different points in the schematic and design development stages: Models were made at 1:200 to 1:50 scales.

7 / Maquettes were produced to show how the façade might look. They were useful tools in instructing the contractor. 2012 prefer to work as part of the construction team, collaborating with the contractor from an early stage in design development to take advantage of his building knowledge. This led to difficulties in the case of Welpeloo as the architects hired a contractor local to their office rather than to the site, which resulted in delays and problems during the build. A second contractor was employed to finish the project.

8 / The Paternoster had been used to change large rolls of yarn quickly. It measured 4.14 x 10 x 6 m (13½ x 32¾ x 19¾ ft).

9 / The machine was dismantled. 2012 deliberated about whether or not to use the second-hand steel as it did not bear any quality marks. The structural engineer calculated for the lowest grade of steel in order to avoid problems with the local planning authorities.

10

12

13

11

10 / The steel sections were blasted, repainted and mostly kept to their original length. In the definitive design the width of the house had to be reduced by 10 cm (4 in) as the steel profiles were not long enough to fit the initial concept that had been based on using redundant railway sleepers. End plates were welded on so that the beams could be linked together.

11 / Cable reels were sourced for timber. They have a diameter of 1.2–3.5 m (4–11½ ft). The circular ends are connected by an axle of heartwood with planks of 0.6–1.33 m (2–4¼ ft) depending on the diameter. The planks were used to clad the house.

12 / The reels were dismantled. Around 2 m^2 (21½ ft^2) of wood is produced from every reel. This is preserved using a heat treatment invented by the Dutch company Plato (www.platowood.nl) The process is carried out using residual warmth pumped through a heat pipe from a nearby factory.

13 / A second-hand platform lift was used during construction and then tucked into a recess next to the kitchen to eventually be used to transport artworks between floors. The original plans had provided for an elevator, which had to be cut for budget reasons. Situating the platform lift means that routing is in place should funds become available to reinstate this aspect of the design.

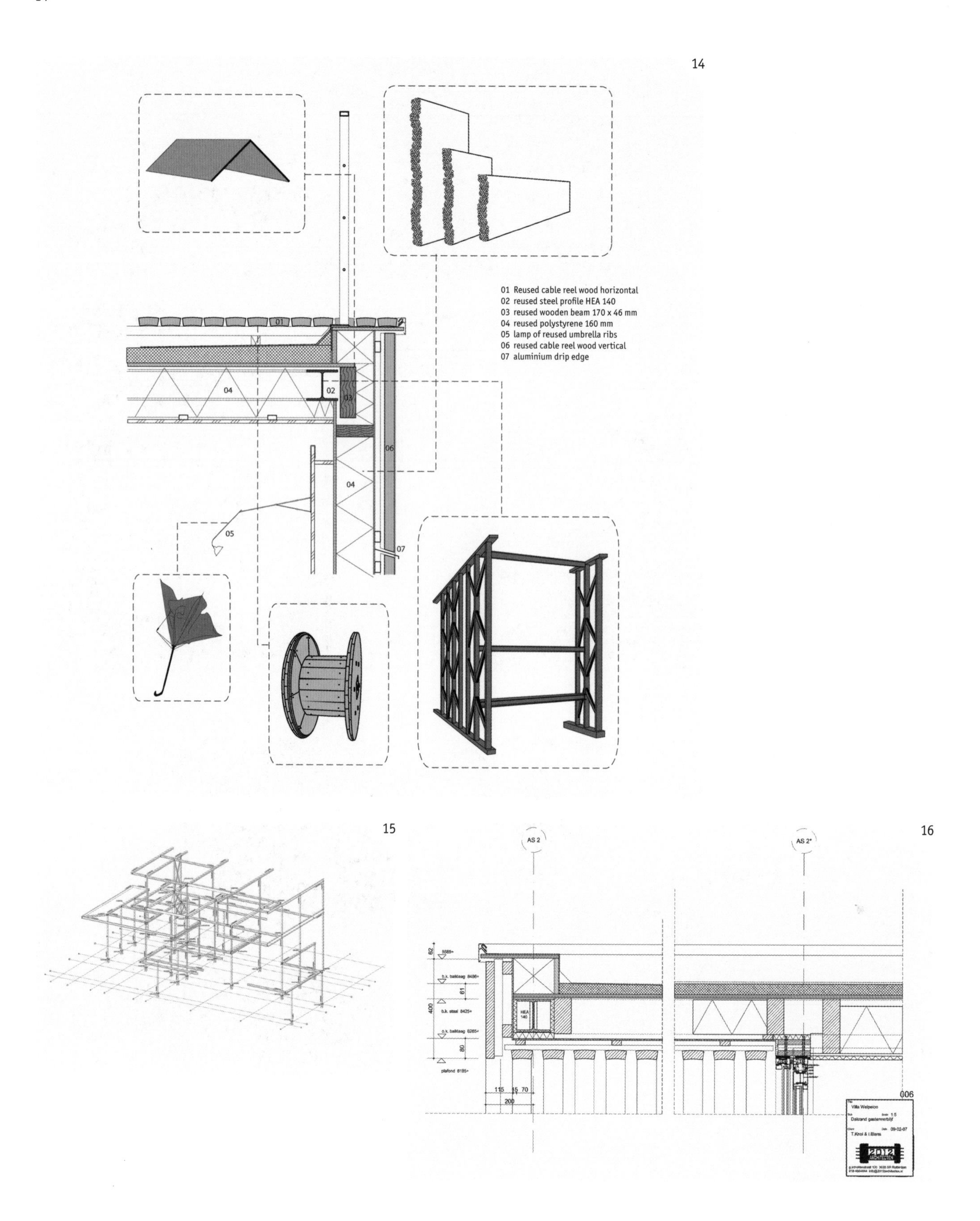

14 / Façade section: Fire safety requirements demanded that the reclaimed steel be concealed within a wooden secondary construction of second-hand beams. These were taken from the floors and roof of a dismantled building and insulated with reused polystyrene. The façade is clad with the cable-reel timber. Custom-made wall lights were designed by Stefan Lehner using recycled umbrella wire.

15 / Construction diagram of the steel frame.

16 / 2012 provided full tender and construction documents. Here a detail drawing shows a vertical section over the cantilevering balcony.

17

18

19

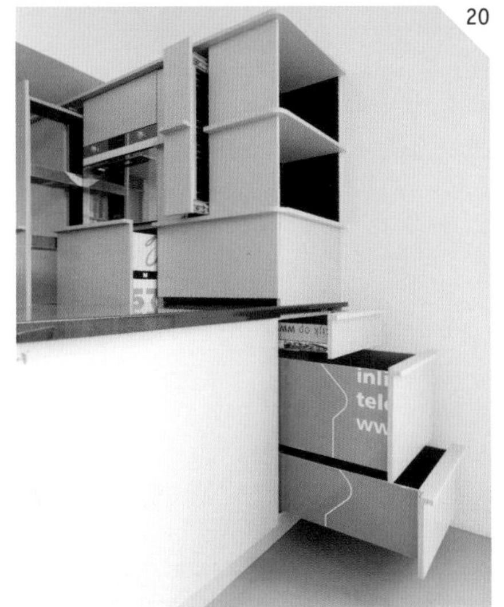

20

21

17 / Construction.

18 / View from the hall to the kitchen: This space is a semi-public private gallery used to stage exhibitions of young artists' work. The platform lift can be seen to the rear of the image.

19 / New materials included the concrete foundations, technical installations, the plasterboard used to finish the interior spaces, the stucco and the glazing. The contractor miscalculated one pane of insulating glass and had to reorder. 2012 managed to recycle the pane by adapting the size of the design of the skylight over the centre of the house.

20 / Part of the shelving was made from signboards from construction sites.

21 / The material used in the bathroom resembles stone but is made from recycled plastic cups melted down and formed into water-resistant panels by a company in the UK.

YTL Residence

Agence JouinManku

Location: Kuala Lumpur
Principal use: Private residence
Client: Malaysian family
Site area: 4,500 m^2 (48,437½ ft^2)
Interior area: 3,200 m^2 (34,445 ft^2)

Total build area: 4,000 m^2
Design period: September 2003 – September 2005
Construction period: September 2005 – September 2008
Budget: Undeclared

Patrick Jouin trained as an industrial designer, and since founding his studio in 1999 has built up an international reputation for his unique blend of design and interior architecture. He is best known for a string of restaurant interiors for Alain Ducasse including the Plaza Athenée in Paris (2011), the signature project that brought him worldwide acclaim. A chance encounter with Kenyan-born Canadian architect Sanjit Manku in 2001 was a fortuitous meeting of like minds. They recognized that combining their experience and concordant conceptual and experimental approaches would provide them with the opportunity for a dynamic collaboration that would break down the boundaries between object, interior and structure. The YTL residence is their first large-scale integrated project.

The house is named after a prominent Malaysian industrialist who, together with his family, has been instrumental in the development of much of modern-day Kuala Lumpur. The patriarch of three generations, he wanted to create an iconic house that would reflect the technical know-how of the YTL Group, accommodate the 11 members of his dynasty and be suitable for extravagant entertaining, both private and for business. To that end he bought a plot of land on a hill top in the residential Daramsara district with impressive views towards the skyline, over the abundant tropical vegetation that characterizes the city.

As Agence Jouin Manku is a design studio, and at this point had been involved only in small-scale projects, it was not an obvious choice for such an ambitious architectural scheme. However, the family wanted a house that blended traditional and modern influences to represent the different ages of its members, and came to the practice after having experienced the synergy of contemporary and classical themes in the bar at the Plaza Athenée. As the YTL Group would be playing a key role in the construction, the client was not concerned that this would be the designer's first residence and was persuaded by Jouin's initial response to the brief, which sought a way to express the relation between the family's generations architectonically.

Jouin and Manku were invited to Kuala Lumpur – a trip that was vital to the concept they developed. They were immediately struck by the intense, sultry atmosphere and lush untamed vegetation. They could see that, without parodying a tropical design language, the house had to suit the climate and that nature should be evident, physically in the landscaping and, more abstractly, represented in the volumes and programming. Manku explains: 'We learnt more from the plants and the forests about spatial conditions and Malaysia than we did from any of [the country's] buildings. While well designed, they still seem so bland when compared to the richness of a walk through a Malaysian forest.'

For the first time Jouin and Manku had the chance to observe the idiosyncrasies of the family's lifestyle. Its members are very close-knit and stay together most of the day. Although they divide into subgroups depending on age or activity, they are often in sight of one another. The circulation of the interior was therefore important and needed to be as organic as possible with few barriers, each space unfolding onto the next.

Initial sketches were made on site and worked up over the following months. The principle was to cut into the hill so that 95 per cent of the 4-hectare (1-acre) site could be used, allowing a number of activities to take place simultaneously. The final design consists of three distinct forms (base, ring and house) influenced by the spatial relationships found in Malaysia's forests: the voids and spaces created as the volumes interlink, echoing the hollows, paths and undulations of the natural terrain. The base encloses the public function areas (a ballroom, formal dining area and chapel) and is surmounted by the ring, which includes guest accommodation and flattens out to become the ground floor of the main residence, containing the kitchen, dining and family rooms. The internal layout of the house revolves around two vertical axes: a grand marble staircase leading to the library and a wooden spiral staircase ascending through the main atrium over the kitchen to all the family bedrooms.

The family house is the defining element of the residence; its monumental form appears to hover lightly over the ground.

The task was to find a way to build the 'floating' biomorphic structure. The design was developed in collaboration with YTL who wanted to demonstrate its capacity to do something remarkable by harnessing the construction skills for which it is known. The giant cantilever that forms the upper floors spans a distance that exceeds engineering norms. In order to keep the views throughout the living spaces clear it 'balances' on only three points but is held in place by an intricate system of tension cables that tilts it back and connects it to the foundations at the rear of the building; a technique that owes a debt more to bridge design than building design.

The YTL house is a new take on tropical architecture. Although its openness and the way it is elevated may refer to vernacular Malaysian buildings its innovative structure and detailing reinterpret traditional methods of shading and shelter. The cantilever offers protection from the rain and sun, while a louvred metallic skin shields the glazed façades. Natural ventilation is provided by the ground-floor glass walls that slide back to allow cool breezes to enter and traverse the interiors, breaking down the boundaries between inside and out – an effect magnified by the landscaping that makes the house appear to rise from its verdant environment.

1 / 'We created a brand-new architecture for the [YTL] house,' says Patrick Jouin. 'New shapes, new ways of connecting spaces and new combinations of cutting-edge technology and traditional local practices.'

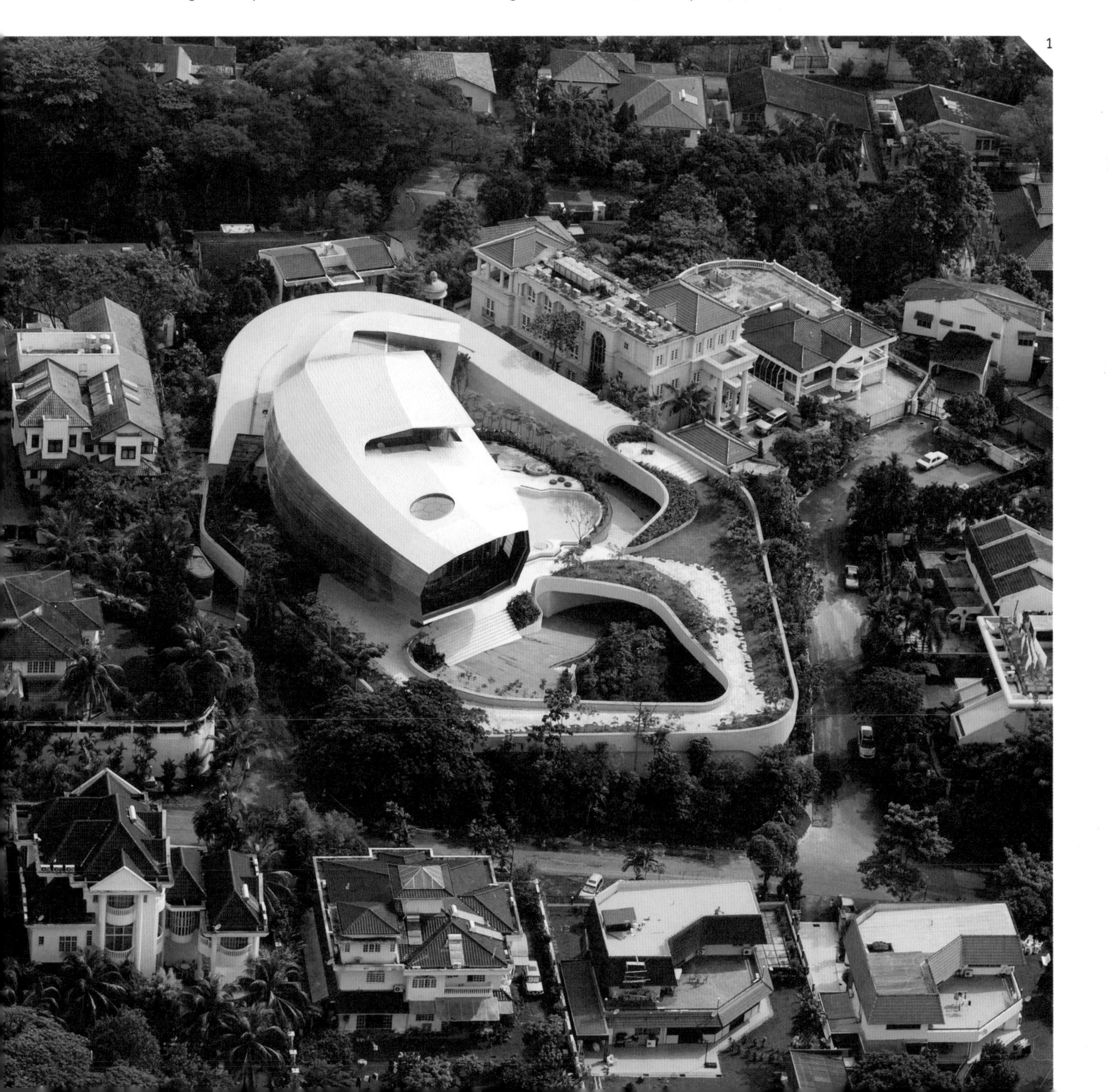

2

1 Gate access
2 Car wash area
3 Car park
4 Staircase 1
5 Entrance
6 Lift
7 Wet kitchen
8 Staff parking
9 Dining toilets
10 Bathroom
11 Corridor
12 Staircase 2
13 Staff toilet
14 Staircase 3
15 Back office
16 Chapel
17 Special dining room
18 Ballroom
19 Filter and pump room
20 Beverage area
21 Store
22 Staircase 5
23 Pre-function lobby
24 Pedestrian tunnel
25 Storage
26 Male toilet
27 Lobby toilet
28 Storage
29 Female toilet
30 Light room
31 Wine cellar
32 Store
33 Drivers' area
34 Staircase 6
35 Toilet
36 Guard
37 Guard

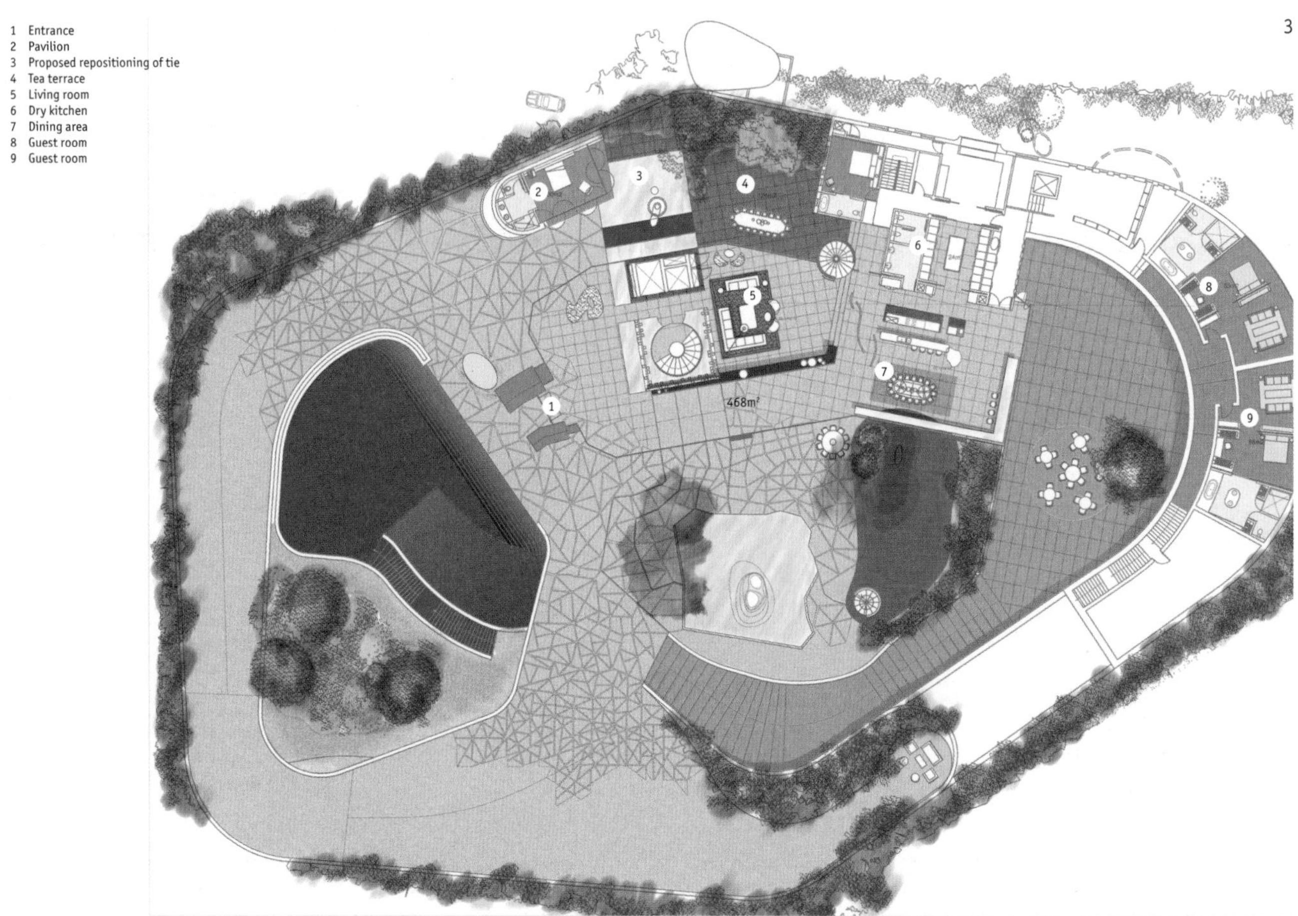

3

1 Entrance
2 Pavilion
3 Proposed repositioning of tie
4 Tea terrace
5 Living room
6 Dry kitchen
7 Dining area
8 Guest room
9 Guest room

4

1 Family room
2 Void over kitchen below
3 Void through building
4 Library
5 Study
6 Lounge

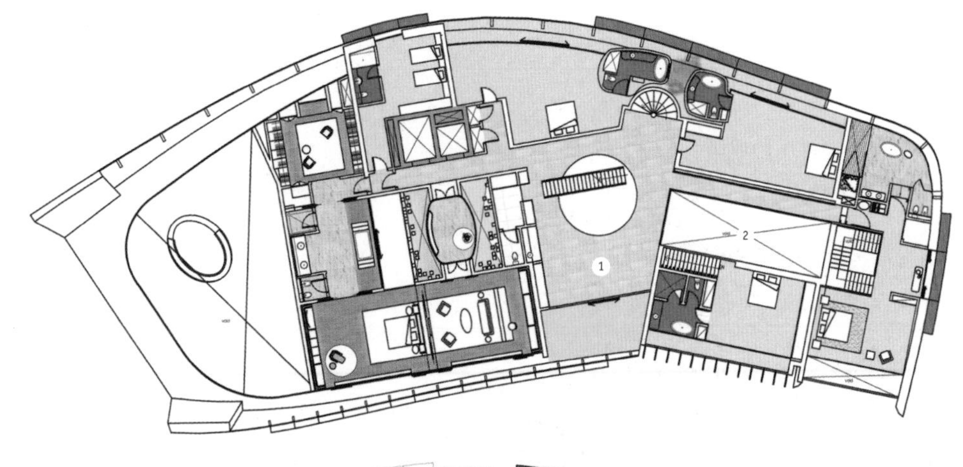

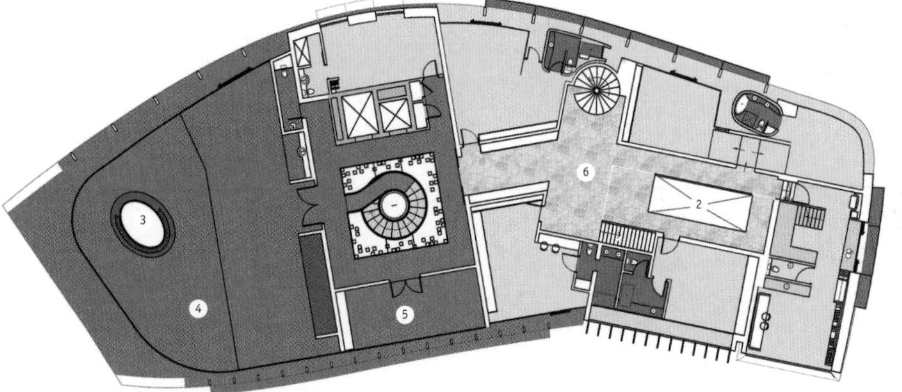

5

6

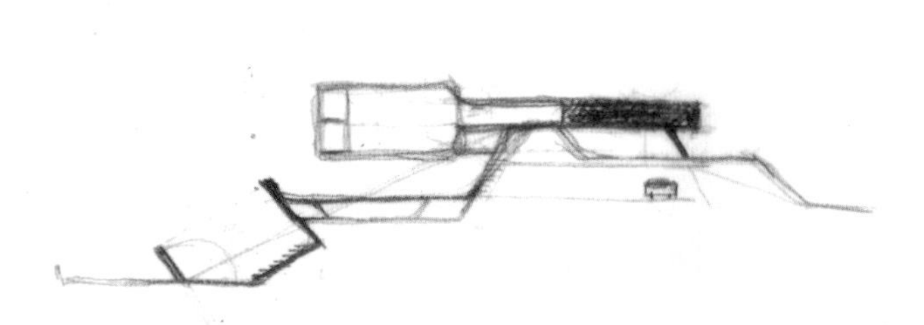

7

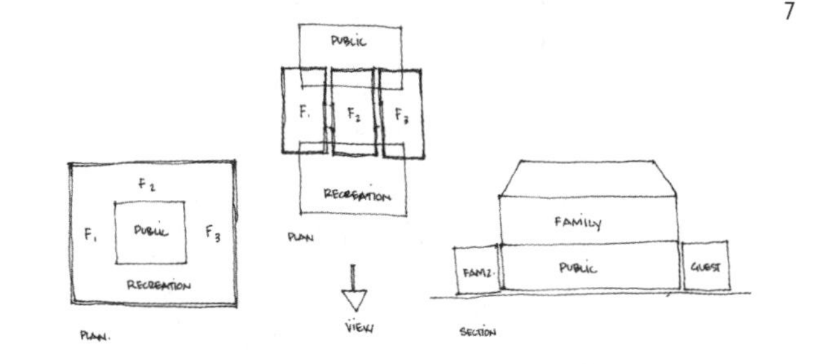

2 / Basement plan: Guests are directed from the main Moon Gate to the reception and public function areas via the sculptural ring that envelops the house and the perimeter of the property.

3 / Ground-floor plan: The ring rises to house visitors in elegantly carved suites, and flattens out at the ground level of the house. It provides an undulating landscape of private gardens, and dips to form the swimming pool.

4 / First- and second-floor plans (above and below respectively): The upper floors of the house accommodate two suites, family bedrooms and a double-height private library.

5 / Front and rear elevations (left and right respectively).

6 / Sketch made during the first meeting with the client: Jouin and Manku wanted to make clear that they were searching for an ultramodern architectural language.

7 / Sketch investigating how the family's generations could be expressed.

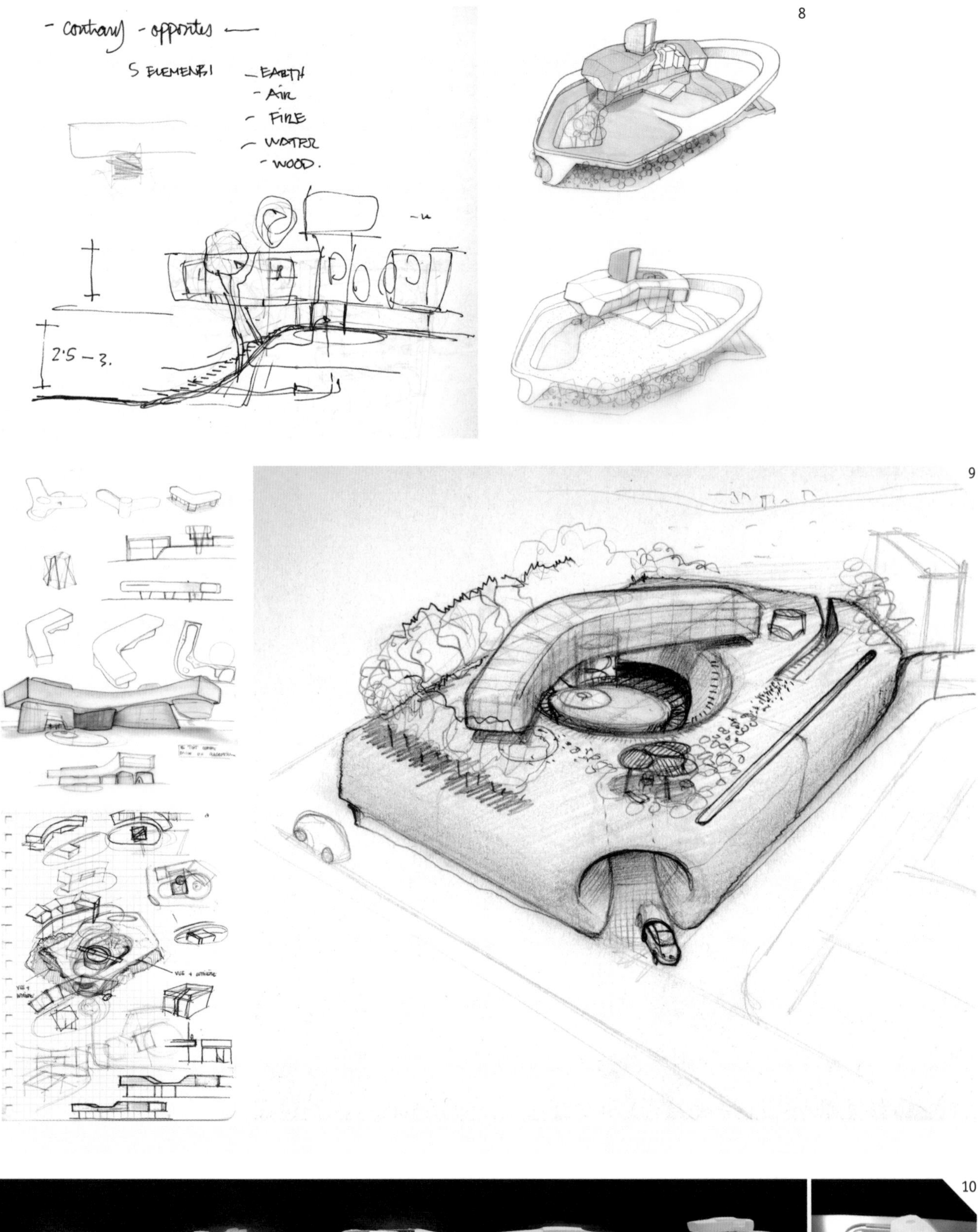
- contrary - opposites —
5 ELEMENTS
- EARTH
- AIR
- FIRE
- WATER
- WOOD.
2.5 – 3.

8

9

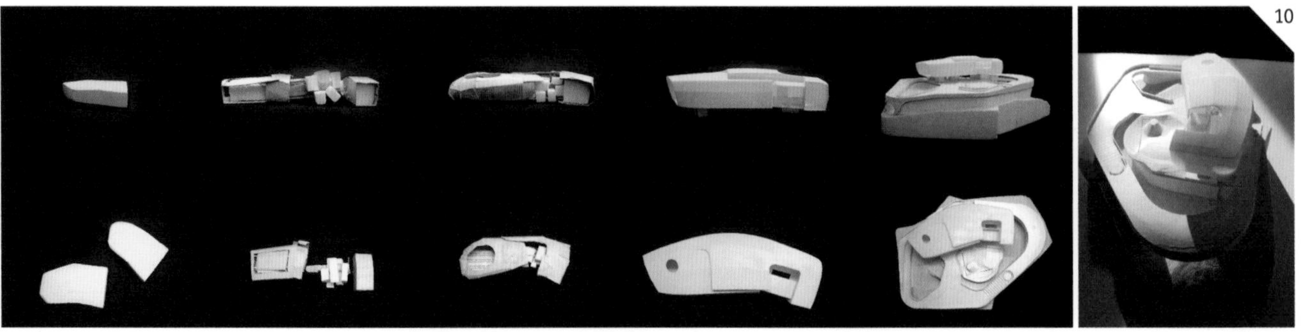

10

11

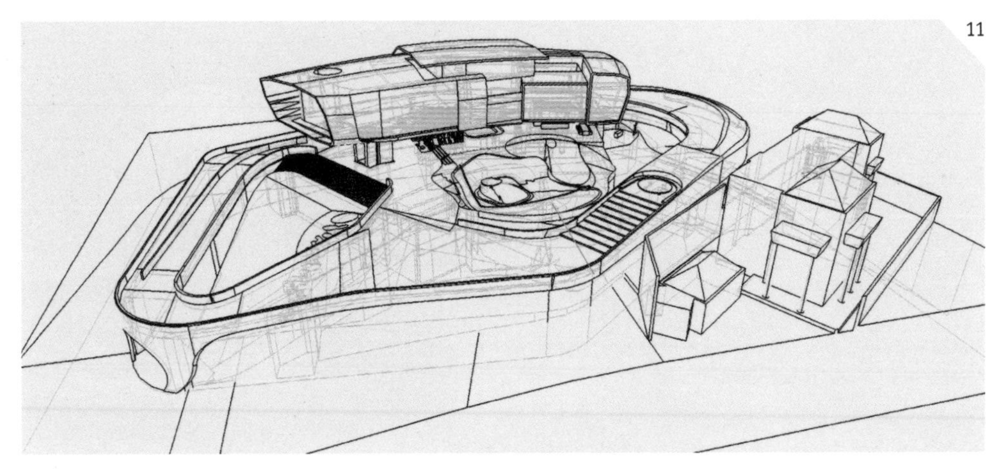

12

13

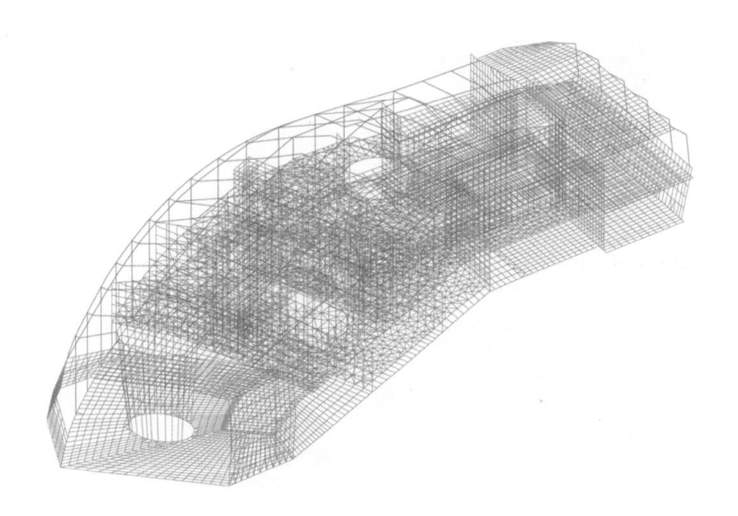

8 / An early idea was based on traditional Asian family hierarchy with a tower that would house the patriarch and his family accommodated in units below.

9 / Series of sketches made during the early stages of schematic design: Jouin and Manku knew from the beginning that they wanted separate volumes, and would utilize the open ground plane. They had also decided that the public function areas would be below ground level and the circulation organic.

10 / Sequential series of models working out the elements of the building: The programming eventually generated the volumes of the structure.

11 / Computer drawing of the final form.

12 / An example of the renderings used for presentation to the client: The interiors were conceived simultaneously with the architecture, and the introduction of light and shade into the building was also considered. Jouin and Manku enjoyed a close, informal and mutually supportive relationship with the client.

13 / The Architect of Record worked for the YTL Group and reinterpreted Jouin and Manku's design intent drawings to make them code-compliant. The process between client, architect, local architect and structural engineer was highly collaborative. As the client was the contractor most issues were worked out in-house.

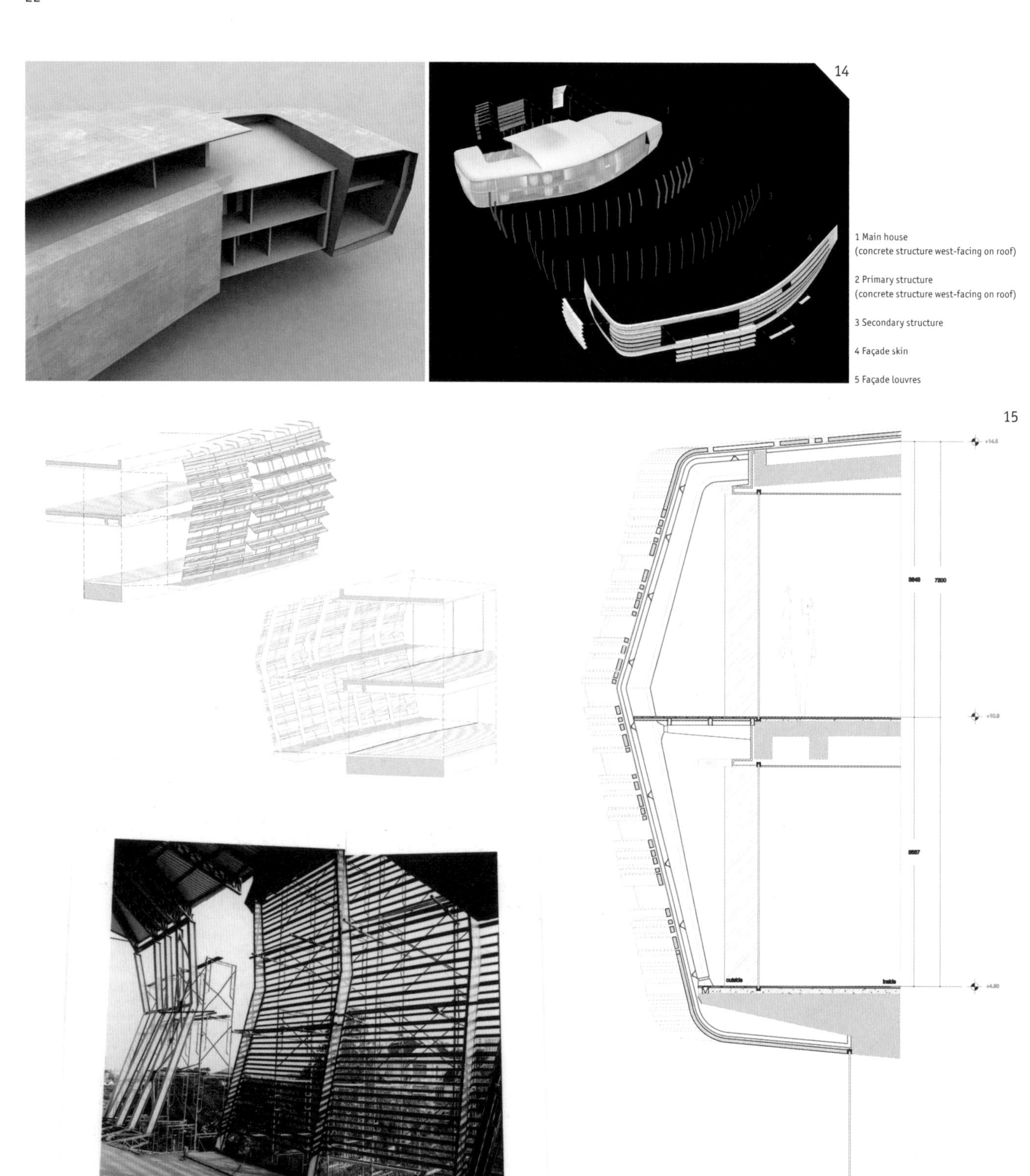

14 / The design that Jouin and Manku proposed was complicated and unorthodox. They knew the house might not be realized if they suggested using a complex construction technique unfamiliar to Malaysian contractors, but they did not want to rationalize the geometry and deliver something too straightforward. The relatively simple steel-reinforced concrete structure, overlaid with a secondary metal 'veil' that they proposed for the façade delivered the form and feeling of weightlessness they desired.

15 / The secondary structural system is light and transparent. It consists of a series of individual metal ribs, each distinct from its neighbour, that together define the shape of the house. Over the ribs there is a tertiary and finer layer to which the façade is attached. This consists of a series of non-parallel extruded metal slats clad with stainless steel on the exterior and wood on the interior.

16

17

16 / As 30 per cent of the project was below ground the site was levelled and the hole gradually filled as the building took shape, reforming the hill in the process.

17 / The amount of reinforcing steel that went into the primary structural supports was enormous, and the first indication of the scale and ambition of the project.

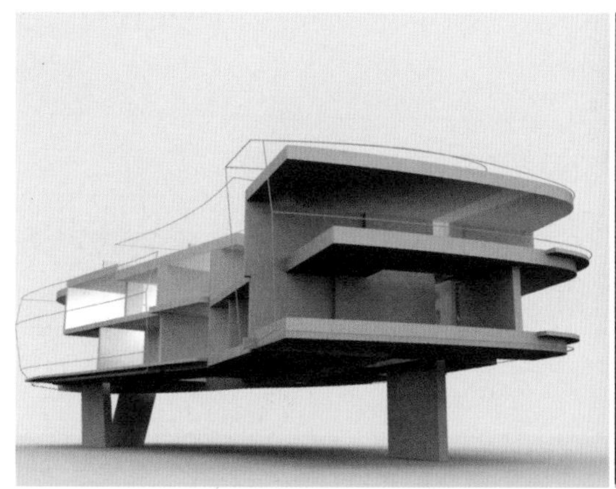

18

19

18 / The intricate formwork the construction team delivered for the concrete structure was in the end as precise as the metal façade. Post-tensioned concrete was used in the upper levels so that slab depths could be decreased and the size of the cantilevers increased. The formwork had to be removed floor by floor and the tension within the slabs recalibrated to ensure the structure was stable and would not slump and impede the sliding glass panels on the ground floor.

19 / The tension cables were laid in a carefully considered grid and the concrete poured and left to cure. The cables were pulled tight and the tension assessed. They attach to three main tension ties only one of which is 'visible', masked by a column rising out of a koi pond at the rear of the building.

20

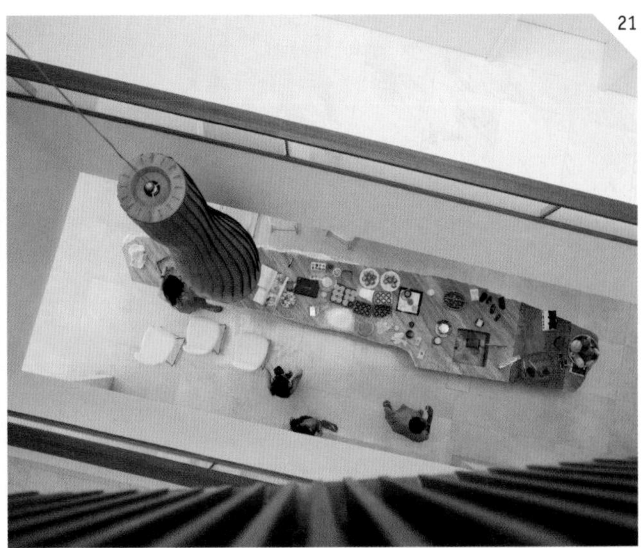
21

22

23

24

20 / The landscaping is fundamental to the project and was designed by Sophie Ambroise who is best known for her work at the Bulgari Hotel in Milan. The integration of building and landscape was paramount, and the planting is choreographed to match the structure. Indigenous and rare species were used to form a biological bank of endangered plants.

21 / The kitchen is the heart of the house. The whole family congregates around the monolithic and elemental carved Carrara marble island that dominates the space. The main atrium is the only vertical accent in the project, emphasized by the giant teak lanterns that descend through the space.

22 / The interiors are distinguished by the use of stone and wood, and are at once modern yet warm. The architects collaborated with local and international craftsmen and artists.

23 / The ground floor is open. The dining area, living room and kitchen blend seamlessly into one another. The giant sliding, glazed panels blur the boundary between interior and exterior.

24 / Jouin had always wanted to design a chapel and says his enthusiasm for this important part of the brief was one of the reasons he was selected for the commission. The design is informal, simple and minimal, and conceived to encourage conversation while still focusing on the cross through which daylight falls into the interior of the chapel.

The Yas Marina Hotel

Asymptote: Hani Rashid + Lise Anne Couture

Location: Abu Dhabi, UAE
Principal use: 500-room, 5-star hotel
Client: Aldar Properties PJSC
Site area: 35,000 m^2 (376,736½ ft^2)
Interior area: building A: 45,000 m^2 (484,375½ ft^2); building B: 26,000 m^2 (279,861½ ft^2)
Total build area: 85,000 m^2 (914,931½ ft^2)
Design and construction period: Construction: November 2007 – October 2009 (design and build overlapped on a fast-track schedule)
Budget: Withheld at owner's request

The Yas Marina Hotel is the main feature of the ambitious $36 billion Yas Marina development in Abu Dhabi, and is the first hotel in the world to be built over a Formula One race circuit.

Asymptote was founded in 1989 and from the beginning Rashid and Couture have challenged the boundaries of their discipline by exploring the overlap between real and virtual spaces. Their early years were dominated by theoretical projects and today, although the partners have built up an international reputation for their innovative and visionary buildings, they still devote energy to their experimental work, both didactically (Rashid headed the digital design initiatives at Columbia University) and in their own practice. One whole floor of their New York studio is dedicated to being a research laboratory where hypothetical schemes and experiments in form, technology and materials are models for possible structures. Hani Rashid refers to this method of exploration as an 'architectural wind tunnel ... where we try to produce certain kinds of effects and potentials in real architectural space'. Over the years the architects' conceptual work and involvement in the arts and academia have produced a lexicon of reference material from which they draw.

Serendipitously, at the time that Asymptote was awarded the commission for the Yas Hotel, Rashid was working with his students on a study of the influences of speed and technology on architectural space, and was developing an idea for an imaginary city that would grow over a race circuit. This prior research proved invaluable when the architects were called on to develop a sketch design for the Yas Marina Hotel in less than a week. The hotel was to open in time for the inaugural 2009 Formula One Ethiad Airways Abu Dhabi Grand Prix on 1 November and the schedule was tight. Building had already commenced on a design made by an engineering company but Sheikh Mubarak, who had in mind an iconic building, halted construction and requested the developer, Aldar, to find an architect who was capable of producing an architectural symbol for the city.

Asymptote was working with Aldar on the Al Raha Beach Strata Tower (Abu Dhabi, 2011), a luxurious apartment tower, and was using what Rashid refers to as 'veiling technology'. The architects' proposal for the Yas Hotel was based on a similar conceptual assumption. The veil is an important Islamic cultural reference and the notion of draping is also valuable in hot climates, as a means of keeping the body and places cool and comfortable. To produce an architecturally strong design that had local significance but did not fall into the trap of a kitsch, Disneyland vernacular style, Rashid and Couture conceived the building as a straightforward glazed slab and column concrete volume swathed by a spectacular skin that would pay homage visually to Islamic decoration and the cultural landscape in which they were building. Starting with the elliptical footprint already on site, a second oval was formed by Asymptote reaching into the water of the marina, thereby not only allowing the building to cross the race circuit but also siting it in a body of water, thereby enabling access by yacht. This became the 'T' of the plan and was joined to the first oval by a monocoque steel-and-glass bridge structure spanning the race circuit. The veil was then extended to cover the entire complex, making the track appear to run through the centre of the hotel.

Keeping the structure simple conserved expenditure and allowed increased investment in the elaborate grid-shell: a 217-square-metre (712-square-foot) expanse of sweeping, curvilinear glass and steel made up of 5,800 pivoting diamond-shaped glass panels. It was developed in close collaboration with the structural engineer, Schlaich Bergermann, and Gehry Technologies as well as later with Arup Lighting, who helped devise a system of LED lighting that met the architects' vision for the building. The outcome of the initiative between Asymptote and Arup consisted of seven customized video sequences onto and around the fritted glass panels in a spectacular 3-D light show.

The shape of the 'veil' is unprecedented and is the largest expanse of shell structure built on a parametric model to date. Using parametric CAD software, such as Gehry Technologies' Digital Project and Rhino, allowed the architects to produce amorphic rather than spherical surfaces. Traditionally, only a repetitive pattern based on a single curve and resulting in a dome shape would have been possible. Computer modelling and parametric optimization were employed to calculate the number of panels needed to achieve the desired effect while keeping the structure affordable to build.

Construction of the hotel took only 18 months, a period that Rashid describes as 'insane'. Dewan, the local architect hired by Asymptote, supervised the build and it's a testament to the successful collaboration between Asymptote, Dewan and others as well as the sensitive, supportive attitude of the client that the quality and integrity of the design concept was retained and celebrated in the finished building.

'One could say my goal is to discover and divulge why we find certain technological objects beautiful. And along with that is a belief that it is essentially because of their kinship to the natural, both in formal outcome and mathematical logic,' says Rashid. '[However] merely imitating a bone or a wing is no longer interesting to us. Rather, it is about looking deeper at things like the dynamics of a system and the ability to peer through computing at the motion-based aspect of things around us.' He adds: 'The hotel embodies various key influences ranging from the aesthetics and forms associated with speed, movement and spectacle to the artistry and geometries of Islamic art and craft tradition. The search here was inspired by what one could call the "art" and poetics of Formula One, coupled with the making of a place that celebrates Abu Dhabi as a cultural and technological tour de force.'

1/ The Yas Marina Hotel viewed from the marina: By day the faceted expanse of the grid-shell sparkles in the sunlight and reflects the sky and surroundings while by night the computer-programmed light sequences fly around the fritted glass panels in an ever-changing 3-D display.

1

2

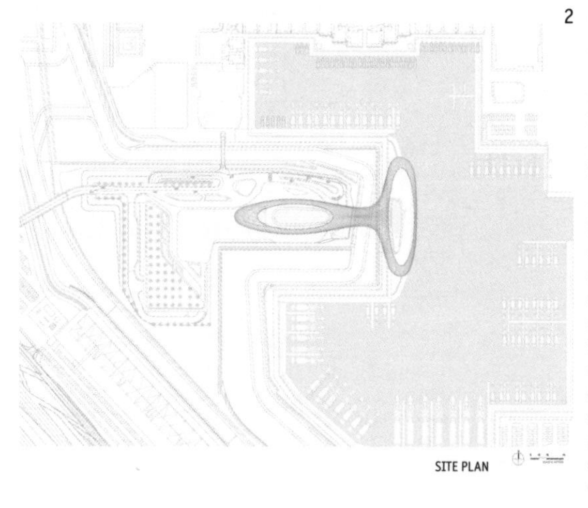

3

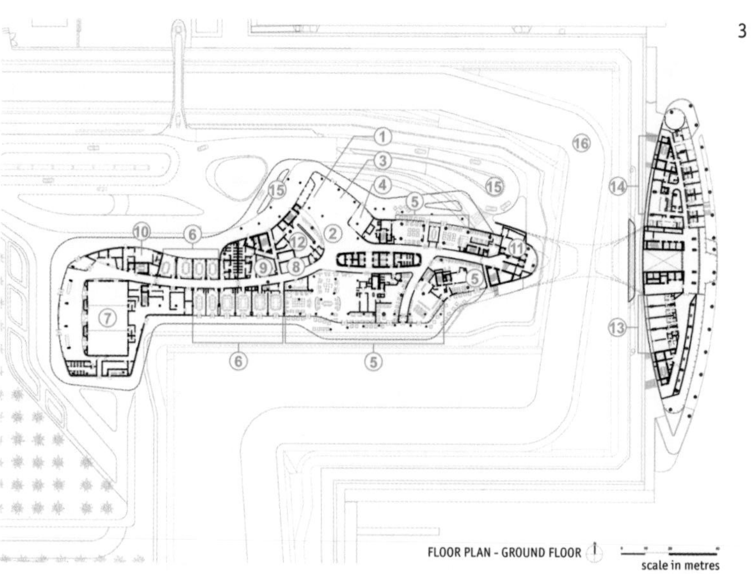

4

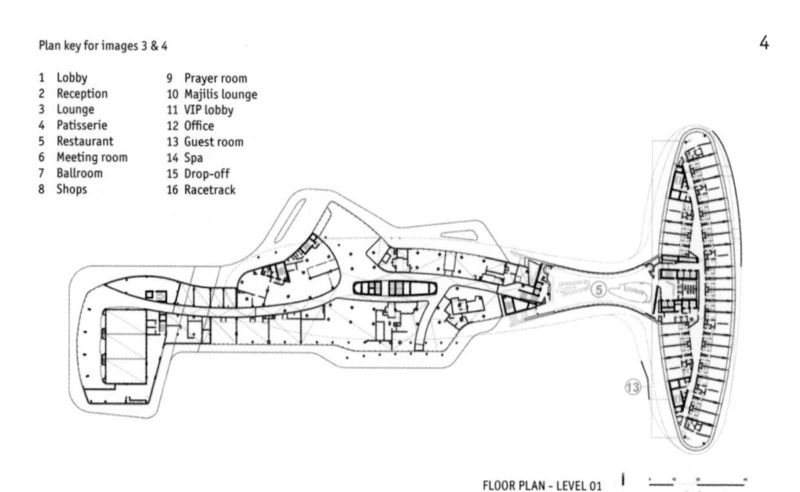

5

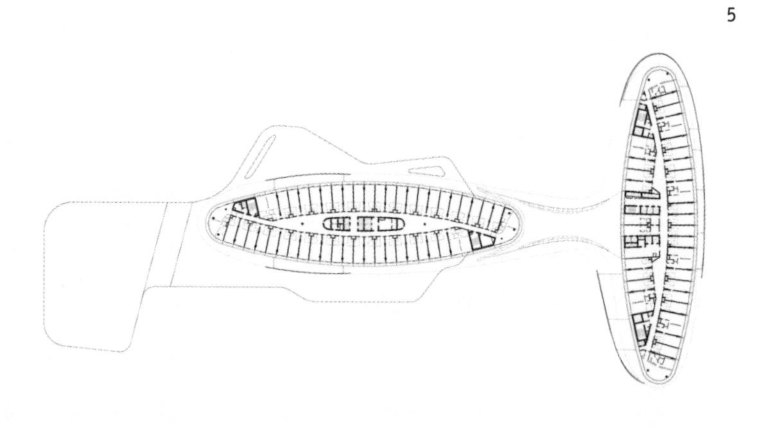

2 / Site plan: The hotel is the key architectural feature on Yas Island. When completed the master plan will include not only the race circuit and marina but leisure facilities, six further hotels, a water park, a Warner Brothers' movie world, 300,000 m² (984,240 ft²) of retail space and Ferrari World along with apartments and villas that will house a population of c.110,000. The hotel's plan is T-shaped and extends out into the marina.

3 / Ground-floor plan.

4 / Mezzanine level.

5 / Typical guest-room level.

6 / South elevation.

7 / North elevation.

8 / West elevation.

9 / East elevation.

10 / Section AA.

6

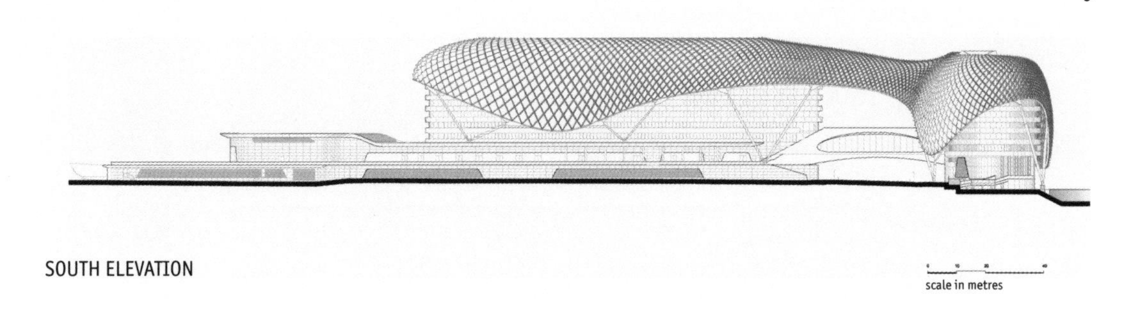

SOUTH ELEVATION

7

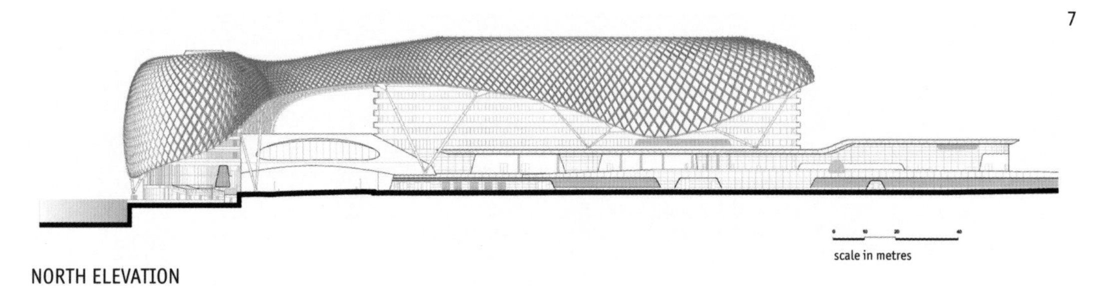

NORTH ELEVATION

8

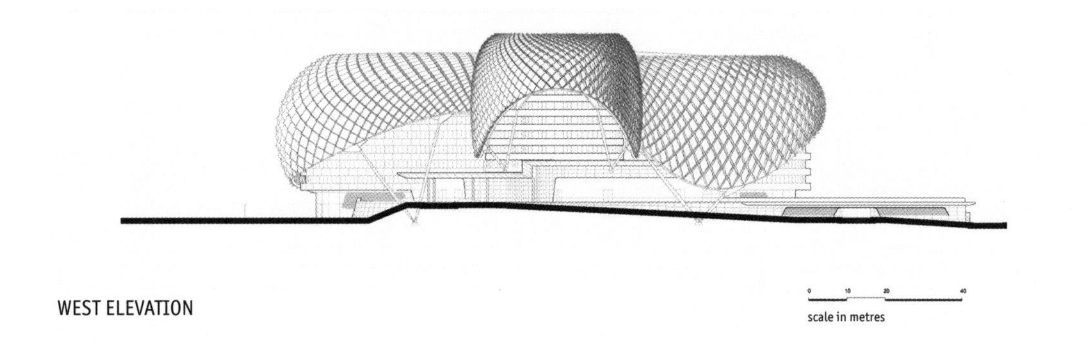

WEST ELEVATION

9

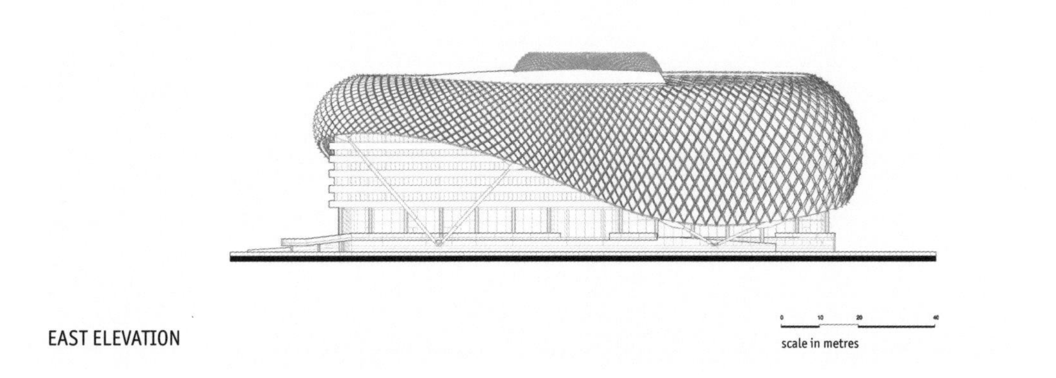

EAST ELEVATION

10

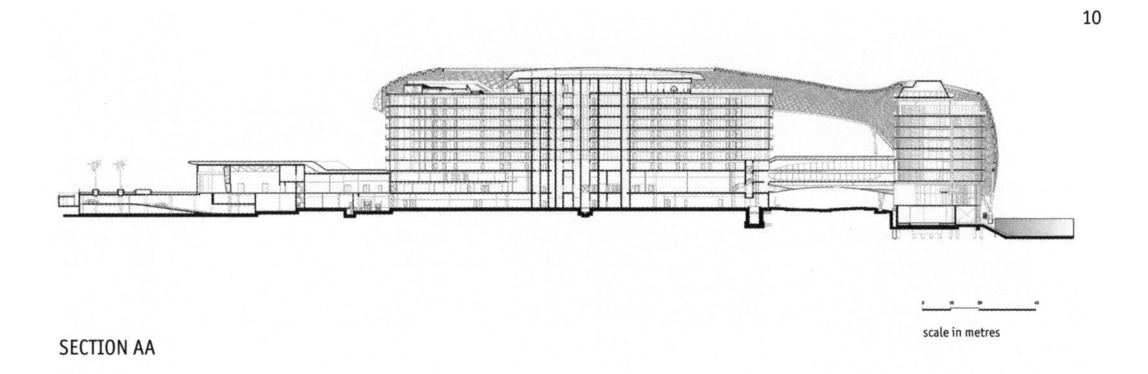

SECTION AA

11

12

13

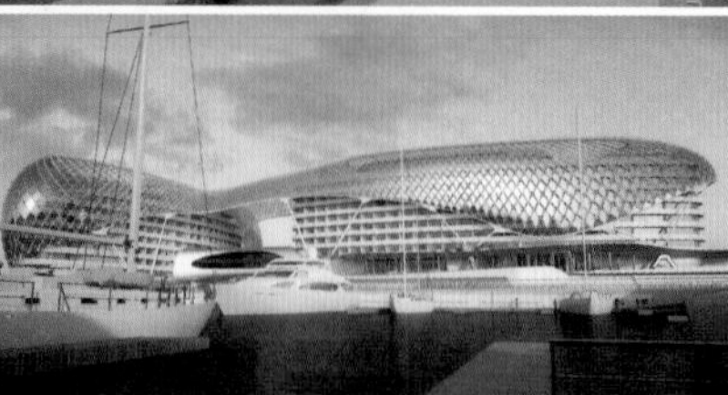

14

11 / Rendering of the Strata Tower: The 50-storey apartment building uses what Rashid refers to as 'veiling technology' and was instrumental in the architects being awarded the hotel commission. It acted as a starting point for the design concept.

12 / Concept sketch: The practice uses sketches and models to develop a design. These are then turned into 3-D computer models and presentation drawings. In the case of the hotel, as the schematic design had to be delivered within a week there was no time to make a presentation model.

13 / Asymptote is conversant with detailing the functional and pragmatic requirements of hotels. 2-D drawings used in the presentation outlined the provision of 500 rooms and the efficient working of the hotel's public spaces. Renderings illustrated the dynamic form of the outer grid-shell structure, the idea of a monocoque bridge linking the two towers and the notion of the race circuit running through the building, as well as the relationship of the hotel with the marina, and the main public interior spaces.

14 / 3-D computer models of the grid-shell were used extensively throughout the design development.

15 / Parametric models of the grid-shell structure: The mathematical processes involved in optimizing what are effectively double curved surfaces would have been impossible without sophisticated computer software. Traditionally only a repetitive pattern based on a single curve and resulting in a dome shape would have been possible. Parametric modelling allowed an amorphic form to be created.

16 / The grid-shell is attached to the concrete substructure by a series of vertical columns aligned with the concrete columns at the top of the hotel building, and an array of horizontal struts anchored to the outside face of the floor slabs. It is carried on its own structure down to the ground and does not produce any unwieldy forces on the concrete work; an important consideration in a seismically unstable region of the world.

15

16

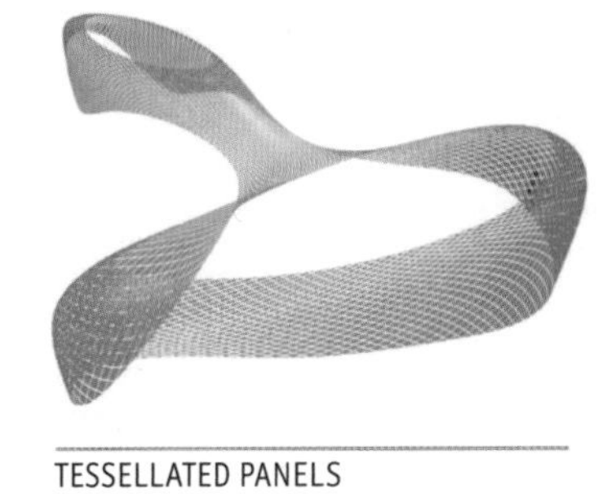

TESSELLATED PANELS

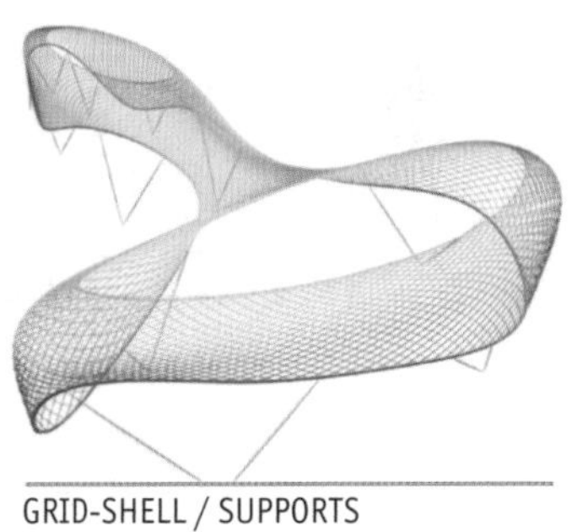

GRID-SHELL / SUPPORTS

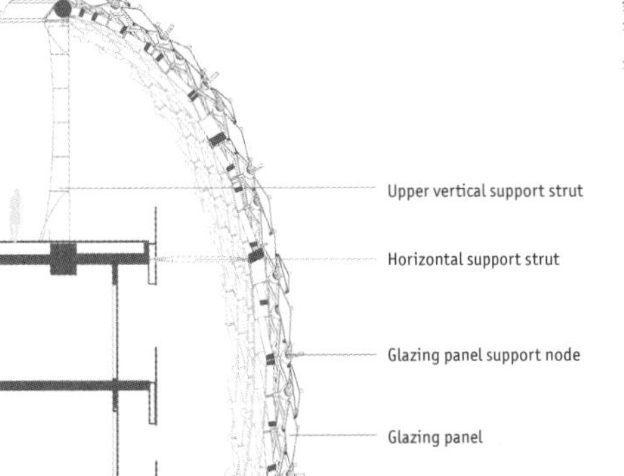

GRID-SHELL SECTION DETAIL

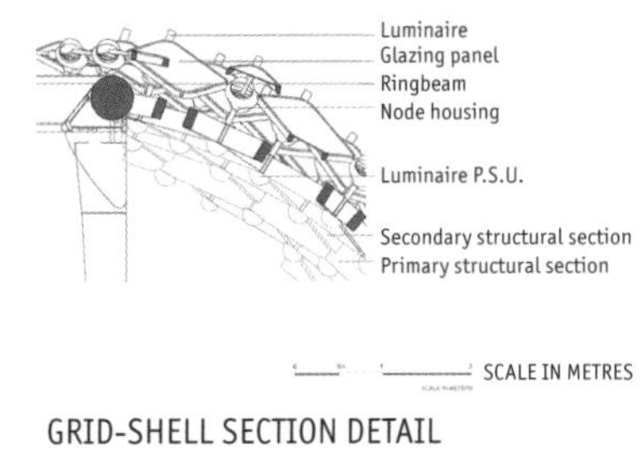

GRID-SHELL SECTION DETAIL

17

18

19

20

21

17 / The local architect produced the construction documents to local codes and standards but worked under Asymptote's umbrella – the practice maintained a staff of 30–40 in Abu Dhabi at all times.

18 / The site included the existing elliptical footprint of a previous design.

19 / The limited time frame was a double-edged sword. Although it created a logistical nightmare it also allowed the architects to realize aspects of their design that might have been cut given a longer construction period. In a normal build lasting three or four years there are many opportunities for extraneous factors to impact on the integrity of a design concept.

20 / The grid-shell veil was designed in collaboration with BIM specialists at Gehry Technologies and structural engineers Schlaich Bergermann. Standing independently of the main structure, it acts as a solar-shading heat chimney. The 'stack effect' behaves similarly to the scales on desert animals. Mimicking nature, hot air is pulled away from the skin and at the same time cool air is pulled in.

21 / Asymptote recognized the opportunity of using the outer skin as a canvas on which to input data and worked with Arup Lighting to devise a lighting programme. The design places 5,000 IP65-rated RGBW LED light sources at the intersections of the grid-shell and projects seven customized computer-controlled video sequences onto and around the glass panels. These are parced over 5,000 pixels, running over the entire surface to produce a subtly changing, flowing and ambient lighting effect.

22 / Asymptote designed all the public areas of the hotel as well as the presidential suites. The architects were responsible for all the interior spaces that were in the same aesthetic scheme as the exterior. The walls and floors are inlaid with metal bands that mimic speed and refer to the race circuit.

23 / The sculpted steel bridge construction passes over the Formula One circuit and houses bars and a restaurant.

24 / The corridors are influenced by the traditional trelliswork found in the Arab world. This was turned into computer-generated surfaces, produced in light plaster milled with a high glass content, which line the interior spaces.

25 / Hani Rashid designed sculptural artworks that are found throughout the public spaces.

26 / The roof-top pool decks are shaded from the sun by the grid-shell.

Nordwesthaus

Baumschlager Eberle

Location: Fussach, Austria
Principal use: Boat- and clubhouse
Client: Hafen Rohner GmbH
Site area: 15,000 m² (161,458½ ft²)
Interior Area: 180 m² (1,937½ ft²)
Total build area: 115 m² (1,237¾ ft²)
Design period: December 2004 – March 2007
Construction period: April 2007 – July 2008
Budget: Undeclared

The Hafen Rohner (Rohner Yacht Harbour) is situated in the Rhine Delta Nature Conservation Zone. The site was once home to a thriving aggregates enterprise that ceased business in 2003. It fell to proprietor Maria Rohner to devise a way to transform the former gravel pits on the edge of Lake Constance into a picturesque destination. The Nordwesthaus clubhouse is the third and final phase in a master plan to create what is today recognized as one of the most exquisite sailing boat marinas in Europe. In accordance with its protected location the responsibility of both client and architect (the nearby Lochau office of Baumschlager Eberle) was to undertake a delicate regeneration that would respectfully combine nature and man-made buildings.

Almost a decade in the making, the project began with the development of the harbour itself along with a sophisticated cantilevered concrete office building. Elevated and aligned to focus on the waterfront the ambitious tube-like structure is anchored to the ground by a 'pedestal' construction and appears to float above the landscape – an effect that associates it with the nearby sails, water and wind. Phase Two saw the radical redesign of the shoreline from which Phase Three, the gem-like clubhouse, rises 14 metres (46 feet) directly out of the lake to form a dynamic focal point at the head of the Hafen Rohner complex. The cube is in direct contrast to the horizontal linearity of the office building and comprises a glass box that envelops an organic, openwork concrete form, designed to blend perfectly with the natural surroundings of reeds and trees. By day the irregularly shaped walls mimic the patterns that the play of light sheds on the surface of the water, while at night a sophisticated LED lighting system within the basic architectural elements provides ever-changing colour sequences that bring the unique façades to life.

Baumschlager Eberle has completed over 300 projects since the company was founded in 1985 and work such as the Beijing MoMA high-rise building, the ETH e-Science Lab in Zurich and the Munich Reinsurance company headquarters has garnered it notable recognition and numerous awards. The Nordwesthaus is one of the firm's smallest schemes and shows a more playful side to the practice's usually restrained style of architecture but, nevertheless, clearly illustrates its philosophy of planning 'from the outside in'. By a careful examination of what already exists the partners, Carlo Baumschlager and Dietmar Eberle, form a set of rules for their economically, technically and emotionally sustainable buildings. 'Analyzing the precise location is a prerequisite for achieving the best possible customization of a new building,' says Eberle. 'The structure is therefore determined by an ideal relationship between shell, site development and primary structure [that] determines its atmosphere and image.'

Maria Rohner and Dietmar Eberle, the partner-in-charge of the harbour development, began their professional association with the design of her private house 15 years ago, since which time they have built up a mutually supportive and trusting relationship. They developed the brief for the clubhouse together. As the popularity of the marina grew, it became clear that a multifunctional building that could accommodate a range of events and act as a gathering place for the yacht owners was needed. The selected site juts out over the lake and building regulations demanded that the facility should have access by boat from the water. The concept was presented to the client using floor plans, elevations, sections and a physical model. Although alternative studies were made in-house, only one was shown. The office has a very hands-on and traditional method of working and avoids using computer visualizations, which Eberle considers to be fraudulent.

The clubhouse is situated over Lake Constance, but also in front of a large grassed area reserved for the yachts' winter berths. In all seasons the tall, straight masts of the boats define the area. Eberle's idea was to create a dialogue with the perpendicularity of this feature in a geometrically-shaped structure whose verticality had been subverted by the softening aesthetic of patterned walls. Volumetrically, the clubhouse had to act as a foil to his earlier office building. It also had to be tall enough to compete with the height of the boats and powerful enough to give the whole site a central attraction. The decision was made to build in cast concrete and to open up the shell as much as structurally possible with organic-shaped apertures. The design of the cube was developed over several months in close collaboration with project architect Christoph von Oefele and structural engineer Ernst Mader. The majority of the time was devoted to devising an intricate load-bearing system, and cost-effective, modular formwork that could be easily produced and used many times in all the different elevations of the façade.

Baumschlager Eberle used contractors from the surrounding area and worked with them closely. The practice likes to encourage local companies to use their knowledge, so that they take pride in their work. It's a philosophy Eberle refers to as 'long-term sustainability'. He adds: 'It's not an issue of techniques but making a contribution to the area in which you are building.'

The 180-square-metre (1,937½-square-foot) clubhouse has garnered much acclaim since it opened in July 2008 and makes sense of the expression 'small but perfectly formed'. 'Building is teamwork,' says von Oefele. 'Only through trust, courage, innovation and the remarkable input of all involved could the Nordwesthaus emerge in its current form. Throughout, all the trades individually developed solutions that go to the edge of what is possible.'

1/ The Nordwesthaus appears to float on the edge of Lake Constance, casting shimmering reflections over the waterscape. At night a custom-designed lighting system creates an X-ray effect that reveals the structure's skeleton.

1

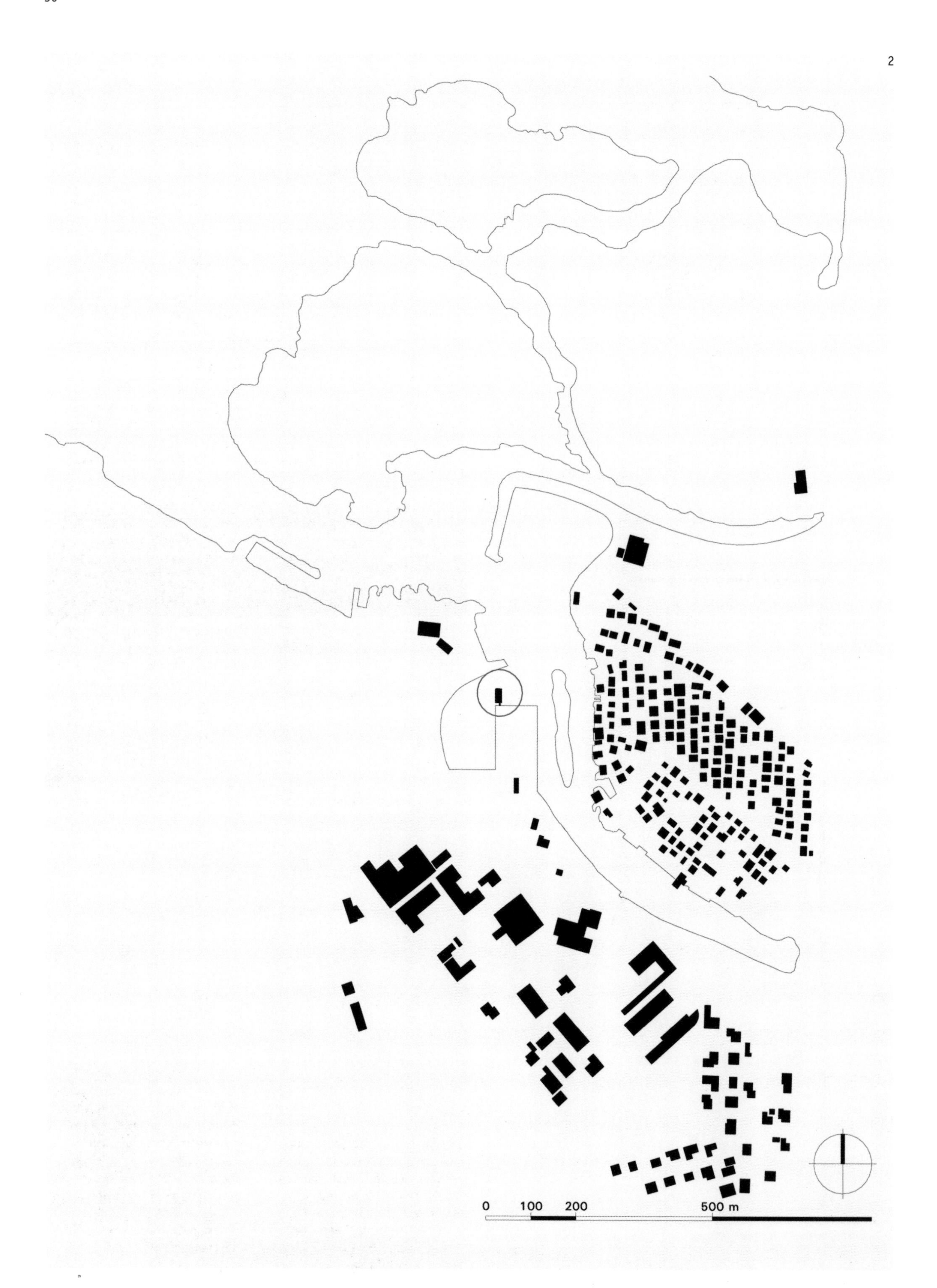
2
0
100
200
500 m

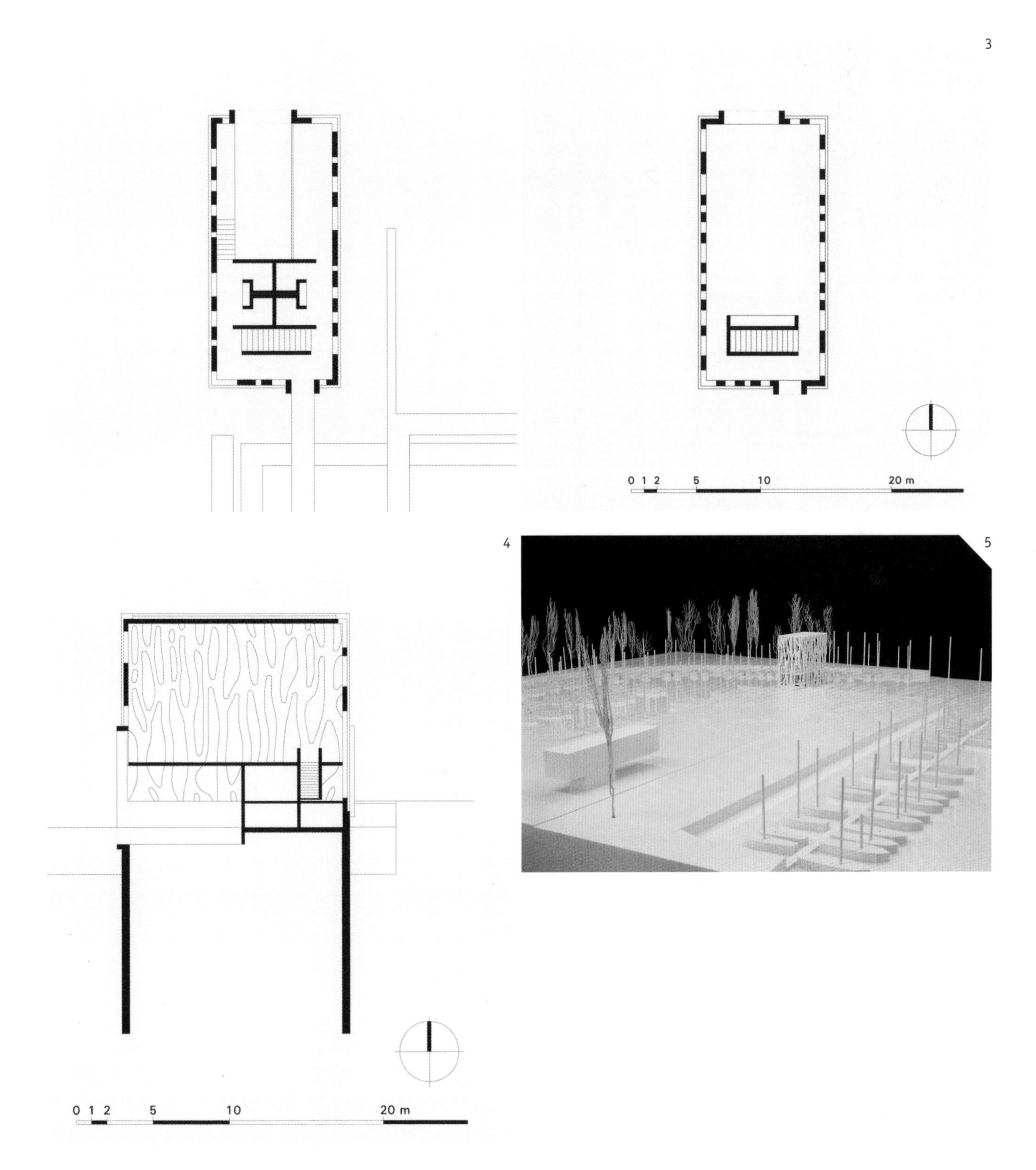

2 / Site plan.

3 / Floor plans: The clubhouse is a two-level, multifunctional event-facility-cum-boathouse. The 'boat box' is at water level creating a lakeside entry. It is followed by a connecting floor with stairs which provide access from the land side to the club room above.

4 / Elevation: The building juts out directly from the boat basin and rests on a concrete foundation supported by a ring of concrete pillars that reach down to the load-bearing strata of the lakebed.

5 / A model was used for presentation.

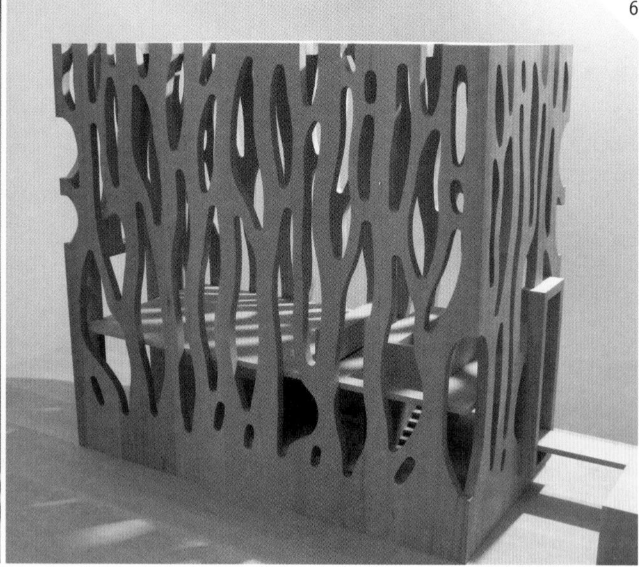

6

7

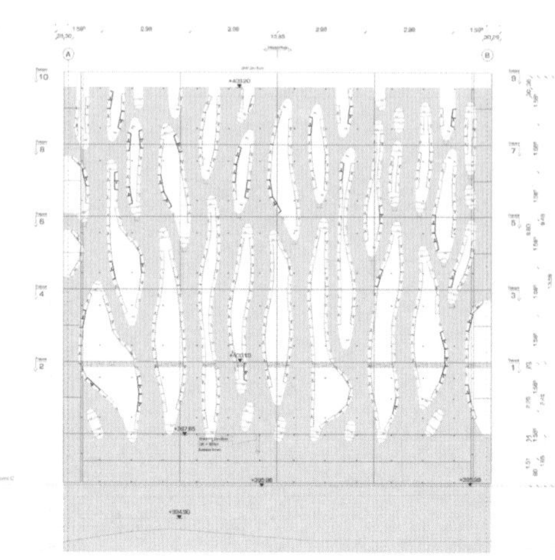

8

6 / Working models made during the design-development phase.

7 / The floor of the clubhouse with the steel reinforcement and tubes for the electrical installation: The shapes of the apertures were developed over a period of several months. Many revisions were needed to fuse the demands of the structural engineer with the forms the architects had in mind. The result was a complex load-bearing system that depended on the stiffening effect of the clubhouse floors.

8 / Concrete contractors submitted very high prices during the tender stage as they were not certain how to make the formwork for the complex walls. Once the contractor was selected the architects worked with him to develop the most cost-effective shuttering. The modular formwork was developed on the computer.

9 / The walls are divided into five concrete elements. By proceeding in sections the shuttering for the lower elements could be used again in each ascending stage. The organic shapes were created using 60 cm (23⅝ in) long modules consisting of only three radii with convex and concave profiles – a total of six sections that through different combinations formed the shuttering for all the curved arches.

10 / Wood was selected for the formwork to take the tension of the reinforcements in the concrete.

11 / The glass box is made from 3 x 1.6 m (9¾ x 5¼ ft) double-glazed, float-glass panels framed in metal T-profiles. They are suspended from horizontal aluminium rails that are fixed to the concrete superstructure by steel clips. The gap between the outer and inner layers is c.25 cm (9⅞ in) and is a feature of the building.

9

6 2007

10

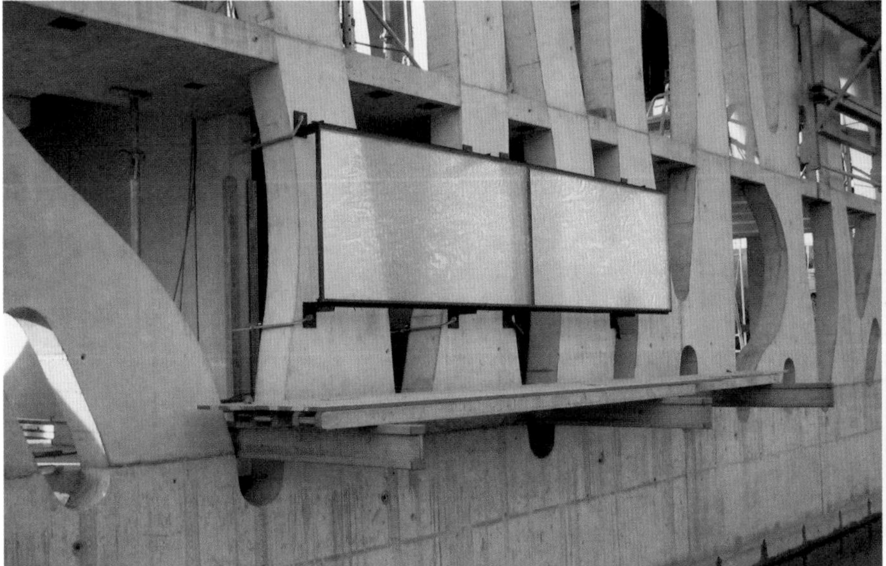

11

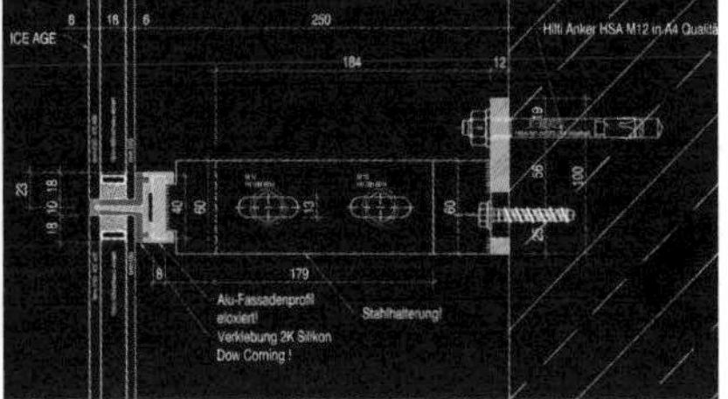
282 (±10)
8
18
6
250
ICE AGE
Hilti Anker HSA M12 in A4 Qualitä
184
12
19
23
18
10
18
40
60
13
60
56
100
25
8
179
Alu-Fassadenprofil
eloxiert!
Verklebung 2K Silikon
Dow Corning !
Stahlhalterung!

12

13

14

12 / The decoration on the glazing is created by a centuries-old procedure revived by Marte in Breganz, and named ICE-H as it resembles ice crystals on a frozen window. The technique involves dissolving glass splinters away from the surface of the glass to generate a broken-up texture. Using varying temperatures determines the dimensions of the motifs: the higher the heat, the larger the pattern.

13 / The irregularity of the cut-outs is in direct contrast to the rectangular shapes of the sheets of glass. The effect is softened by the randomness of the textured patterning on the glass.

14 / Baumschlager Eberle's contract included all stages from schematic design to construction documentation and site supervision.

15 / The lighting system was custom-designed by Zumtobel. 125 LED spotlights are arranged within the elements of the façade to avoid glare. Each luminaire has 12 integrated RGB (red/green/blue) LEDs that offer an immense spectrum of 16 million colours. They are fitted with asymmetrical optics that guarantee all parts of the intricate cut-outs are illuminated, while also ensuring that light is cast to the sides of the room as well as to the outside. DMX (digital multiplexing) control enables dynamic lighting sequences to be created.

15

Ozeaneum

Behnisch Architekten
Behnisch & Partner (Competition)

Location: Stralsund, Germany
Principal use: Oceanographic museum
Client: Deutsches Meeresmuseum, Stralsund
Site area: 7,250 m² (78,038¼ ft²)
Interior area: 8,400 m² (90,416¾ ft²)
Total build area: 17,400 m² (187,291¾ ft²)
Design period: September 2003 – September 2005
Construction period: October 2005 – July 2008
Budget: €50,000,000

Behnisch & Partner was founded in 1952 by Günter Behnisch (architect of the Munich Olympic Games stadium) who sadly passed away in July 2010, almost two years to the day after the opening of one of his last designs: the Ozeaneum in Stralsund. Throughout his career he often made reference to *Situationarchitektur*, a form of building that responds to place and circumstances, and adopts a human-centred emphasis on programme and function. In 2008, conscious of his failing health, Behnisch retreated from professional life and, acknowledging that he would be unable to complete the successful competition-winning concepts on which he was working, he entrusted his son Stefan (who founded his own Stuttgart-based company, Behnisch Architekten in 1991) with a number of projects, including the oceanographic museum.

Günter Behnisch's approach to architecture continues to influence Behnisch Architekten's daily activities. Today the company has built up an important portfolio in both the public and private sectors throughout Europe and America. Its work is respected for a design language characterized by transparency, lightness and a modern approach. Responding to the peculiarities of client and place has resulted in buildings that are emblematic of their location and respectful of their *genus loci*.

Such is the case with the Ozeaneum. The competition brief encompassed a number of challenges. Not only should the design create a technically and architecturally ambitious natural history museum complex incorporating large aquaria, but it also had to take into account an educational programme that would familiarize visitors with underwater flora and fauna, and convey the importance of conserving their natural habitat. In addition, the facility had to be a prominent building that respected and complemented the traditional Hanseatic city of Stralsund, which has been classified as a UNESCO World Heritage Site. The museum is located on its distinctive waterfront with a skyline of restored nineteenth-century warehouses and a striking panorama over the Strela Sound towards Rugen Island.

The client, the Deutsches Meeresmuseum, had a clear understanding of how the exhibition should unfold through separate halls dedicated to a general presentation of the world's oceans, the Baltic Sea aquaria, the North Sea aquaria and a Giants of the Sea display. To define the competition proposal Behnisch Architekten collaborated closely with an expert in museum design on the logistics of how the interiors should work, and an engineer specializing in the construction of aquaria to determine how the water in the tanks could be treated and the requisite extensive system of compressors, coolers, pumps and filters concealed. Key to the concept was the creation of a didactic journey through the zones. In working out the functional programme Martin Haas, the partner-in-charge, realized that it presented the perfect architectural solution. The design comprises four hermetic, free-form elements joined by a rigorous glass atrium. This allows visitors to focus on the exhibitions, and then to emerge from darkness and immediately be orientated by expansive views to either the Baltic Sea or the city. Establishing an open and closed language produced a specific rhythm. Like water swirling around stones on the seabed, the building could be flooded from all sides by daylight and visitors. The building elements, the 'stones', were given shape by cladding them with freely slung ribbons of steel, reminiscent of sails billowing in the wind.

The concept that Behnisch presented to the client (a panel consisting of representatives of the city as well as the museum) through a 1:500 physical model and a full set of plans, elevations and sections, illustrated not only the museum's physical appearance, layout and programming but also included the basis for the structural and mechanical engineering. Behnisch's proposal was selected from over 400 entries, with the jury commending the way the separate units were in scale with the surrounding medieval city. Most competitors had suggested one single edifice that would have dominated the vernacular architecture. Behnisch had been concerned that producing a contemporary design for a heritage site would raise a lot of discussion, but the client was strong enough to recognize that such an iconic building would only encourage tourists to visit the area. Throughout the design development the architect gave a series of lectures and mounted public-related exhibitions to familiarize the local population with the architecture, and invited comments. Unusually, this did not amount to any compromises in the design being made.

Behnisch do not adopt what they refer to as a clichéd architectural approach, 'the genius hand sketch translated by a couple of staff members into computer drawings', but prefer instead to move from quick concept sketches to physical models which they produce and refine at various stages during the design process before working on the construction drawings. The practice's philosophy is collegiate, with the team discussing the possibilities, advantages and disadvantages of every approach.

The Ozeaneum typifies *Situationarchitektur*. It is both a landmark for Stralsund as well as a new kind of museum, and illustrates Behnisch Architekten's commitment to context, content and performance.

1 / The museum consists of four separate elements. The disparate parts are given unity by the use of free-flowing ribbons of steel.

1

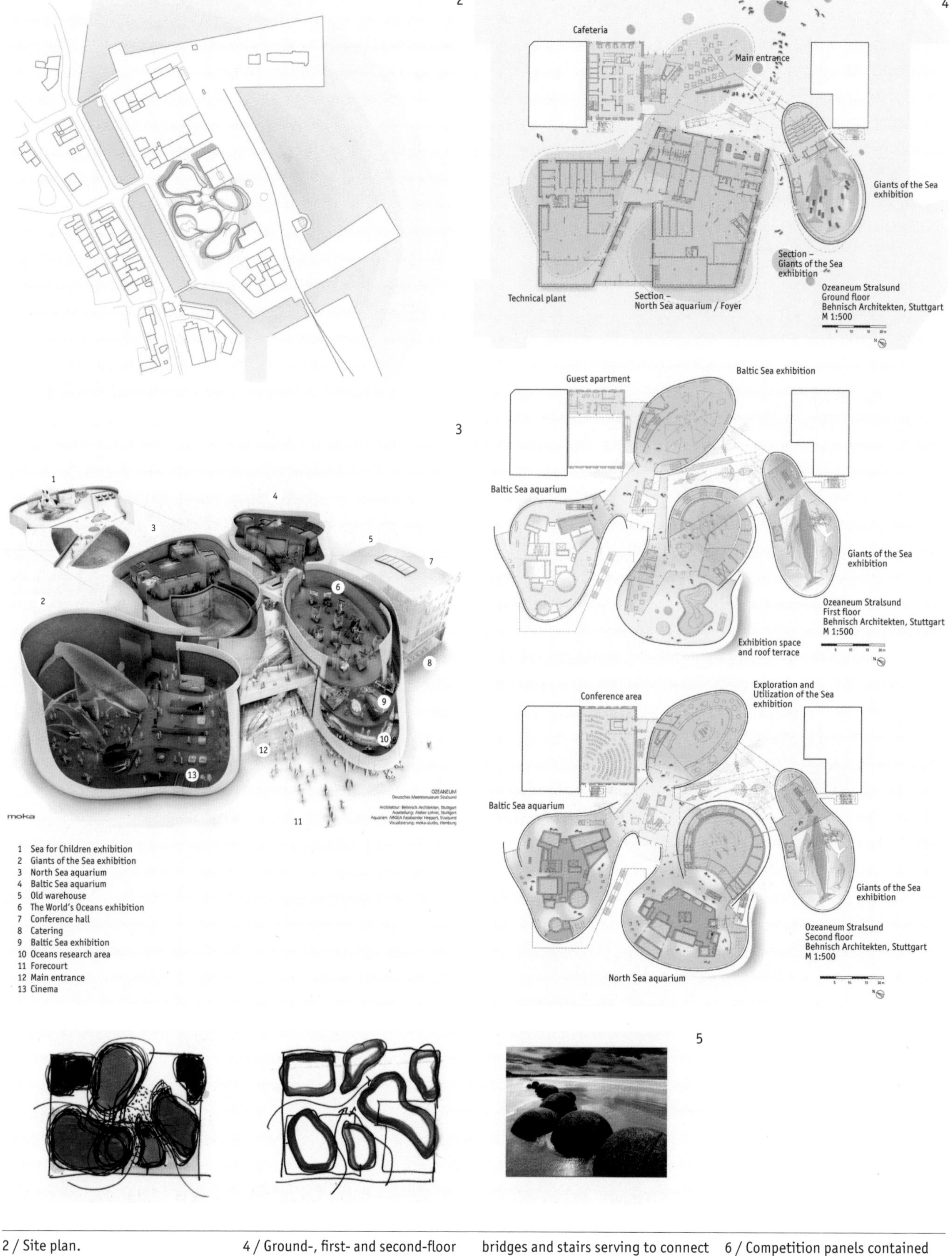

2 / Site plan.

3 / Visualization of the exhibition areas.

4 / Ground-, first- and second-floor plans: The four structures are between two and four storeys in height and are arranged around a central glazed entrance foyer. This extends over several levels with bridges and stairs serving to connect the individual elements.

5 / Behnisch use hand-drawn sketches to develop a concept quickly.

6 / Competition panels contained images of the 1:500 model, plans, sections and elevations (see also page 46).

6

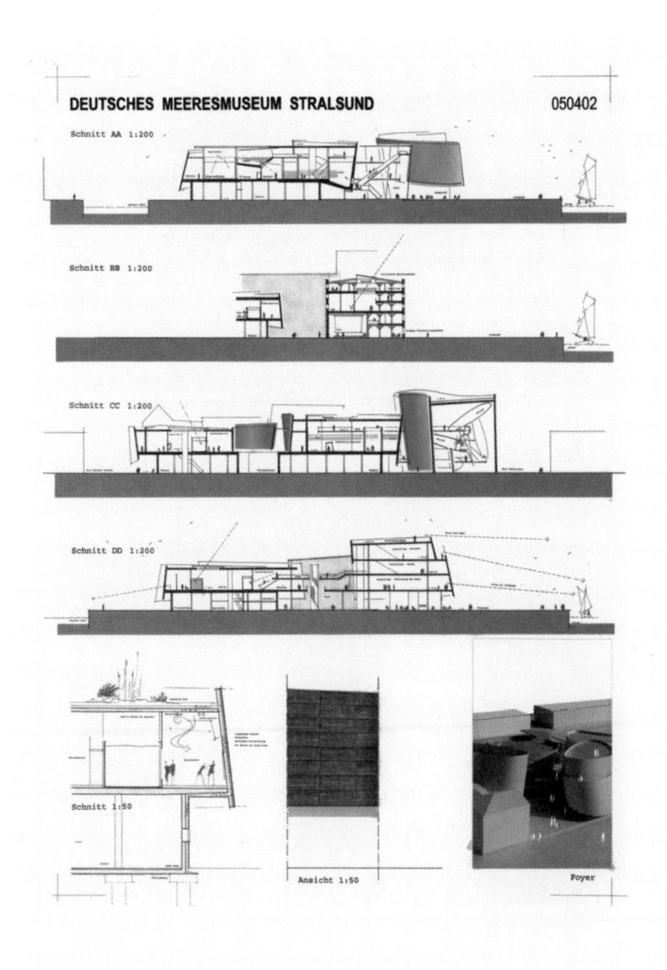
DEUTSCHES MEERESMUSEUM STRALSUND
050402
Schnitt AA 1:200
Schnitt BB 1:200
Schnitt CC 1:200
Schnitt DD 1:200
Schnitt 1:50
Ansicht 1:50
Foyer

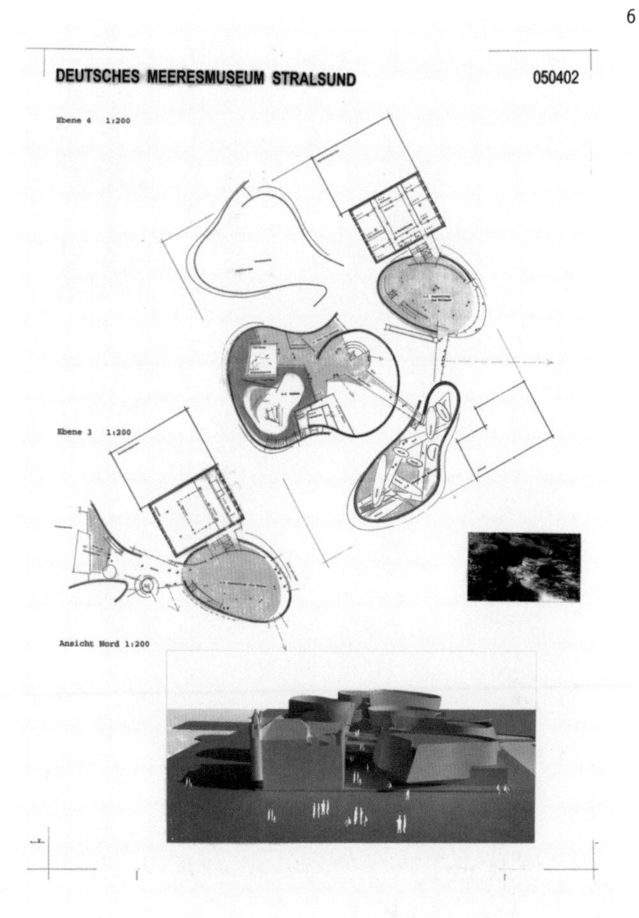
DEUTSCHES MEERESMUSEUM STRALSUND
050402
Ebene 4 1:200
Ebene 3 1:200
Ansicht Nord 1:200

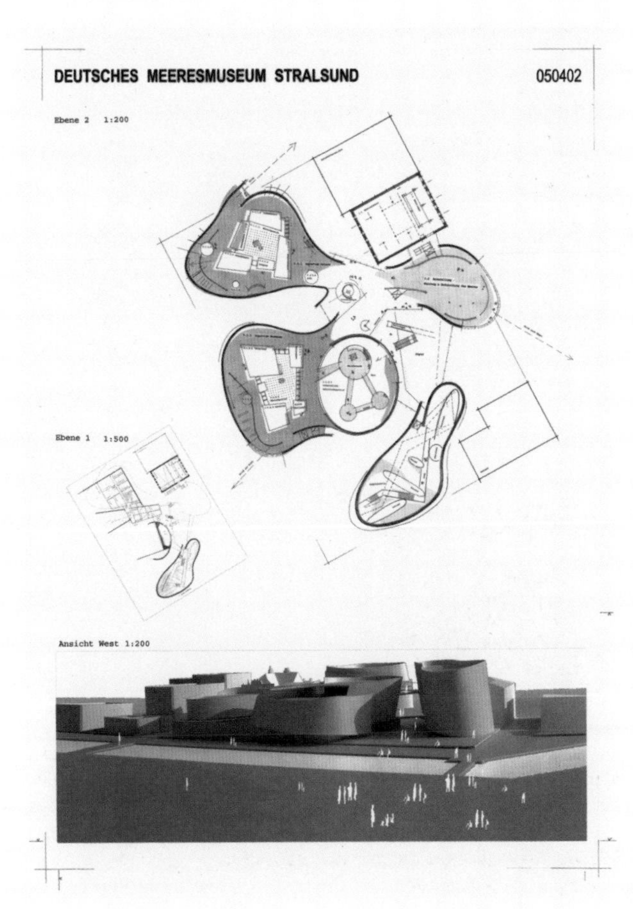
DEUTSCHES MEERESMUSEUM STRALSUND
050402
Ebene 2 1:200
Ebene 1 1:500
Ansicht West 1:200

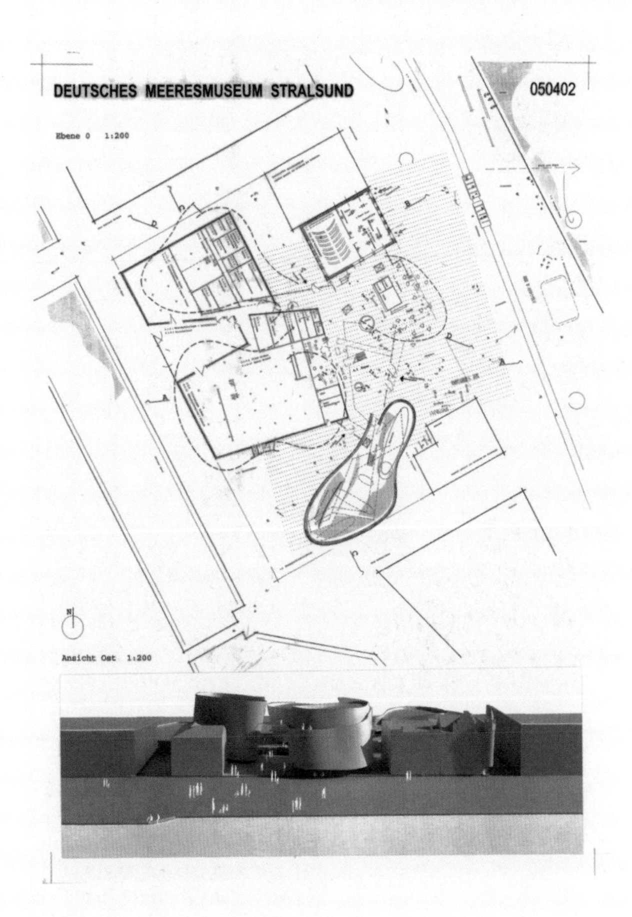
DEUTSCHES MEERESMUSEUM STRALSUND
050402
Ebene 0 1:200
N
Ansicht Ost 1:200

6

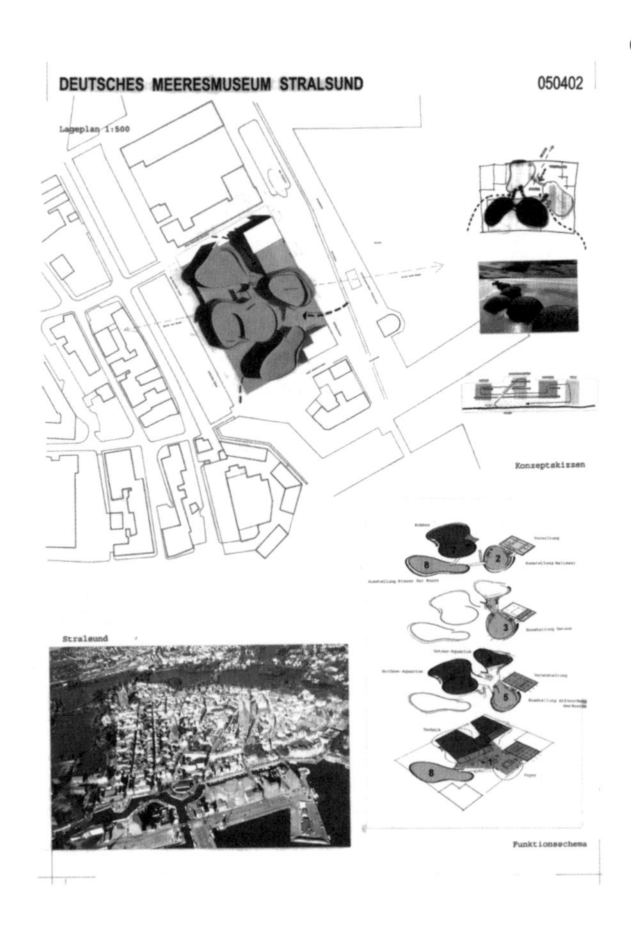

8a

8b

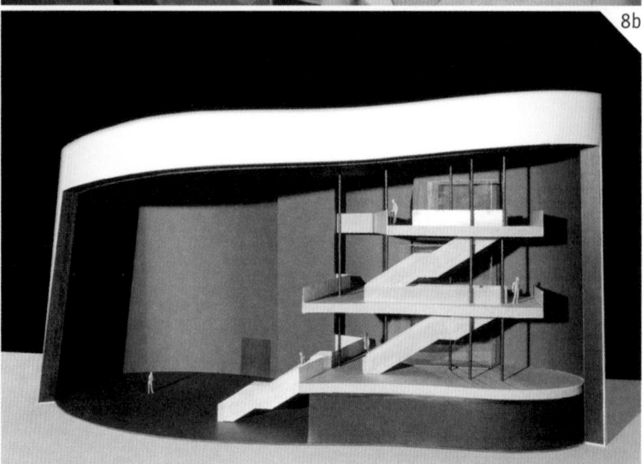

7

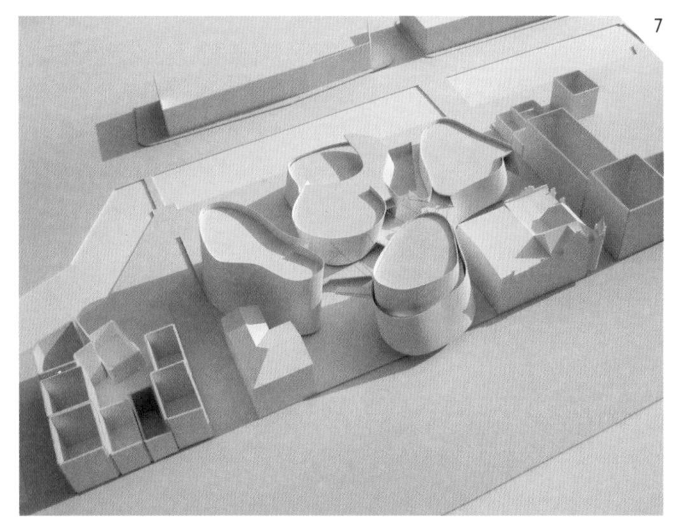

8c

7 / Close-up of the competition model.

8 / Design development models of (a) The World's Oceans exhibit, (b) the Giants of the Sea hall and (c) the final presentation model: Behnisch consider physical models the best tools to understand an architectural project. They can be used to work out layout, spatial issues and materiality as well as being used when presenting to the client.

9

10

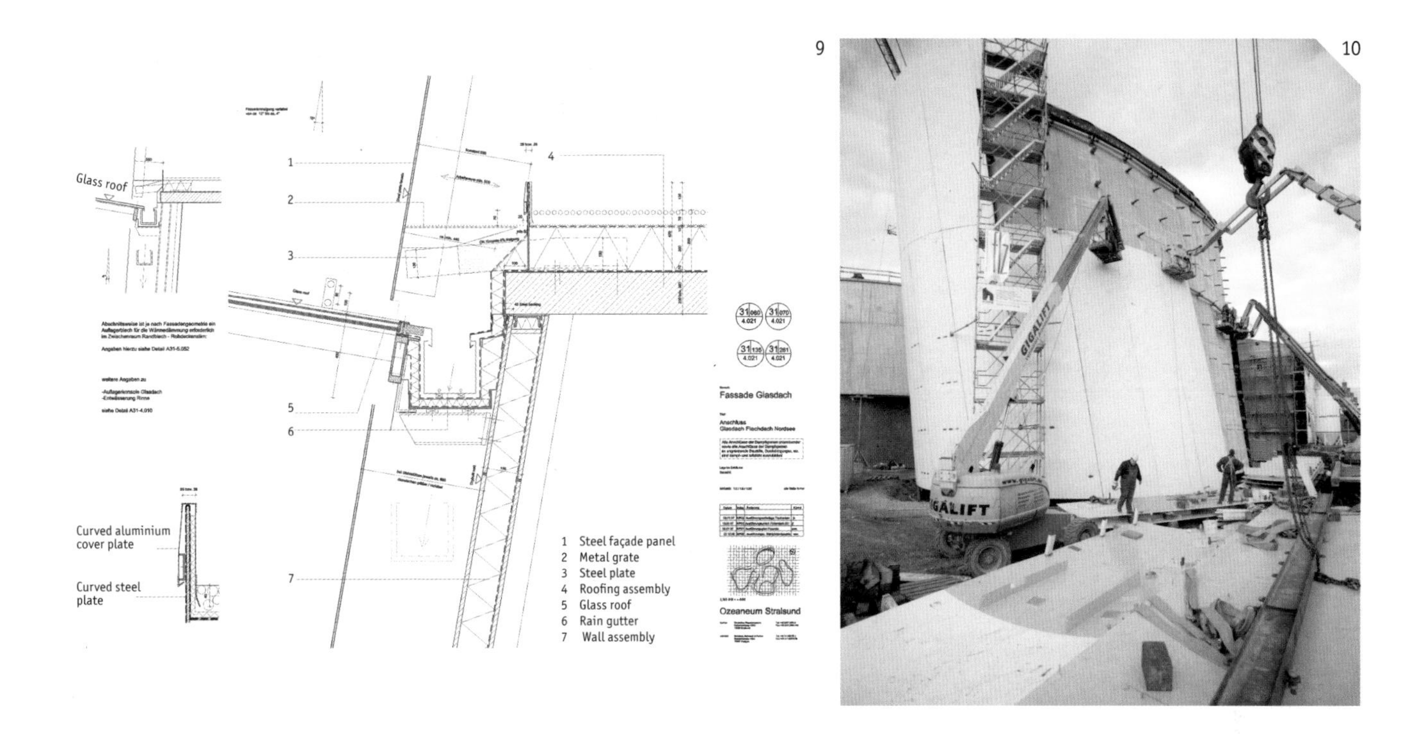

11

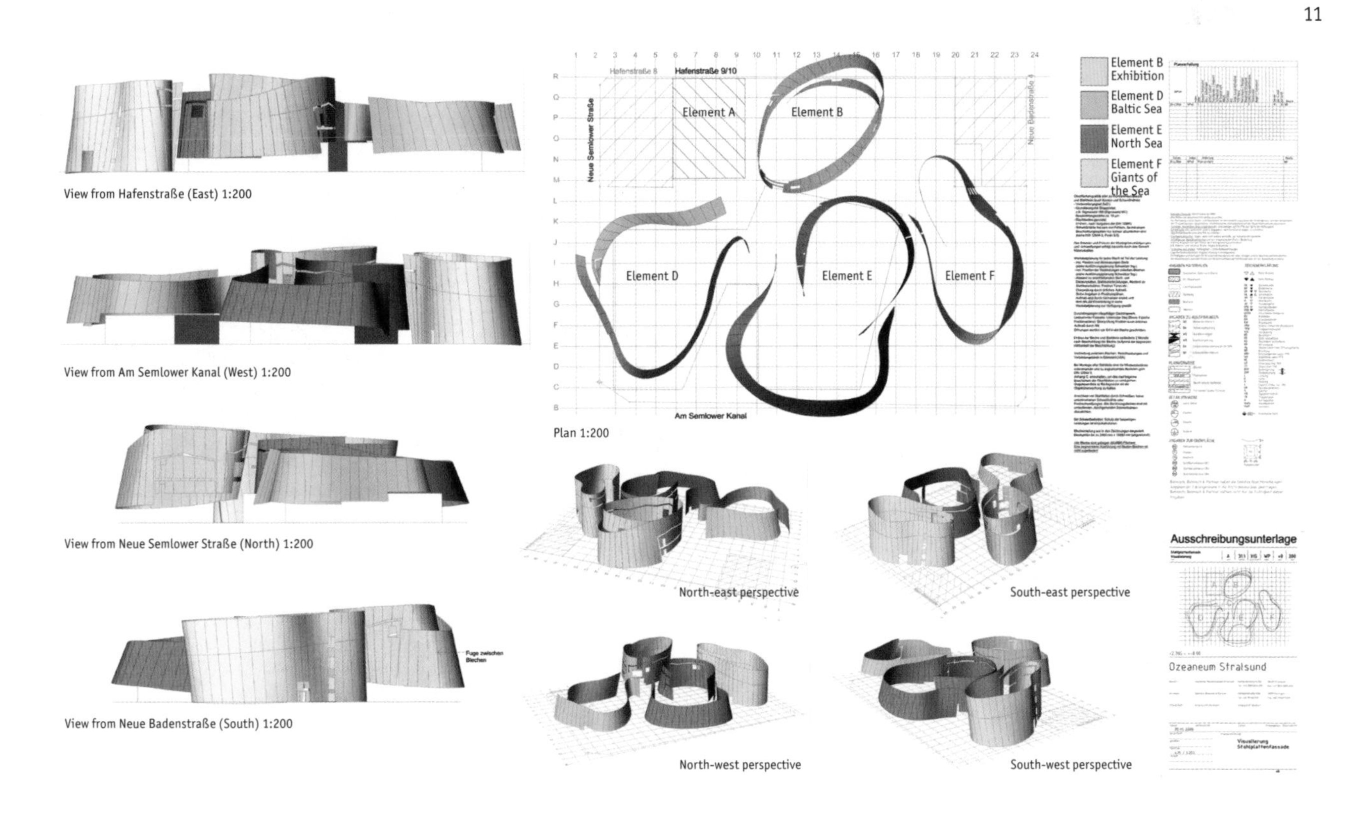

9 / Construction drawings of the connection of the glass with the roof: The contract was for a full architectural build and Behnisch were responsible for tendering and producing workshop drawings. A local architect was employed by the client to supervise the site and to calculate the technical descriptions of materials and packaging.

10 / Mounting the steel panels: An early concept was to use wood for the cladding, to bring to mind the barrels once used in the harbour, but the client thought the high humidity levels might cause structural problems. A manufacturer was sought to produce steel, free-formed panels on a large scale.

11 / 3-D workshop drawings for the steel plates: At the beginning of the design development, 3-D computer technology was in its infancy. Behnisch collaborated with Porsche, who had access to the most advanced programs on the market and scanned the practice's physical models. The 3-D versions were used to develop the concept.

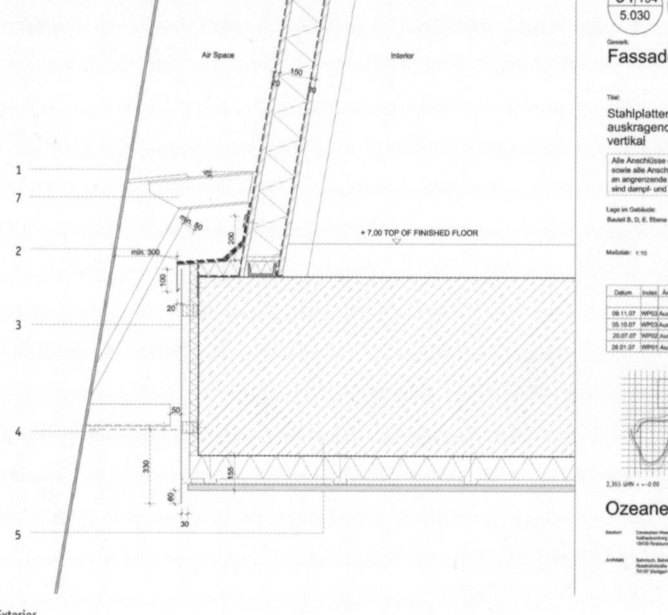

Exterior

1 Steel façade panel
2 Waterproofing
3 Aluminium plate
4 Stainless steel grating
5 Suspended ceiling
6 Wall assembly
7 Steel support bracket

Air space

Interior

+7,00 TOP OF FINISHED FLOOR

12 / The panels were produced by a local company specializing in cold-forming steel. Ostseestaal are used to precisely cutting and shaping construction panels three-dimensionally for use in ships' hulls. The sheets are shaped by hydraulic presses. A special gauge was made from hard fibreboard for each sheet in order to control the geometry.

13 / Because of the high water table, creating the foundations was a challenge. Pillars had to be drilled deep into the site to support the reinforced-concrete plinth and building substructure.

14 / The blades clad a steel frame construction. The 16 x 3 m (52½ x 9¾ ft) sheets are secured at isolated points without any further structural support. Overhangs are thus braced yet appear to be free-standing.

15 / Colour mock-ups for the concrete plinth were set up on site. At first the architects wanted to mimic the limestone brick houses of the region but eventually changed to a more earthy shade. Although major decisions are taken early, Behnisch's designs evolve, and decisions about detailing and materials are often made just prior to construction.

16 / The tank in the North Sea exhibit for the schooling fish contains c. 2.6 million litres (572,000 gallons) of water. It has a 10 x 5 m (32¾ x 16½ ft) curving acrylic glass front. Only one company, based in Colorado in the USA, could manufacture such a product and it took four months to ship it to Europe. The engineers found it a trial to match the precision of the glass to the concrete substructure, which has a degree of tolerance.

17 / Construction drawing of the steel plate façade.

18 / The heights of the new structures are aligned with neighbouring buildings by staggering the surface areas of some of the upper storeys or, where technically feasible, by flattening them.

19 / A 30 m (98½ ft) suspended escalator, the longest in Europe, traverses the entire breadth of the foyer and takes visitors to the upper storey where the exhibitions begin.

20 / Life-size models of whales, sponsored by Greenpeace, are an awe-inspiring sight in the Giants of the Sea display.

21 / The centrepiece of the North Sea exhibit is the huge aquarium of schooling fish.

22 / The World's Oceans: The individual exhibition halls have been given different atmospheres and were developed in collaboration with museum designers Atelier Lohrer.

23 / The materiality is raw, robust and simple. A judicious use of steel and reinforced concrete achieves a sense of lightness. Natural stone is used in the foyer. Granite cobblestones for the flooring mimic the cobblestones characteristic of the harbour.

24 / The heating and cooling demands of the building are reduced as much as possible, and the foyer is naturally ventilated throughout. The overhang of the exhibition areas shades the glazing of the atrium, and the large front entrance is north-facing. Each element of the building has specific requirements and energy-saving solutions were developed.

Etrium

Benthem Crouwel Architekten

Location: Cologne, Germany
Principal use: Headquarters/office, Econcern
Client: HIBA Grundbesitz GmbH & Co. KG
Site area: 3,000 m² (32,291¾ ft²)
Interior area: 1,490 m² (16,038¼ ft²)
Total build area: 4,970 m² (53,496½ ft²)
Design period: August 2007 – August 2008
Construction period: January 2008 – October 2008
Budget: €6,800,000

Dutch architects Jan Benthem and Mels Crouwel are best known for the redesign of Schiphol airport (2011), and the renovation and enlargement of the Stedelijk Museum in Amsterdam (2011). Founded in 1979, their practice is one of the most consistent and productive in the Netherlands today. Since 2005 Bentham Crouwel has run a German office in Aachen, which was responsible for the Etrium project. The firm is recognized internationally for its functional, sober and logical approach and distinguished by its use of transparency and the harmonious way it manages to integrate the human dimension into large-scale projects. Called upon to describe their design philosophy, Mels Crouwel takes a pragmatic stance. 'Our ideas seem to have lost nothing of their value after 30 years. Good architecture begins with clear thinking, better solutions come from digging deeper. Which is why we like clients who ask questions and have opinions of their own. We are not after sensation and extravagance but seek the core of the matter. This, in our experience, is how to achieve designs that steer clear of the obvious. Creativity thrives in a climate of orderliness and rationality.'

Etrium is one of the smallest projects undertaken recently by Benthem Crouwel but bears many of the architects' traits and is by no means to be underestimated. The German headquarters of the Dutch company Econcern is the first office building in Cologne to qualify as a 'passive house', and as such acts as a calling card for this market leader in sustainable energy.

Benthem Crouwel knew both the client (HIBA Grundbesitz GmbH, which owns the Triotop business and country park), and Grundbesitz's eventual tenant, Econcern, and were instrumental in introducing the two parties. Triotop is located on the shores of the Wassermann Lake, to the west of Cologne, and is committed to providing a stimulating working environment. Offices and commercial premises are built from traditional materials and provide spacious, bright and flexible workspaces. 'There's one place where we work and other places that inspire our creativity. And for recreation, we go somewhere new,' the park's developers wrote. 'Wouldn't it make sense to combine these spaces into one harmonious unit and into one location that integrates everything: work – create – play.'

Anton Bausinger from HIBA Grundbesitz is an architect and owns Friedrich Wassermann GmbH, the company that worked as the contractor for the headquarters, with Benthem Crouwel developing a feasibility study, being responsible for the design and the construction drawings, and acting as artistic director (stages 1–5 and 8 according to German architectural orders). Grundbesitz was heavily involved in decision-making and in the detailing of the design, with Wassermann responsible for the tender and construction documentation, which was based on the architects' meticulous and extensive construction planning drawings. The contractor was also responsible for supervising the build.

The brief was developed collaboratively. The initial requirement was for an office building that could accommodate 150 members of staff, and be sustainable and in tune aesthetically with the other facilities on the site. During the preliminary design stage, four brainstorming sessions were held with the client and the tenant during which the programme and the structure were defined. Powerpoint was used as a presentation tool, and printouts were made and handed out so that the discussions would continue after the meetings finished. Physical models were also used in various scales from 1:500 up to 1:100. The scheme took a further two months to develop but in essence the core concept changed little.

The design that was delivered is compact on the outside while being very open and generous internally. It has three storeys arranged around an atrium, a spectacular glass-covered court that draws daylight and air into the entire building. Internal terraces on the upper floors are rotated relative to one another to give unexpected views and vibrant spaces. The use of wood finishes on the walls and floor adds warmth as well as a sense of informality to the rigorous geometry. The exterior of the concrete walls is covered with a ground red-glass render that blends with the colour of the brick used in the surrounding buildings but remains unique and eye-catching as it glitters in the daylight.

The building is orientated towards the sun and well insulated. An integrated air-conditioning system exploits the thermal capacities of the concrete used in the main structure, allowing for smaller fluctuations in temperature. The building has no need for traditional heating and cooling systems, as passive energy sources provide almost all the necessary heating: a waste-heat recovery system for exhausted air, and a heat pump that uses the difference in temperature between the groundwater and the air, guarantee an ambient and stable atmosphere all year round. In addition, solar panels on the roof contribute to an agreeable indoor climate and rainwater is collected and used for sanitation purposes.

Despite being on a much smaller scale than most of Benthem Crouwel's commissions, the practice admits to having learnt a great deal from working on Etrium. Although the architects are known for their very technical building solutions they have not been particularly associated with green design. However, the experience they gained in satisfying all the energy regulations of the Deutsche Gesellschaft für Nachhaltiges Bauen (the German equivalent of Leadership in Energy and Environmental Design, or LEED) in a building that consumes less than a fifth of the energy used by comparable office complexes, has convinced Benthem Crouwel that sustainability will have a greater influence on their future portfolio.

1 / The German headquarters of Econcern qualifies as a 'passive house' and is extremely low in energy consumption with a pleasant indoor climate.

1

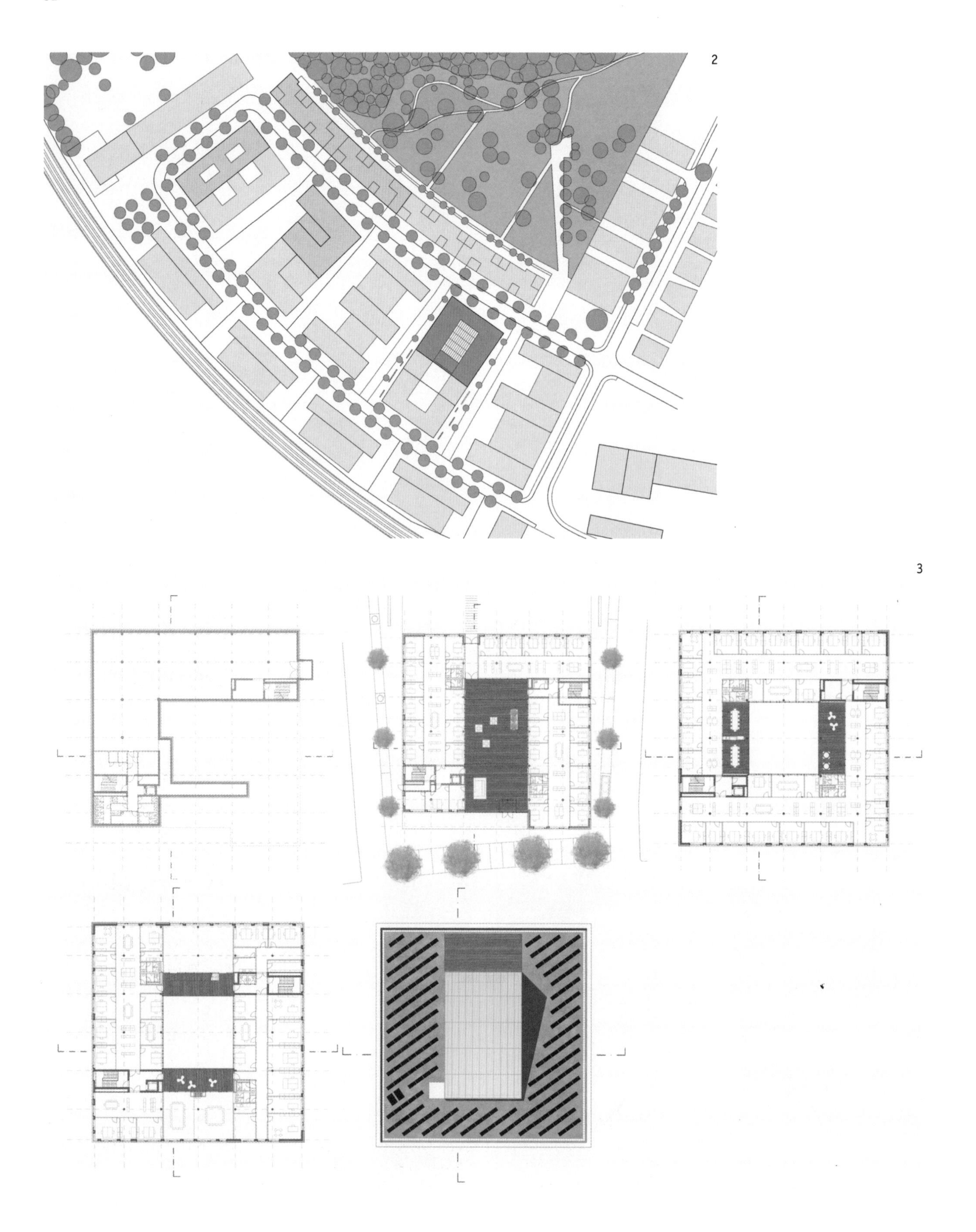
2
3

4

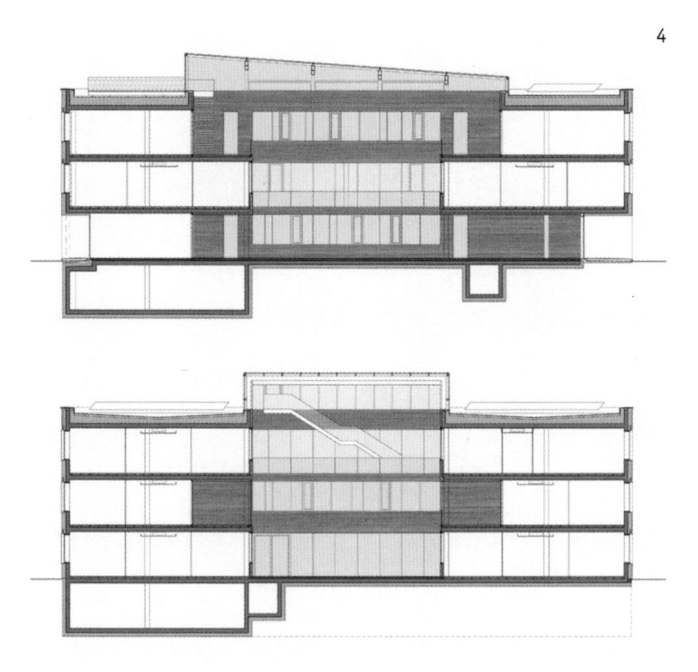

5

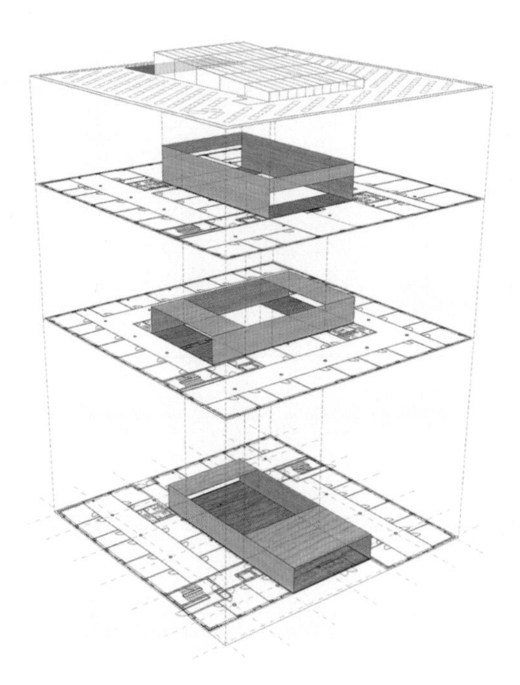

6

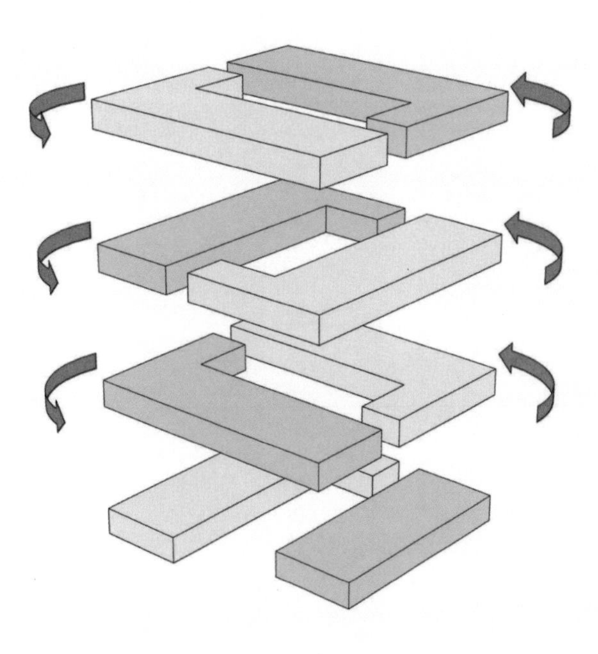

2 / Site plan.

3 / Basement to roof-level floor plans: The building is based on a 38 m² (409 ft²) plan. To achieve a comfortable internal climate the structure needed to be compact with a good AV relation between the volume being heated and heat lost through the surface.

4 / Sections AA-south and BB-west.

5 / Axonometric showing the three storeys and roof terrace. The internal terraces surrounding the atrium have been rotated 90 degrees relative to one other, to create spaces used for relaxation and break-out sessions.

6 / First presentation: The concept was developed in collaboration with the client and tenant using four PowerPoint presentations over a period of five weeks, with each iteration adding to the previous proposal. The idea that the design should be compact on the outside with open-plan offices centred around a generous central atrium was already in place in the first presentation, as was the idea that the floors should shift in orientation on each level.

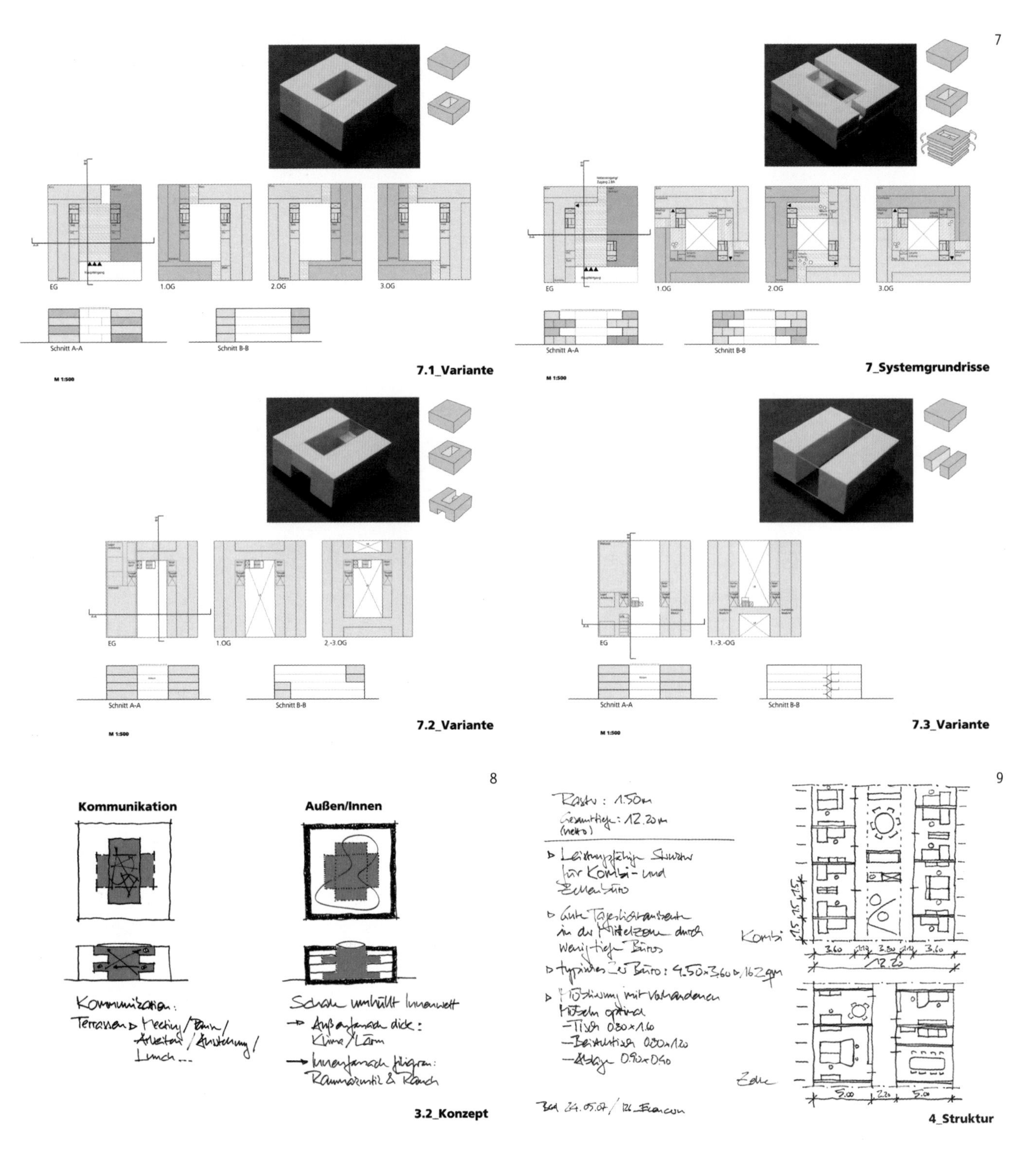

7 / First presentation: The architects used physical models to develop the concept. These were shown to the client in the presentation, in tandem with diagrammatic floor plans and sections to give a better understanding of how the floors would rotate relative to one another.

8 / First presentation: Sketches were used to examine how the internal spaces could relate to one another as well as to the possible circulation routes.

9 / First presentation: Hand-drawn floor plans of the office spaces show two variations of possible layout.

10 / First presentation: Early concept investigating the use of passive energy sources.

11 / Second presentation: The concept that was selected.

12 / Second presentation: Sections.

13 / Second presentation: Studies were made of how the façade could work to take advantage of solar energy.

14 / Floor plans taken from the second presentation show how the layout had been developed since the first meeting. Plans were printed out and annotated by hand during informal round-table discussions.

10

5_Klimakonzept

11

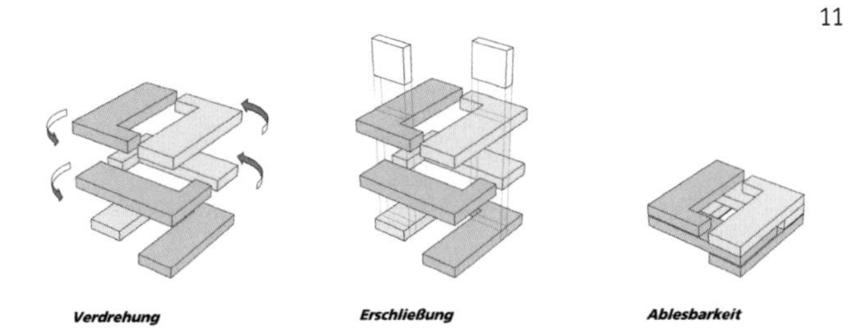

1_Konzept

12

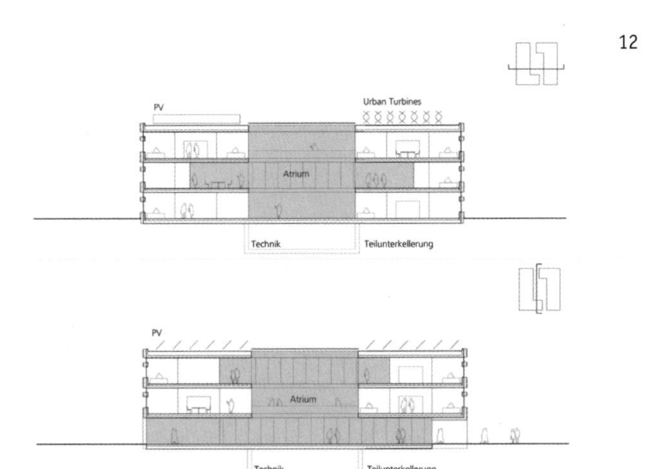

13

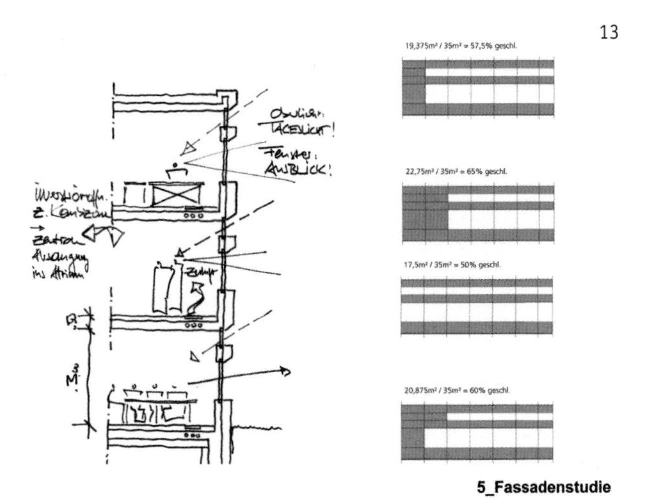

5_Fassadenstudie

14

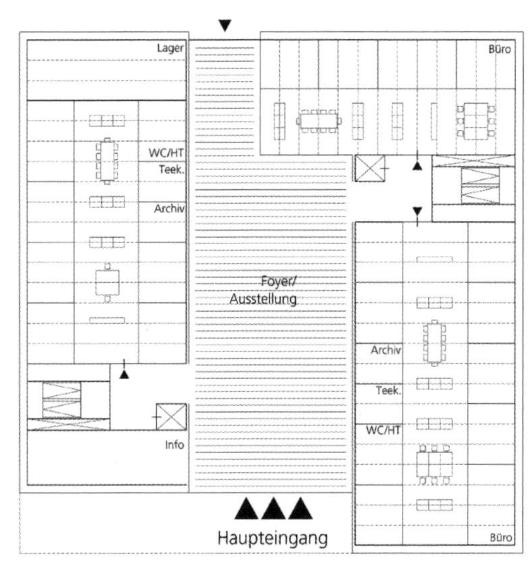

Stand 01.06.2007 EG M 1:200
126_Econcern
Benthem Crouwel

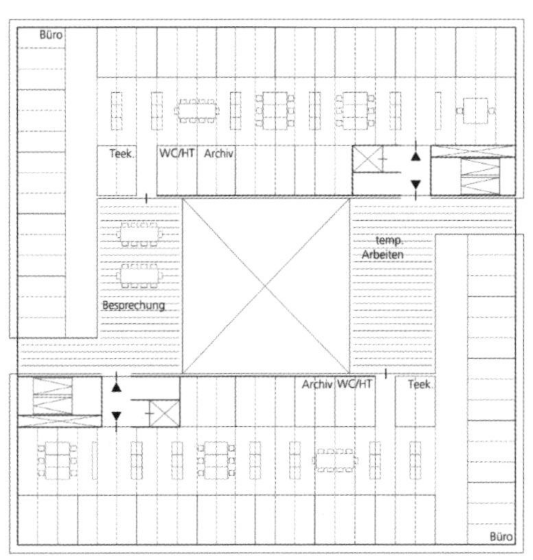

Stand 01.06.2007 1.OG M 1:200
126_Econcern
Benthem Crouwel

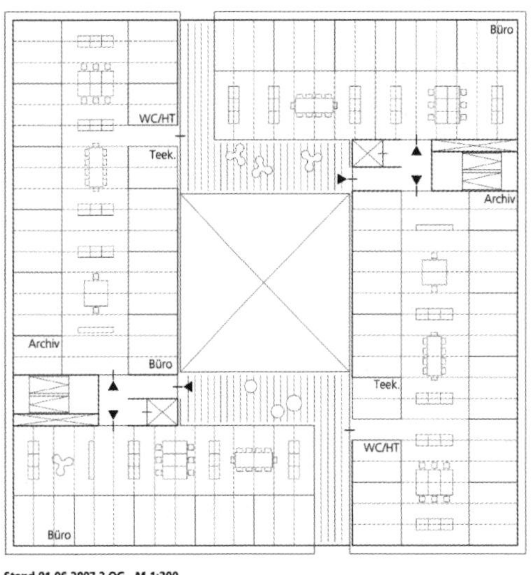

Stand 01.06.2007 2.OG M 1:200
126_Econcern
Benthem Crouwel

15

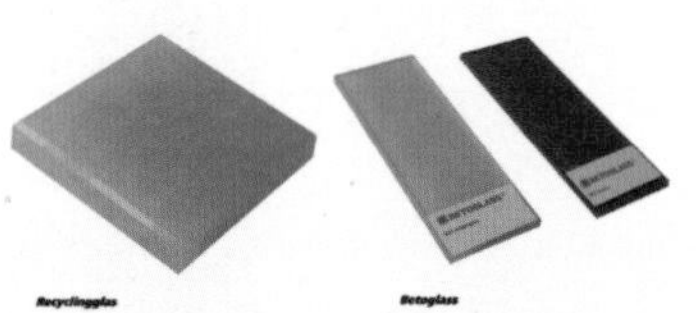

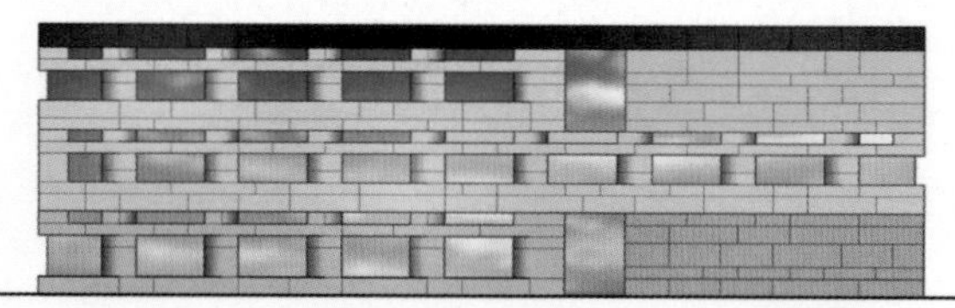

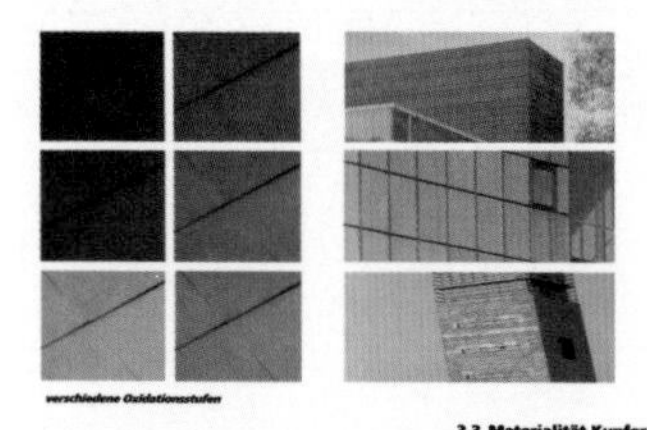

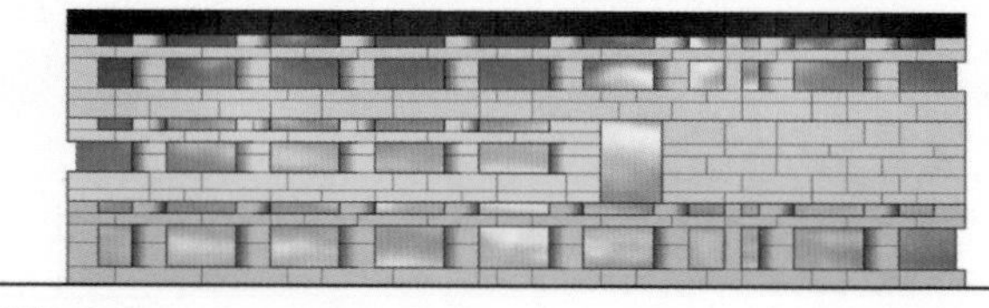

16

17

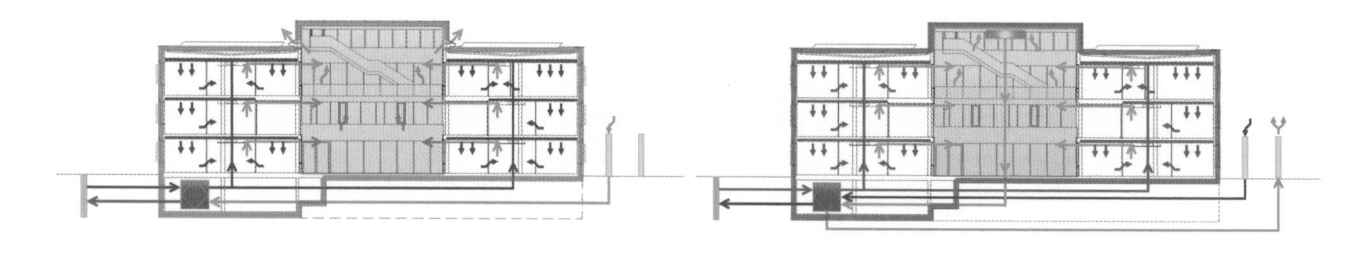

15 / By the third presentation materiality was being considered as well as the articulation of the façade.

16 / Fourth presentation: Renderings, here of the lobby, were made to give an idea of how the interiors would look.

17 / Climate studies for summer and winter: All the outgoing air from the offices is brought to the central atrium. From here the air is exhausted through the welded steel-frame glass roof in the summer, or brought back to the basement to a waste-heat recovery facility in the winter.

18 / Final renderings were made at the end of the design phase to control the design and as a draft for the tender and construction.

19 / Construction-planning drawing of the façade: To qualify as a passive house, outer walls have to fulfil insulation criteria. In the case of Etrium the external concrete walls had to have 28 cm (11 in) of insulation. A compound thermal system was selected. The polystyrene rigid-foam sheets with rebated joints are adhesive-fixed over the full surface area.

18

19

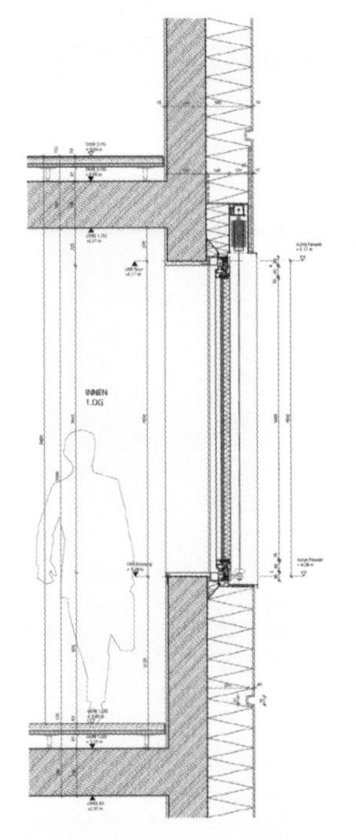

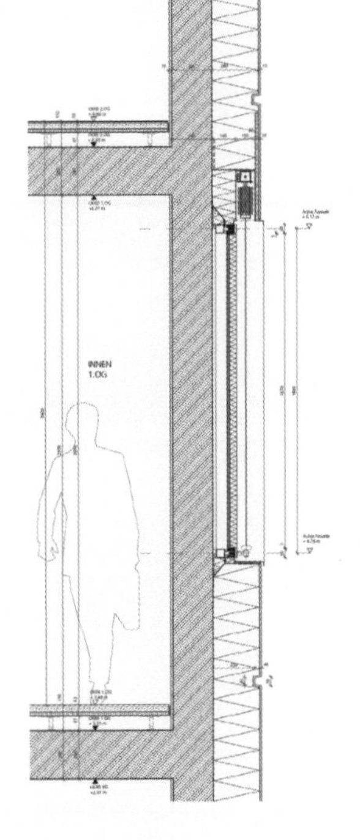

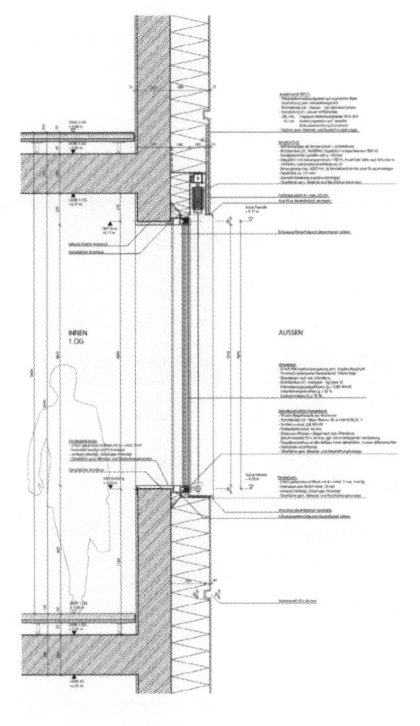

OPAQUE CASEMENT WINDOW V-SECTION

Element 4 – opaque casement window:
- Pivot made of thermally separated aluminium profiles
- Reference make, e.g., Raico WING 75 B
- Uf = min. 1.80 W/m²K
- Implementation as block window with concealed casement
- Building depth in accordance with static requirement
- Concealed fitting system
- VI panel in accordance with specifications for element 2
- Surface in accordance with the material and coating concept

TRANSPARENT CASEMENT WINDOW V-SECTION

Element 3 – transparent casement window:
- Pivot made of thermally separated aluminium profiles
- Reference make, e.g., Raico WING 75 B
- Uf = min. 1.80 W/m²K
- Implementation as block window with concealed casement
- Building depth in accordance with static requirement
- Concealed fitting system
- Triple-tinted glass in accordance with specifications for element 1
- Surface in accordance with the material and coating concept

VI PANEL V-SECTION

Element 2 – vacuum insulation panel
- VI panel in accordance with component catalogue
- Reference make, e.g., ESCO VI-plus panel
- Heat transfer coefficient Up = 0.24 W/m²K
- Filling of VI sheet and MF insulation
- Thermally improved warm-edge seal, PSI = 0.04 W/mK
- Double-sided panelling with 3 mm sheet aluminium
- Surface in accordance with the material and coating concept

FIXED GLAZING V-SECTION:

- Triple-tinted glass in accordance with component catalogue
- Reference make, e.g., Interpane iplus 3E Heat transfer coefficient Ug ≈ 0.60 W/m²K Total energy penetration g ≈ 50 % Light transmission TL ≈ 70 %
- Thermally improved warm-edge seal, PSI = 0.04 W/mK
- Overall design in accordance with static requirement

Key
Materials

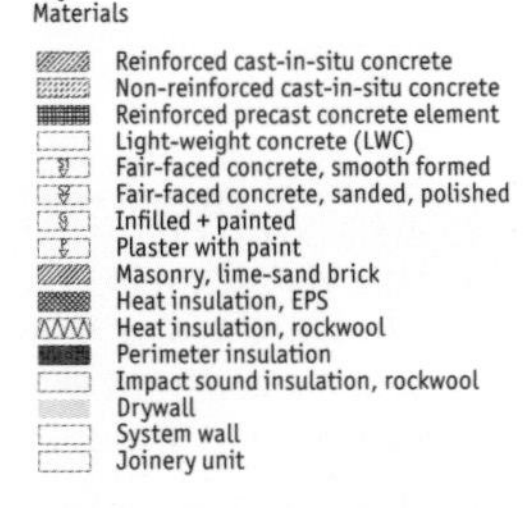

Reinforced cast-in-situ concrete
Non-reinforced cast-in-situ concrete
Reinforced precast concrete element
Light-weight concrete (LWC)
Fair-faced concrete, smooth formed
Fair-faced concrete, sanded, polished
Infilled + painted
Plaster with paint
Masonry, lime-sand brick
Heat insulation, EPS
Heat insulation, rockwool
Perimeter insulation
Impact sound insulation, rockwool
Drywall
System wall
Joinery unit

Breakthroughs

- OKFB Top edge of finished floor
- OKRB Top edge of unfinished floor
- UKRD Bottom edge of unfinished floor
- UKFD Bottom edge of prefabricated floor
- OKAD Top edge of suspended ceiling
- UKAD Bottom edge of suspended ceiling
- UKUZ Bottom edge of drop beam
- UKST Bottom edge of lintel
- RBR Apron unfinished height
- FBR Apron finished height
- VKR Unfinished leading edge
- VKF Finished leading edge

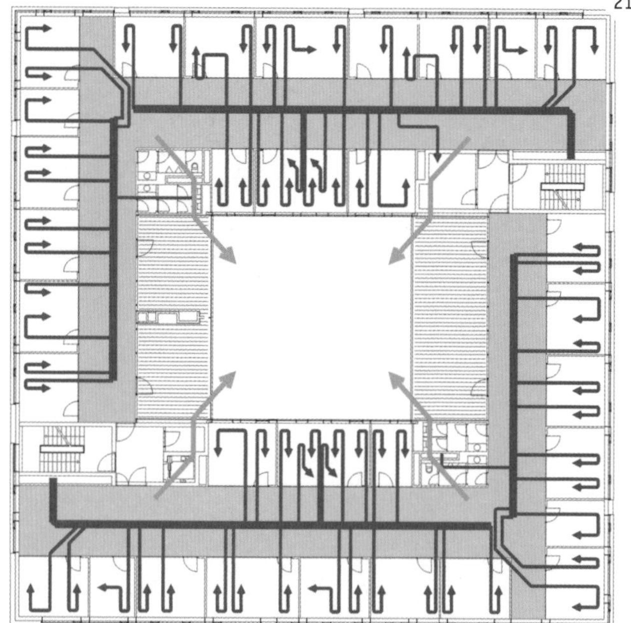

20 / The basic structure is reinforced concrete with weight-bearing outer walls, round columns and flat ceilings.

21 / Plan of the air supply system: According to the project architect, designing the mechanical services was 'the most interesting aspect of the project'. Five experts were involved in working out the sustainable requirements of the building as well as the complex heating, cooling, water and electrical supplies.

22 / Construction shot showing the pipes for the ventilation system being placed in one of the concrete ceilings.

23 / The main ventilation channel feeds all the smaller pipes. It needed to be accessible for maintenance and was too large to be concealed in the concrete so is suspended below the ceiling.

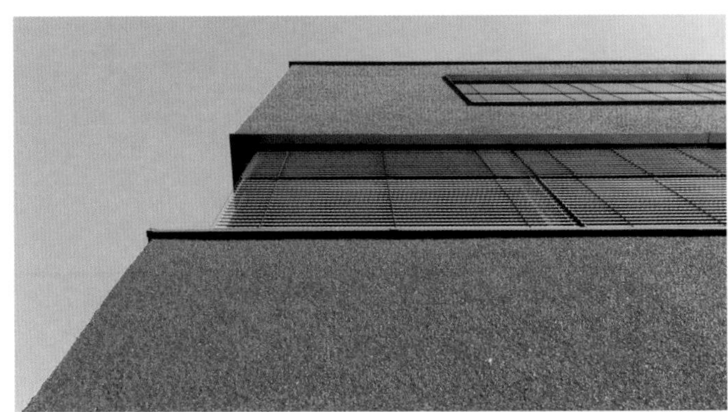

24 / A Solior system was used for the solar heating of water.

25 / Passive heat sources include energy created by office staff, and technical equipment including computers and lighting.

26 / The unique exterior surface was achieved through the use of glass granules in hues from orange to red that were applied to the outer layer of the render in a special 'thrown-on' technique.

27 / Atrium: The floor, walls and ceilings are finished in oak to improve the acoustics of the large open atrium and to lend the space an informal atmosphere. Only the walls and ceilings have a sound-absorbing finish.

Neues Museum

David Chipperfield Architects with Julian Harrap

Location: Museum Island, Berlin, Germany
Principal use: Museum
Client: Stiftung Preußischer Kulturbesitz represented by Bundesamt für Bauwesen und Raumordnung
Interior area: 15,400 m^2 (165,764 ft^2)
Exhibition area: 8,900 m^2 (95,798¾ ft^2)
Total build area: 20,500 m^2 (220,660 ft^2)
Design period: October 1998 – December 2005
Construction period: June 2003 – March 2009
Budget: €230,000,000 (completed for €200,000,000)

The Neues Museum is one of the five Neoclassical buildings that form UNESCO-protected Museum Island, situated in Berlin's Spree River. The first three-storey museum building in the world, it was designed by Schinkel's protégé, Friedrick August Stüler, and constructed between 1841 and 1859 in a Greco-Roman style. At the time the lightweight structure was a sensation. Combining traditional construction methods with the innovation of new industrialized building procedures, the museum played an important role in the history of technology. Extensive bombing during the World War II left the impressive edifice in ruins, with entire sections missing completely and others severely damaged. Although it was stabilized in the 1980s, and new foundation piles added to supplement the decaying timber grillage on which the building was originally founded, it was in essence left in its sorry post-war state until, in 1993, the Prussian Cultural Heritage Foundation launched a restricted international architecture competition calling for its restoration.

The initial brief asked not only for the museum to be renovated, but for an extensive master plan that would link it with the Pergamon and Altes museums, and for an urban and architectural solution for the redevelopment of Museum Island. Five architects were shortlisted: Giorgio Grassi, Francesco Venezia, Frank Gehry, Axel Schultes and David Chipperfield. The commission was initially awarded to Grassi, whose overall proposal for the up-to-date ensemble of museums was the most successful but who had not fully considered the functionality of the Neues Museum itself. He was asked to rework his concept but doubts remained and in 1997 the five architects were asked to present new solutions, this time for a reduced mandate focusing on the refurbishment of the museum in its original cubature. The jury selected David Chipperfield Architects who from the beginning had been working with conservation architect Julian Harrap.

The project required an extensive rebuilding programme as well as the restoration of the parts that remained. Certain interiors had survived the war almost entirely with elaborate finishes and frescoes intact, while other elements existed only as the enclosures of gaping voids. Chipperfield's approach was to unite the new and the old, the original and the repaired, the renovation and the intervention in a comprehensible setting that would reconnect the disparate components back into an architectural whole.

Once the commission was awarded Chipperfield founded a Berlin office and worked closely with the client. The decision-making process took place within two types of framework: the User Jour Fixe (formal group meetings that included all the parties involved, from the museum's directors to builders, planners and conservationists) and informal workshops.

The proposal for the restoration followed the principle of conservation rather than reconstruction. The new elements had to be of sufficient scale to have a physical character of their own while not contrasting too dramatically with the original building. In addition, the interventions and the philosophical concerns of restoration had to address the complex technical task of achieving thermal and environmental standards as well as the organizational requisites of a modern museum.

Julian Harrap started the assessment by compiling a Conservation Guideline and Restoration Strategy analyzing what was extant, room by room and surface by surface, and providing a series of visions for repairing the existing fabric in each case. The result was a methodology that provided an intellectual framework within which the new work and conservation could be evaluated, and formed the basis for the restoration concept developed by Chipperfield's team. The approach was rooted in the philosophy set out by William Morris at the time of the foundation of the Society for the Protection of Ancient Buildings (SPAB). Its aim was not to restore the building as an idealized version of the original; instead it proposed a preservation programme that would show the vicissitudes of time and so conserve the broader cultural heritage of the museum. The Piranesian vision of the ruinous structure was to remain, and the corrupting concrete and unsympathetic, red engineering-brick consolidation work that had been undertaken by the GDR with no heed to aesthetic considerations, removed. The design centres around the most emphatic of the new interventions: the giant staircase in precast concrete that follows the form but not the detail of the stair it replaces, and sits in the main staircase hall, which is preserved only as a brick volume, devoid of its original ornamentation. The nineteenth-century spatial sequence of galleries was re-established and the northwest wing, with the Egyptian courtyard and the Apollo risalit, as well as the apse of the Greek courtyard and the south dome were rebuilt using recycled handmade bricks.

The Neues Museum is an architectural masterpiece and resounds with the echoes of its history, from its original construction, its subsequent use and the devastation of bombardment, to the erosion of years of neglect and, finally, facing the future, its gradual phoenix-like rebirth and renewal. The collection it houses is of international importance and traces the history of the ancient world through the millennia from the Palaeolithic period to the early Middle Ages – a rich resource that was divided between the Egyptian Museum and the Museum of Pre- and Early History during and just after the war. With the collection reunited once more, and married to the restored building that shows both historical splendour and scars, the place of the Neues Museum alongside the Louvre and the British Museum is ensured.

1 / East façade and entrance of the Neues Museum.

1

2

1 Bode-Museum
2 Pergamon Museum
3 New entrance building – James Simon Gallery
4 Neues Museum
5 Altes Museum
6 Old National Gallery

3

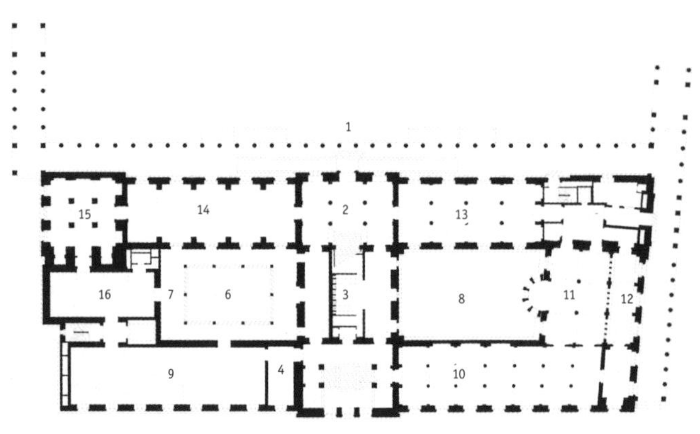

GROUND-FLOOR PLAN

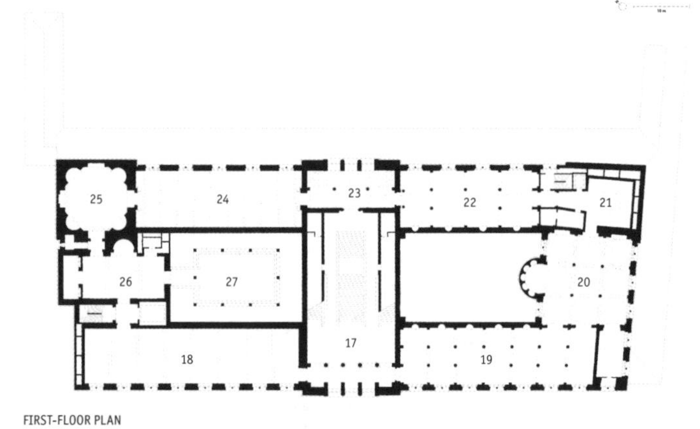

FIRST-FLOOR PLAN

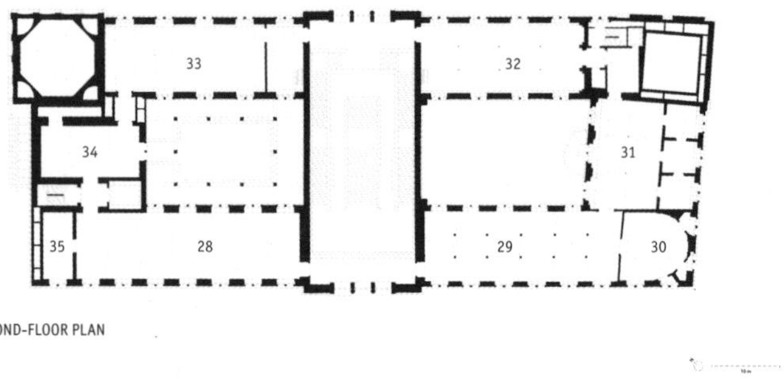

SECOND-FLOOR PLAN

1 Main entrance
2 Vestibule
3 Cloakroom
4 Museum shop
5 West entrance
6 Void above Egyptian courtyard
7 New gallery
8 Void above Greek courtyard
9 Historical Room
10 Ethnographical Room
11 Flat dome room
12 Café
13 Fatherland Room
14 Mythological Room
15 Tomb Room
16 Hypostyle
17 Staircase hall
18 Greek Room
19 Modern Room
20 Medieval Room
21 South dome room
22 Roman Room
23 Bacchus Room
24 Room of the Niobids
25 North dome room
26 Apollo Room
27 Platform above Egyptian courtyard
28 Blue Room
29 Western Art Chamber
30 Star Room
31 Majolica Room
32 Eastern Art Chamber
33 Red Room
34 Green Room
35 Education

4

5

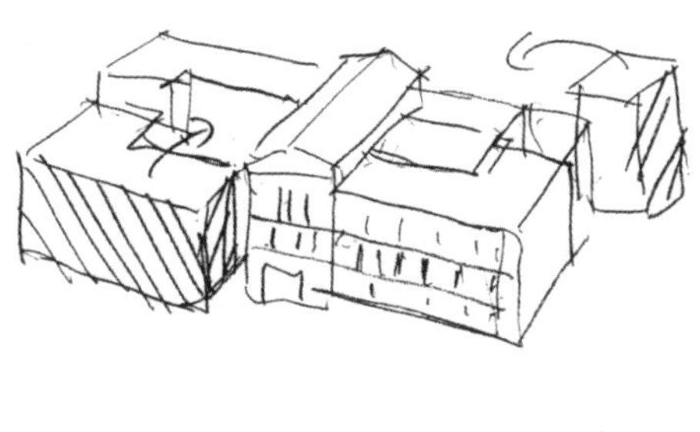

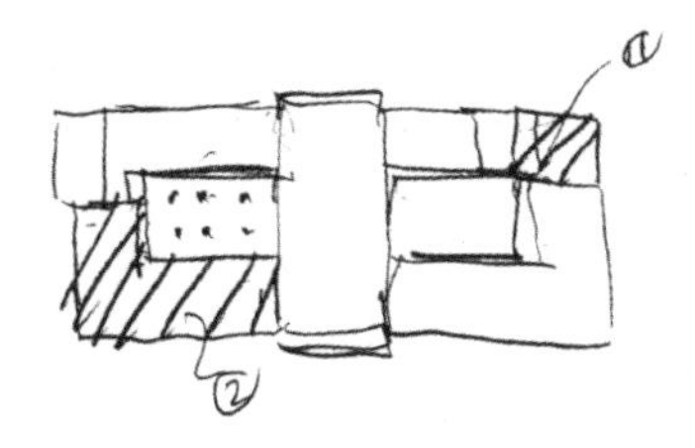

6

7

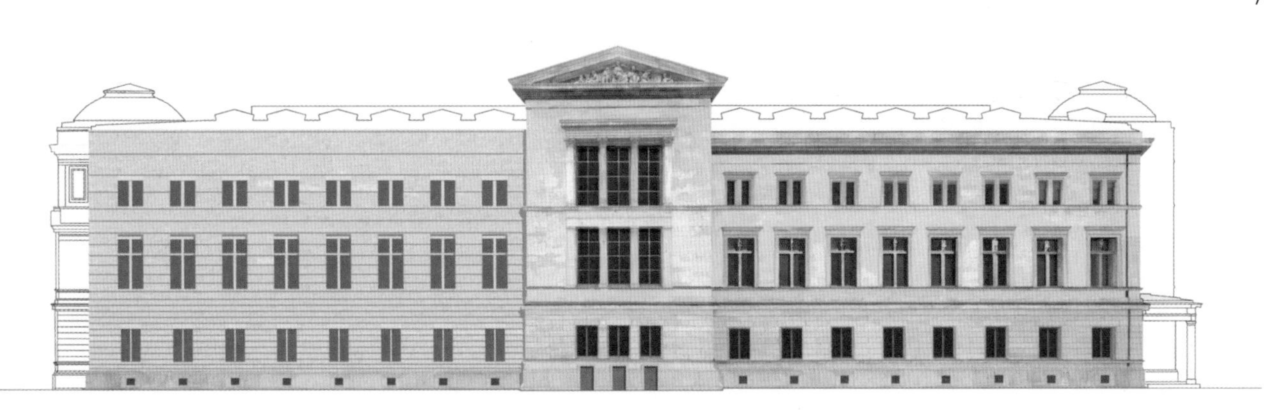

2 / Site plan: The James Simon Gallery forms the entrance to Museum Island's building ensemble.

3 / Ground-, first- and second-floor plans.

4 / The museum building and the main staircase hall prior to restoration work.

5 / David Chipperfield's first sketch showing how the form of the original museum would be reinstated by the addition of new-build elements.

6 / East elevation: Chipperfield used 2-D coloured elevations and sections to present his design to the client, as well as working and presentation models and renderings.

7 / West elevation.

8

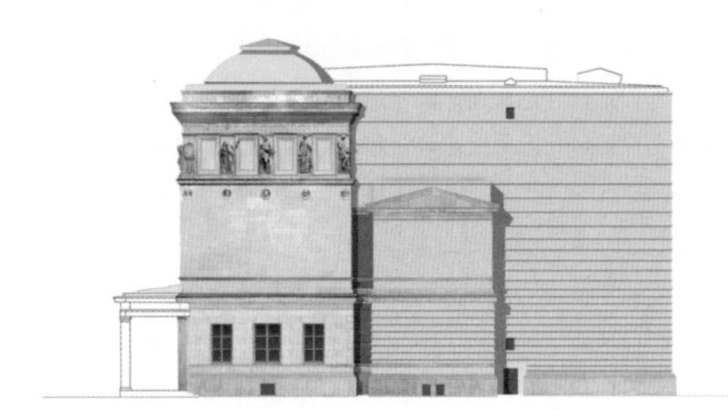

9

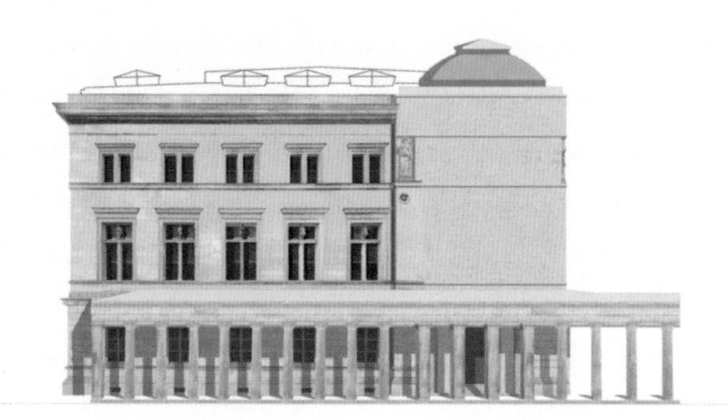

10

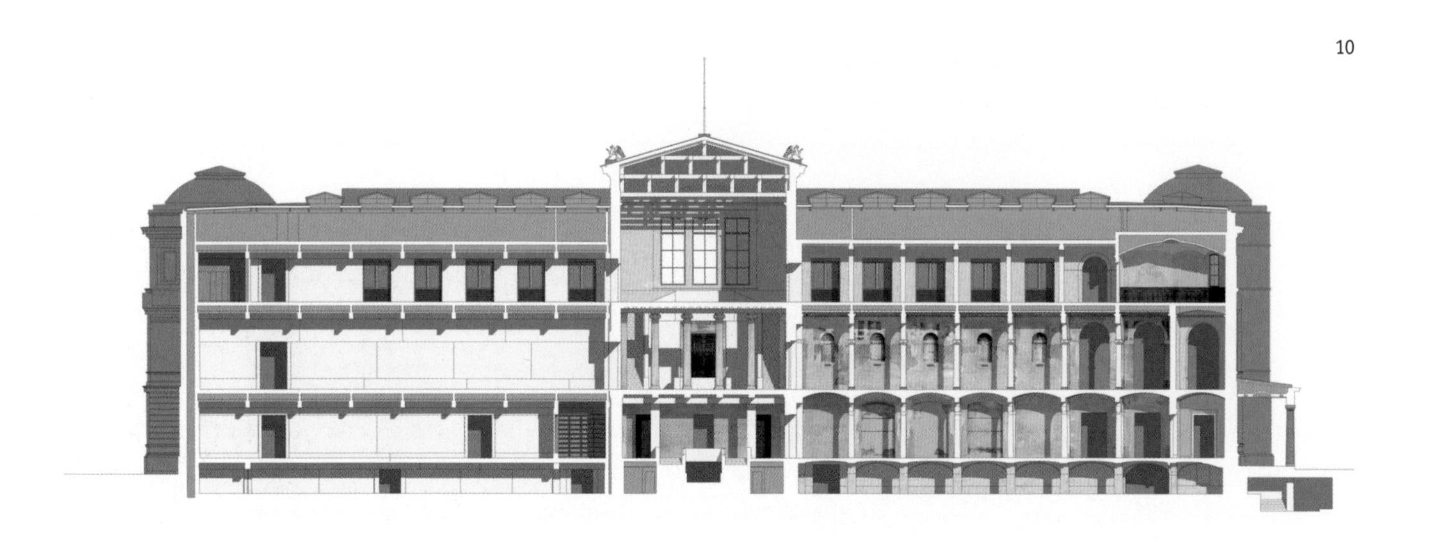

11

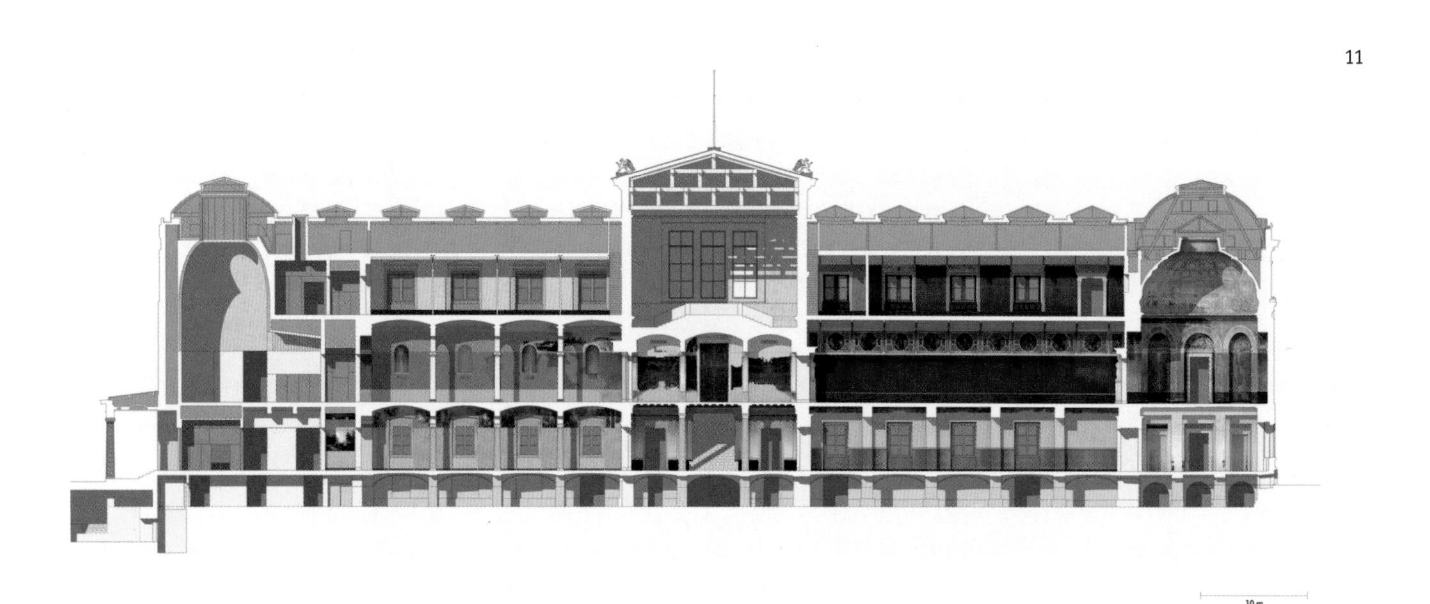

8 / North elevation.

9 / South elevation.

10 / Section through the west wing.

11 / Section through the east wing.

12

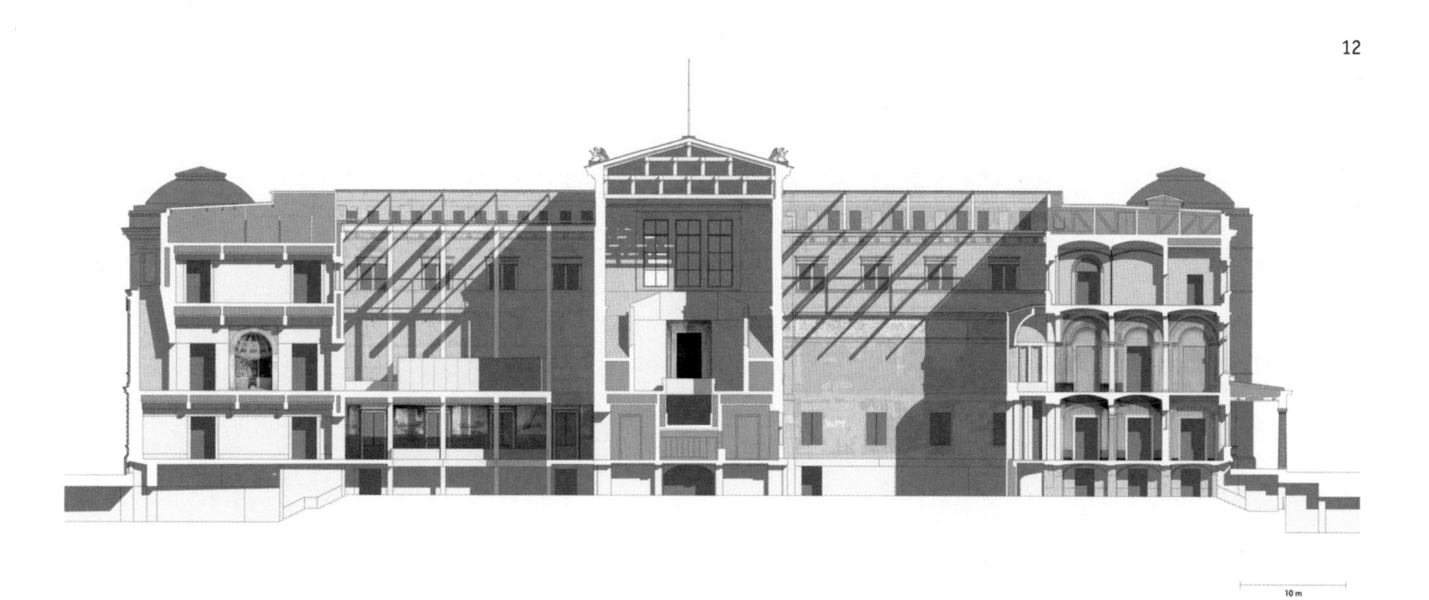

13

12 / Section through the courtyards.

13 / Working model of the main staircase hall from the preliminary design stage (top left), presentation model from the final design stage (bottom left) and a rendering (right). Models were used throughout the development process, as both design aids and presentation tools.

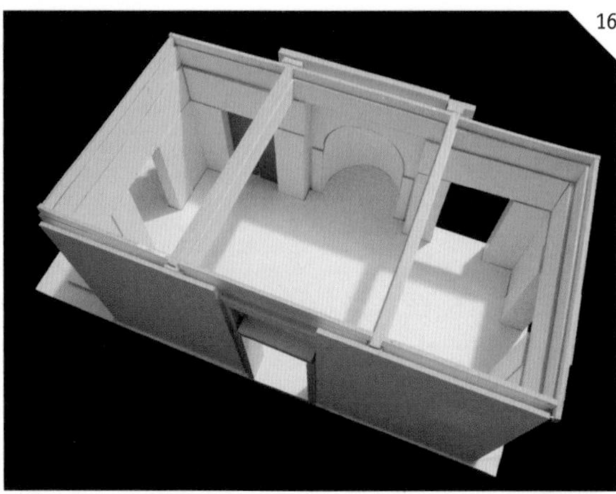

14 / Working model of the Egyptian Courtyard from the preliminary design stage (left), a presentation model for the final design stage (middle) and rendering (right): The Greek and Egyptian courtyards were excavated to the basement level and extended to the north and south to provide a future link between the Neues and the Pergamon and Altes museums.

15 / Presentation model of the Roman Room from the final design stage.

16 / Working model of the Apollo Room (new build) from the final design stage. To avoid damaging the original fabric, the modern elements carry the majority of the new plant and services requirements of the museum. Elsewhere the existing utility lines were cleared out, extended and broadened.

17 / The building was fully tested using a variety of means from scientific investigation of the foundations to stress analysis and empirical load assessment – illustrated here.

18 / Temporary structures held the building together while the GDR-era securing material was removed and the load paths of the original Stüler construction were re-established.

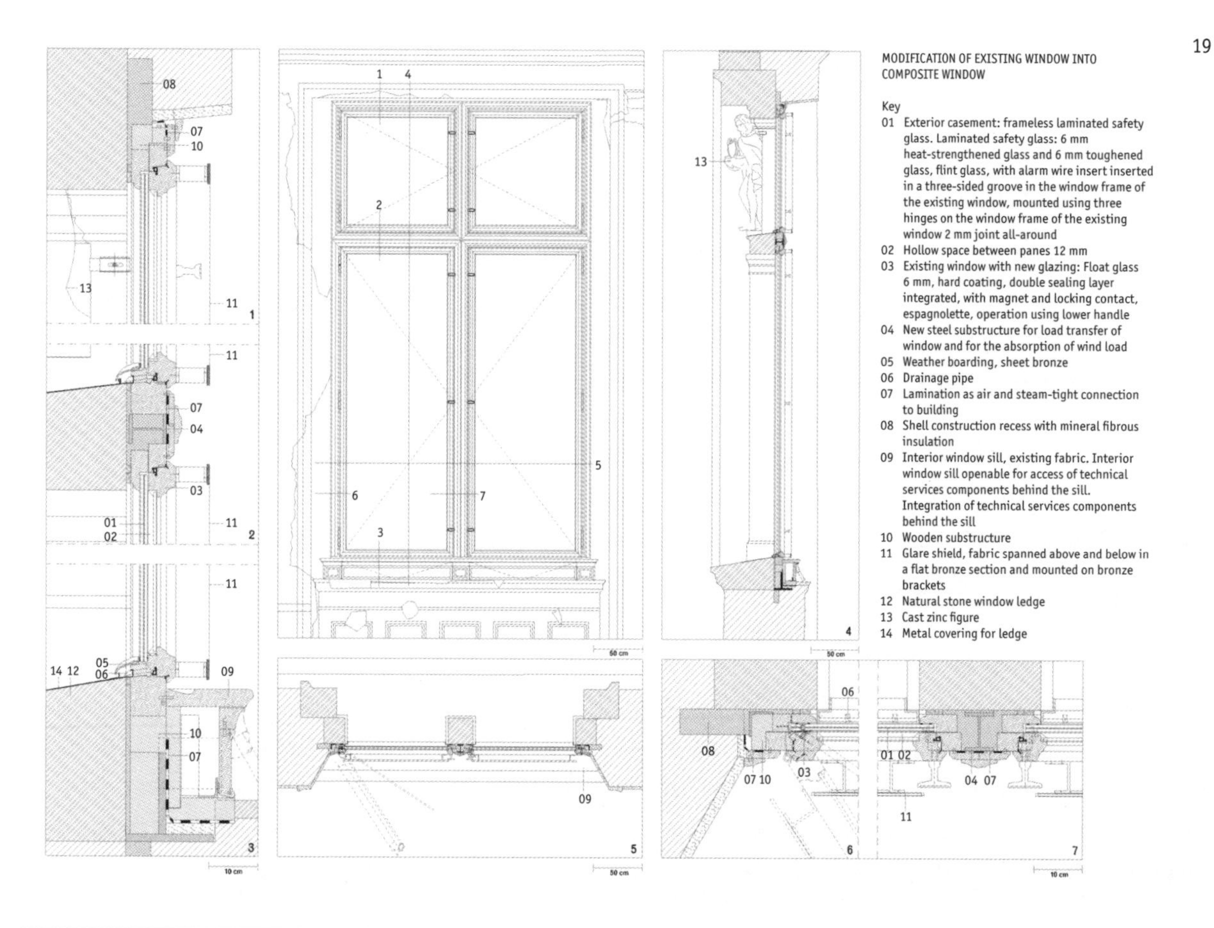

19
MODIFICATION OF EXISTING WINDOW INTO COMPOSITE WINDOW
Key
01 Exterior casement: frameless laminated safety glass. Laminated safety glass: 6 mm heat-strengthened glass and 6 mm toughened glass, flint glass, with alarm wire insert inserted in a three-sided groove in the window frame of the existing window, mounted using three hinges on the window frame of the existing window 2 mm joint all-around
02 Hollow space between panes 12 mm
03 Existing window with new glazing: Float glass 6 mm, hard coating, double sealing layer integrated, with magnet and locking contact, espagnolette, operation using lower handle
04 New steel substructure for load transfer of window and for the absorption of wind load
05 Weather boarding, sheet bronze
06 Drainage pipe
07 Lamination as air and steam-tight connection to building
08 Shell construction recess with mineral fibrous insulation
09 Interior window sill, existing fabric. Interior window sill openable for access of technical services components behind the sill. Integration of technical services components behind the sill
10 Wooden substructure
11 Glare shield, fabric spanned above and below in a flat bronze section and mounted on bronze brackets
12 Natural stone window ledge
13 Cast zinc figure
14 Metal covering for ledge

19 / Technical drawing showing the modification of the existing window into a composite window: The original oak frames were preserved and an extra layer of glass with a thermal break was inserted.

20 / The 19th-century museum rested on timber piles sunk into the sandy riverbed. Many devices were used to keep the building lightweight including hollow, terracotta pot domes and vaults. A fabricator was sought to replicate the pots used in the restoration of the partially surviving vaults.

21 / Construction of a clay pot ceiling: Before construction began a prototype was built to test how much load the vault could bear before breaking.

22 / Vaults in the Medieval Room: Originally the pots would have been covered in plaster. One of the principles was to show the layers of construction while avoiding harsh contrast. Wherever plaster was extant, the substrate was left visible but was washed with lime, so the plaster does not stand out too violently, in this case against the terracotta colour of the clay pots.

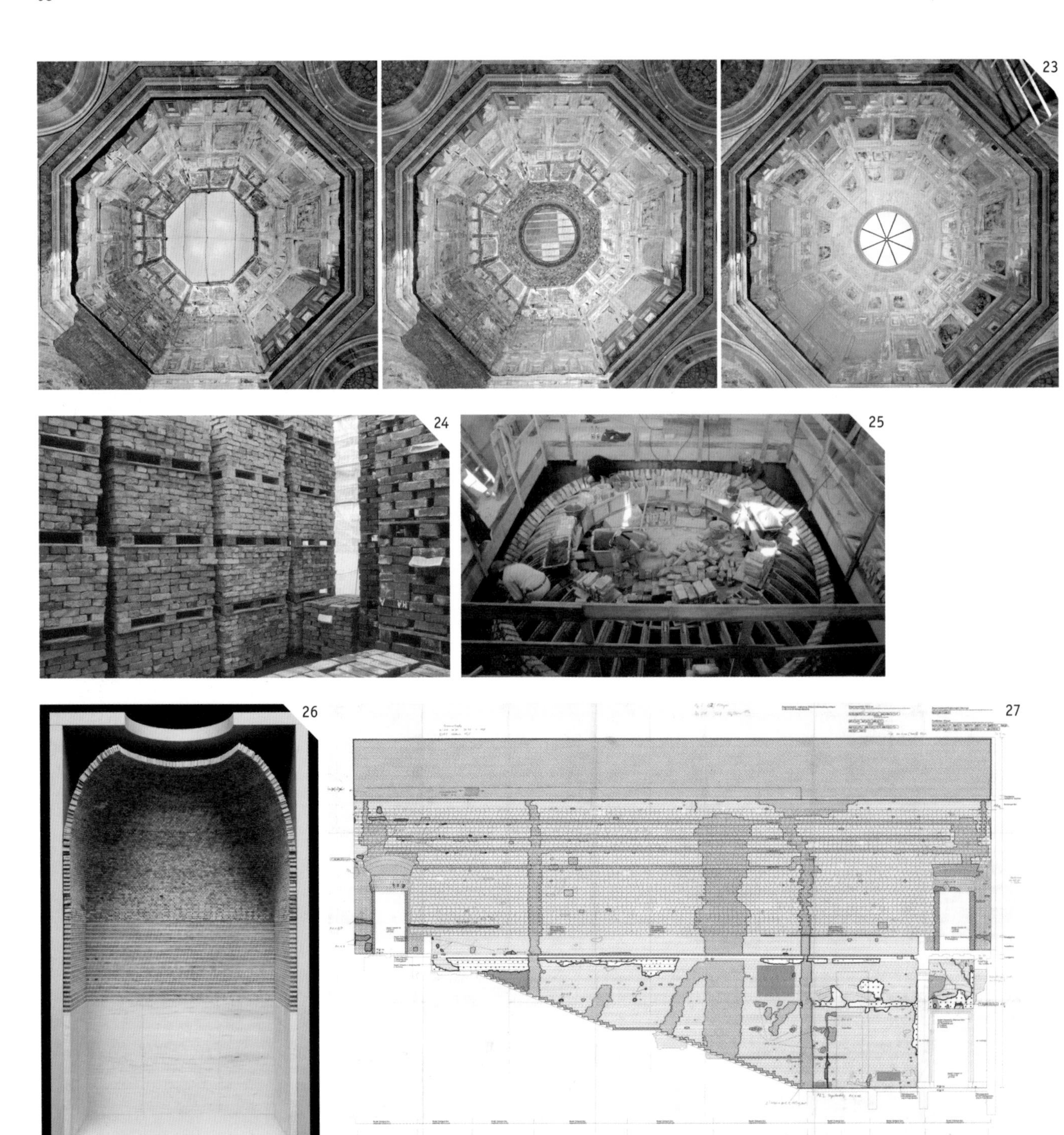

23 / Before, during and after restoration of the octagonal dome in the northwest dome: The oculus was reinstated by adding rings of recycled brick. Damage was manipulated rather than removed. The dark stain caused by water ingress was treated and colour washes used to tone the contrasting plasterwork up or down. Severely damaged but conserved wall paintings were brought out of storage and put back in place. Almost like framing a work of art, the lines of architectural decoration were recreated in stucco in order to restore the geometry and provide a fitting context for the fragmentary frescoes.

24 / The concept of building in recycled brick is alien to German construction. Five Berlin architects were asked to source samples of old bricks, to demonstrate that it was possible to find original material that was neither distorted nor broken, had the correct compression and conformed to DIN standards.

25 / Building up the brickwork around the oculus in the north dome.

26 / Model demonstrating the recycled brickwork in the south dome.

27 / Restoration drawing of the south wall in the main staircase hall, used to direct the work of the conservators.

28 / Renderings were made of the work that needed to be done – here of the condition of the ceiling in the Roman Room in 2000 (top) and a restoration study (middle). Restoration drawings were then produced (bottom).

28

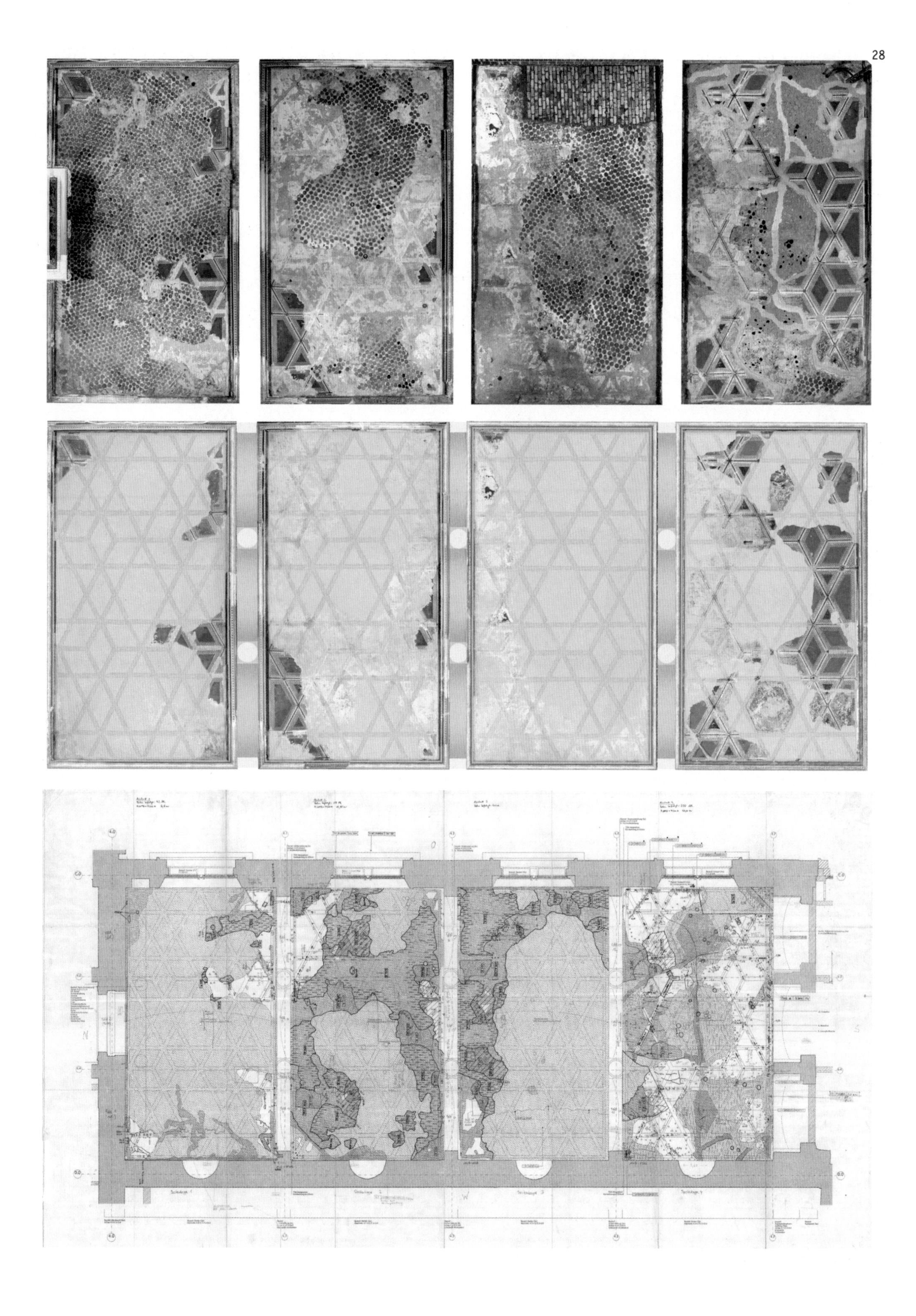

29 / Restorers at work in the Fatherland Room (left) and The Room of the Niobids (right).

30 / Left to right: Before, during and after images of the Medieval Room (top), Modern Room (middle) and Room of the Niobids (bottom): Each room was treated as an individual, special case with tailored solutions that combine to achieve a coherent whole. The surviving interiors act as a record of a 19th-century curator's view of the world, and the museum, even without its collection, is in itself an exhibit.

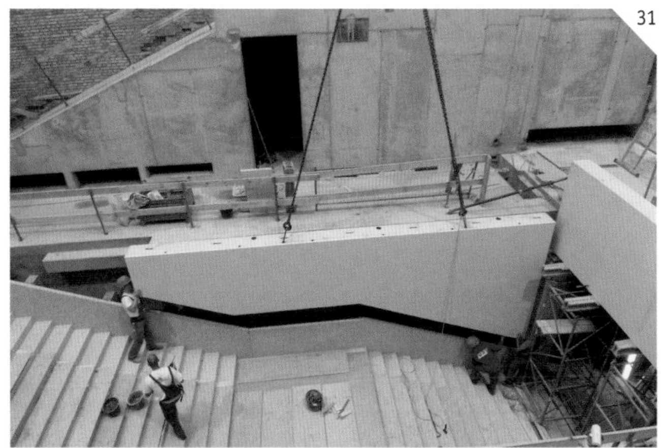

31 / A precast concrete section of the staircase is lowered into place.

32 / The new staircase is massive and monumental. Parts that are touched are polished smooth while untouched ones are distressed and rough, providing a sensory and visual experience. The concrete contains an aggregate of Saxonian marble chips.

33 / The Greek Courtyard is dominated by a new semicircular bay on the south side.

34 / The Egyptian courtyard is filled with a new structural frame supporting a mezzanine gallery and translucent glass roof.

35 / The old and new elevations are harmonized using recycled bricks. The contemporary elements borrow from the main contours of the original structure but are identified as modern additions by their absence of ornamentation. Stonework was cleaned and repaired, but care was taken not to destroy shrapnel damage that forms part of the cultural history of the building.

The Hotel Cha Am

Duangrit Bunnag Architect Ltd (DBALP)

Location: Cha Am, Petchaburi, Thailand
Principal use: Luxury resort
Client: KS Resort and Spa Co. Ltd
Site area: 30,000 m² (322,917 ft²)
Interior area: 16,000 m² (172,222½ ft²)
Total build area: 18,000 m² (193,750¼ ft²)
Design period: November 2004 – October 2005
Construction period: June 2005 – January 2009
Budget: 350,000,000 baht

Duangrit Bunnag received his bachelor degree in architecture from Chulalongkorn University but furthered his studies at the Architectural Association (AA) in London, where he received his graduate diploma in 1995. It was a period he considers fundamental to the way he started to perceive architecture and design. He was introduced to many disciplines, above all that of adopting a theoretical approach in his work, a practice that is missing in the educational system in Thailand. To a person who had never been taught to think this way before it was a crucial and effective way of learning. His diploma was not so much about the architecture (a concept design for the Yokohama air terminal in Japan) as it was about developing a methodology which, he maintains, still informs the way he works today.

Duangrit's buildings are undoubtedly Modernist in their language but are Thai in their detailing. 'I don't brand myself as a traditional Thai architect but I'm Thai. Maybe my Thai building "vocabulary" is not loud, or obvious, but it's there.' Although Duangrit is involved in all fields from residential to commercial, he is recognized most for his luxurious yet Minimalist resorts, which appeal to the new wave of young and daring developers who are turning against the kitsch, 'Disneyland' Thai villas that dot the country's coast and which Duangrit dismisses as a clichéd marketing ploy.

The client of the Cha Am approached DBALP after becoming acquainted with the Costa Lanta Resort that Duangrit had designed in a rustic but modern vernacular style. He had interviewed over 30 architects from both Thailand and abroad but saw in the Costa Lanta a marriage between the traditional Thai resort he envisaged for his family-run business (KS Resort and Spa Co. Ltd), and a contemporary idiom that would lift it ahead of the competition.

After being awarded the commission Duangrit visited the site. He is keen to point out that he doesn't have any preconceived ideas when he takes on a project, but allows the context to determine his design approach. In the case of the Cha Am the site was a featureless narrow strip facing the ocean, which told him he would have to create his own poetry and that the narrative needed to be sequential.

In Thailand an architect is responsible for everything including all construction documents, and Duangrit's company is qualified to produce quality tender manuals and expert detailed drawings. The 17-strong practice is divided into architecture and interior design sections, and there is one landscape specialist. For the hotel, Duangrit worked with one member from each section. Generally, DBALP has three organizing principles when it starts a project: synthesis analysis (development of a programme); the pattern book catalogue (each member of staff brings in a motivational photograph that is pinned to the walls and used to boost creativity); and grafting methodology, the tactic Duangrit learnt at the AA. This demanding technique involves graphically overlaying an unrelated but inspiring form on an image of the site, liberating the mind to accept what the 'graft' might infer in terms of perception of architectural space. The team work with what they call the 'design instrumental technique' – the individual merits of sketches, computer drawings and physical models are used in tandem to develop the sensations and experiences desired in the end product. It took DBALP three months to formulate the sequence for the hotel that was presented to the client, using over 80 renderings. The client's family, who were financing the project, were hesitant when faced with such a radical design but the client himself was convinced.

Customers park their cars on an engineered grass courtyard, an experience that already suggests their journey will be unorthodox. A contrasting Taj Mahal-like white stone plaza announces a monumental staircase that rises to the lobby – an open space beneath two giant columns spanned by timber beams. Looking out towards the sea, the area between is filled by a long reflecting pool that forms the roof of a spa beneath and is flanked by the hotel's 72 rooms and seven pool villas. The walk to the Clouds Loft restaurant at the far end of the complex is orchestrated by caged stone walls influenced by Herzog & de Meuron's work at the Dominus winery in California.

The design changed little, apart from minor modifications to functional elements that were made when the client went into partnership with the first hotel operator, Alila. (At the time of going to print a second hotel operator was about to be appointed.) Some of the drama of the central space was lost in favour of additional rooms to increase profitability.

Although detailed drawings were made, the contractors (chosen by the client, who managed the tendering process) worked without shop drawings and lacked the experience to build the more complex elements of the hotel without constant advice and supervision. Duangrit likens the process to music: 'With an orchestra you can write a note and everyone plays by it but in Thailand you can compose the score but not everyone follows it. You have to at least make certain they are playing on the same scale and you have chosen good musicians. You have to be ready for improvisation and flexibility.'

Writing of his work, Duangrit states, 'I can always feel my architecture during the design process.' He continues: 'Through computer renderings, models and hundreds of sketches, I am seeing a form develop that must contain and sustain life. Similar to all living organisms, it must appear simple but ideologically complex ... It has to create its own coherence to its context; physically, functionally and visually.'

1 / View along the reflecting pool to the Clouds Loft restaurant: Duangrit Bunnag's Minimalist lines, bold forms and subtle colour palette are enriched by the use of natural materials.

2

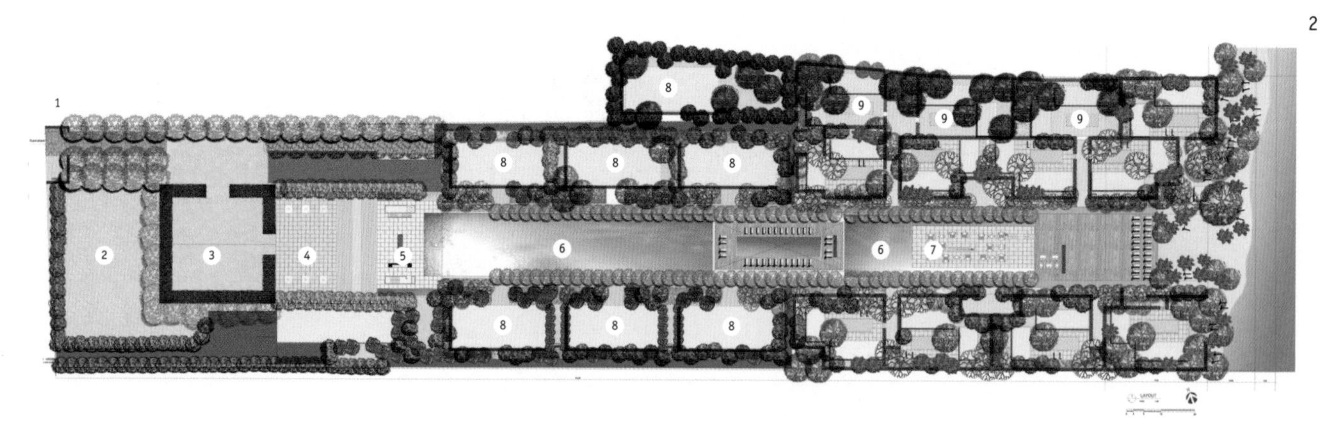

1 Guest access
2 Overflow parking
3 Courtyard
4 Plaza
5 Lobby
6 Pool
7 Restaurant
8 Room
9 House (phase 2)

3 4

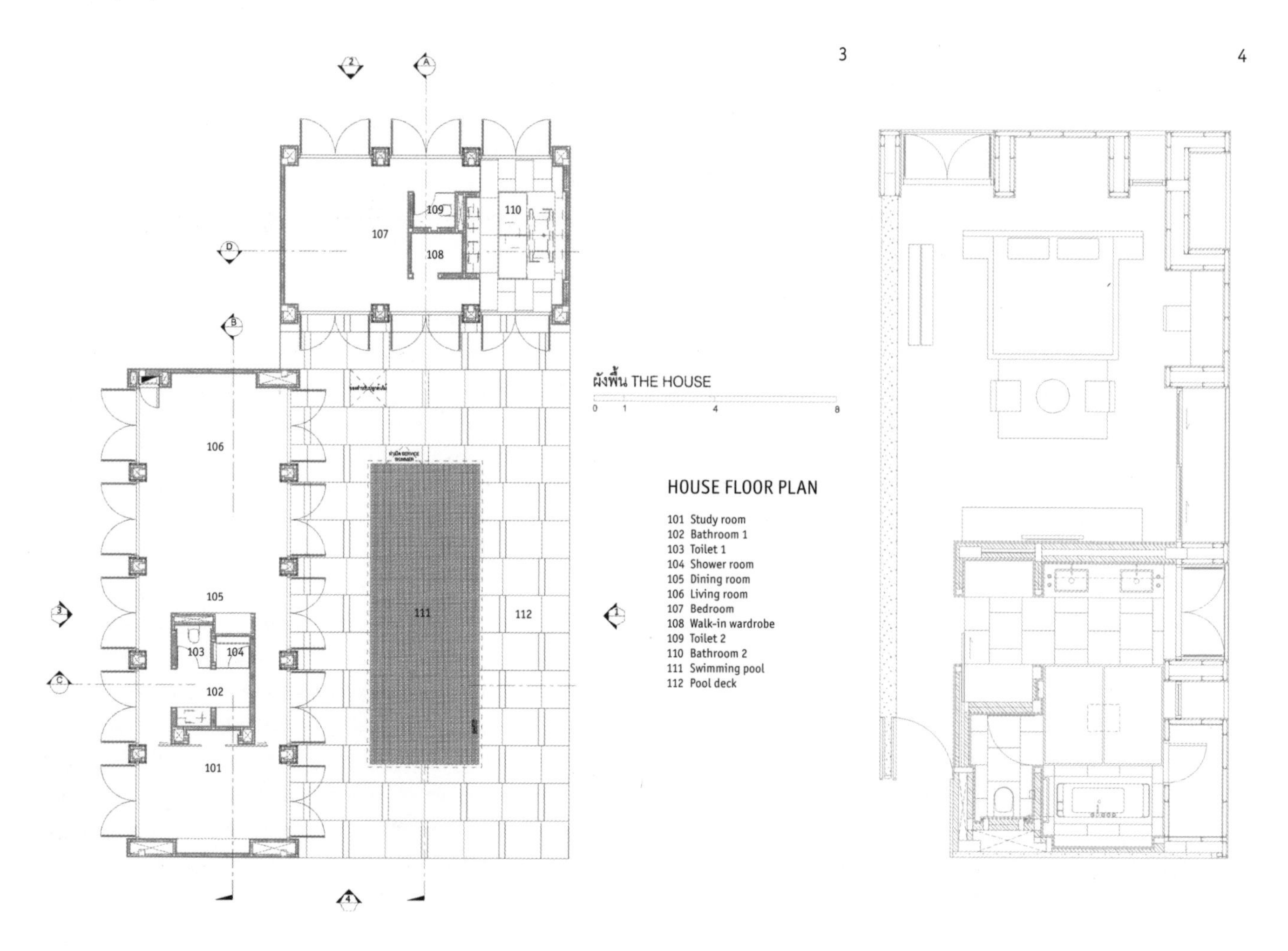

2 / Initial master plan: An additional swimming pool was later added on the beachfront at the client's request.

3 / Floor plan of a pool villa.

4 / Floor plan of a typical room.

5 / Each of the villas is articulated by a different fenestration, adding an emotional and organic quality to the otherwise monumental and block-like structures.

6 / Site prior to development.

5

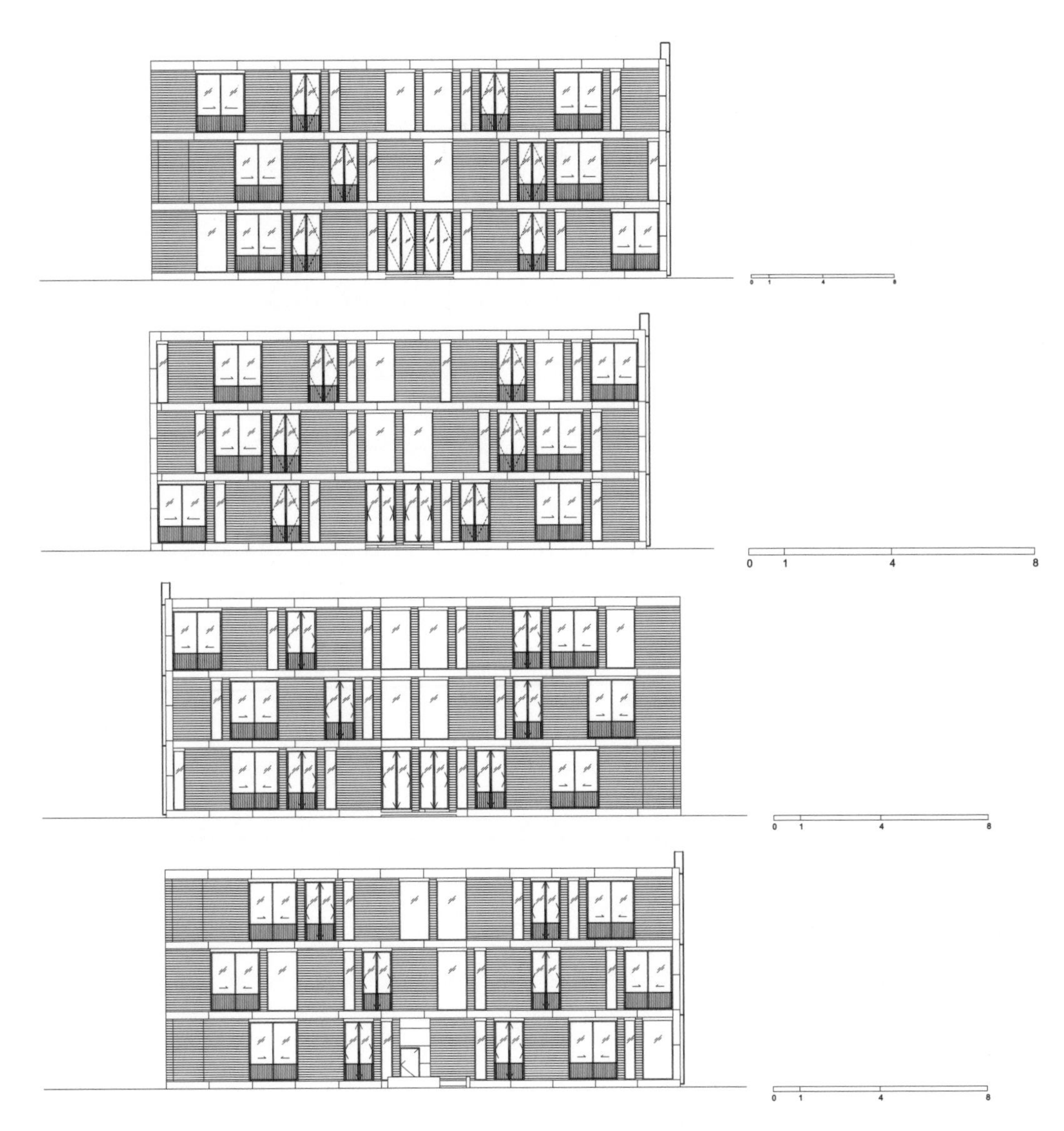

6

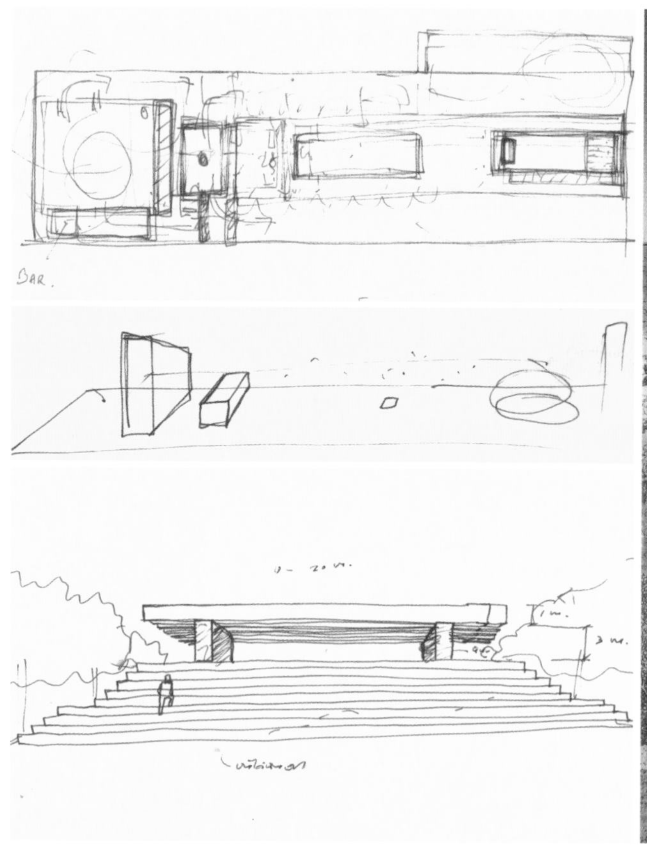

7

8

9

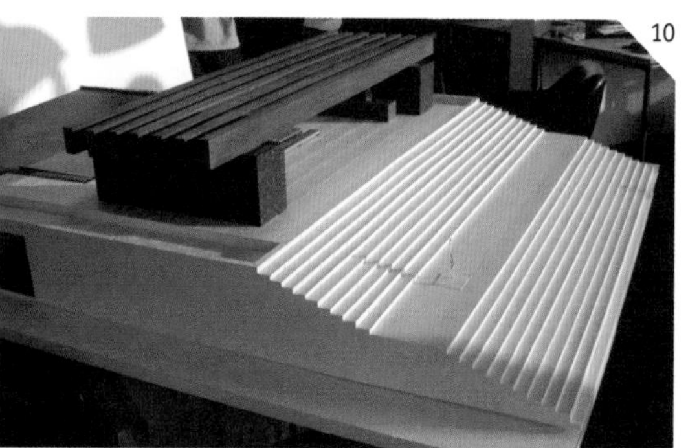

10

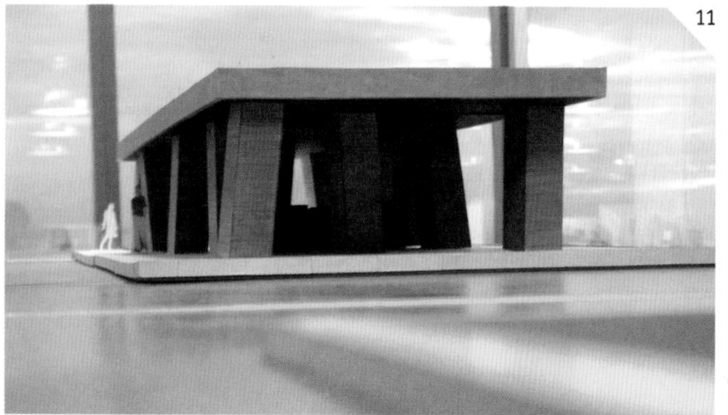

11

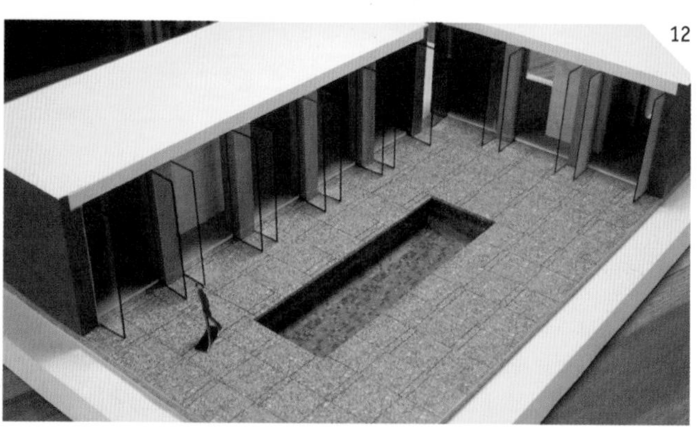

12

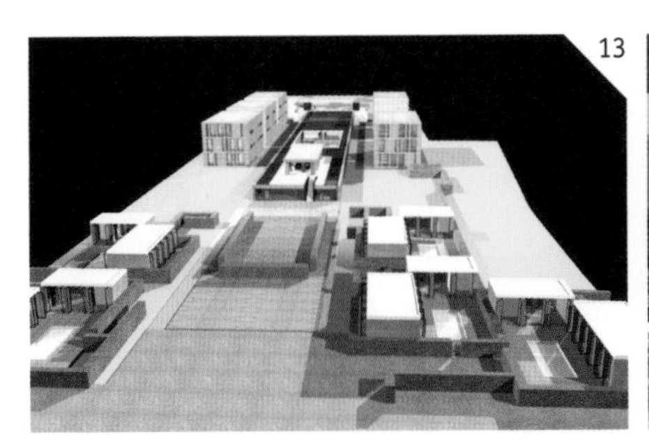

13

14

15

16

17

18

19

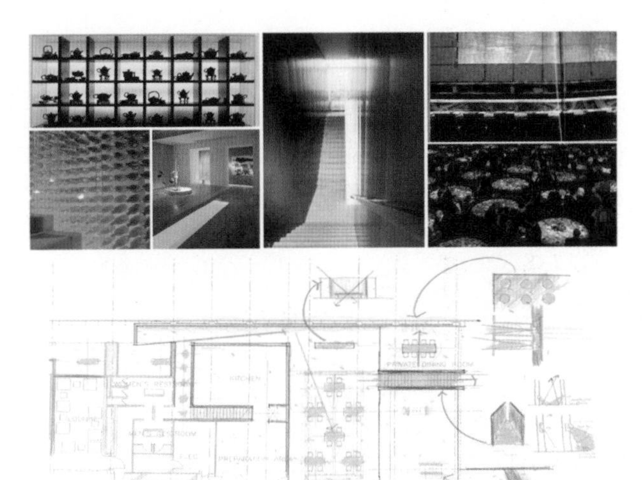

7 / During the schematic design phase DBALP use sketches in tandem with computer drawings and models.

8 / Dance table: The sequence was developed piecemeal and put together like a jigsaw. The plaza and lobby were conceived first and then the rooms and villas. On the day before presentation the restaurant structure was created, based on the sloping legs of the Dance table designed by Duangrit in 2006.

9 / Modelling is an important part of the design process. All models are fabricated in-house and develop in complexity as the project progresses. Normally the first are made from paper or styrofoam. Acrylic versions are created to examine three-dimensional space from outside in. The final model is in wood.

10 / A 1:50 model of the lobby was produced to check its proportions.

11 / Model of the restaurant.

12 / Model of a pool villa.

13 / Once the proportions have been worked out using models, the information is translated into renderings. Duangrit sits in front of the computer with his team to 'walk through' each of the spaces.

14 / Rendering of the reflecting pool seen from the lobby: The presentation was made at DBALP's Bangkok offices. Every detail of the design was shown in over 80 renderings.

15 / The walk towards the restaurant at the far end of the complex is orchestrated by a caged stone wall.

16 / Exterior view of one of the villas.

17 / A typical room.

18 / The spa swimming pool.

19 / Lighting plan for the restaurant: The lighting was designed by Kanokporn Noochsang of APLD Co. Ltd, whom Duangrit has worked with on many occasions. It complements rather than overwhelms the architecture. In the restaurant the lighting creates a random pattern on the ceiling while illuminating the columns.

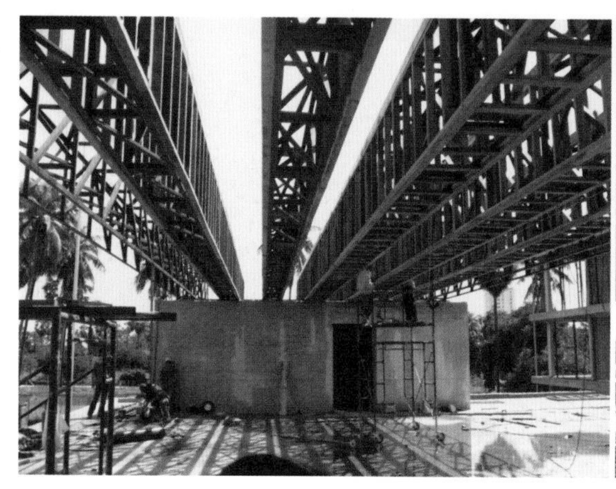

20 / DBALP produced construction drawings and Duangrit maintained a high profile on site to guide the contractors.

21 / The stone wall has two sides with a service corridor running between them, and needed a high level of ventilation. The idea of a retaining wall encased in a metal frame was taken from Herzog & de Meuron's Dominus winery in California. The individual stones let the wall breathe.

22 / The wall had to be torn down twice because the contractor did not add enough structural support to the wire cage. The local stone is added one piece at a time in a labour-intensive process.

23 / The basic construction of the hotel is poured concrete. The rooms are clad in locally sourced timber.

24 / The span across the lobby measures 18 m (59 ft). The beams are made from steel trusses clad in timber.

25

26

27

28

29

25 / Rendering of the grass courtyard: The parking area is engineered to take the weight of a fire engine, so cars pose no problem.

26 / The lobby is open on two sides and is thus ventilated naturally. It is quoted as being a new example of tropical architecture, achieving as it does the right balance between good design and climatic response.

27 / The reflecting pool was a late addition to the design. The roof of the spa, part of the restaurant and the Red Bar initially formed a functionless and faceless space.

28 / Interior: Most of the furniture was designed by DBALP to match the strong personality of the architecture. All the materials used for both furniture and finishes (stone, wood, glass and concrete) were inspired by nature.

29 / The staircase from the lower restaurant area to the upper is made from artificial stone that can be lit from below. During the day it is consistent with the marble floor but at night it glows like a lantern.

House at No. 85 Swain's Lane

Eldridge Smerin

Location: London, UK
Principal use: Private residence
Client: Richard Elliott
Site area: 144 m² (1,550 ft²)
Interior area: 414 m² (4,456¼ ft²)

Total build area: 513 m² (5,522 ft²)
Design period: March 2003 – October 2005
Construction period: November 2005 – January 2008
Budget: Undeclared

Despite a string of award-winning schemes, Eldridge Smerin is probably still best known for its first major commission, The Lawns (2000), a family home in London's Highgate Conservation Area for John Sorrell (formerly chairman of the Design Council) and his wife, Frances. In many ways, this early project still encapsulates the practice's attitude to architecture. The design conceals the core of an existing 1950s house in sleek and highly engineered double-height, predominantly glazed extensions. The building won recognition from both RIBA and the Civic Trust and was shortlisted for the Stirling Prize. At the time the jury commented: 'We considered The Lawns to be an exemplary example of how the twenty-first-century house can be incorporated into historic conservation areas as part of the continuing evolution of domestic architecture. It should also inspire other clients and architects to positively confront the challenges of the UK planning process.' The panel's words were prescient.

Desiring an equally iconic and attention-grabbing residence as The Lawns, Richard Elliott, a nearby property owner, engaged Eldridge Smerin to work on the redesign of the house he occupied on a highly sensitive site overlooking Highgate's Grade I-listed Victorian cemetery, with spectacular views of London's skyline beyond. The existing edifice, a cantilevering steel construction dating from the 1970s and designed by noted architect John Winter, was in a bad state of repair, with corroding supports that needed propping. Elliott had already collaborated with an architect on a concept that would incorporate the original structure. Because of the need to respect 'right of light', the first design was the same height as the house next door, and it was only once Elliott had acquired this property that he saw the opportunity for a radically new version. Reorientating that building would enable him to build No. 85 Swain's Lane higher, almost doubling the floor space. It was at this point that Eldridge Smerin became involved.

The client is a surveyor and professional photographer. In addition to the programming, the brief stipulated that the house should be celebratory, with interiors suitable for photo-shoots, and specified the integration of cabling for cutting-edge audio-visual equipment. Elliott did not want to constrain the architects' creative thinking and asked for a design that would be peculiar to the site. At concept design stage, Nick Eldridge and Piers Smerin work independently on separate schemes, each developing a response to the client's brief in their own way. The designs are presented to the client and the preferred idea is selected for taking forward to the planning process and then construction. In this case, proposals were made for retaining the Winter house (Smerin) and for a new build (Eldridge). Keeping the dilapidated structure would have required complete reconstruction and compromised the greater potential for a new house on the unique but restrictive 12 x 12-metre (39½ x 39½-foot) site. Rebuilding would enable a layout that was more suitable for modern living, and this was the scheme that Elliott chose.

Winter's ground plan was divided in two, with 6-metre (13¼-foot) spans on either side of a central support from which the cantilever sprang. Eldridge's intention was to split the building into three modules of 4 metres (13¼ feet); one third given to bedrooms and bathrooms, and two-thirds for the living spaces, separated by a wall containing built-in storage and services. To maximize the views, increase the apparent volumes and spaces and to merge the exterior with the interior he conceived the façade on two sides as structurally glazed double-height curtain walls, while to mitigate traffic noise the street elevation was drawn as a honed black granite monolith with minimum fenestration that added to the house's mystery. The proposed structure consisted of flat concrete slabs with long cantilevers back to four central columns that supported each of the three floors without any perimeter structure interrupting the glazing. At this point in the design process, provision was made for a small basement to house the building services and AV plant.

The planning submission that was made to Camden Council was key to the schematic design as there was no guarantee permission would be granted for such an extreme building, which doubled the volume of the original structure. The architects' track record with The Lawns and their reputation with the planning authority was beneficial to the application process; only one adjustment was made – to the street façade where an extra window was requested by Camden to break up the uninterrupted surface.

The original concept changed little (the basement was enlarged at the client's request to accommodate a home cinema) and was developed from an early stage in collaboration with specialist engineers and consultants. Although the floor area was increased, it was Eldridge's intention from the beginning to produce a structure that would use significantly less energy than Winter's original. The concrete slows down heat gain in the summer and limits heat loss in the winter, while the south-facing glazed façade allows passive solar gain to be harnessed during winter months. The house is heated by a low-temperature hot water, underfloor system which works in tandem with the thermal mass of the house to reduce energy consumption.

The result is, as John Winter himself enthuses, 'as near to a faultless building as I have seen for a long time'. Writing for *Architecture Today* magazine he continued: 'It is unbelievably difficult to achieve quality. Quality in design, in finish, in workmanship. Here it has been achieved and I am lost in admiration for the excellence of the building work and the thorough rigour of design.'

1 / The double-height glazed façades of No. 85 Swain's Lane are held up on the cantilevered concrete floor slabs. With no visible means of support the glass box dematerializes into its imposing setting.

1

2

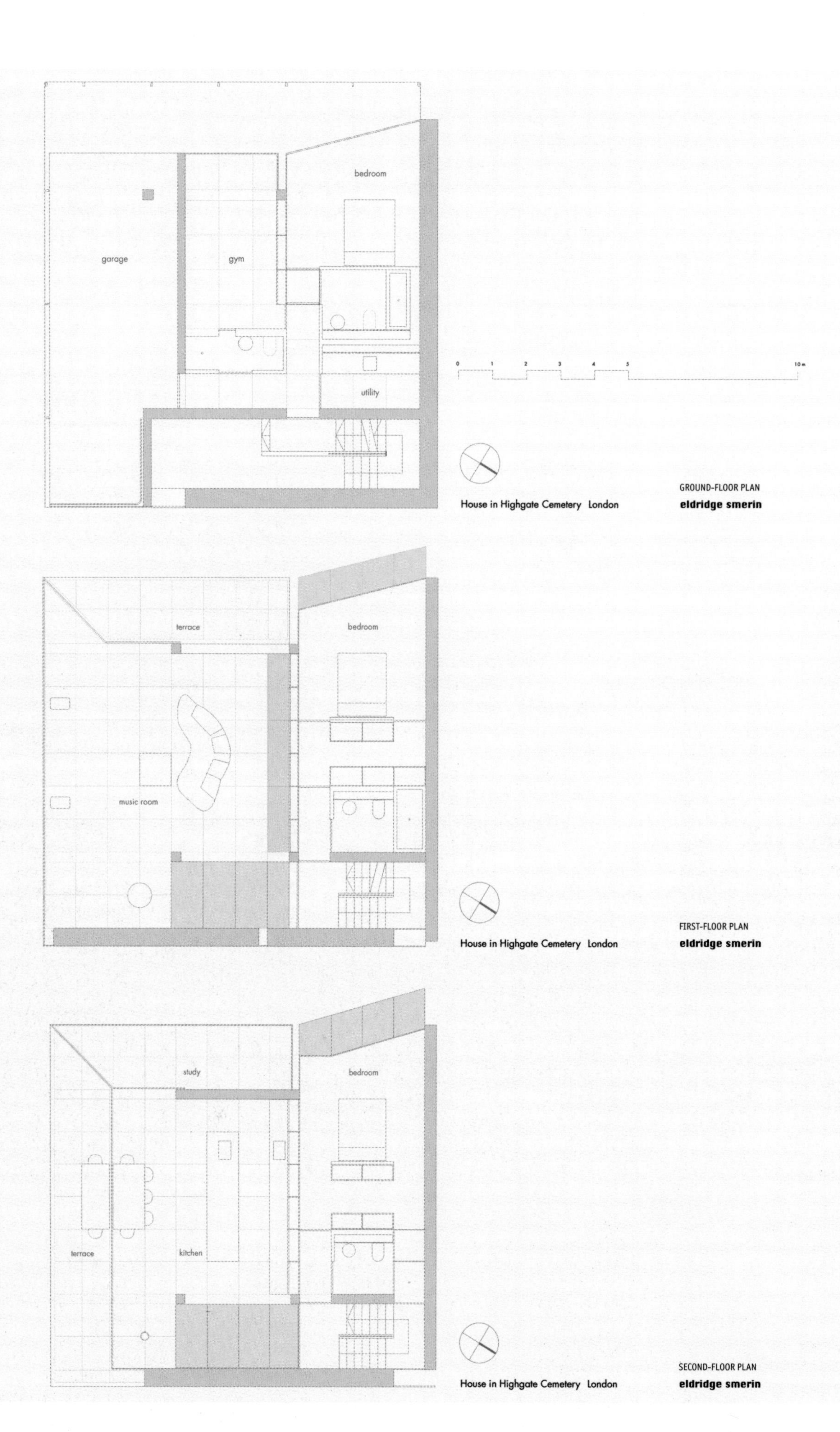
bedroom
garage
gym
utility
0 1 2 3 4 5 10 m
GROUND-FLOOR PLAN
House in Highgate Cemetery London
eldridge smerin
terrace
bedroom
music room
FIRST-FLOOR PLAN
House in Highgate Cemetery London
eldridge smerin
study
bedroom
terrace
kitchen
SECOND-FLOOR PLAN
House in Highgate Cemetery London
eldridge smerin

3

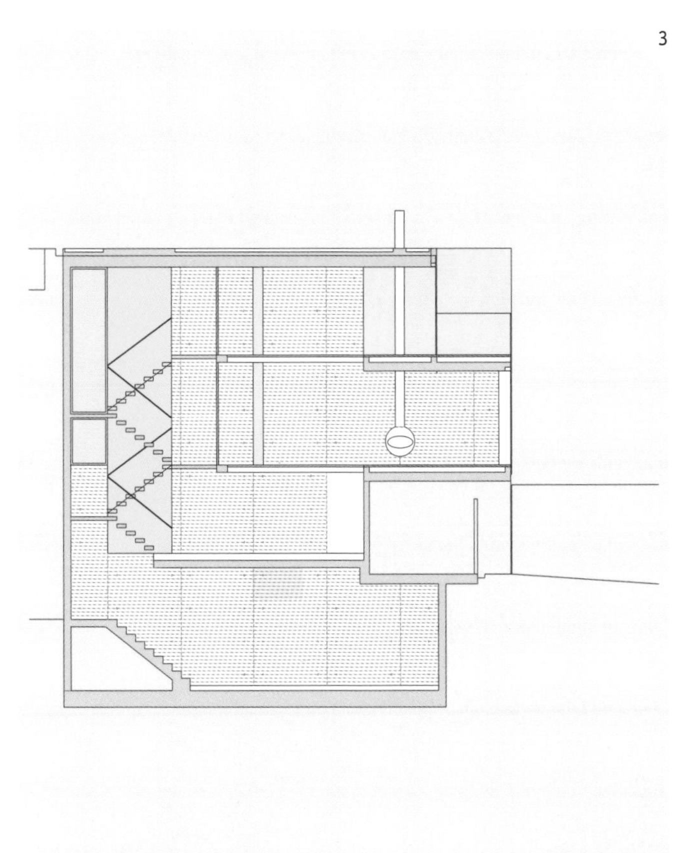

4

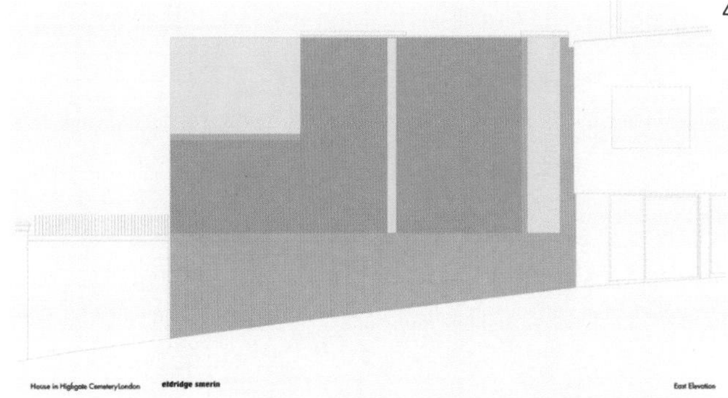

5

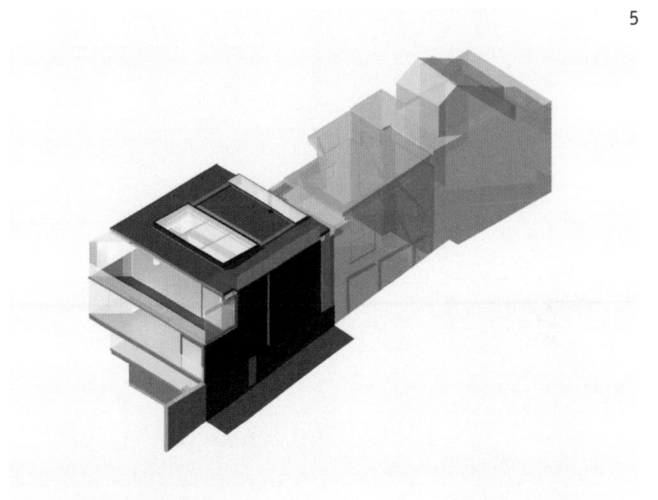

6

2 / Ground- to second-floor plans.

3 / Cross-section.

4 / Street elevation.

5 / 3-D computer drawing showing the house's position on Swain's Lane.

6 / Renderings of Eldridge Smerin's proposal for No. 85 Swain's Lane (right) and the Winter house building (left). The original house was an interesting steel and corrugated steel structure, but was badly insulated and in a poor state of repair.

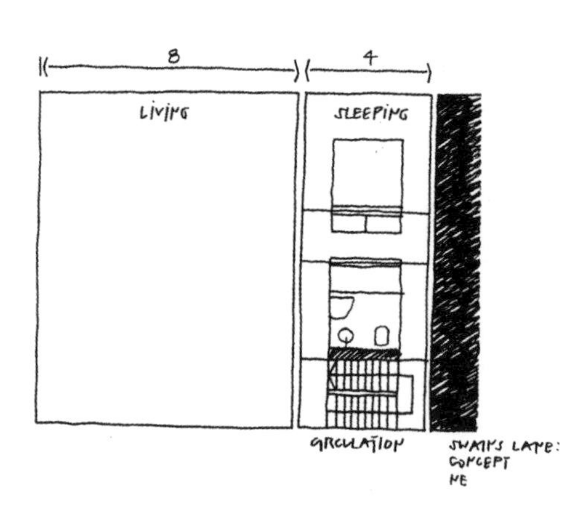

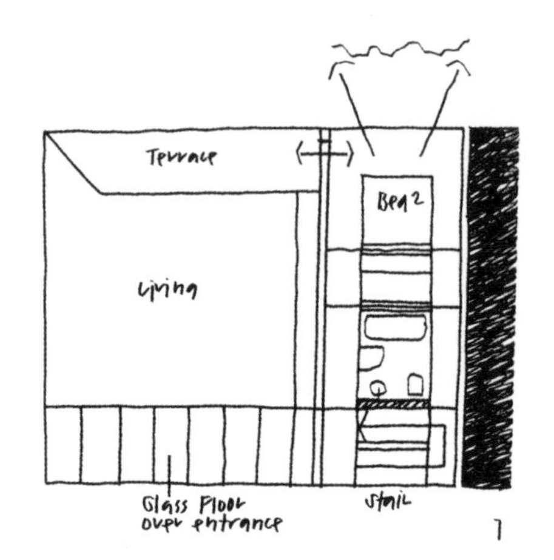

7

8

9

7 / Felt-pen drawings illustrating how the plan could be laid out were shown to the client during the concept design phase.

8 / Renderings of the kitchen and the living room: The worked-up proposal was presented to the client using 2-D plans and 3-D renderings.

9 / Planning drawings were submitted along with a presentation model. The house was made from the same material – maplewood – as the neighbouring property to present a coherent whole. The model was purposely small to minimize, psychologically, the effect the building appears to have on the site.

10

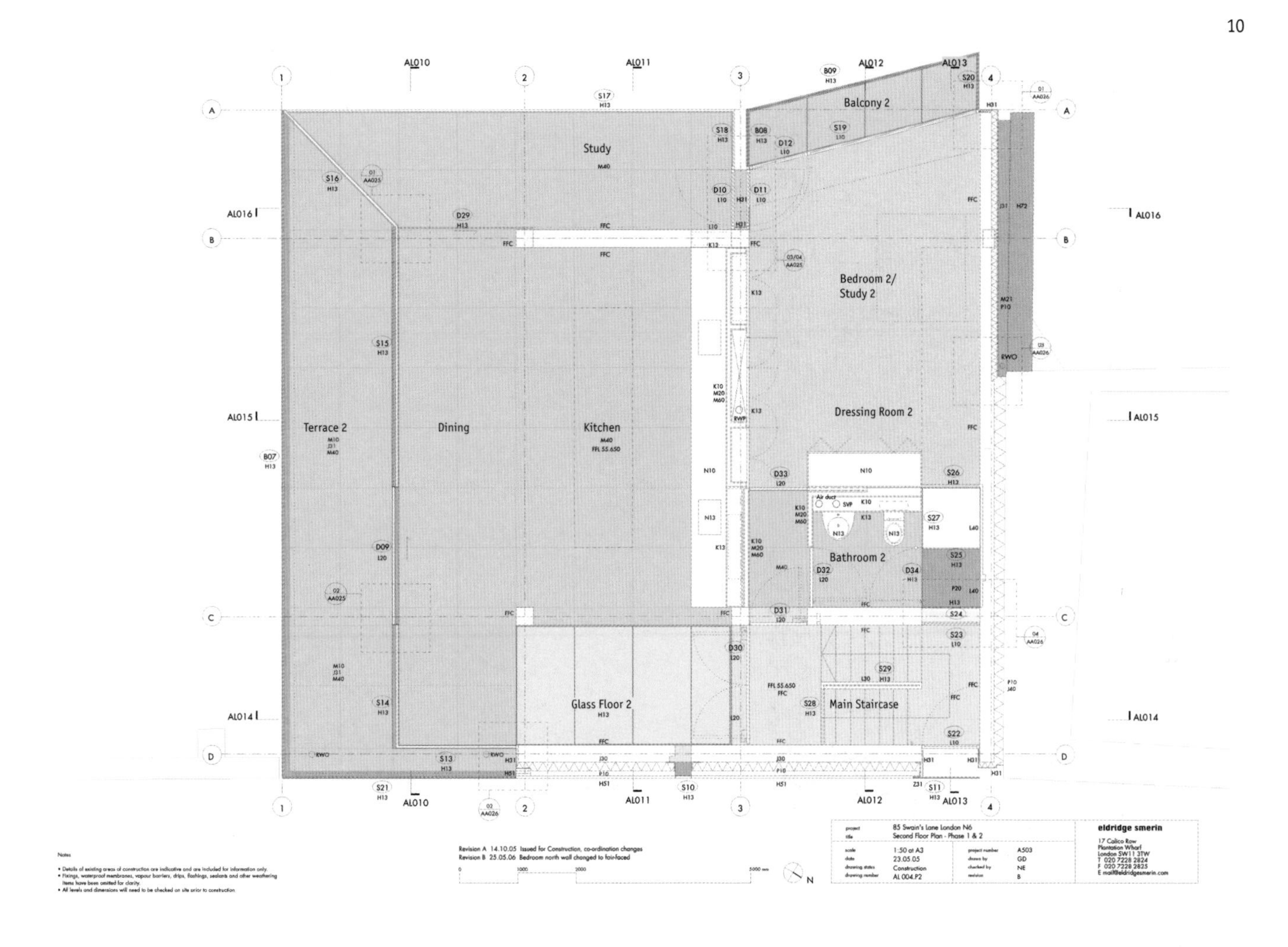

CONTENTS LIST
FFC Fair-faced concrete
F10 Brick/blockwork walling
G20 Carpentry/timber framing/first fixing

H13 Structural glass assemblies
H21 Timber weatherboarding/cladding
H31 Metal flat sheet cladding
H51 Natural stone slab cladding
H72 Aluminium strip/sheet coverings/flashings

J30 Liquid applied tanking/damp-proof membranes
J31 Liquid applied waterproof roof coatings
J40 Flexible sheet tanking/damp-proof membranes
J41 Grass roof systems

K10 Plasterboard dry linings/partitions/ceilings
K13 Rigid sheet fine linings/panelling
L10 Windows/rooflights/screens/louvres
L20 Doors
L30 Stairs/balustrades
L40 General glazing

M10 Cement/sand screeds
M20 Plastered/rendered coatings
M21 Insulation with rendered finish
M40 Stone tiling
M51 Edge-fixed carpeting
M60 Painting

N10 General fixtures
N13 Sanitary appliances/fittings
N25 Permanent access and safety equipment

P10 Sundry insulation/fire stops
P20 Unframed isolated trims/skirtings/sundry items
P21 Ironmongery
Z31 Powder coatings

10 / General arrangement drawing to a 1:50 scale showing the top floor: The architects were responsible for full construction documentation, and for such a complex design it was vital to keep control. A suitable contractor, capable of constructing the glazing and achieving the demanding finish of the fair-faced concrete, was hard to find.

11

3D DRAWING

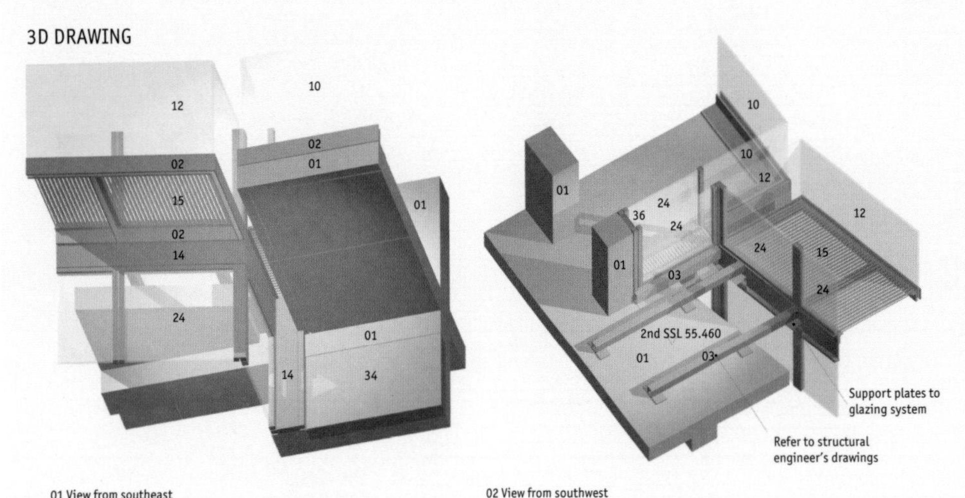

01 View from southeast

02 View from southwest

01 Concrete construction
02 Powder-coated galvanised mild steel structural section
03 Galvanised mild steel structural section
04 Stainless steel structural section
05 Powder-coated aluminium structural section
06 Existing brickwork
07 Blockwork
08 Timber packing
09 Plywood board
10 Frameless glass screen
11 Frameless glass rooflight
12 Structural glass balustrading
13 Glass/acrylic screen
14 Aluminium cladding
15 Aluminium decking
16 Granite stone cladding
17 Aluminium flashing
18 Eaves cover flashing
19 Liquid-applied damp-proofing
20 Liquid-applied waterproof roof covering
21 Damp-proof membrane/tanking
22 Insulated sedum roof
23 Stone ballast
24 Steel/aluminium glazing system
25 Frameless sliding roof-light
26 Metal louvres
27 Stainless steel screen
28 Frameless metal-clad timber door
29 Framed painted timber door
30 Frameless metal-clad ventilation hatch
31 Sliding aluminium-framed glass door
32 Sliding garage door
33 Screed
34 Insulation with rendered finish
35 Letter box/door entry system
36 Rigid insulation
37 Insulated damp-proof course
38 Rainscreen cladding insulation
39 Fire protection insulation
40 Mild steel infill plate
41 Stainless steel flat infill bars
42 Rainwater outlet (see service engineer's spec.)

AA DRAWING

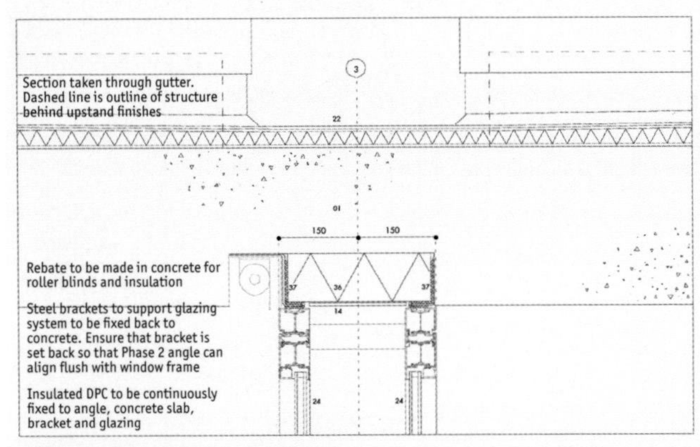

Section taken through gutter. Dashed line is outline of structure behind upstand finishes
Rebate to be made in concrete for roller blinds and insulation
Steel brackets to support glazing system to be fixed back to concrete. Ensure that bracket is set back so that Phase 2 angle can align flush with window frame
Insulated DPC to be continuously fixed to angle, concrete slab, bracket and glazing
150
150

01 Detail showing junction between heads of doors D10 and D11

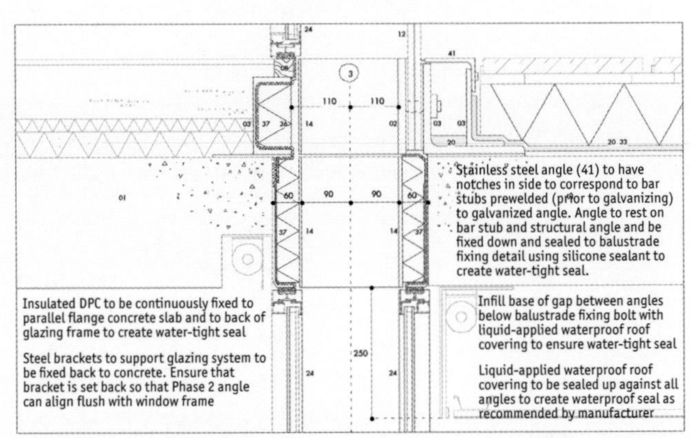

Stainless steel angle (41) to have notches in side to correspond to bar stubs prewelded (prior to galvanizing) to galvanized angle. Angle to rest on bar stub and structural angle and be fixed down and sealed to balustrade fixing detail using silicone sealant to create water-tight seal.
Infill base of gap between angles below balustrade fixing bolt with liquid-applied waterproof roof covering to ensure water-tight seal
Liquid-applied waterproof roof covering to be sealed up against all angles to create waterproof seal as recommended by manufacturer
Insulated DPC to be continuously fixed to parallel flange concrete slab and to back of glazing frame to create water-tight seal
Steel brackets to support glazing system to be fixed back to concrete. Ensure that bracket is set back so that Phase 2 angle can align flush with window frame
110
110
90
90
250

03 Detail showing junction between heads of screens S02 and S03

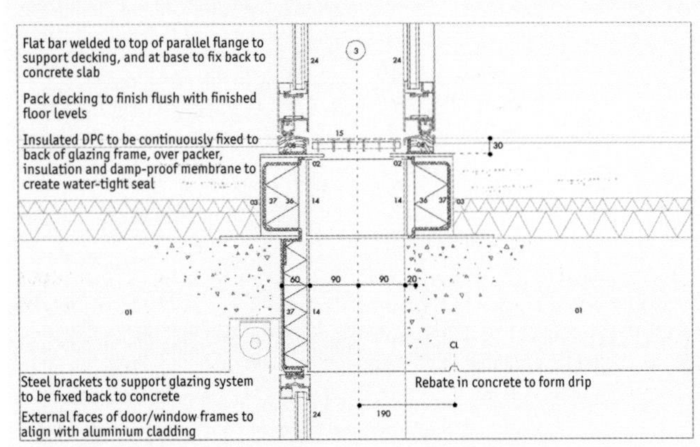

02 Detail showing junction between sills of doors D10 and D11, and head junction of screen S07

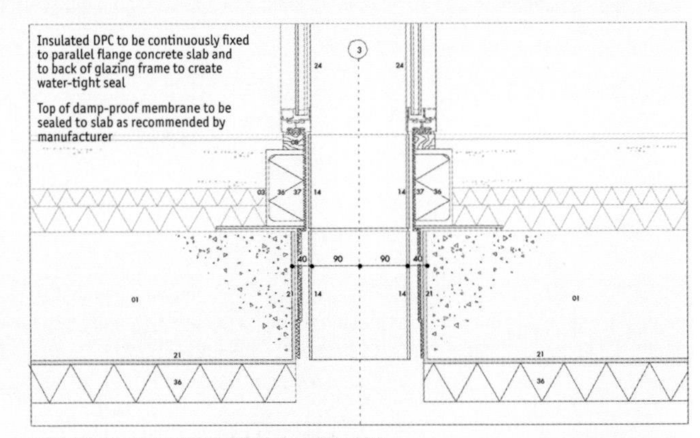

Insulated DPC to be continuously fixed to parallel flange concrete slab and to back of glazing frame to create water-tight seal
Top of damp-proof membrane to be sealed to slab as recommended by manufacturer
90
90

04 Detail showing junction between sills of screens S02 and S03

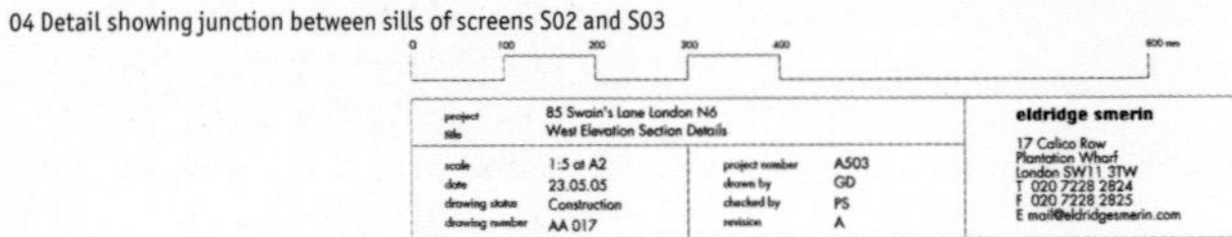

project 85 Swain's Lane London N6
title West Elevation Section Details
scale 1:5 at A2
date 23.05.05
drawing status Construction
drawing number AA 017
project number A503
drawn by GD
checked by PS
revision A
eldridge smerin
17 Calico Row
Plantation Wharf
London SW11 3TW
T 020 7228 2824
F 020 7228 2825
E mail@eldridgesmerin.com

12

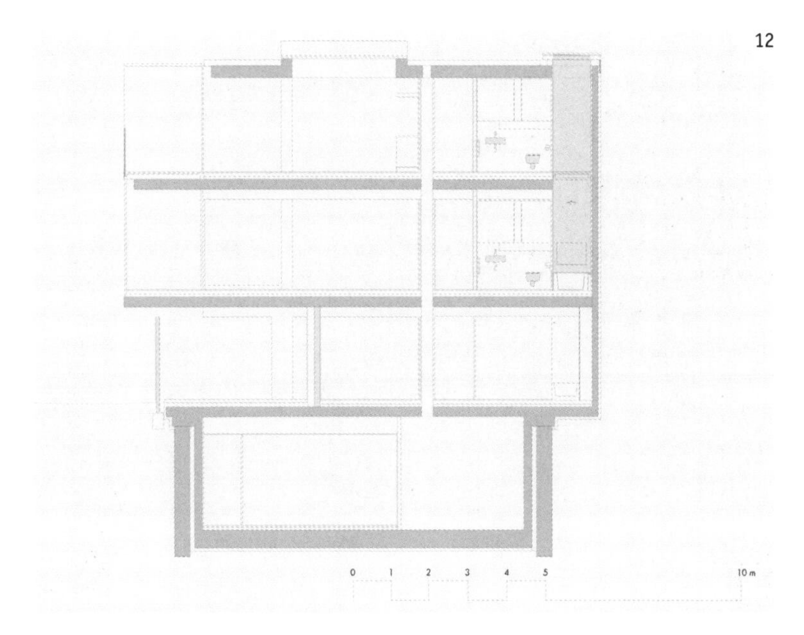

13

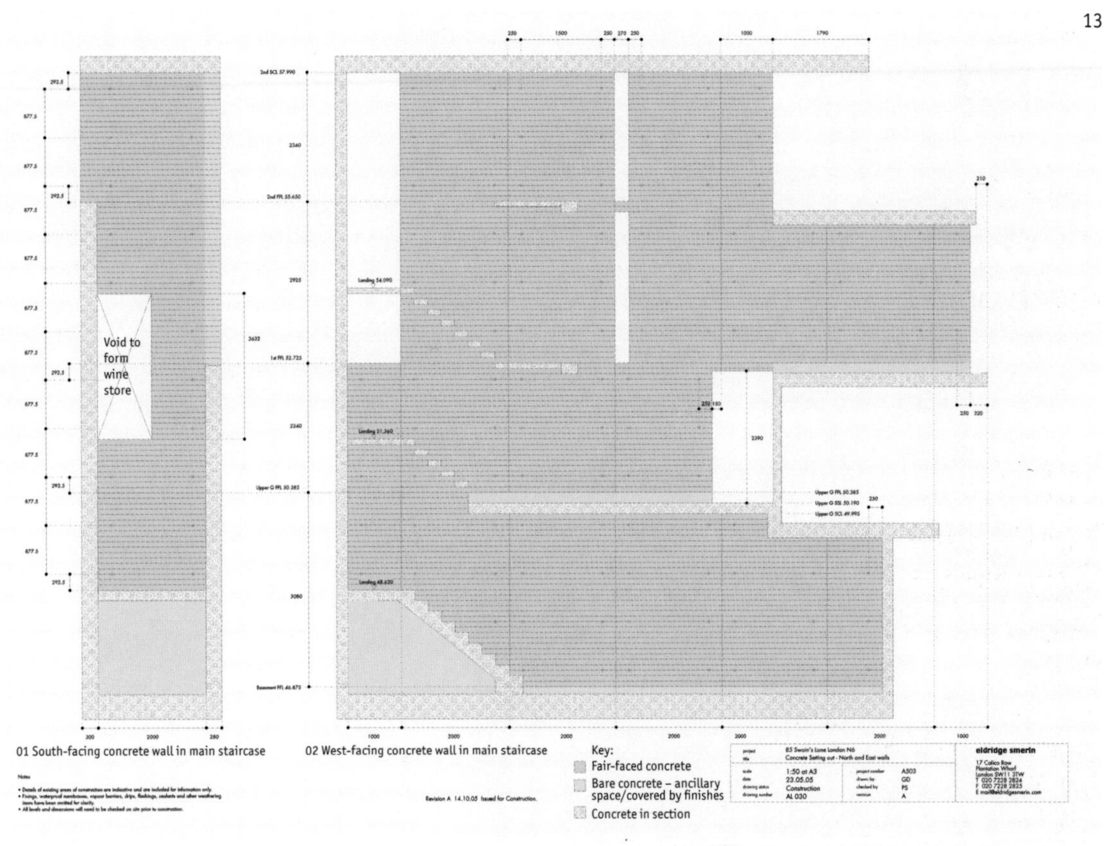

11 / 3-D drawing showing the second-floor balcony off bedroom two and AA drawing at 1:5 scale detailing the glazing of the top-floor balcony door: There is a gap between the bedroom balcony and that of the study. The narrow slot runs from the top to the bottom of the house and is visible from the exterior, architecturally expressing the division of the two blocks of the building.

12 / Long section: To maintain a thin profile on the edge of the cantilever, concrete beams run back to the party wall and stop short 2 m (6½ ft) back from the elevation.

13 / The design is set to a rigorous 1 m (3¼ ft) grid. The board-marked concrete was poured in situ. The vertical grid was designed to fit the depth of the stair treads. The design was then detailed vertically and horizontally to fit in with the set pattern.

14

15

16

17

14 / Although the structural engineers had organized trial excavations and soil investigation, it had not been possible to dig pits in all areas of the existing house, which was still inhabited by the owner. During construction, the contractor encountered a water course emanating from the nearby underground River Fleet. Pumping the site basement and stabilizing the foundations of 87 Swain's Lane delayed the construction by a number of months.

15 / The construction process was difficult as the equipment could not be located in the cemetery.

16 / A rendering of the original concept (left) and the house as built (right) shows how little the design changed during development.

17 / Street elevation: The planning authorities thought the original design too monolithic and demanded an extra window. Eldridge reworked his original drawings to include a transluscent slot window that he believes is a compositional improvement.

18

19

20

21

18 / A sliding glass roof-light enables the top floor to become an open-air court.

19 / In contrast to the smooth fair-faced concrete columns and soffits, and the smooth stone flooring, the interior of the walls to the street and adjoining property have a strong horizontal pattern from the timber boards used to shutter the concrete.

20 / The interior spaces are linked vertically by a series of large areas of clear glass floor-panels that filter daylight from the main sliding roof-light down to the entrance area off the street.

21 / The study is connected to the master bedroom via an exterior bridge. The desk was custom-designed by Eldridge and manufactured by Santambrogio Milano. It is a masterpiece of engineering and had to be craned into place.

Moses Mabhida Stadium

von Gerkan, Marg und Partner Architects (gmp), in cooperation with Ibhola Lethu Consortium (ILC)

Location: Durban, South Africa
Principal use: Multifunctional stadium
Client: Municipality of Durban (eThekwini Municipality), Strategic Projects Unit (SPU)
Site area: stadium, platform, media compound, access, green area, linear park: 296,000 m^2 (3,186,118 ft^2). Linear park area: 131,500 m^2 (1,415,454 ft^2)
Total build area: 92,300 m^2 (990,279 ft^2)
Competition: July 2006
Design and construction period: November 2006 – November 2009
Budget: ZAR 3 billion

In the introduction to *Architecture for an African Dream* (a monograph elucidating the circumstances of planning and realizing the three stadia designed by von Gerkan, Marg und Partners Architects (gmp) in Cape Town, Port Elizabeth and Durban for the 2010 World Cup), Volkwin Marg compares architecture to 'a dance in chains'. Outlining the constraints imposed by client, budgetary considerations and the need to produce a structure suitable for its intended function, he emphasizes that the discipline is the least free of the arts and is further bound by its sociopolitical agenda. Narrowing the argument to gmp's work in South Africa, he continues: 'The projects don't stand isolated on green fields in the middle of nowhere; they are held in chains, but also firmly anchored in the urban picture, and in South African society and reality. The whole of Africa views this football World Cup as the fulfilment of an African dream. The stadia are part of this dream, and they are places where the dream will come true.'

Durban is South Africa's second largest city after Johannesburg and the country's biggest port, as well as a much-frequented tourist destination. In 2005 the city's authorities adopted the '2010 and beyond strategy', aimed at positioning Durban as Africa's sports and events capital by upgrading the Kings Park Sports Precinct, a recreational area north of the inner city, and making a bid for the FIFA World Cup. Investigations carried out on the existing ABSA Rugby Stadium revealed that the investment necessary to meet the minimum FIFA requirements would be prohibitively high and still not ensure a world-class facility that could sustain itself in the future without being a burden on the city's financial resources. Recognizing the need for international expertise while drawing on the wealth of home-grown professional resources, the municipality of Durban launched a worldwide competition to find a collective capable of designing a new multipurpose stadium that could accommodate rugby, football and athletics, have flexible seating capacity to minimize the operational costs and would have the scope to host enough other activities to ensure it would be used 365 days a year. Most importantly, the brief stipulated that the structure had to have the 'Sydney Opera House effect' and be a symbol for the upward-striving city. The commission was awarded to the Ibhola Lethu Consortium (ILC) led by the South African engineering firm BKS, together with over 30 local companies under the architectural direction of Berlin-based gmp, in collaboration with innovative structural engineers Schlaich Bergermann & Partners from Stuttgart.

gmp's extensive international portfolio covers a range of projects from the smaller scale to transport systems and city master plans. Since its acclaimed modernization of Berlin's Olympic stadium in 2004, the firm has become established as expert in the field of sports-arena construction. It was responsible for three of the stadia for the 2006 World Cup in Germany, as well as a series of projects in the Arab Gulf States, North Africa and China that have set new standards in this specialized branch of design. The practice is known for a style of architecture that eschews expressionist forms based solely on artistic caprice in favour of buildings that are rooted in their context, function and the demands of the client. Once schematic design started a branch of the company was opened in South Africa to encourage a dialogical approach and expedite collaboration between the various members of the Durban consortium. Both gmp and the client quote the team spirit between the national and international design and construction groups as the driving force behind the success of the flagship building. gmp was responsible for the overall design concept as well as for the roof and the façade. It further developed the design and construction drawings in cooperation with ILC for all building parts: roof, concrete structure and seating. One of the main challenges for the local team was to translate the construction documents to meet South African building codes and regulations.

The stadium is situated on a raised platform overlooking the Indian Ocean and is accessed from the south via a broad flight of steps. The main entrance coincides with the divergence of the two prongs of the soaring arch that gives the iconic structure its silhouette and acts as a gateway to the city. The geometry of the roof is predetermined by the architectural concept. All around the stadium, radial prestressing cables are attached to the external edge of the roof (the compression ring) stretching between the great arch on one side and the inner edge of the roof on the other, thus forcing the latter into an almond shape. The PTFE-coated roof membrane admits 50 per cent of the sunlight into the arena while also providing shade. The façade is formed from perforated metal lamellae that provide protection from the elements and offer glimpses of the interior, giving the building a light and airy feel.

Almost two decades after the end of apartheid, hosting the nineteenth World Cup tournament was South Africa's opportunity to demonstrate to the world that it had overcome years of racial discrimination and was now a prosperous country where everyone had the same chance at success and happiness whatever the colour of their skin. The Moses Mabhida Stadium is an architecturally expressive emblem that gives the city of Durban a landmark that can be seen from miles around. Towering 105 metres (344½ ft) above the pitch, the bifurcating arch unites overhead and symbolically represents a divided nation coming together as one.

1 / A 105 m (344½ ft) two-pronged arch curves high over the Moses Mabhida Stadium, creating an emblem that is visible far and wide. The main entrance coincides with the bifurcation of the arch, which acts as a gateway to the city of Durban.

1

2

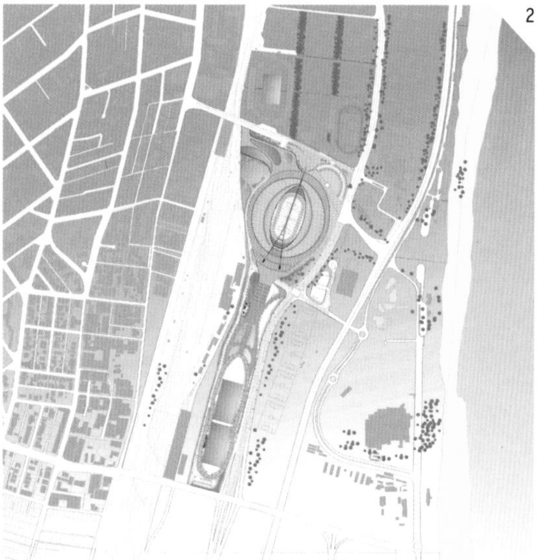

3

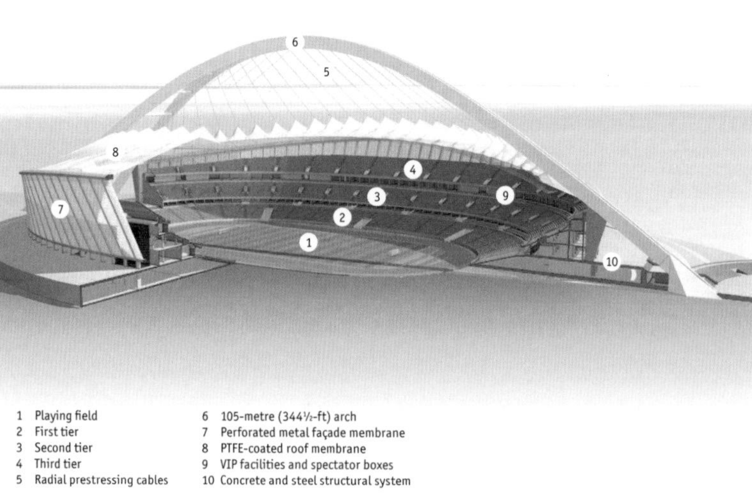

4

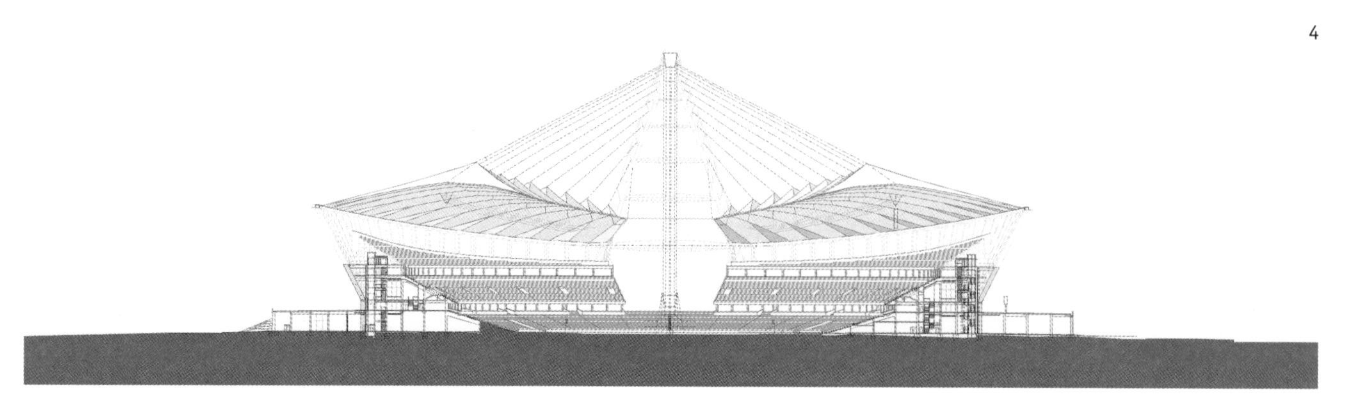

5

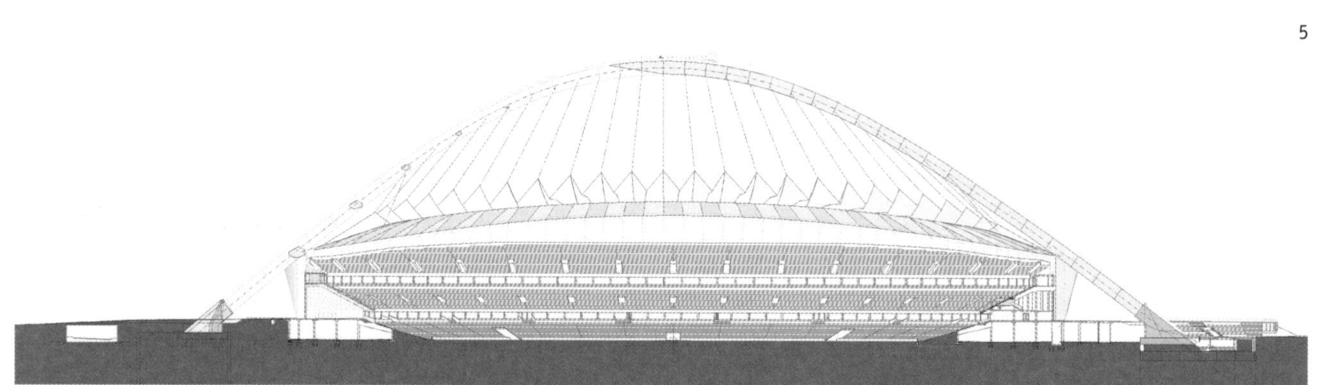

2 / Site plan: A 1-km (0.6-mile) linear park guides people from downtown Durban to the stadium. Seen from above, the split arch over the stadium represents the motif on the South African flag.

3 / Axonometric of the stadium.

4 / Cross-section: The outer skin is in effect a geometrical overlay of a cone imposed on a cylinder.

5 / Longitudinal section.

6 / Level 1 plan: The stadium offers VIP facilities, the President and Ocean atria (both over six storeys high), clubrooms and 130 spectator boxes.

7 / Level 3 plan.

8 / Level 6 plan.

9 / Roof plan.

10 / Concept sketches.

11 / Early sketch of the arch shape and the connection point of the southern legs with the geometry.

12 / Early sketch study of the façade and compression ring: Only one design solution was developed. gmp is a non-hierarchical office with members of the team working together on the initial concept.

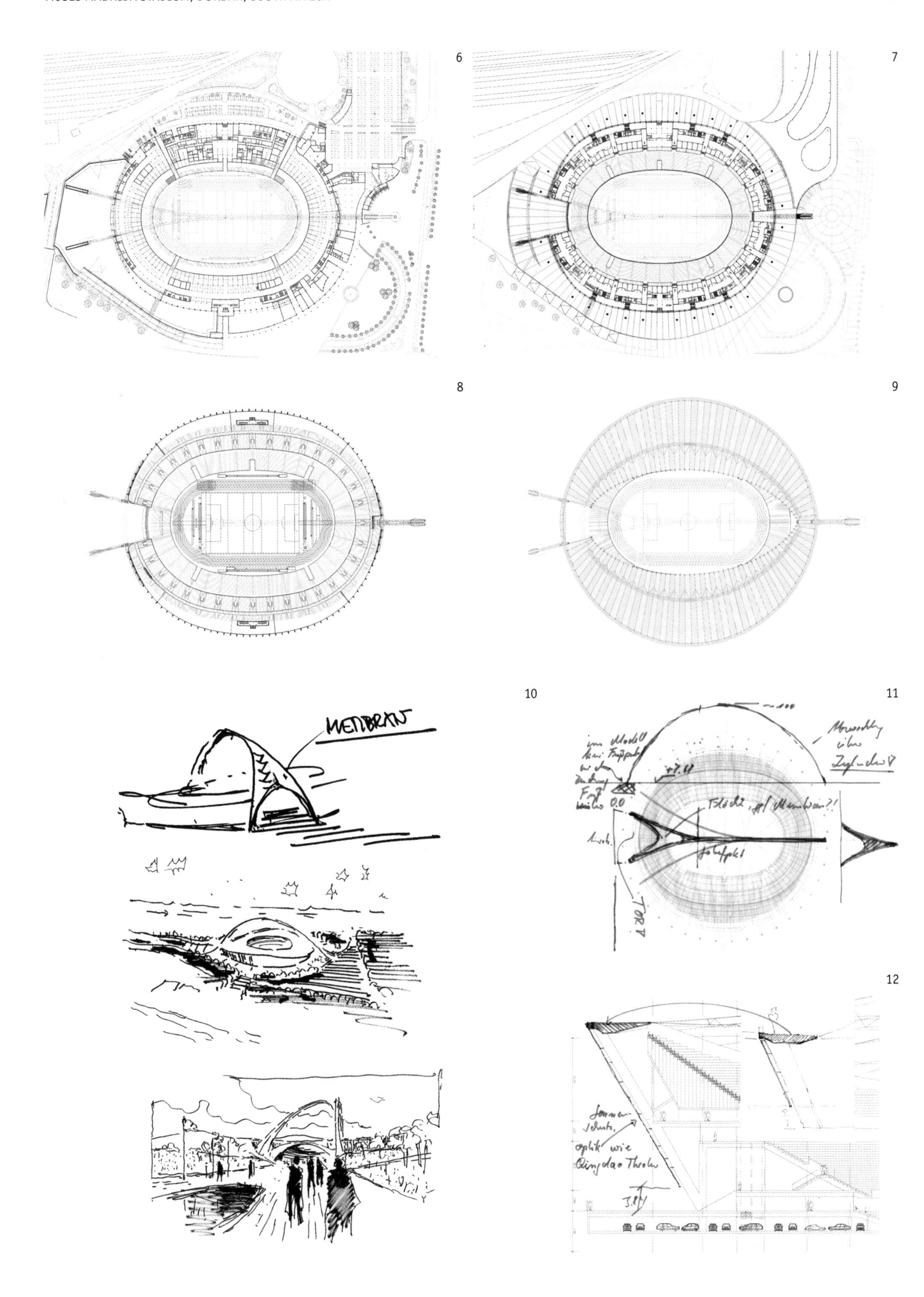
6
7
8
9
10
11
12
MEMBRAN
TOR

13

14

15

13 / A presentation was made at the Congress Centre in Durban using renderings, material boards, 3-D animations, computer models and physical models.

14 / 2006 presentation model: Providing the model was one of the regulations of the design competition. During design development it helped the team specify dimensions of the inner building as well as details and technical features.

15 / Presentation rendering: The stadium is surrounded by green areas for sports, leisure and cultural activities, fulfilling the brief for an attractive urban area that will establish itself as a high-quality venue for sports events in South Africa.

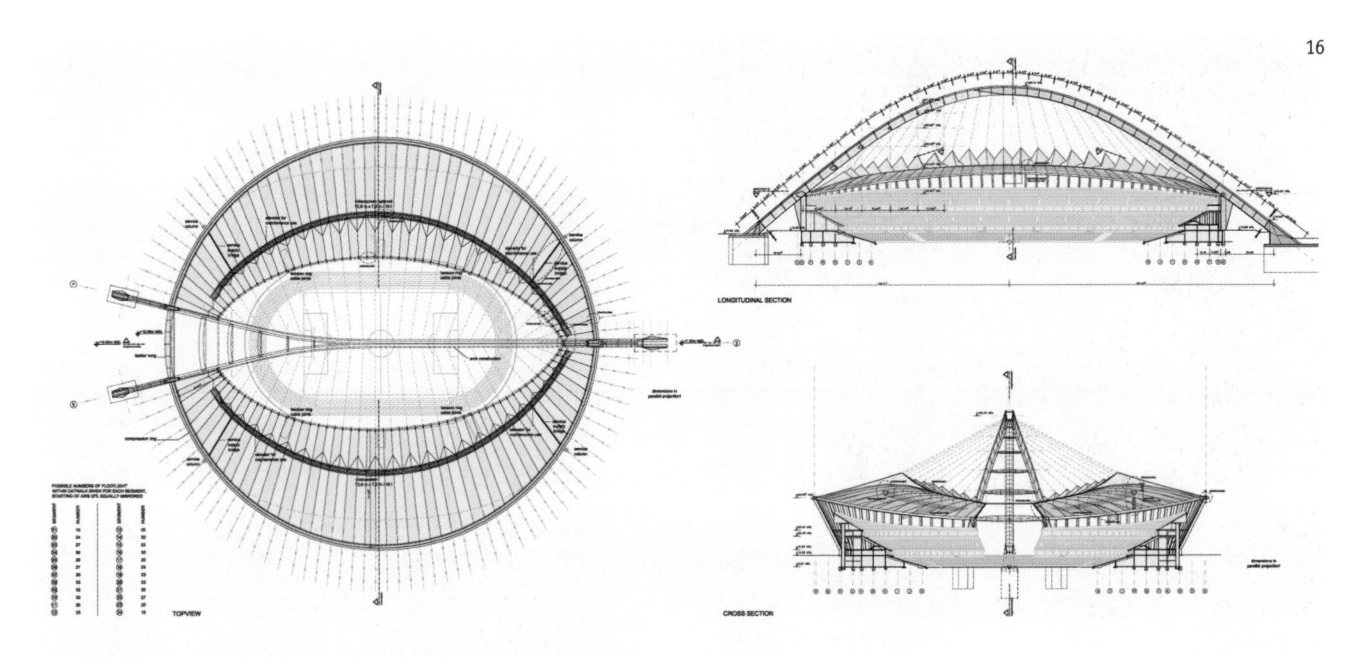

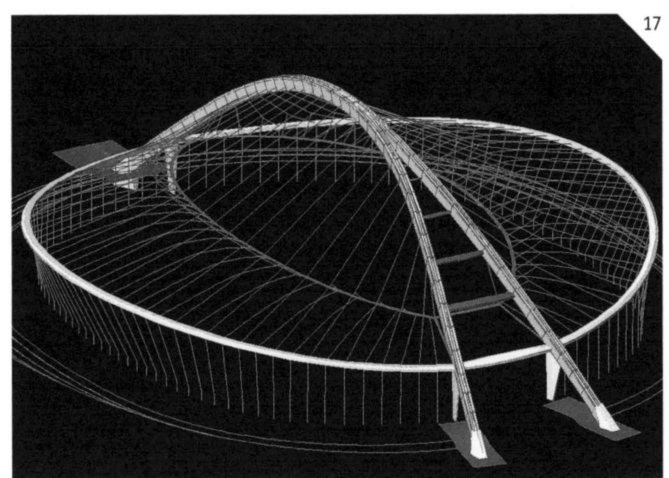

16 / The cable structure and steel compression ring along the outer edge of the roof resemble a wheel-and-spoke system with the cables acting as spokes and the ring as the rim of the wheel. In addition, the cable structure is suspended from the arch in order to stabilize the ring.

17 / The geometry of each element was evaluated via measurements in a 3-D CAD system and the necessary corrections made.

18 / The keystone was the last element to be erected and was a perfect fit.

19 / The installation of the arch began with lifting the first four elements of the divided section into place above the stadium. Adjustments needed to be made to their geometry to ensure that the remaining elements (56 in total) fitted accurately.

20 / Complying with the demands of the Black Economic Empowerment programme (geared towards giving previously disadvantaged ethnic groups economic opportunities) was an essential prerequisite in gmp being awarded the contract. The joint-venture team worked collaboratively with the client in weekly design review meetings. gmp were encouraged to pursue an extensive and intensive exchange of information with, and knowledge transfer to, the South African partners. They were constantly on site during the construction process.

21 / Workers inside the top arch element just prior to installation.

22 / The steel elements of the arch were fabricated in Hanover and shipped to South Africa.

23 / A worker manoeuvres one of the arch elements into position to make the pin connection between the element and the supporting column.

24 / The compression ring, the northern arch element and the arch column.

25 / Connection nodes for the roof cable structure.

26 / The cable structure prior to attachment to the compression ring.

27 / The arch-bearing points are clad in reinforced precast concrete.

28 / The whole stadium complex was built mainly as an in-situ concrete structure and used 80,000 m^3 (282,500 ft^3) of reinforced concrete.

29 / The compression ring and façade are carried on precast concrete columns below, and hollow box steel columns above. The height and angle of inclination vary around the stadium from c. 30 m (98 ft) with a 90° slope to c. 50 m (164 ft) with a 60° gradient.

30 / A 'skydeck' offering panoramic views of the city and the Indian Ocean sits at the apex of the arch (left) and is reached via a cable car from the northern end of the stadium, represented here by a concept computer drawing from an early stage of planning.

31 / A 'maritime' colour scheme, consisting of 13 shades typical of those found in Durban's coastal landscape, was selected for the seat shells. Even when the stadium is half empty it appears to be fully occupied by brightly dressed people. A third tier of seating can be added, increasing the capacity of the stadium from 56,000 to 85,000 for major events. The design includes escape routes and infrastructure for the additional seats.

Ecomusée du Pays de Rennes

*Guinée*Potin*

Location: Rennes, Brittany, France
Principal use: Farm museum
Client: Rennes Métropole
Site area: 2,668 m² (28,718 ft²)
Interior area: 990 m² (10,656¼ ft²)

Total build area: 990 m² (10,656¼ ft²)
Design period: July 2006 – September 2008
Construction period: September 2008 – December 2009
Budget: €1,900,000

The concept of the *écomusée* originated in France, where two museologists coined the term in the 1970s. Although *éco* is a shortened form of *écologie*, in the context of museums the definition of the term is much broader. It refers to a new idea for the holistic interpretation of cultural customs and traditions, which allows communities to preserve, interpret and manage their heritage for a sustainable development.

The Ecomusée on the outskirts of Rennes traces five centuries of the history of the Bintinais farm, one of the oldest in the region. Through exhibitions of machinery, everyday objects, costumes, furniture and crafts, rare breeds and crop conservation programmes as well as interactive audio-visual educational facilities, visitors can learn about the daily workings and domestic life of Brittany's rural community since the seventeenth century. The site is bordered to the west by a dense copse, to the east by the Bintinais family gardens, to the north by a wild cherry grove and the agricultural park beyond, and to the south by the access road. The museum was housed in a complex of buildings with the reception and administrative facilities in an entrance building dating from the early 1990s and the permanent exhibition area in one of the original stables.

In 2000 the museum received a large donation of ancient vernacular furniture from the Pays de Rennes, which compounded the lack of space from which it was suffering; the antiquated and unfriendly layout made it difficult to receive the increasing numbers of tourists visiting the unique attraction. In addition, the 19 employees were working in cramped offices in the main building. It became necessary to look to growth and in 2006 the city of Rennes launched an international competition for a radical redesign. The brief asked for the 'soul' of the museum and the rural history and tradition it represented to be recreated in architectural form, in a legible plan that would benefit both workers and clientele alike. The cherry grove had to be protected and a new car park created to the south. The building was to offer additional offices and create an easy and 'friendly' circulation between the entrance hall and new temporary exhibition space.

Writing in 2002, Patrice Goulet of the Institut Français d'Architecture praised Hervé Potin and Anne-Flore Guinée's ability to mix the natural and the artificial, the rough and the sophisticated, the hard and the soft, in architecture that is sensual, expressive and magical. In the case of the Écomusée, all these qualities are present, as is the architects' quest to produce a building that is site-specific. They believe that the exterior skin is the link between a structure and its surrounding context. Potin and Guinée therefore proposed a flagship extension that used locally sourced sustainable materials (chestnut, Douglas pine, organic-coloured concrete and hemp insulation) and were influenced by the region's architecture in the way the façades were articulated.

They positioned the temporary exhibition to the west, which enabled the conservation of the cherry grove and 70 per cent of the existing woodlands, while the north–south orientation allowed the museum to benefit from sunlight in the winter and shading during the summer. To encourage biodiversity, the entire structure would be covered with a sedum roof, and in order to maintain harmony with the landscape the design was kept compact. The breakthrough for the layout came when they resolved a way to extend the original entrance into the new addition, in the form of a welcoming and multipurpose reception hall, and place the offices in such a way that the staff maintained visual contact with visitors. Once the plan was formulated the architects' attention turned to materiality and colour palette.

The inspiration for the south façade came from an unlikely source: haute couture. Guinée and Potin had in mind the sculptural dresses designed by Paco Rabanne in the 1960s, made from plastic and metal tiles or discs held together with wire. Their proposition was to develop a cladding system of overlapping chestnut shingles that reinterpreted the vernacular of Brittany's windmills in a contemporary idiom.

Guinée*Potin's office is small and the team of five work non-hierarchically and collaboratively to build up a concept. Although they sketch during the early stages, designs are developed on the computer. Physical and 3-D models are built simultaneously to get a clear picture of the elevations and volumes and to test materials and detailing.

The competition was anonymous and Guinée*Potin's winning entry was commended for its legibility and the way both the exterior and interior spaces conveyed a sense of place and purpose. Once the commission was awarded the architects met formally with the client, at first monthly and then weekly. They were given complete creative freedom to work up the design within the constraints of the budget and local planning regulations. The contract was for all stages of design and construction, including selection and management of the 17 contractors and site supervision. For planning and technical reasons it was not possible to have a sedum roof on the entire structure, and a textile one was substituted on the sloping eaves of the original building and its southern extension. Otherwise the initial design altered little.

Guinée*Potin's organic modern building is a welcome relief from the normal language of farm museums, which all too often falls into rural parody. The Ecomusée harks back to its past in its choice of materials and detailing, but its bold form speaks of the future, bringing new life to traditional techniques and ideas.

1 / The long two-storey building is straddled by a second volume, clad in recycled maritime planks and supported on pillars made of raw tree trunks. The studied use of natural materials announces the 'eco' nature of the museum.

1

2

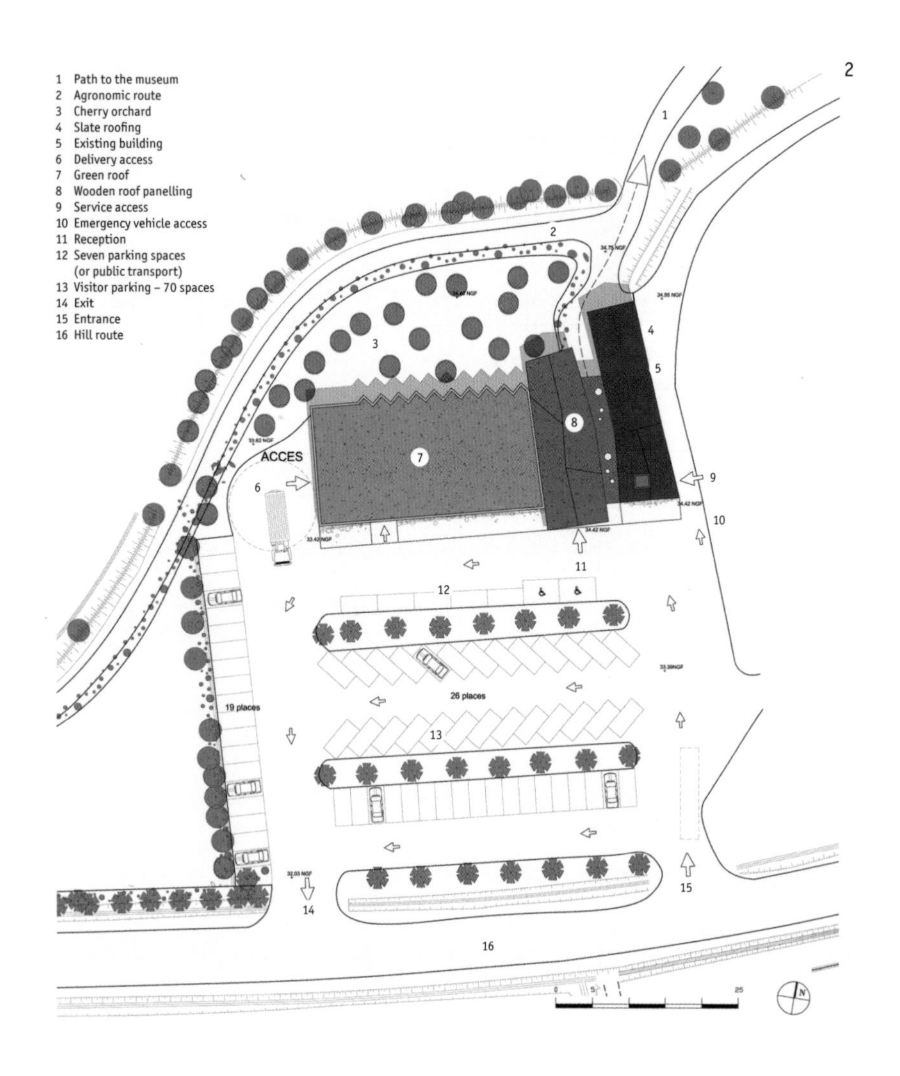
1 Path to the museum
2 Agronomic route
3 Cherry orchard
4 Slate roofing
5 Existing building
6 Delivery access
7 Green roof
8 Wooden roof panelling
9 Service access
10 Emergency vehicle access
11 Reception
12 Seven parking spaces (or public transport)
13 Visitor parking – 70 spaces
14 Exit
15 Entrance
16 Hill route
ACCES
19 places
26 places

3

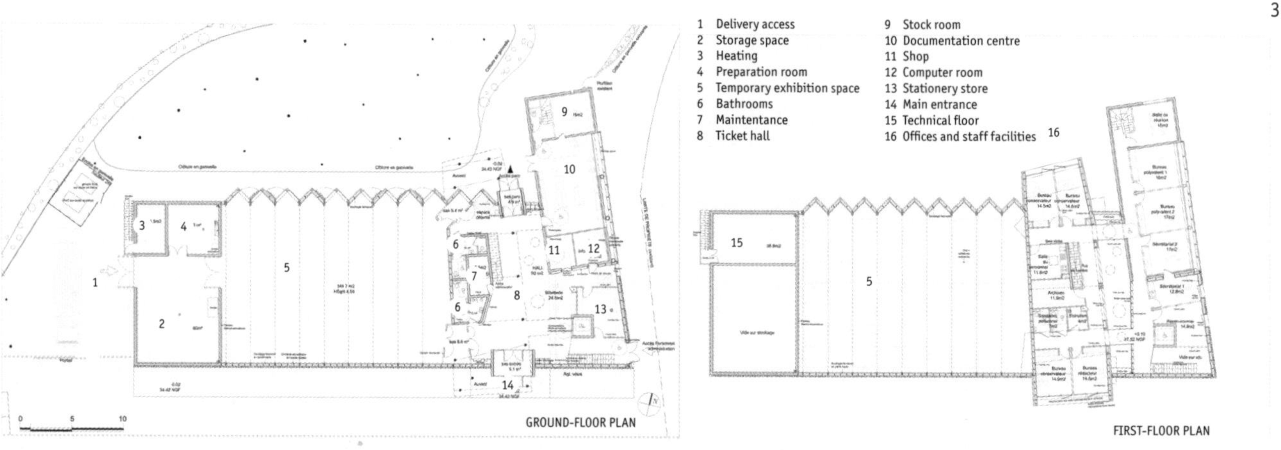
1 Delivery access
2 Storage space
3 Heating
4 Preparation room
5 Temporary exhibition space
6 Bathrooms
7 Maintenance
8 Ticket hall
9 Stock room
10 Documentation centre
11 Shop
12 Computer room
13 Stationery store
14 Main entrance
15 Technical floor
16 Offices and staff facilities
GROUND-FLOOR PLAN
FIRST-FLOOR PLAN

4

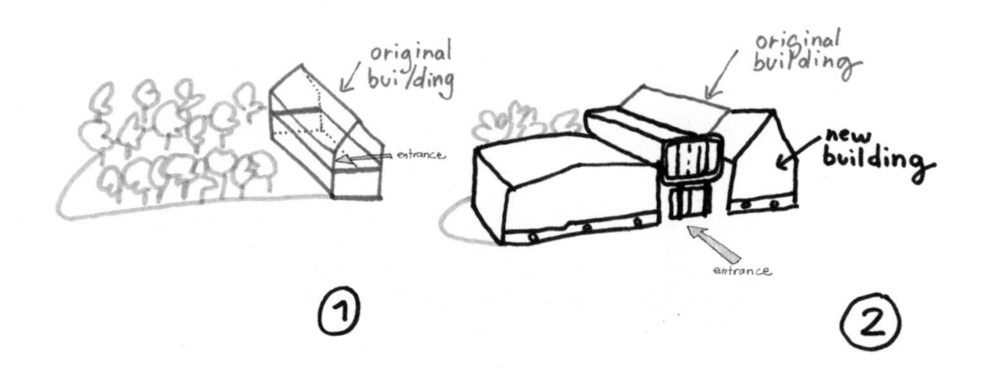
original building
entrance
original building
new building
entrance
1
2

5

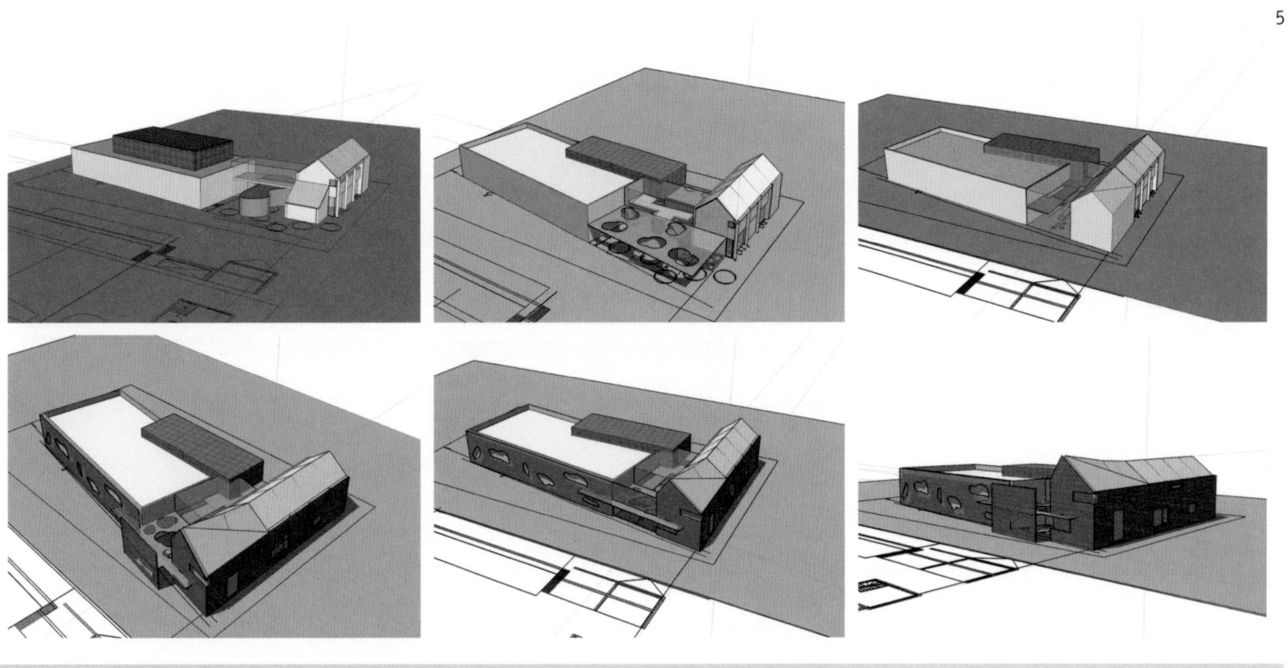

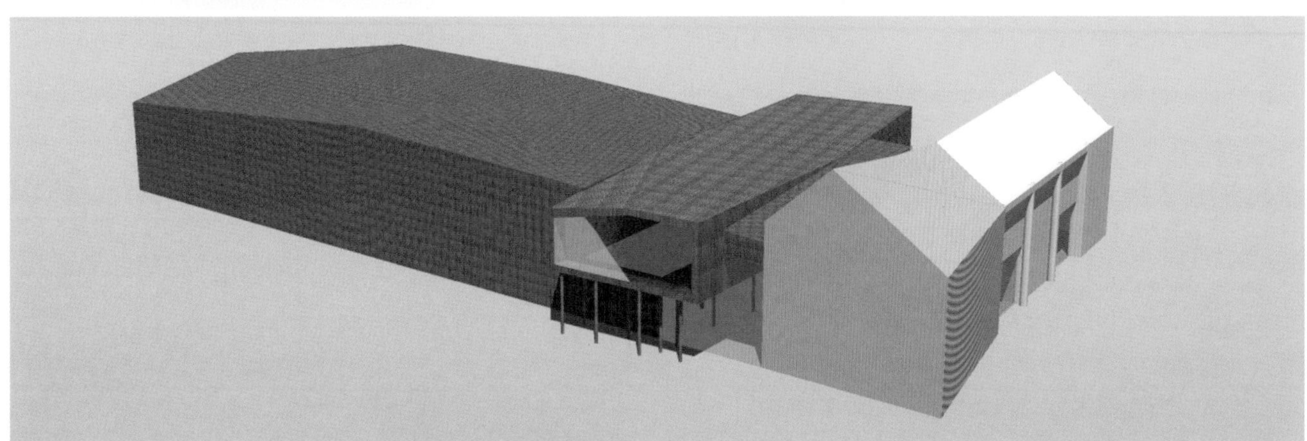

6

2 / Context plan.

3 / Ground- and first-floor plans.

4 / Retrospective sketch showing the relation of the original building (in red) to the new extensions (in black).

5 / SketchUp drawings: The architects use computer-drawing tools from an early stage to work up a concept. This shows the sequential development of possible layouts, forms and materials resulting in the final design presented to the client.

6 / Models are used through the first stage of the design process to examine façades and internal volumes.

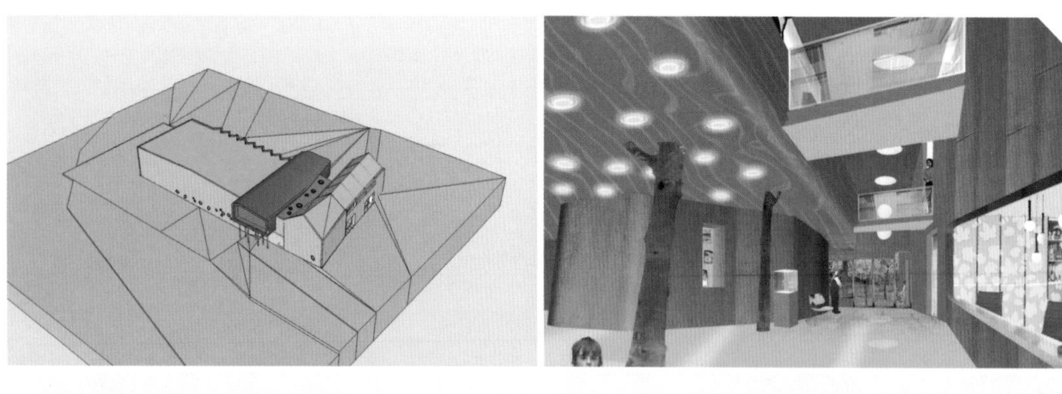

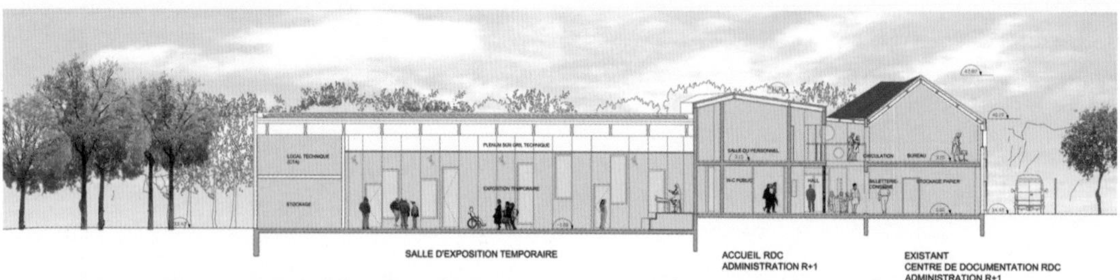

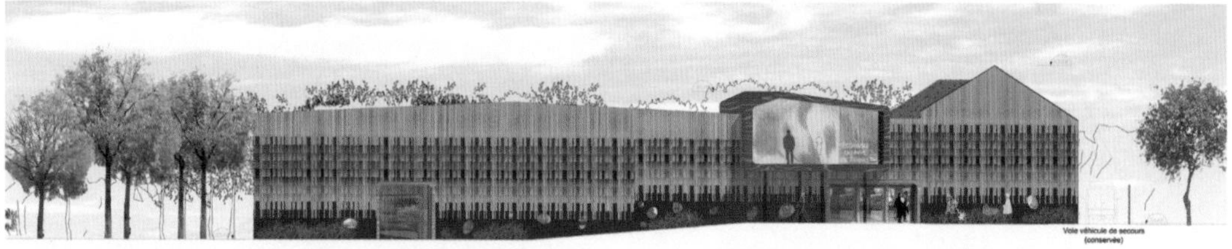

7 / SketchUp drawings produced for the competition, which was anonymous: The jury consisted of representatives of the city of Rennes, including economists and local councillors. The museum was represented by its director and curators. Jury members were shown presentation panels illustrating plans, sections and elevations as well as renderings of the interior and exterior, backed up by printed handouts and technical explanations.

8 / A 1:1 scale mock-up of the shingle cladding was made in collaboration with the contractor, who specialized in wooden structures, to test the construction and how to fix the cladding to the façade. The architects wanted a geometric wooden skin for the museum, and were inspired by the exteriors of local vernacular architecture and the tiles and discs of Paco Rabanne's iconic haute-couture 1960s dresses.

9 / The dimensions of the cladding had to be recalculated to make the shingles shorter. Planning specifications demanded that a maximum height should be respected as well as a strict size for the overlap. Chestnut is a soft wood and easily damaged.

10 / Wall section.

8

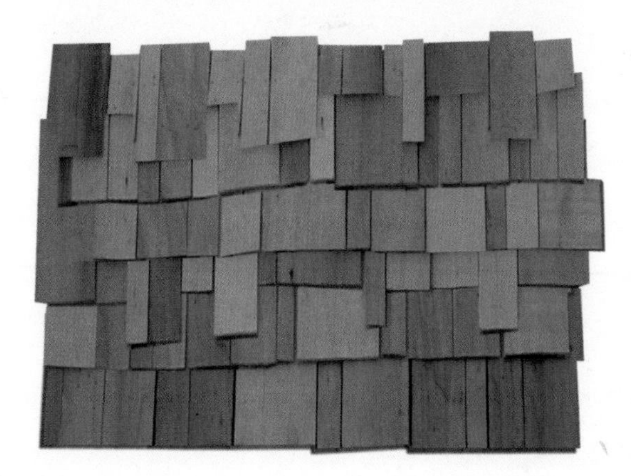

9

CUTTING wooden structure on wood frame + natural wood shingles / south façade

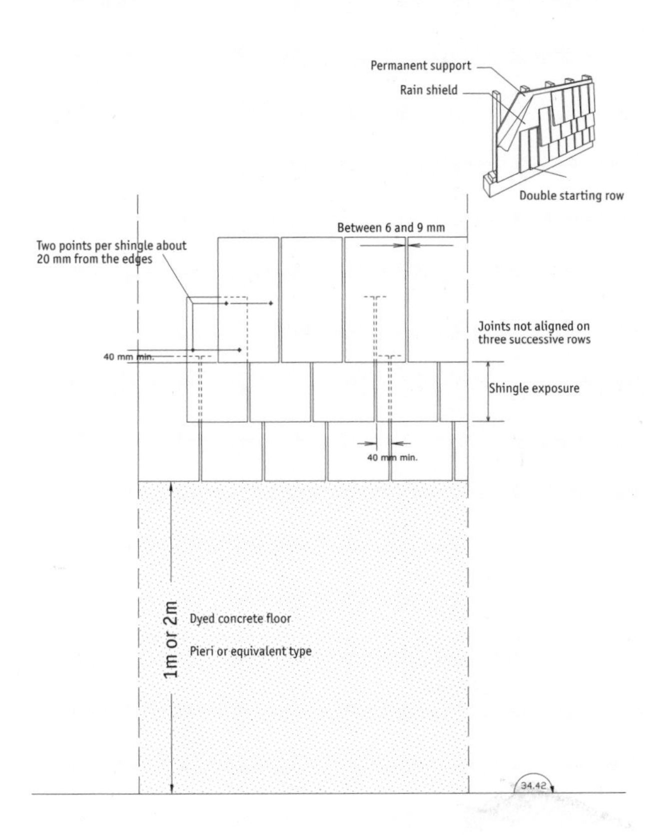
Permanent support
Rain shield
Double starting row
Between 6 and 9 mm
Two points per shingle about 20 mm from the edges
40 mm min.
Joints not aligned on three successive rows
Shingle exposure
40 mm min.
1m or 2m
Dyed concrete floor
Pieri or equivalent type
34.42

10

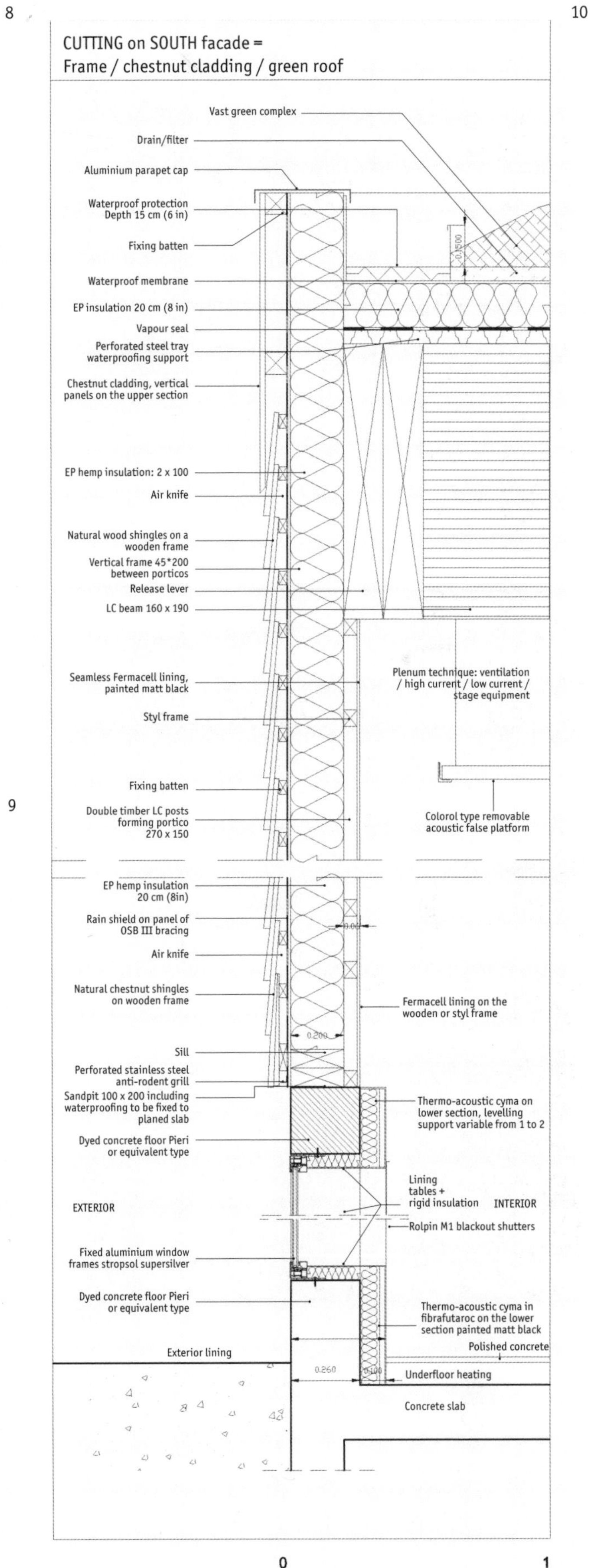
CUTTING on SOUTH facade =
Frame / chestnut cladding / green roof
Vast green complex
Drain/filter
Aluminium parapet cap
Waterproof protection Depth 15 cm (6 in)
Fixing batten
Waterproof membrane
EP insulation 20 cm (8 in)
Vapour seal
Perforated steel tray waterproofing support
Chestnut cladding, vertical panels on the upper section
EP hemp insulation: 2 x 100
Air knife
Natural wood shingles on a wooden frame
Vertical frame 45*200 between porticos
Release lever
LC beam 160 x 190
Seamless Fermacell lining, painted matt black
Styl frame
Fixing batten
Double timber LC posts forming portico 270 x 150
Plenum technique: ventilation / high current / low current / stage equipment
Colorol type removable acoustic false platform
EP hemp insulation 20 cm (8in)
Rain shield on panel of OSB III bracing
Air knife
Natural chestnut shingles on wooden frame
Fermacell lining on the wooden or styl frame
Sill
Perforated stainless steel anti-rodent grill
Sandpit 100 x 200 including waterproofing to be fixed to planed slab
Dyed concrete floor Pieri or equivalent type
Thermo-acoustic cyma on lower section, levelling support variable from 1 to 2
EXTERIOR
Lining tables + rigid insulation
INTERIOR
Rolpin M1 blackout shutters
Fixed aluminium window frames stropsol supersilver
Dyed concrete floor Pieri or equivalent type
Thermo-acoustic cyma in fibrafutaroc on the lower section painted matt black
Polished concrete
Exterior lining
Underfloor heating
Concrete slab
0.260
0
1

11

12

13

14

11 / The extension rests on a concrete foundation surmounted by a wooden frame. The southern façade has an ecological concrete base coloured by natural pigments.

12 / Fixing for the shingle cladding panels.

13 / The green roof is laid on the temporary exhibition hall. The sedum is precultivated and rests on top of an airtight membrane that consists of layers of insulation and a vapour barrier.

14 / The log-like form that announces the entrance of the museum pierces the first storey. Resting on giant oak trunks, it becomes a ceiling for the foyer and provides additional temporary exhibition space. The interiors use warm materials (partitions and walls in wood, floors in natural lino) and a rich colour palette reminiscent of the flora and fauna of Rennes.

15 / Interior of the temporary exhibition hall: The space is 4.2 m (13¾) ft) high and 350 m² (3,767 ft²). Equipped with a technical grid, the mainly black box can compete with the best in contemporary museography.

16 / The northern elevation is clad in Douglas pine and faces the cherry grove. The accordion-like façade lends it a sense of movement and offers a softer 'face' to the trees. The windows are placed at varied heights to magnify the effect.

17 / Workspaces for the management team are placed on the first floor with views out towards the entrance and new parking area, and downwards, via walkways, into the foyer. Further offices, including educational support offices, remain in the original building.

18 / Close-up of the concrete base surmounted by the shingle cladding.

The Dovecote Studio

Haworth Tompkins

Location: Snape Maltings, Suffolk, UK
Principal use: Artists' studio
Client: Aldeburgh Music
Site area: 30 m^2 (323 ft^2)
Interior area: 30 m^2 (323 ft^2)
Total build area: 30 m^2 (323 ft^2)
Design period: March 2007 – January 2009
Construction period: January 2009 – August 2009
Budget: £155,000

The Dovecote Studio is the smallest structure on Aldeburgh Music's new creative campus at Snape Maltings (previously, as the name suggests, a barley-malting plant), yet its symbolic significance should not be underestimated. It is the first building you see as you enter the complex and sits on the boundary between land and sea. A Cor-ten steel box has been inserted into the dimensions of the original, nineteenth-century brick dovecote that announced the former industrial site. As such, it serves as a memory of what was once there and is also an enigmatic object belonging to Snape's new life as a cultural centre.

The man who first saw the post-barley potential at Snape was George Gooderham, a local agriculturalist. Modern advances in technology had made the 10.9-hectare (27-acre) facility, consisting of no fewer than 20 individual buildings, redundant and he managed to acquire it for £54,000 in 1964. In the late 1960s Gooderham was approached by the composer Benjamin Britten, who agreed to lease a large kiln building for use as a venue for the Aldeburgh Music Festival. The space was later converted into a 750-capacity concert hall by Arup Associates in a spirit of preservation. In the early 1970s Aldeburgh Music's board commissioned a master plan to adapt the other redundant buildings to form what would effectively be an arts complex, but although a corner site was developed it wasn't until recently that the original vision began to be realized.

In 2005, following its successful renovation of London's famous Royal Court Theatre, Haworth Tompkins won a competition to design a phased regeneration of the Maltings. The scheme comprised a commercial development (65 residential units and retail space) and the Hoffmann Building, a new suite of rehearsal and occasional performance rooms including the 80-seat Jerwood Kiln Studio, as well as the project's centrepiece and only new-build structure: the Britten Studio, with retractable seating for 350. The Dovecote Studio is the latest of the nationally important grade 2 listed buildings to be completed.

The client, Aldeburgh Music, provided an open brief for a flexible space that could be used by artists, musicians and writers alike; above all, it had to be inexpensive. Haworth Tompkins rejected the idea of restoring the dovecote, as this would have lacked the authenticity of the original and be out of keeping with the design principles practised throughout the rest of the site. The importance of the Maltings is in the way it has been used, and has aged, throughout the last 200 years.

From the beginning of the regeneration scheme the architects, in dialogue with the local authority and English Heritage, had determined to preserve the site's unique character, defined by dereliction, and the delicate balance between industrial buildings and the marsh landscape. As much as possible of the original fabric was kept or recycled. Many surfaces were left as found and materials (bricks, timber beams and boards, trusses, doors and slates, etc.) were salvaged and reused wherever possible, to meet an extremely challenging budget, maintain continuity with the site and minimize the embodied energy of the project. Additions that had been built over time, and the weathering suffered by the kilns and granaries due to the aggressive sea-coast environment, were also preserved. As the project associate Paddy Dillon states: 'They had become a kind of palimpsest of different changes that had placed the ghosts among the buildings and given them a very strong and particular feeling.' It was important for Haworth Tompkins not to create too brittle a contrast between the very soft and patinated structures and a thin contemporary urban architectural language. To this end, materials were selected (board-marked concrete, unpainted steel) to be recognizably modern, while sharing the industrial quality and rich texture of the site.

The concept for the Dovecote was presented to the client using a combination of sketches and a photomontage. It was decided that to build on top of the ruin would destroy its romantic character, and the architects looked at ways to create a box within the shell. Different materials were examined, including fully planted green walls, but Cor-ten was selected because weathered steel is commonly found along the coastline. In addition, its rich red colour matched the burnish of the Suffolk red brick used in the surrounding buildings. The structural engineer and architects collaborated closely on the detailed drawings to create a steel box that was a completely sealed weatherproof shell. The construction was prefabricated off site and craned into place during the course of a day, keeping costs low. The monocoque box was given a strong architectonic form derived from the original dovecote, but the eaves were detailed as flush junctions of steel sheet, lending the structure a sculptural quality. The building was fully welded in a single piece, like the hull of a ship, to achieve weathertightness, then fitted with a simple plywood inner lining. The original building was stabilized but the window sills were left to rot naturally; and the vegetation was protected during the build so that it could continue to gradually cover the new structure.

From a distance the silhouette of the Victorian dovecote seems to have changed little, but on closer inspection the studio's bold and assertive engineered steel box, tucked snugly in its picturesque nineteenth-century husk, performs a poetic symphony that celebrates both contemporary design and conservation.

1 / Aldeburgh Music has a long tradition of commissioning pieces of art including the iconic Barbara Hepworth 'Family of Man'. The sculptural shape of the Studio was conceived in part to fit in with this history.

1

2

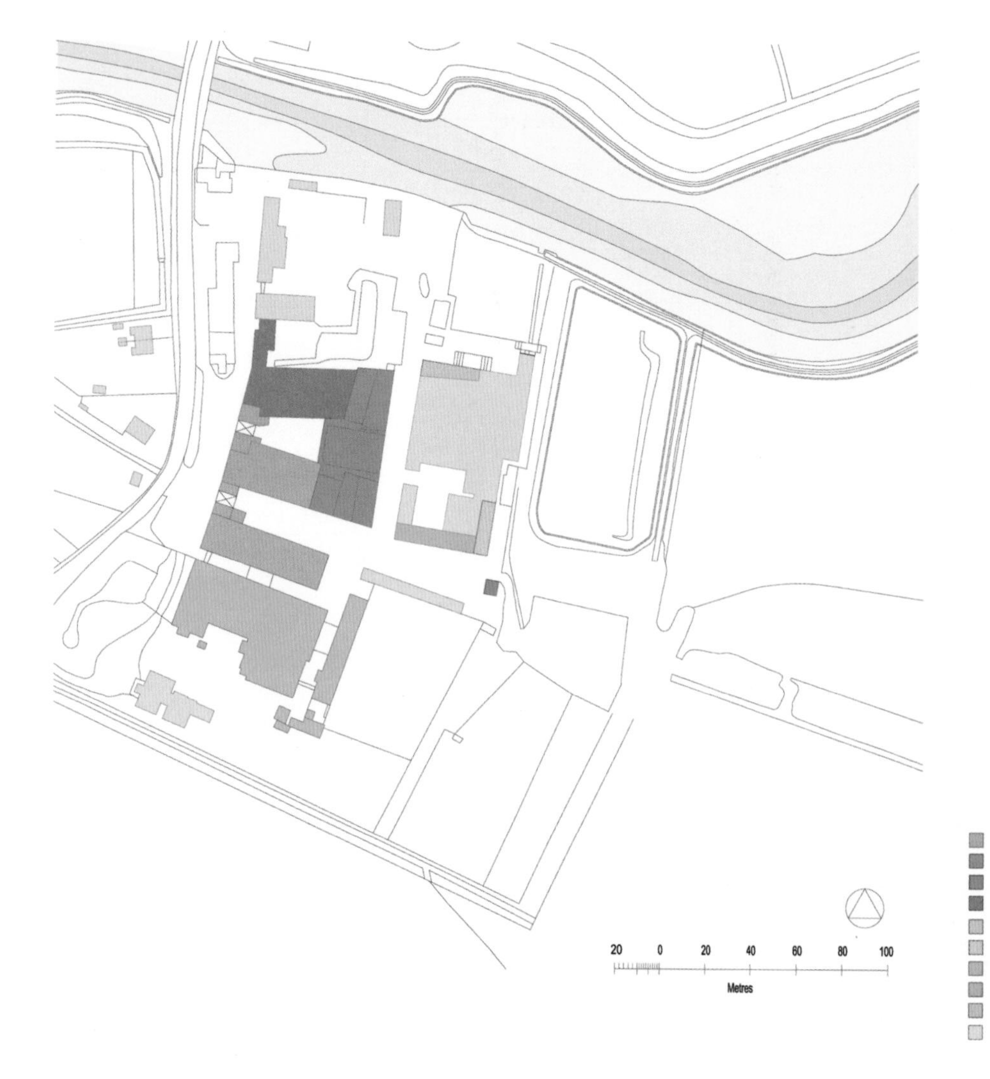

SNAPE MALTINGS, SUFFOLK

PHASING DIAGRAM

- Residential phase 1
- Hoffmann Building, Britten Studio and Jerwood Kiln Studio
- Dovecote Studio
- Retail unit (ground floor only – residential phase 1 above)
- Aldeburgh Music visitor centre
- Aldeburgh Music café
- Britten-Pear Building
- Residential phase 2 (unbuilt)
- Residential phase 3 (unbuilt)
- Existing buildings

3

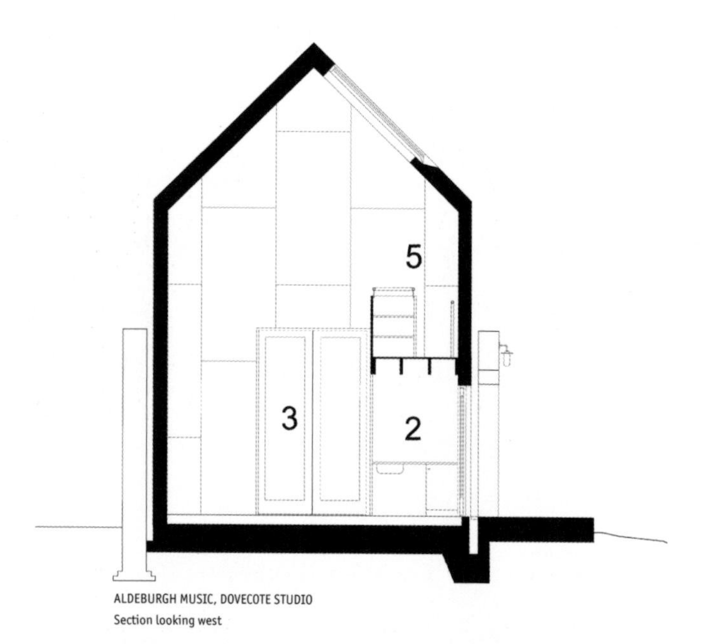

ALDEBURGH MUSIC, DOVECOTE STUDIO

Section looking west

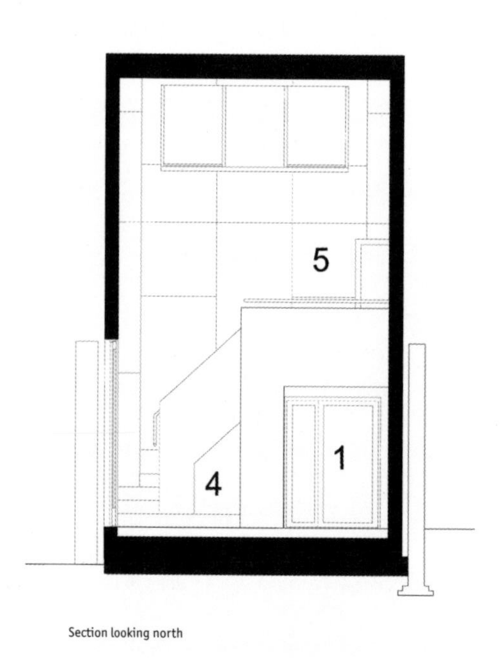

Section looking north

1 Entrance
2 Kitchen
3 Studio
4 Store
5 Mezzanine

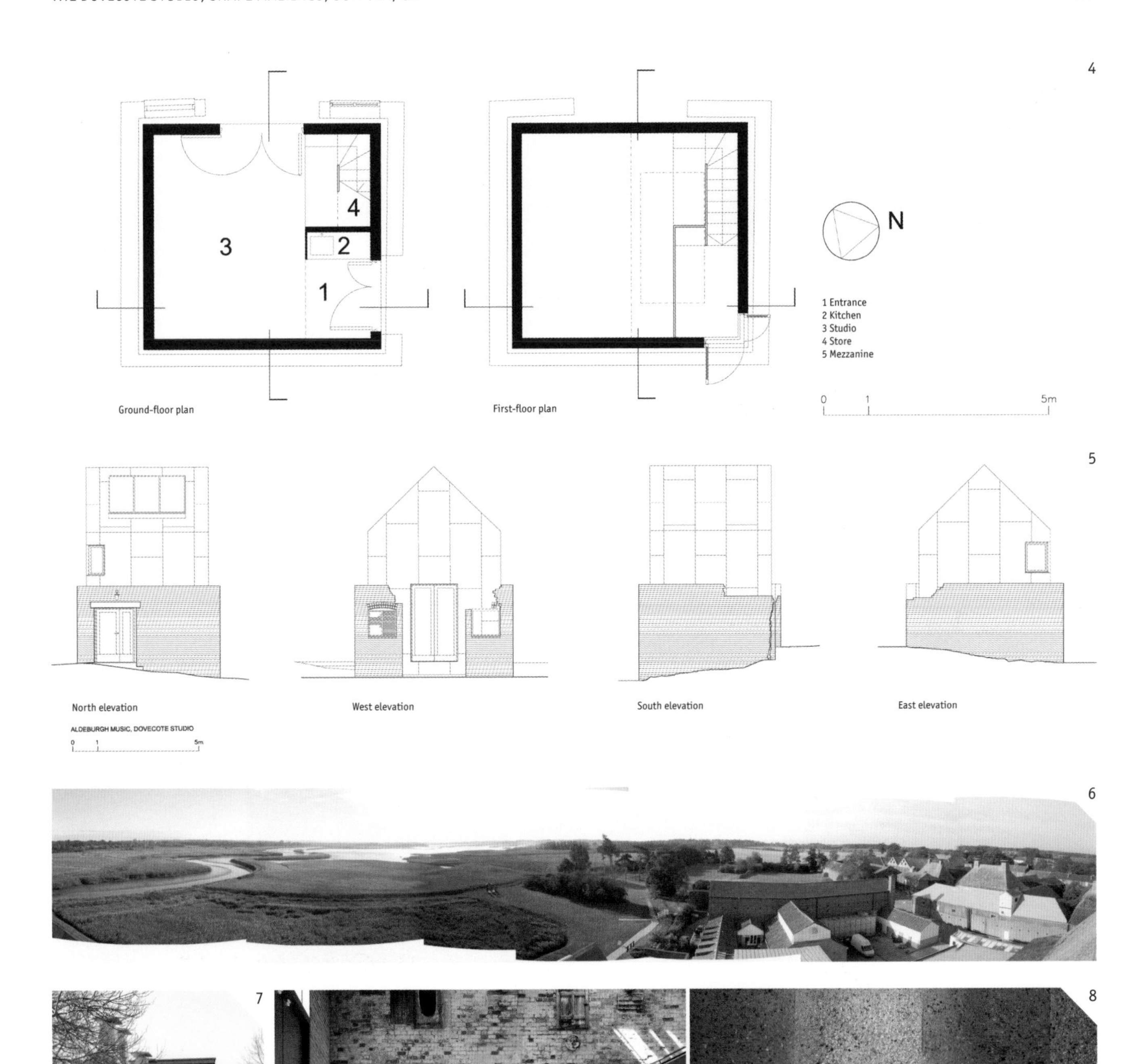

2 / Phasing diagram of Snape Maltings: The Dovecote and the Hoffmann Building were developed simultaneously.

3 / Sections looking west and north.

4 / Ground-floor and first-floor plans.

5 / Elevations.

6 / Benjamin Britten was first attracted to the Maltings because of its unique location on the border between the Suffolk farmland and coastline marshes.

7 / The first phase of the housing was designed under Haworth Tompkins' direction but passed on to a contractor to finish.

8 / Britten Studio: New elements of design were developed to respond to existing buildings and landscape. Concrete internal walls in the Britten Studio were washed to expose locally sourced aggregate, giving them the appearance of shingle beaches. The original brick was recycled.

9

10

Snape Maltings
Aldeburgh Music
Proposed Dovecote studio looking east - grass courtyard option

11

12

13

9 / The Jerwood Kiln Studio.

10 / The concept for the Dovecote was shown to the client using a combination of sketches and a photomontage: The architects prefer to collaborate informally with a client through discussion and hand-drawing, rather than composing elaborate PowerPoint presentations.

11 / Watercolour sketch of the Maltings from the marshes: Haworth Tompkins use a range of media during the design process, quick, hand-generated sketches, physical models and computer-rendered presentation images.

12 / Early sketch: Different materials for the Dovecote were researched including fully planted green walls. By this point, the form of the studio had been resolved and the decision that it would be a contemporary addition to the existing ruin had been made. The idea of living walls led to a consideration of the material behind the planting, as this would be exposed while the vegetation was establishing itself.

13 / A simple in-house cardboard model was made and altered to try out different ideas, such as the planted walls. A musicians' café occupies the adjacent structure and is linked to the Dovecote by a terrace. The model also addresses the relationship between the two buildings.

14 / The contract was full design to tender. The structural engineer and architects collaborated closely on the detailed drawings that were presented to the steelwork contractor. As the building was unique and the detailing unconventional Haworth Tompkins maintained a constant presence on site.

15 / Wall section: To avoid the build-up of condensation, a continuously sealed vapour barrier was added between the steel and plywood. The new structure was purposely designed not to touch any of the existing walls.

14

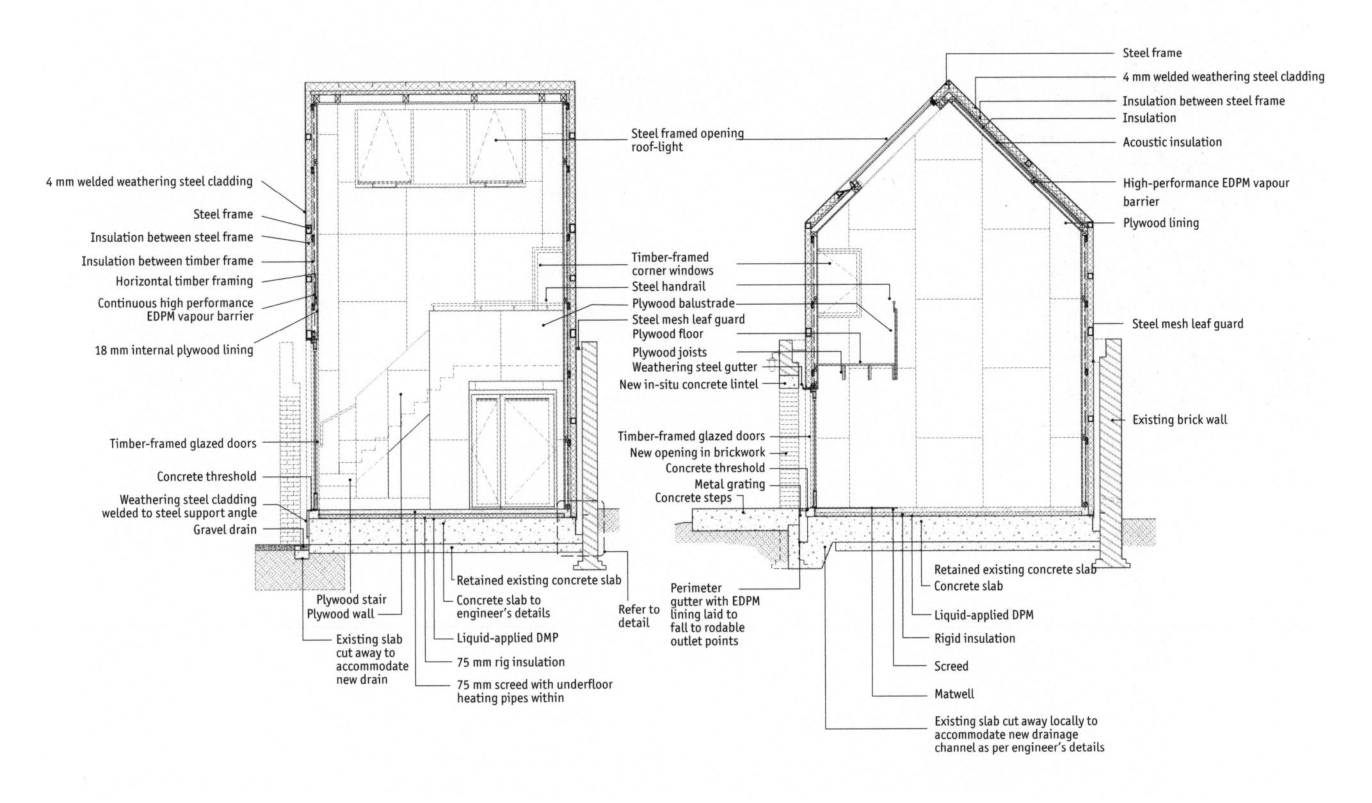
4 mm welded weathering steel cladding
Steel frame
Insulation between steel frame
Insulation between timber frame
Horizontal timber framing
Continuous high performance EDPM vapour barrier
18 mm internal plywood lining
Timber-framed glazed doors
Concrete threshold
Weathering steel cladding welded to steel support angle
Gravel drain
Plywood stair
Plywood wall
Existing slab cut away to accommodate new drain
Retained existing concrete slab
Concrete slab to engineer's details
Liquid-applied DMP
75 mm rig insulation
75 mm screed with underfloor heating pipes within
Refer to detail
Steel framed opening roof-light
Timber-framed corner windows
Steel handrail
Plywood balustrade
Steel mesh leaf guard
Plywood floor
Plywood joists
Weathering steel gutter
New in-situ concrete lintel
Timber-framed glazed doors
New opening in brickwork
Concrete threshold
Metal grating
Concrete steps
Perimeter gutter with EDPM lining laid to fall to rodable outlet points
Steel frame
4 mm welded weathering steel cladding
Insulation between steel frame
Insulation
Acoustic insulation
High-performance EDPM vapour barrier
Plywood lining
Steel mesh leaf guard
Existing brick wall
Retained existing concrete slab
Concrete slab
Liquid-applied DPM
Rigid insulation
Screed
Matwell
Existing slab cut away locally to accommodate new drainage channel as per engineer's details

15

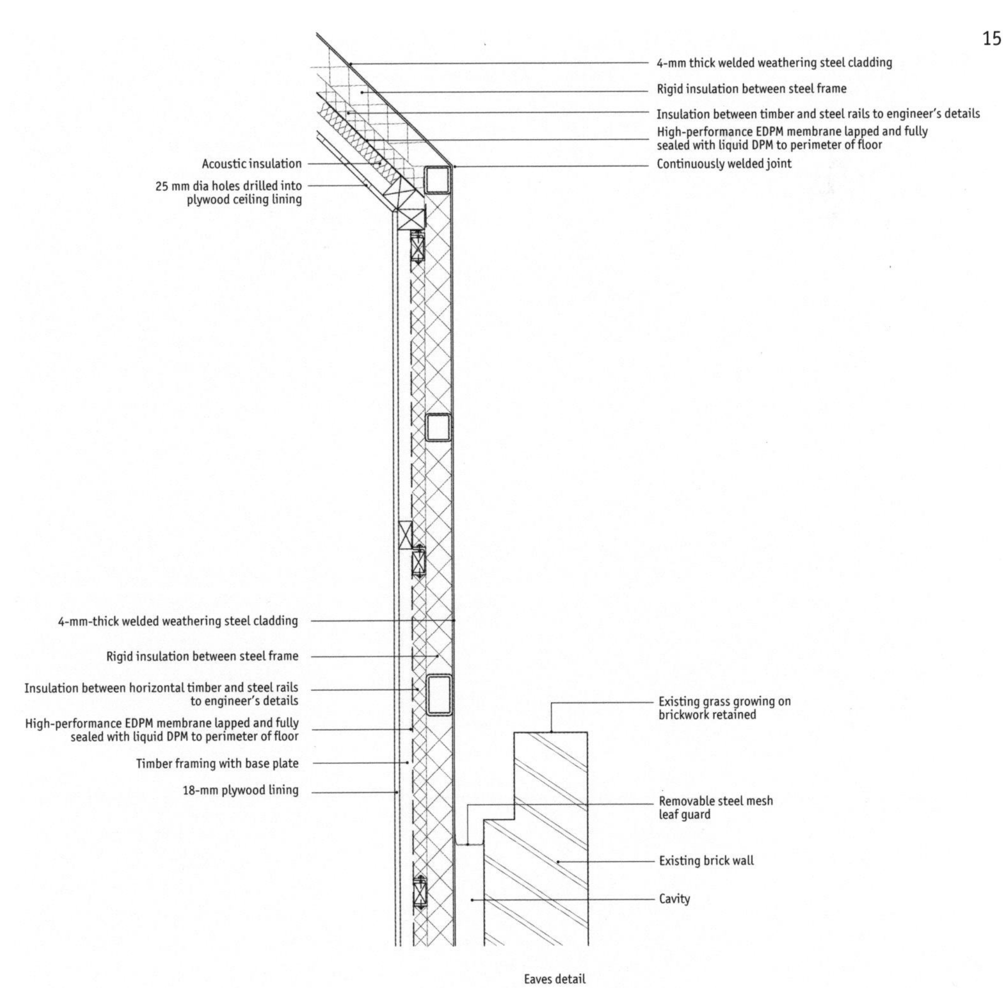
4-mm thick welded weathering steel cladding
Rigid insulation between steel frame
Insulation between timber and steel rails to engineer's details
High-performance EDPM membrane lapped and fully sealed with liquid DPM to perimeter of floor
Continuously welded joint
Acoustic insulation
25 mm dia holes drilled into plywood ceiling lining
4-mm-thick welded weathering steel cladding
Rigid insulation between steel frame
Insulation between horizontal timber and steel rails to engineer's details
High-performance EDPM membrane lapped and fully sealed with liquid DPM to perimeter of floor
Timber framing with base plate
18-mm plywood lining
Existing grass growing on brickwork retained
Removable steel mesh leaf guard
Existing brick wall
Cavity

Eaves detail

16

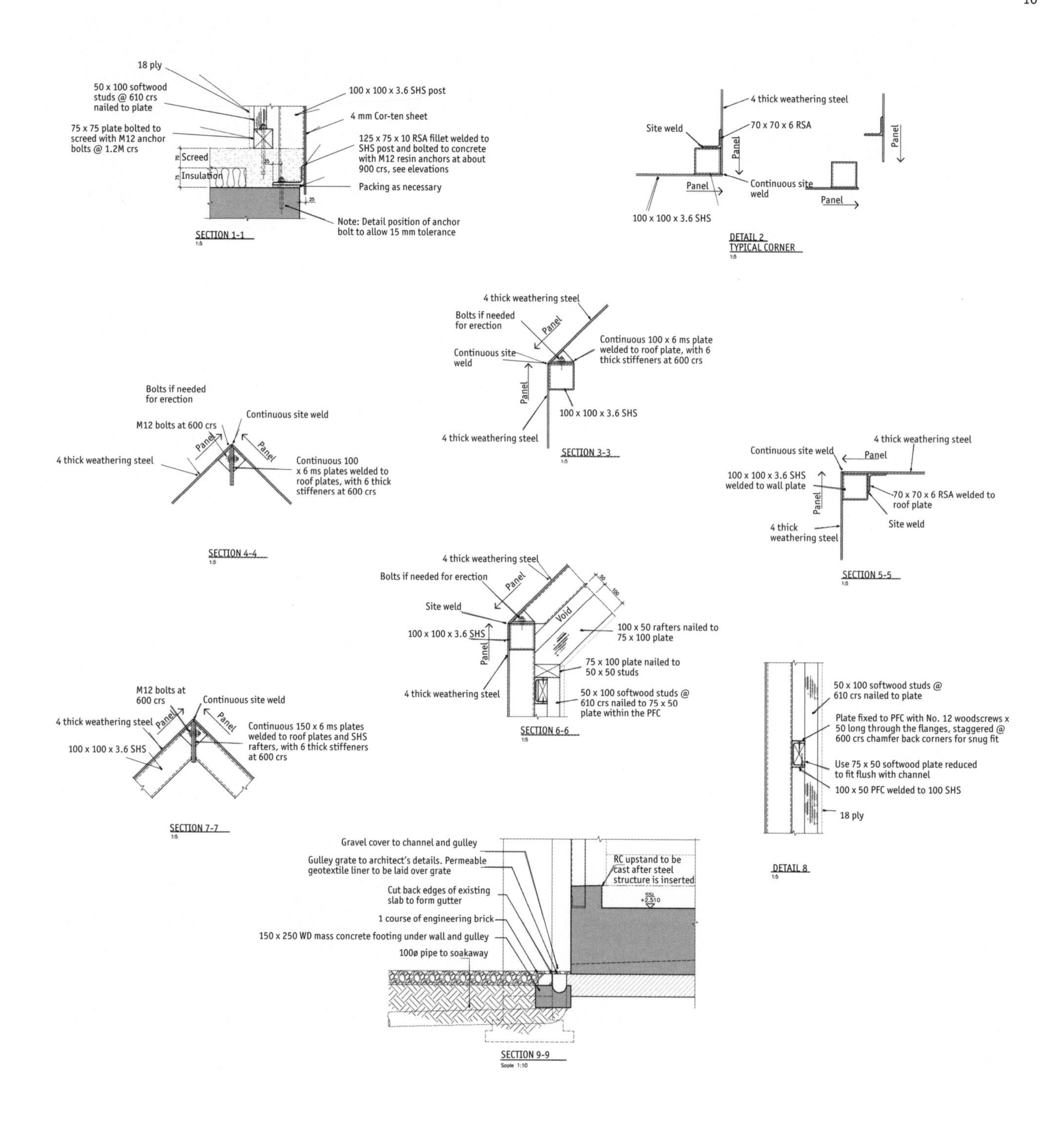

16 / Engineer's drawing: Collaboration with the structural engineer and the steel contractor on the details and positions of the seam welds was crucial. The steel box had to form a completely sealed weatherproofing shell. A wide, steep drainage channel that can be rodded to extract leaves and allow rainwater to drain away easily was added between the steel and the brickwork. The junction between the steel and the concrete foundation was detailed to minimize corrosion due to water ingress.

17 / The ruin was stabilized but no attempt was made to rebuild it. The architects worked closely with the local planning authorities and the relationship was mutually respectful. By the time work began on the Dovecote there was a good understanding of how new construction could be expressed in appropriate contemporary materials. Cor-ten was considered to be aesthetically soft but rhetorically hard and modern.

17

18

19

20

21

22

18 / The Cor-ten box is lowered into place. The structure is fabricated from 120 x 240 cm (47¼ x 94½ in) sheets with regular staggered welded joints, into which door and window openings are cut in locations dictated by the internal layout.

19 / Preparing the 'box' for its lining.

20 / View of the Dovecote from the east.

21 / The interior has a simple spruce plywood lining. By adding a staircase, a mezzanine and a large north-facing skylight, a small space has been given many functions and is adaptable to the needs of the various kinds of artist using it. Plywood was chosen for cost and durability. It can be easily over-hauled or painted when necessary.

22 / The mezzanine level incorporates a fully opening, glazed corner window that gives views over the marshes to the sea.

UK Pavilion, Shanghai World Expo 2010

Heatherwick Studio

Location: Shanghai, China
Principal use: Exhibition space
Client: Foreign and Commonwealth Office
Site area: 6,000 m² (64,583½ ft²)
Interior area of Seed Cathedral: 105 m² (1,130¼ ft²)
Interior area of accommodation: 1,630 m² (17,545 ft²)
Total build area: 4,035 m² (43,432 ft²)
Design period: January 2008 – December 2009
Construction period: January 2009 – April 2010
Budget: £13,200,000

The 2010 Shanghai World Fair was the biggest event of its kind since the expo phenomenon began in 1851 with the Great Exhibition, held in the Crystal Palace erected in London's Hyde Park. Historically, expos have given rise to architectural landmarks: the Eiffel Tower in Paris, Mies van der Rohe's German Pavilion in Barcelona and Buckminster Fuller's geodesic dome in Montreal, to name a few. For the Shanghai Expo, with the aim of attracting investment from the industrial behemoth China, the British government's Foreign and Commonwealth Office pulled out all the stops and dedicated £25 million to the design of a pavilion that would be equally iconic and represent the UK's cultural and commercial ambitions. The brief was for a building that would become one of the five most popular attractions at the event. It may seem surprising, then, that Thomas Heatherwick, who trained as a 3-D designer and has to date only two completed buildings to his name, was awarded the commission, beating off competition from the likes of Zaha Hadid, John McAslan and Marks Barfield.

However, Thomas Heatherwick is one of the UK's most innovative designers. Equal parts sculptor, product designer, engineer and inventor, he refuses to be categorized. He recognized that to stand out from the other venues and competitors, his design needed to be unique.

From the beginning, Heatherwick and the project architect, Katerina Dionysopoulou, wanted to design a structure whose architecture was a direct manifestation of what it was exhibiting, to the point where one could not be considered without the other. Early sketches centred on the idea of a natural object and textures. The site is next to the Huangpu River and benefits from water-borne breezes, and the architects worked with the notion that the structure could somehow move in the wind. The origins of the pavilion's 'hairy' form can be traced back to an unrealized commission for Notting Hill Gate in London. The brief asked for a number of single artworks to be installed on a 1960s concrete building hated by many for its harsh appearance. Instead, the studio proposed to soften the building's entirety with 'architectural hairs'. This project further influenced two research projects for very small buildings called 'sitooteries', which were developments of this approach to architectural texture. The team also researched previous expos and looked for a means to mitigate the frenetic, overcrowded conditions such occasions engender. 'At this Expo, in a sea of stimulation, we thought that calmness would actually be the thing that would refresh you and that you might be the most thirsty for,' says Heatherwick. The design proposal was for a small building surrounded by a significant area of open public space so that visitors could relax, and choose to enter the pavilion itself or see it clearly from a calm, non-queuing vantage point.

The presentation to the competition jury was made on panels that showed 2-D drawings of the layout and visualizations, plus a short animation that demonstrated the rods swaying in the breeze. The form, although not the materiality, of the pavilion was decided, as was the scale and circulation. Once the commission was awarded, Heatherwick was asked to propose a programme and the content for the exhibition. Rather than showcasing a broad range of British expertise, or falling into the trap of portraying Britain as a heritage country (which is the traditional Chinese perception), he decided to concentrate on one particular aspect for which the UK is known, and make it modern and relevant. The theme of the 2010 Expo was 'Better City, Better Life'. Having already presented the idea of a natural object, Heatherwick developed the theme by highlighting the role Britain has played in integrating nature into cities. London with its parks and gardens is the greenest city of its size in the world, and the UK was the first country to open a major botanical garden – the Royal Botanic Gardens at Kew. Looking for something that could be encased in the ends of the rods, Heatherwick approached the Kew Millennium Seed Bank, which was established to collect the seeds of 25 per cent of the world's wild plant species by 2020.

The design, which was developed and constructed over 26 months, employed Chinese contractors and engineers (overseen by The Mace Group, who acted as project managers) and used local materials, the majority of which were sourced within 300 km (186 miles) of the site. It consists of two interlinked experiential elements: the architecturally iconic and contemplative pavilion building and a multilayered landscape treatment of the site. Access to the Seed Cathedral is gained via a walkway that runs around the perimeter of the plot, and contains a narrative exhibition designed by London-based design studio, Troika. Below the circulation zone further spaces can be used for cultural and commercial events hosted by the FCO.

Over 250,000 different seeds, arranged randomly, are cast into the ends of the acrylic rods that penetrate the structure's steel and timber shell, giving the interior its form. On the exterior they extend as a halo of filaments that ripple and change texture in the gentlest breeze. The fibre-optic staves draw light in to illuminate the visitor space; at night, light sources within each stave allow the whole structure to glow. Criticism may have been levelled at the lack of content in the interior (Heatherwick himself admits he has had people come up to him and say, 'Where is it? There's nothing here'), yet this pavilion, the smallest in the expo, is the one that will remain in people's minds, symbolizing as it does the imaginative richness of British design. 'We were deliberately playing with the contrast between grandiosity and insignificance ... In a way, the power of the potential in those 250,000 seeds is mind-blowingly massive. And you're standing in the middle of the most biodiverse point you could possibly stand in, Shanghai! Everything is there and yet there's a kind of absence, it's totally calm.'

1 / The optic 'hairs' create a halo around the British Pavilion and move gently in the wind to create a dynamic effect.

1

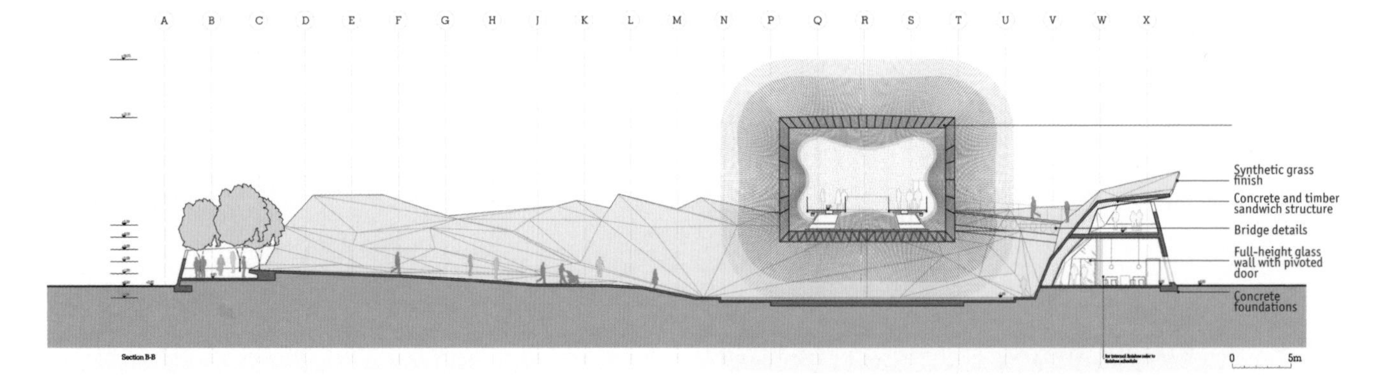

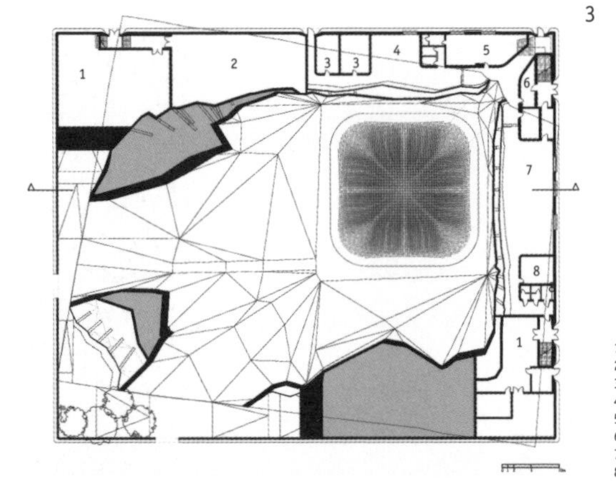

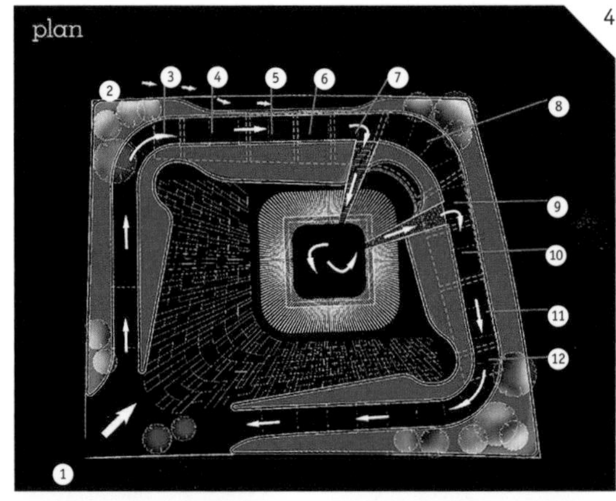

2 / Sections: Beneath the pavilion and the landscaped area is a canopied and naturally ventilated entrance and exit sequence. Spaces dedicated for use by the FCO are situated below.

3 / First-level floor plan: The Seed Cathedral is the axial focus of the 4,035 m² (43,432 ft²) site, which has been treated as a multilayered, folded landscape. Visitors access the plot through a corner entrance, and can either filter into the park and relax or enter the pavilion via a walkway.

4 / Plan.

5 / The concept was for a natural object that would move like grass in the wind.

6 / The origins of the pavilion's 'hairy' form lay in an unrealized arts project intended to soften the harsh appearance of a 1960s building in London.

7 / The notion of 'architectural hairs' influenced two research projects for very small buildings called 'sitooteries'.

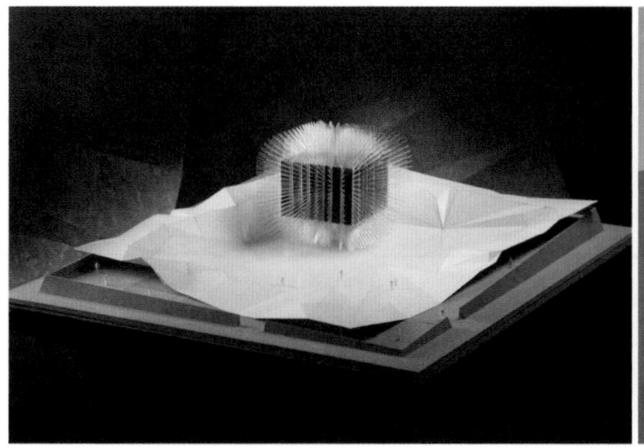

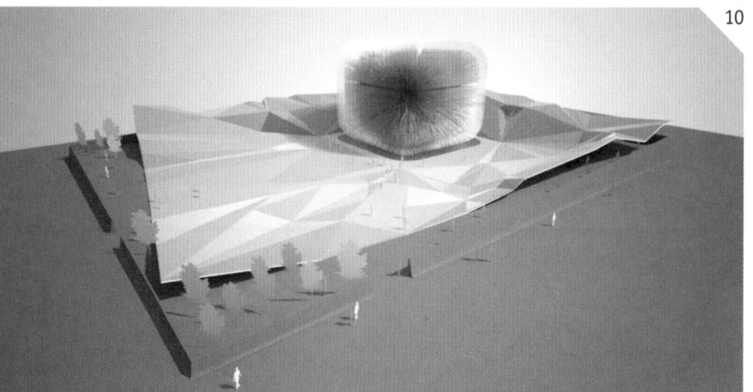

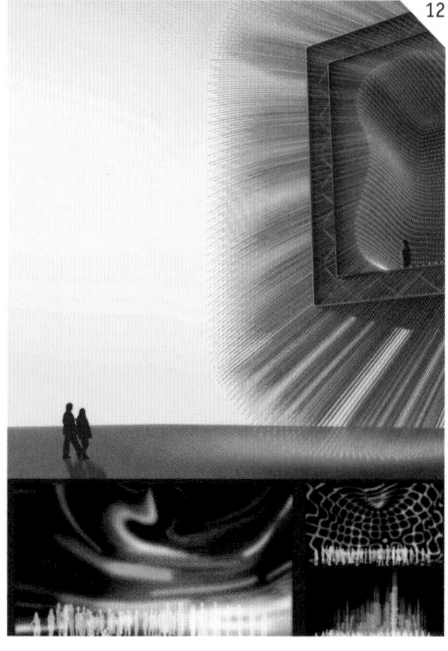

8 / Heatherwick's office is non-hierarchical. All members of the project team are invited to make suggestions. Discussions involve the use of pin-up walls where the results of research and ideas are posted.

9 / An early sketch shows the idea of a natural object sitting within a larger landscaped area.

10 / Axonometric and model produced during schematic design.

11 / Presentation panels: The competition entry had the scale, form and circulation in place, and showed inspirational ideas and rudimentary structural details.

12 / Presentation panels: The client was advised by the consulate general in Shanghai and the British Council, as well as John Sorrell (chairman of the London Design Festival) and Mark Jones (Director of the V&A) who acted as consultants on the content. Heatherwick began his collaboration with the lead engineer, Adams Kara Taylor (AKT), and service engineers Atelier Ten at the competition stage.

13

14

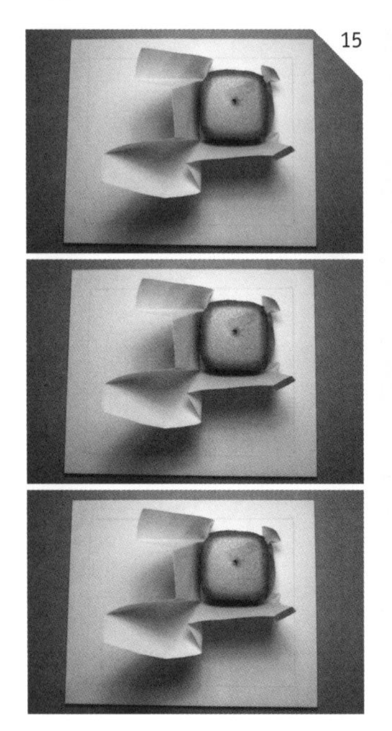
15

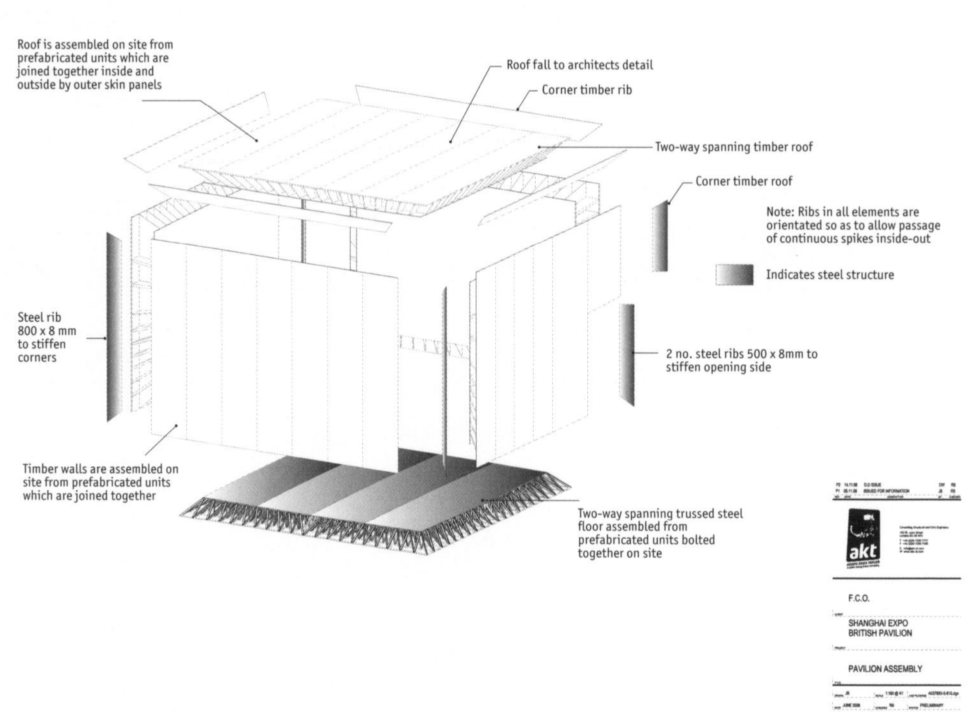
16
Roof is assembled on site from prefabricated units which are joined together inside and outside by outer skin panels
Roof fall to architects detail
Corner timber rib
Two-way spanning timber roof
Corner timber roof
Note: Ribs in all elements are orientated so as to allow passage of continuous spikes inside-out
Indicates steel structure
Steel rib 800 x 8 mm to stiffen corners
2 no. steel ribs 500 x 8mm to stiffen opening side
Timber walls are assembled on site from prefabricated units which are joined together
Two-way spanning trussed steel floor assembled from prefabricated units bolted together on site
akt
F.C.O.
SHANGHAI EXPO
BRITISH PAVILION
PAVILION ASSEMBLY
A037893
S610
P2

13 / Heatherwick works extensively with physical models. 1:1 mock-ups of possible materials for the rods were tested including bamboo, which was found to be too rigid to move in the wind. Acrylic was selected as it allowed light to penetrate into the interior of the box.

14 / Axonometric investigating the use of acrylic rods.

15 / Paper models were used to arrive at the folded, origami-like shape of the concrete landscape. The concept was that it should look like wrapping paper that had been unfolded to reveal the gift inside.

16 / The box structure consists of two plywood panels set 90 cm (35½ in) apart and supported by laminated veneer lumber. The corners and floor are reinforced with steel. The holes for the rods were CNC-drilled in the exact position and angle required. The structure is covered with three layers of waterproofing.

17 / The contractor selected to manufacture the rods competed with two others; all were asked to produce 1:1 mock-ups. Once commissioned, a prototype was developed incorporating the light and seeds, and was then refined by Heatherwick.

18 / The aluminium and the acrylic were extruded in two sections. The internal ends that contain the seeds were cast by hand, polished and glued in place. About 1,000 rods were produced per day.

19 / The aluminium was placed around the acrylic, and LEDs were added and cabled. The rods were delivered on site with all the components in place and were connected to the pre-wired interior of the box.

20 / The rods extend 5 m (16½ ft) outside of the building. Two-thirds of their 7.5 m (24½ ft) length is encased in aluminium, which keeps them stable while allowing movement. Externally, 1.5 m (5 ft) of acrylic is visible, creating a glowing effect around the pavilion's silhouette. A red plastic extrusion at the point where the acrylic meets the aluminium allows the two materials to oscillate without the acrylic becoming scratched.

17

18

19

20

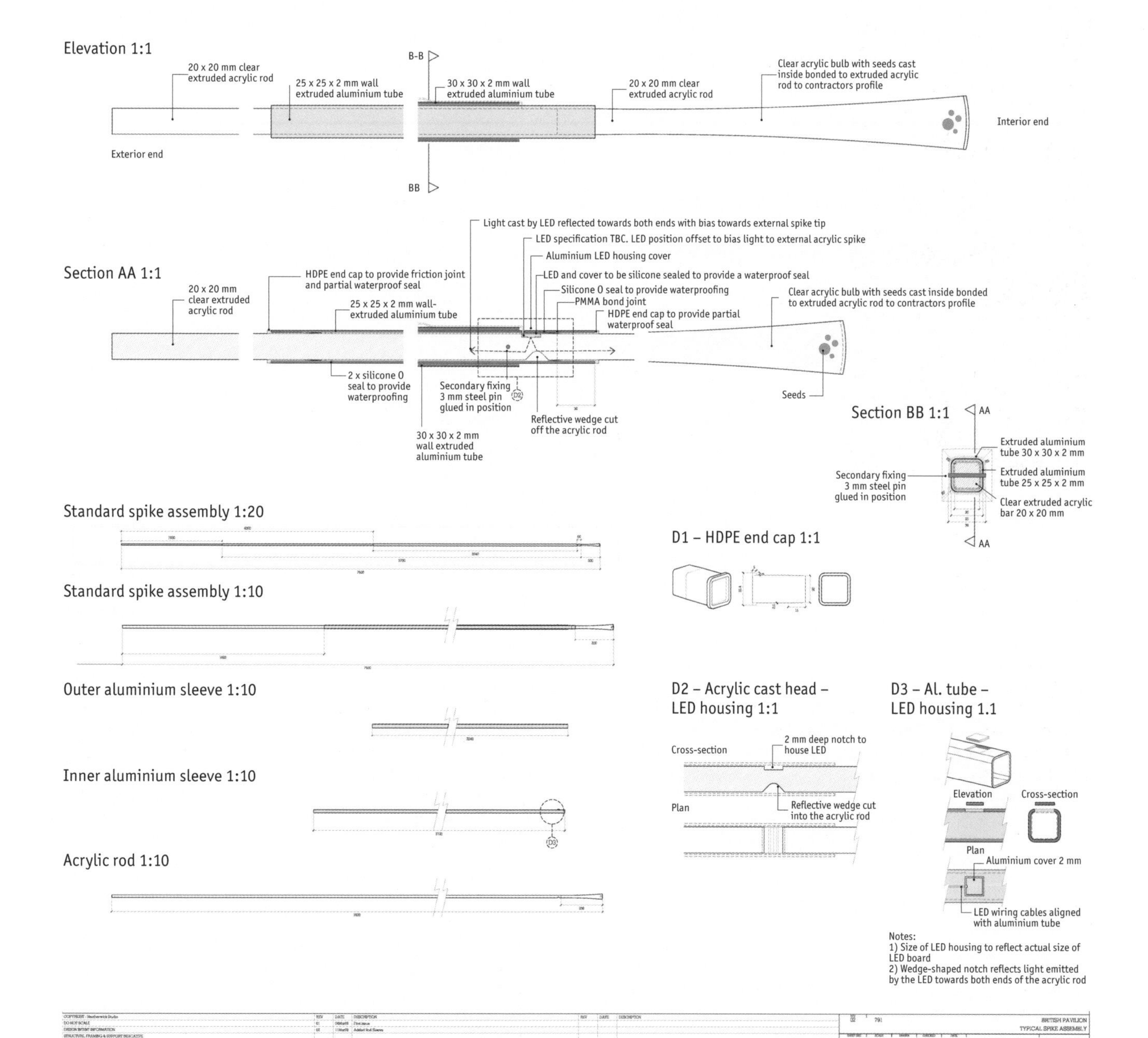

Elevation 1:1
20 x 20 mm clear extruded acrylic rod
25 x 25 x 2 mm wall extruded aluminium tube
B-B
30 x 30 x 2 mm wall extruded aluminium tube
20 x 20 mm clear extruded acrylic rod
Clear acrylic bulb with seeds cast inside bonded to extruded acrylic rod to contractors profile
Interior end
Exterior end
BB
Light cast by LED reflected towards both ends with bias towards external spike tip
LED specification TBC. LED position offset to bias light to external acrylic spike
Aluminium LED housing cover
Section AA 1:1
HDPE end cap to provide friction joint and partial waterproof seal
LED and cover to be silicone sealed to provide a waterproof seal
20 x 20 mm clear extruded acrylic rod
25 x 25 x 2 mm wall-extruded aluminium tube
Silicone O seal to provide waterproofing
PMMA bond joint
HDPE end cap to provide partial waterproof seal
Clear acrylic bulb with seeds cast inside bonded to extruded acrylic rod to contractors profile
2 x silicone O seal to provide waterproofing
Secondary fixing 3 mm steel pin glued in position
30 x 30 x 2 mm wall extruded aluminium tube
Reflective wedge cut off the acrylic rod
Seeds
Section BB 1:1
AA
Extruded aluminium tube 30 x 30 x 2 mm
Extruded aluminium tube 25 x 25 x 2 mm
Clear extruded acrylic bar 20 x 20 mm
Secondary fixing 3 mm steel pin glued in position
Standard spike assembly 1:20
D1 – HDPE end cap 1:1
Standard spike assembly 1:10
Outer aluminium sleeve 1:10
D2 – Acrylic cast head – LED housing 1:1
D3 – Al. tube – LED housing 1.1
Cross-section
2 mm deep notch to house LED
Plan
Reflective wedge cut into the acrylic rod
Elevation
Cross-section
Plan
Aluminium cover 2 mm
Inner aluminium sleeve 1:10
Acrylic rod 1:10
LED wiring cables aligned with aluminium tube
Notes:
1) Size of LED housing to reflect actual size of LED board
2) Wedge-shaped notch reflects light emitted by the LED towards both ends of the acrylic rod
TENDER
Heatherwick studio

21

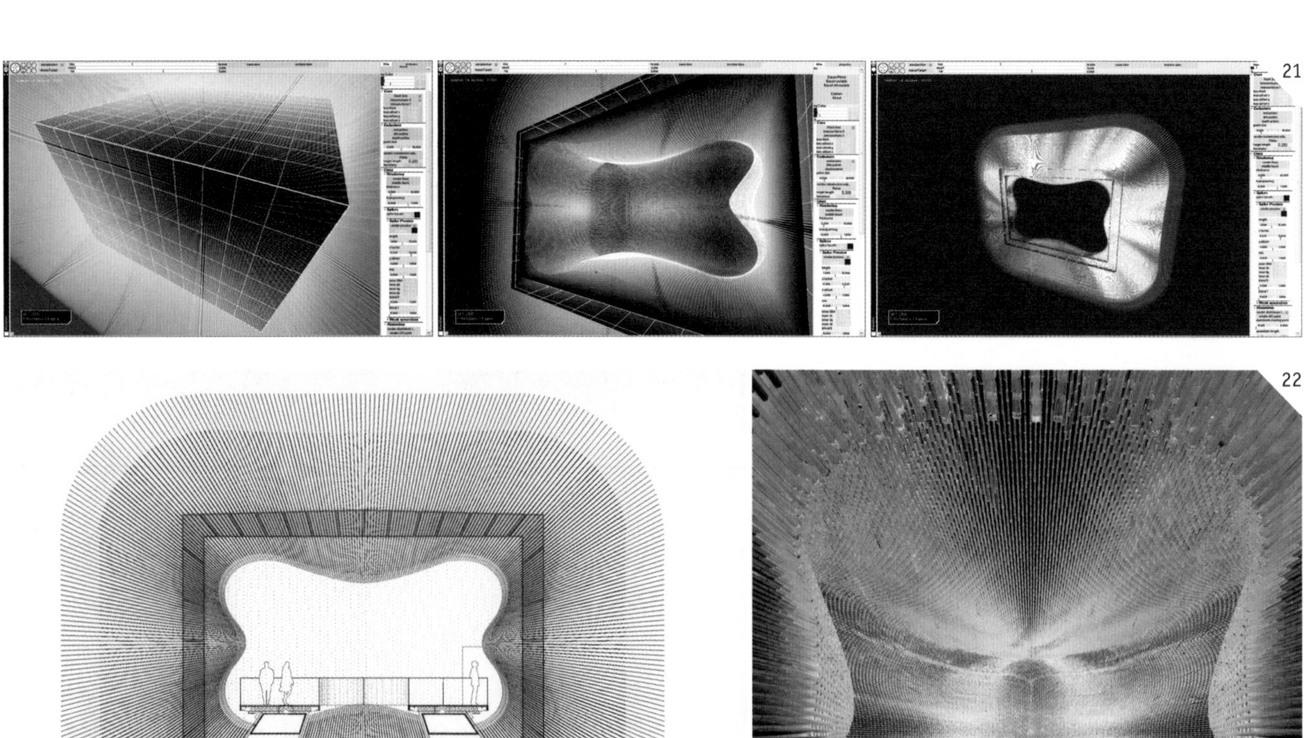

22

23

24

25

26

21 / 3-D computer models were produced by AKT during the design development period to avoid clashes between the rods.

22 / As the box is a squeezed cube measuring 10 x 15 x 15 m (33 x 49 x 49 ft), and the rods (which are of identical length) are focused on a central sphere, an organic shape was created internally. There is a void in the middle of the floating platform people walk on, and visitors gaze down from a glass bridge onto the seeds. Looking up, the rods are suspended 5 m (16½ ft) above head height. The platform conceals the mechanical and engineering services.

23 / The contract was design and build, but Heatherwick's team stayed involved as part of the client body to supervise the construction. Tests were produced for all the elements of the design from waterproofing to the exact red used in the plastic extrusion detail of the rods. The concrete for the landscape contained recycled aggregate and was poured on site.

24 / The darkened, silent inner sanctum creates an atmosphere of reverence around the collection of the world's botanical resources. By day, the tips of the vitrines glow with light drawn from outside and by night they are illuminated by light sources within each rod. Seeming to hover above the visitors, they contain either one or more seeds sourced with the help of China's Kunming Institute of Botany, a partner in the Kew Millennium Seed Bank project.

25 / The circulation zone that forms the entrance and exit sequence runs along the perimeter of the site and contains three installations. These describe the relationship that the UK has with nature: Open City (left), Living City (top right) and Green City (bottom right).

26 / The landscaped park is covered by a special artificial grass surface that acts as a welcoming and restful public space for the expo's visitors.

Loblolly House

KieranTimberlake

Location: Chesapeake Bay, USA
Principal use: Private residence
Client: Stephen Kieran
Site area: 1.5 hectares (3.65 acres)
Interior area: 167.2 m^2 (1,800 ft^2)

Total build area: 204.4 m^2 (2,200 ft^2)
Design period: January 2005 – June 2005
Construction period: September 2006 – November 2006
Budget: Undeclared

Loblolly House is situated on Taylors Island, off the coast of Maryland in Chesapeake Bay. It's the brainchild of KieranTimberlake, a Philadelphia-based architectural practice known for its sustainable architecture and in-depth research into the fundamentals of building. The two-storey, 167.2-square-metre (1,800-square-foot) residence proposes a more efficient method of assembly than the average prefab; it is assembled from 70 per cent off-site fabricated modular parts, with floor and ceiling cartridges containing heating, ventilation and electricity, and integrated mobile bedroom and bathroom units. Through the use of state-of-the-art Building Information Modelling (BIM) the architects were able to streamline the building process into basic constituents: structure/scaffold, cartridge, block and furniture, fixtures and equipment (FF&E). Thousands of parts were simplified into a few dozen panels and blocks that slide into an aluminium frame set on wooden piles made from pressure-treated pine. The whole assembly took less than six weeks. Rather than being an experimental model, this award-winning design heralds an element-based form of mass housing that is set to have an impact on the future of domestic architecture.

Stephen Kieran purchased a plot on Taylors Island with the intention of creating a family home, but at the same time put into built form some of the ideas he and Timberlake had formulated in *Refabricating Architecture*, a book that explains, and argues for, the prefabrication of buildings using parametric computer modelling. The methodology, they maintain, reinstates the architect as master builder, capable of singularly overseeing all aspects of design and erection. Timberlake and Kieran argue that off-site production of buildings has the potential to reduce cost and time, increase quality and reduce the environmental impact of typical on-site construction.

The architects are strong believers in context and the house seeks to fuse the landscape with architectural form. It is positioned between a grove of loblolly pines and the bay, with its wooden piles and staggered vertical board façade mimicking the solids and voids of the forest wall.

Kieran's concept was for a 'tree house' that would bring the exterior indoors and blend the house with its surroundings. Conceptual sketches were made of an elevated structure before the design was developed using BIM. The digital modelling offered the ability to visualize how the project would be delivered and compiled. It provided the level of precision in geometry, three-dimensionality and specification that allowed a simultaneous prefabrication process that integrated components and on-site assembly. BIM builds architecture virtually before it is physically constructed. It produces a prototype, with the finished architecture produced from the information contained in the digital files. Parametric drawing tools allow for the formation of a 3-D model based on the dimensions and specification of the physical elements that will make up the eventual building. If a single dimension is wrong the model discloses a 'failure to close' message inviting the model-maker to correct the problem and rectify the conflict before the construction begins. By breaking down the 40,000 parts of a conventional American house into basic new elements of architecture, information could be fed into the BIM software and the house built as a virtual artefact. The elements are: site (piles and utilities); structure (scaffold); floor cartridge (wood-sheathed floor, ceiling and roof panels with integrated structural, mechanical and electrical systems); block (kitchen and bathrooms enclosed in wood, with fixtures, piping, wiring and ductwork); wall cartridge (wood-sheathed panels with windows, insulation, cement board and vapour barrier) in place; and FF&E. At first the modelling program focuses on specific qualities and appearances, then on joinery and finally on integration into a full model. The components are ordered directly without needing to go through a shop-drawing process.

The architects divided the supply chain/collaborators between three main fabricators and a final assembler, in much the same way that automotive companies outsource major components of each vehicle with final assembly at factories throughout the world. The project architect, Marilia Rodrigues, had an intensely collaborative relationship with Bensonwood Homes, the builder of the house, and together they devised the first parametric model. The build was not a linear process. While the foundations and utilities were underway, the off-site elements were added hierarchically within the model and delivered on site to be assembled; first the scaffold, followed by the floor cartridges and the kitchen and mechanical room blocks, and finally the wall cartridges. Then the house was fitted out with furnishings, fixtures (including the kitchen and stairs) and equipment such as the two-layered glazing system on the west wall that provides an adjustable awning as well as weather and storm protection.

In his Preface to *Loblolly House: Elements of a New Architecture*, Barry Bergdoll writes, 'Loblolly House fulfils the aspiration of rethinking architecture in terms of a new means of industrial production and organized communication within a digital environment.' He continues: 'It reveals that architecture conceived as a product can be customized for an individual client and a specific site without compromising the clarity of its union of design and fabrication, thereby putting to rest two of the oldest anxieties about factory-made architecture.'

1 / Loblolly House was designed in response to its idyllic location. It is a house among and within trees. The complex, faceted façades are the first hint that it was developed on the computer.

1

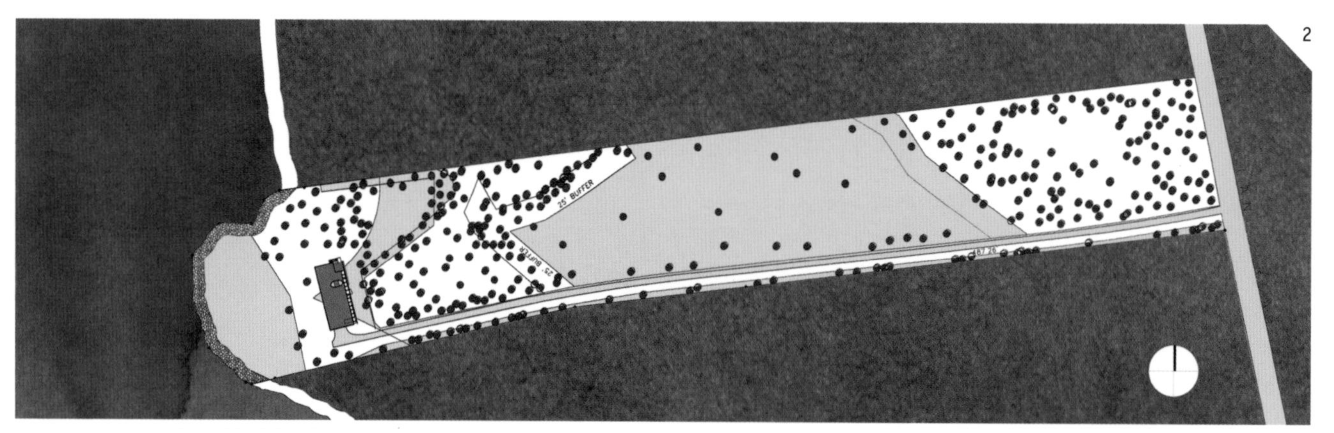

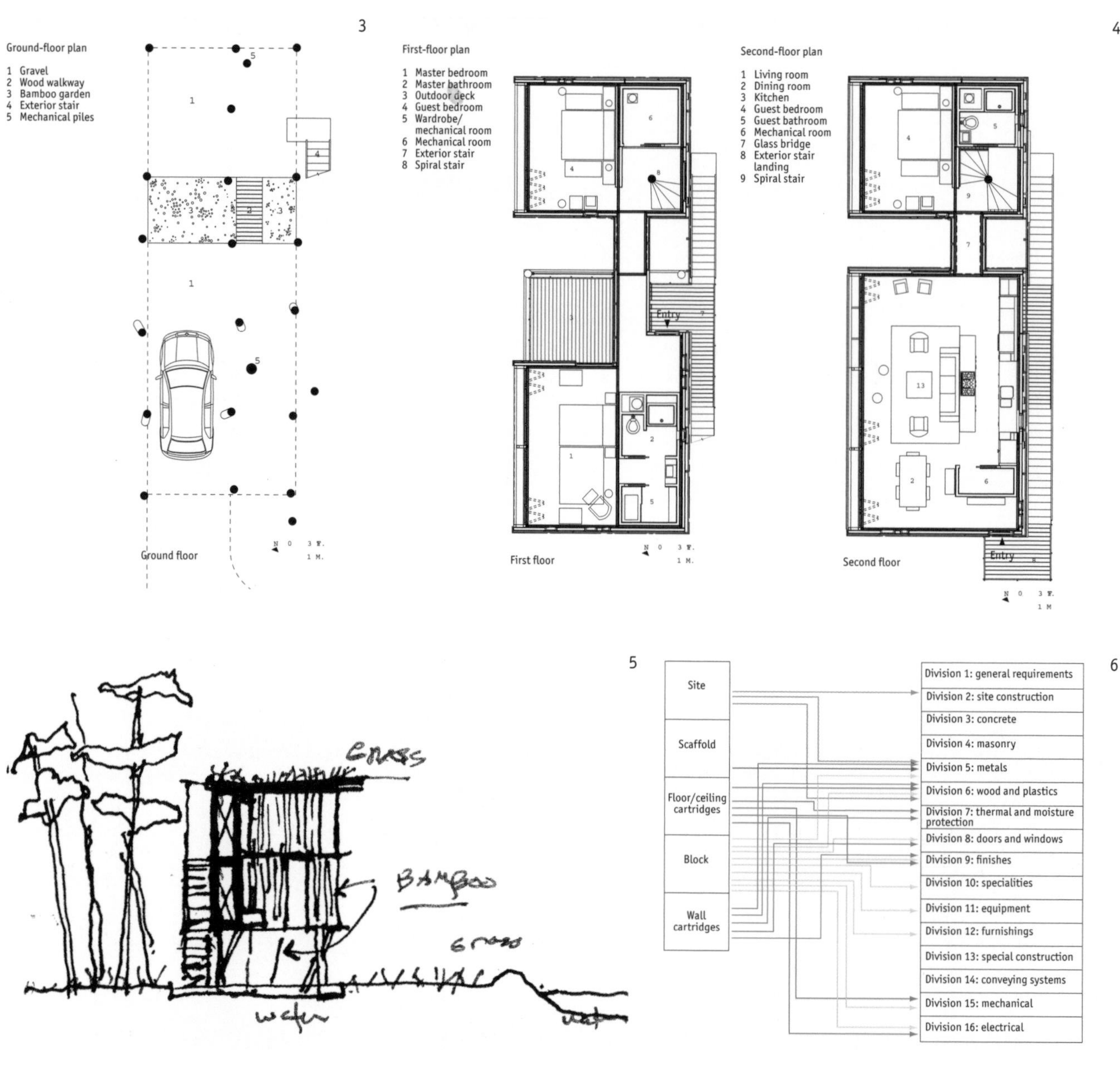

2 / Site plan showing the house positioned between a grove of loblolly pines and Chesapeake Bay.

3 / The ground plan shows the positions of the piles.

4 / First- and second-floor plans.

5 / One of the first sketches illustrating the idea for an elevated structure built from a palette of materials that would blend into the surrounding landscape.

6 / Diagram demonstrating how the 40,000 building parts that make an average American house have been simplified into five integrated building elements.

7

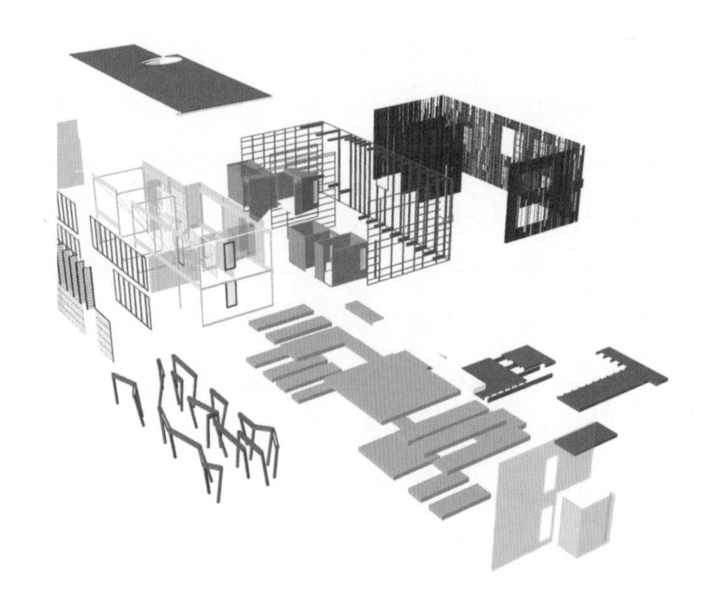

8

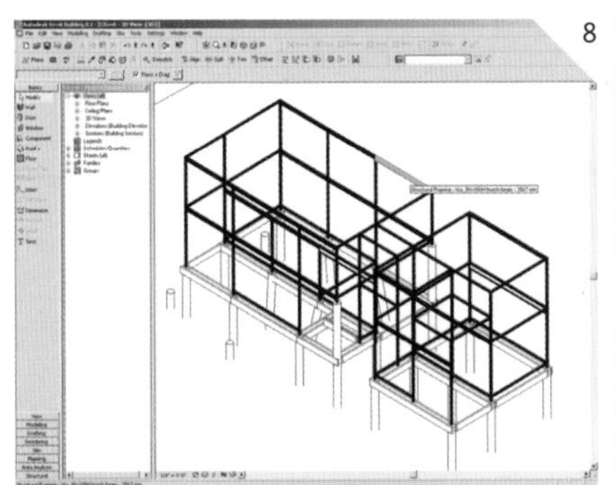

9

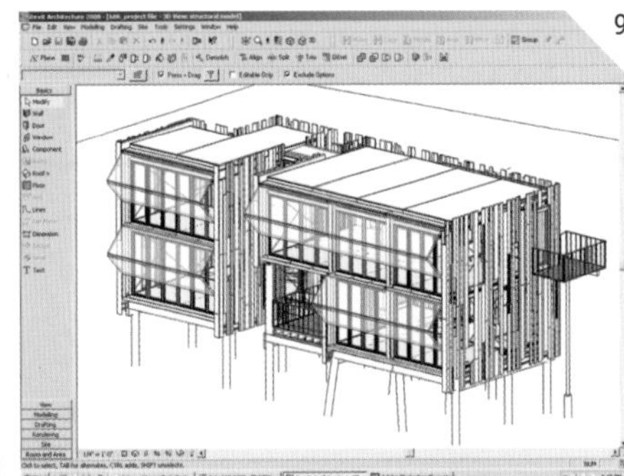

10

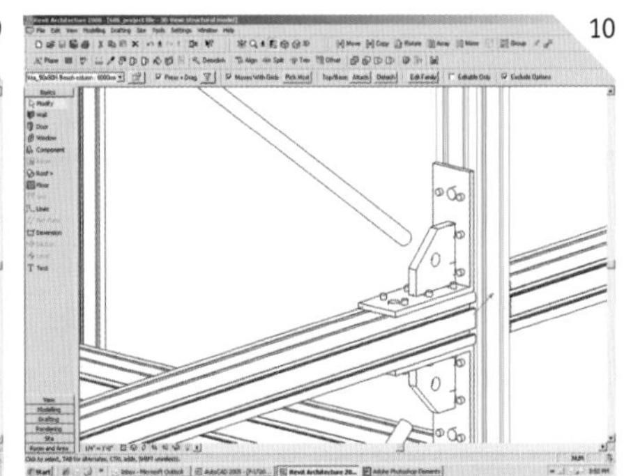

11

12

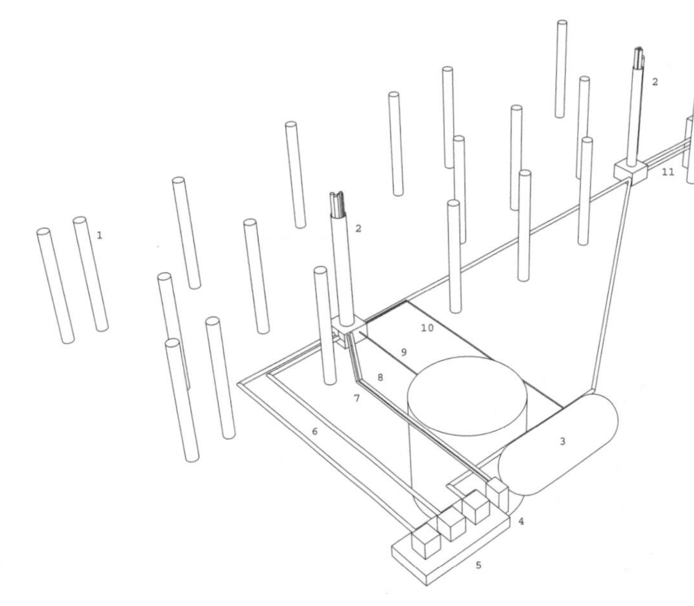

7 / An early axonometric of the elements of the house that were fabricated off site.

8 / BIM (Building Information Modelling) file of the aluminium scaffold.

9 / Screenshot of the fully assembled parametric model: Even the services drawings are integrated into the file. The model drove the Hundegger machine that measured, cut, drilled and otherwise fabricated the wooden elements of the house. The studio uses the Revit software program.

10 / Screenshot of a typical scaffold joint and diagonal bracing: Elements as minuscule as individual screws are set within a hierarchy of increasingly larger elements.

11 / The house is built on pressure-treated pine piles that are sunk into the sandy soil to the point of refusal. In comparison to the precision of the rest of the structure, the process was hard to govern, with irregular final heights and vertical alignment. Two layers of collar beams were needed to bring the substructure in line with the frame.

12 / Utility diagram: Two hollowed-out piles contain all the conduits for water, power, sewage and telephone lines.

13

14

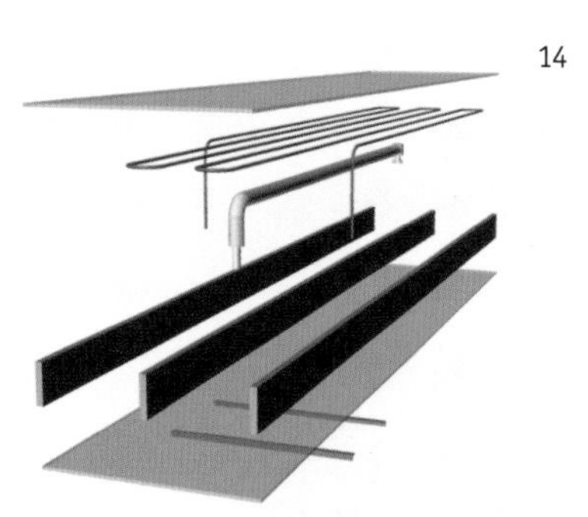

15

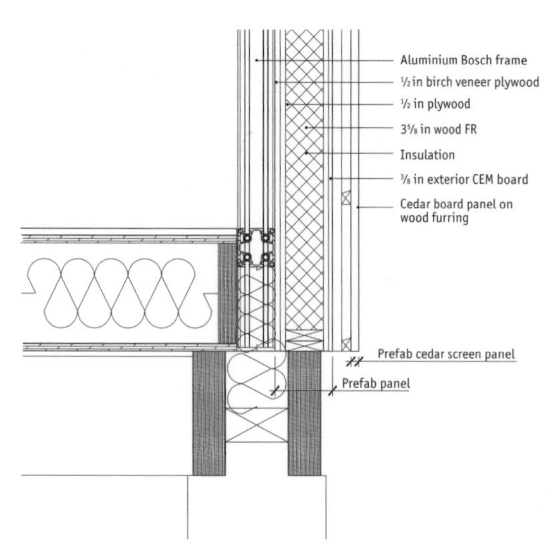

16

17

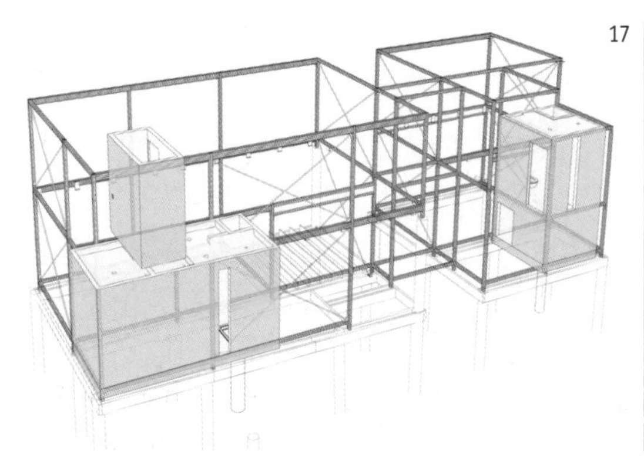

18

13 / The model was the tool by which the supply chain was managed. The aluminium extrusions were created with embedded data including size of profile, length and cost. They came predrilled and with connectors.

14 / Diagram of a typical floor cartridge, containing structural members, radiant heating, micro-ducts, electrical conduits and exterior sheathing.

15 / Diagram of the connection of a floor cartridge and the façade.

16 / Floor cartridge being lifted into place: The cartridges are 'hung' from the frame using Z-connectors.

17 / Parametric model of mechanical, electrical and plumbing blocks within the scaffold: The blocks are the organs of the house and contain manifolds that organize and manage all ingoing and outgoing utility connections. The systems are distributed through the cartridges.

18 / The master bathroom block being constructed off site.

19 / A wall cartridge is bolted in place.

20 / Parametric model of the exterior stairs and interior spiral staircase: Together with the kitchen, the stairs were the main fixtures in the house. They arrived preassembled and were attached on site.

21 / Assembly of the aluminium frame nears completion (top left); cartridge and blocks for the first level are inserted (top right); first layer of glazing is installed on the west façade (bottom left); installation of the adjustable aeroplane hangar doors (bottom right). The house is assembled rather than constructed. The process is quick and needs rudimentary skill and tools. The scaffold and parts can be easily disassembled without a demolition crew or destruction of materials. The elements are fully recyclable.

19

20

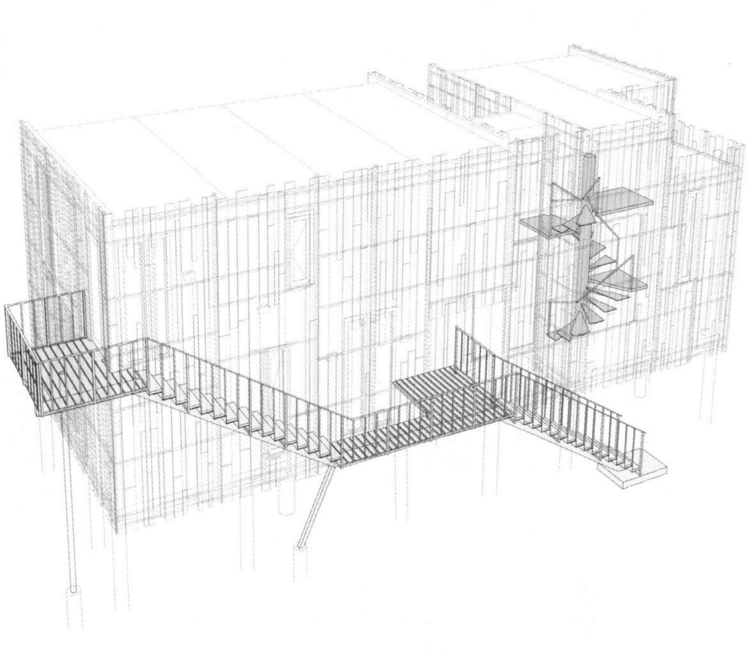

21

22

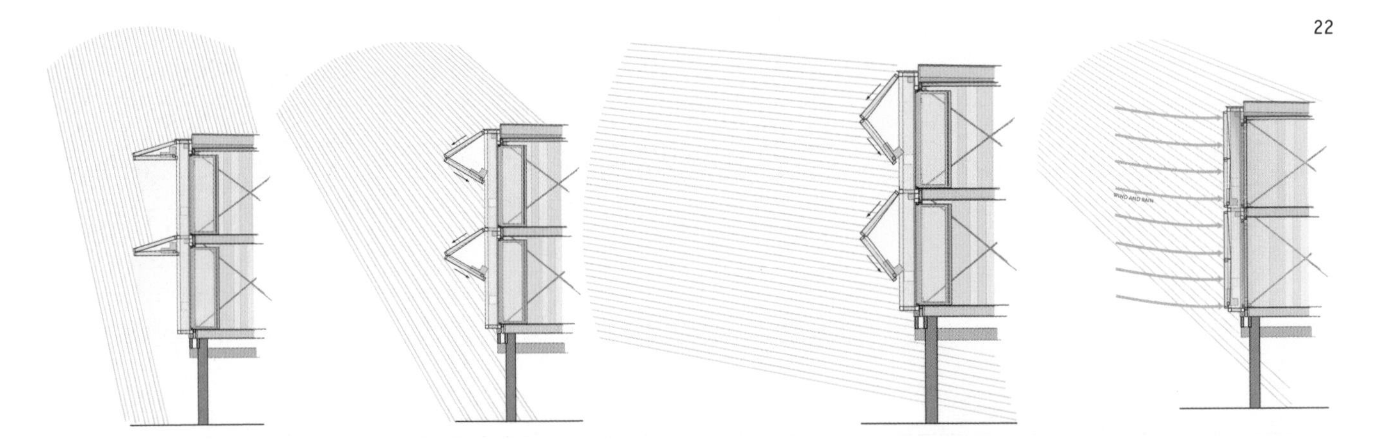

23

22 / Diagrams showing how the bi-folding doors on the west elevation filter the sun at different times of the day. When closed they provide storm protection and trap solar heat in an air pocket between the two glazing systems.

23 / Main living and dining room: Furnishings were chosen to blend the house with its setting and to bring the exterior indoors. The carpets resemble woven cordgrass and the upholstery is in striations of green, brown and yellow, the colours of the surrounding landscape.

24 / The orange glass glows from behind the cedar slats on the east façade and evokes the setting sun.

24

Weiner Townhouse

LOT-EK

Location: New York City, USA
Principal use: Live/work space
Client: Lawrence and Alice Weiner
Site area: 108.7 m² (1,170 ft²)
[5.5 x 19.8 m (18 ft x 65 ft)]
Interior area: 232.2 m² (2,500ft²)

Total build area: 3,500ft²
Design period: August 2005 – October 2008
Construction period: August 2006 – October 2008
Budget: Undeclared (the budget was adequate for the design intentions)

LOT-EK use reclaimed heavy-duty industrial products – petroleum trailer tanks, shipping containers, truck bodies, in one instance the fuselage of a jet engine – as well as raw materials to create buildings that blur the boundaries between architecture, design, art and performance installation. Although employing the latest technological advances, the partners' (Ada Tolla and Giuseppe Lignano) work is aesthetically anti-computer age, emphasizing the fact that we live in an environment littered with the detritus of the industrial age. The emphasis is not on recycling but rather on matching the needs and characters of clients with found objects. 'It's the philosophy of the ready-made bricolage, of improvising, of using your intuition,' Tolla explains.

Frequently called upon to lecture, the duo is known for starting talks with a slideshow of the New York City landscape while quoting a seemingly miscellaneous stream of nouns to describe what is being flashed up on screen. Gradually, words such as 'abandon', 'cast-off', 'demolished', 'erosion' and 'obsolete' are introduced and come together with images of fire hydrants, electrical wires, fire escapes and decaying brick walls to form a kind of urban poetry which is the essence of the firm's architectural vision. It's this narrative approach, as well as LOT-EK's innovative attitude to construction, materials and space, that appealed to Lawrence Weiner (one of the twentieth century's leading conceptual artists) and his wife, Alice, when they were looking for an architect to renovate their West Village townhouse.

The Weiners had lived and worked in the property for over 20 years. The house, a former bakery, dates from 1910 and was becoming increasingly dilapidated. The initial idea was to renovate the façade, but the structure was letting in water and it was quickly apparent that it needed to be demolished and re-built. Zoning codes for the area had also recently been revised allowing for an additional storey. The relationship between the clients and architect was one of immediate understanding. The brief was informal and developed gradually through a process of dialogue. The programming had to provide separate workspaces for Lawrence and Alice. In addition, the renovation had to be sustainable, the volume flooded with light and provision made for Lawrence's studio in the basement to have access to the existing outside area. The Weiners were heavily involved in the conceptual design and detailing of the project and tested LOT-EK's ideas and decisions at every stage throughout development and construction. In particular, Alice Weiner was determined that the house should be as ecologically friendly as possible, and invested time and money in sourcing the best green solutions in terms of energy, materials and systems, appreciating that the initial investment would be repaid over time. Although this made the process lengthy, and at one point it felt as if the project could become redundant, Tolla (the partner-in-charge) points out that, 'on the other hand it was really interesting to have a client that was so engaged, wilful but eager to understand and contribute'.

The design concept evolved from the idea of opening up the traditional enclosed townhouse interior, which consisted of a floor plan divided in two by a centrally placed staircase and bathroom. Adding the fourth floor gave the necessary space to move the stairs to the back façade, freeing the interior spaces and organizing the mixed programme vertically. The live/work spaces are layered on alternating levels: the cellar houses Lawrence's studio; the ground floor the living room and kitchen; the second floor the archive/management office; and the third floor the master suite, which is topped by the penthouse sun room. At every level, a perpendicular core (housing a lift, bathroom, storage and mechanical equipment) was designed to pierce the open plan. To emphasize this feature, it was to be constructed as a galvanized-steel duct structure.

The proposal had to conform to the Landmark Commission's idea of 'appropriateness', a process that Tolla describes as Kafkaesque. Although the interior was passed quickly, the front façade was more complex. The idea of adding very large bay windows constructed from sections of stainless-steel truck bodies was present from the beginning and sanctioned; Tolla managed to demonstrate that they were in tune with earlier artists' atelier conversions where large panes of glass had, in some cases, altered the conventional fenestration of West Village townhouses. However, the first design that was presented to Landmark was rejected. Returning to the residence's commercial origins, Tolla had suggested using white tiles similar to some she had found during tests made on the exterior, which probably dated from the original bakery façade. Linking to the real history of the site was not considered 'appropriate' and she had to revert to using brick, albeit a more modern and natural version of traditional red brick, in an approximation of the faux street frontage that had largely been constructed in the 1960s.

The project was highly collaborative, with Tolla and project architect Haruka Saito working closely with the mechanical and structural engineers from the beginning, as well as with the fabricators of the trucks and the ductwork to devise a way of adapting their products for constructional use. 'We like this project very much,' says Tolla. 'We sometimes think it would have been nice if we could have done this or that a little more forcibly, but in the end it has been a great ride and challenge to engage in some of the restrictions of the site and the Landmark as well as the strengths of the client.'

1/ Lawrence and Alice Weiner sit in one of the bay windows constructed from sawn-off sections of stainless-steel truck bodies.

1

2 / The original façade of the Weiner residence above the completed renovation.

3 / Section B and elevation A showing the stack of bathrooms contained within the stainless-steel ductwork, topped by the penthouse, which is used as a sun room.

4 / The rear elevation is one level lower than the front. It has a much higher degree of transparency than the street façade. The stairs are positioned across the rear.

5 / Early exploded axonometric: The concept changed little, with later design development concentrating on materiality and detailing. An element that was lost in the final design was how much the truck sections extruded on the interior. The original idea had been that they should form different functions: a bench in the kitchen, a booth in the archive room, a sleeping platform in the bedroom.

6 / Early sketch.

7 / Presentation to the clients was made using volumetric renderings and perspectives.

8 / Physical models were used throughout the design development. At first these were rough, constructed from foamcore and chipboard, and were used in-house to understand the relationship of the bay windows to the interior and the façade. Later models (an example of which is shown here) were made in a clear plastic to understand the internal volumes and how the stack performs.

5

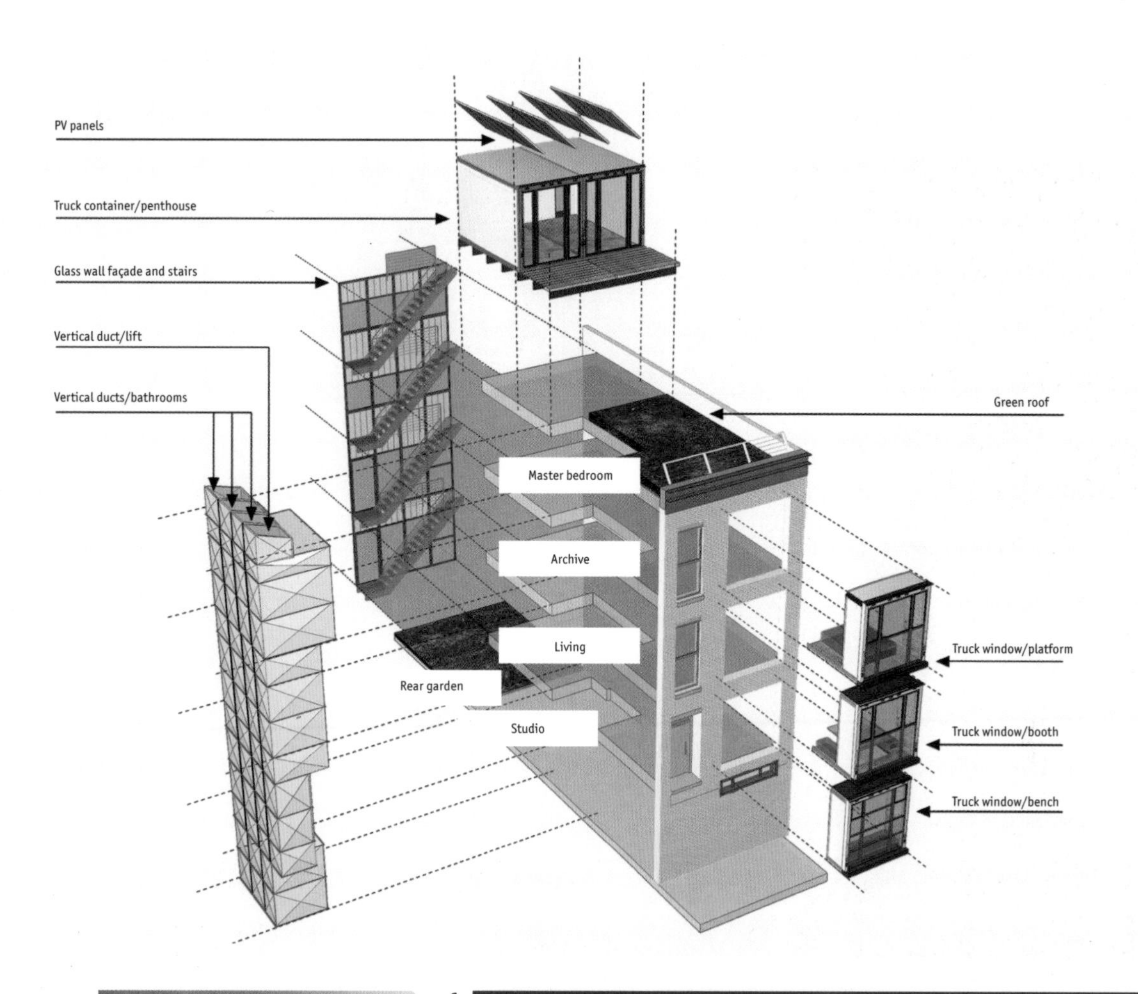
PV panels
Truck container/penthouse
Glass wall façade and stairs
Vertical duct/lift
Vertical ducts/bathrooms
Green roof
Master bedroom
Archive
Living
Rear garden
Studio
Truck window/platform
Truck window/booth
Truck window/bench

6

7

8

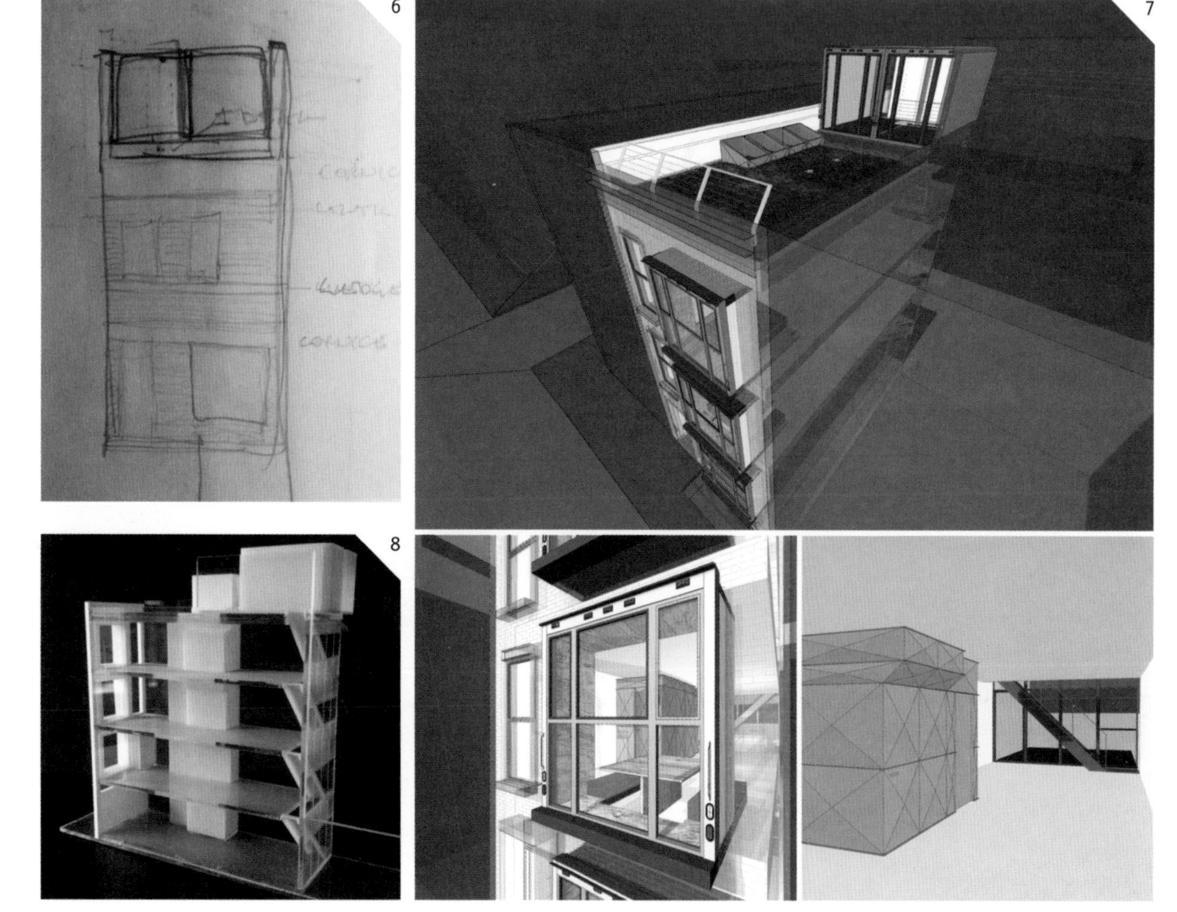

9

10

11

LOT-EK
297 WEST 4th STREET
FACADE COMPONENTS L.19
297 WEST 4th STREET
FRONT FACADE L11
297 WEST 4th STREET
PENTHOUSE VISIBILITY L.18
297 WEST 4th STREET
EXIST & PROPOSED STREETFRONT ELEVATION B L.14
297 WEST 4th STREET
FLOOR PLANS L.05
297 WEST 4th STREET
STREET PERSPECTIVES L16
TRUCK BODY REAR FRAME
FRONT FACADE WINDOW FRAME
297 WEST 4th STREET
WINDOW FRAME L.10
297 WEST 4th STREET
FRONT FACADE L11

12

13

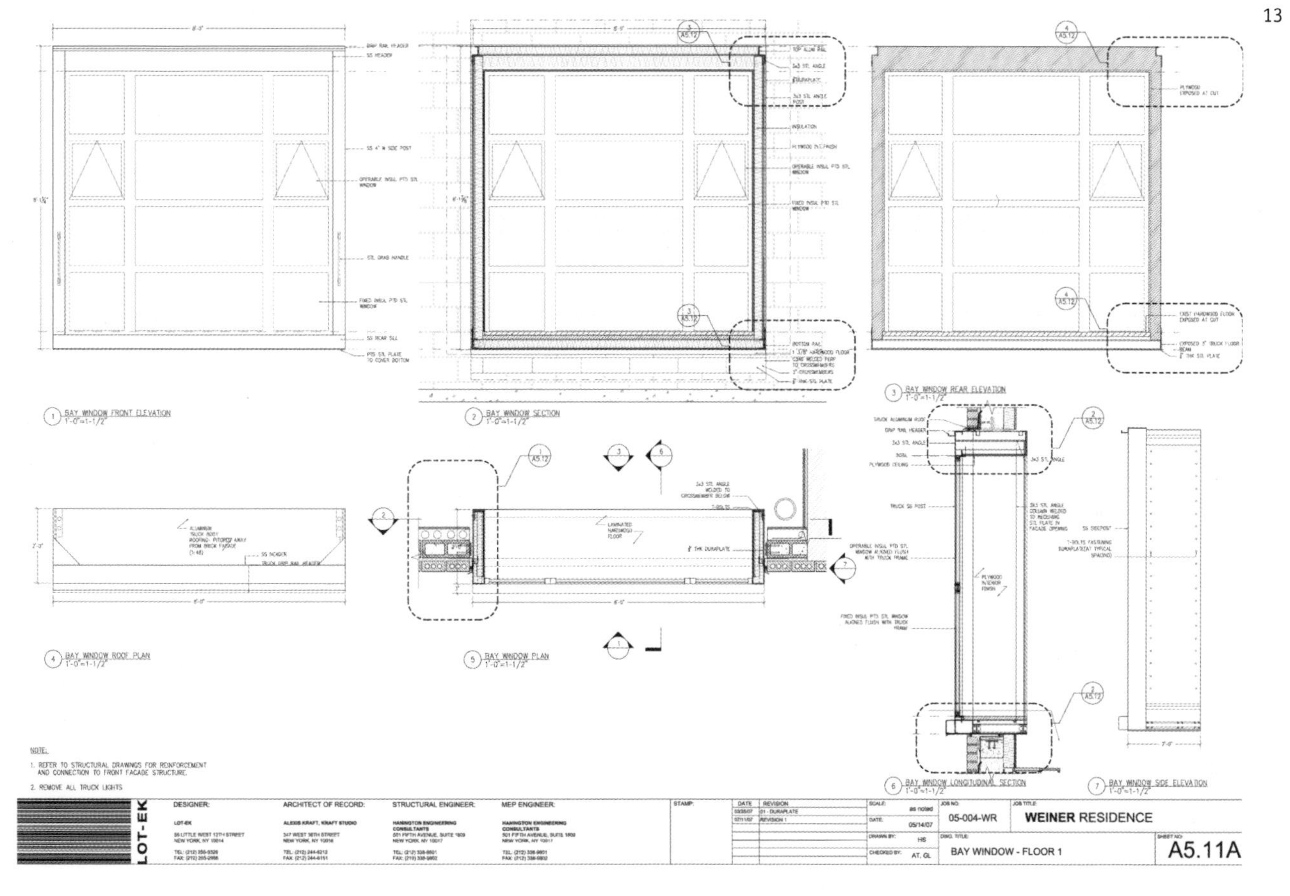

9 / The first presentation to the Landmark Commission showed the architect's idea of using white tiles on the front façade, as well as multiple bay windows positioned above each other.

10 / The first presentation was formal. The façade was shown in context and drawings and collages were used to assess visibility. CAD was employed to demonstrate how the space worked and 3-D renderings to illustrate the general volume.

11 / The second presentation to the Landmark Commission: A modern version of red brick replaced the tiles and the number of bay windows was reduced to resemble the fenestration of a traditional townhouse. One of the Landmark's policies is to support the upgrade of materials. They accepted the idea of using truck sections as the frames are stainless steel, the sides aluminium and the floor engineered timber, creating a box that is resistant to weathering and wear.

12 / Rendering of the façade for the second presentation.

13 / Design development drawing of the juncture between the truck sections and the façade: The sections have steel frames along their 'cut' faces that allow for their structural connection with the horizontal steel beams and vertical steel posts installed within the walls of the townhouse. The detailing is unconventional for a window construction, and care had to be taken in maintaining an adequate thermal bridge and waterproofing.

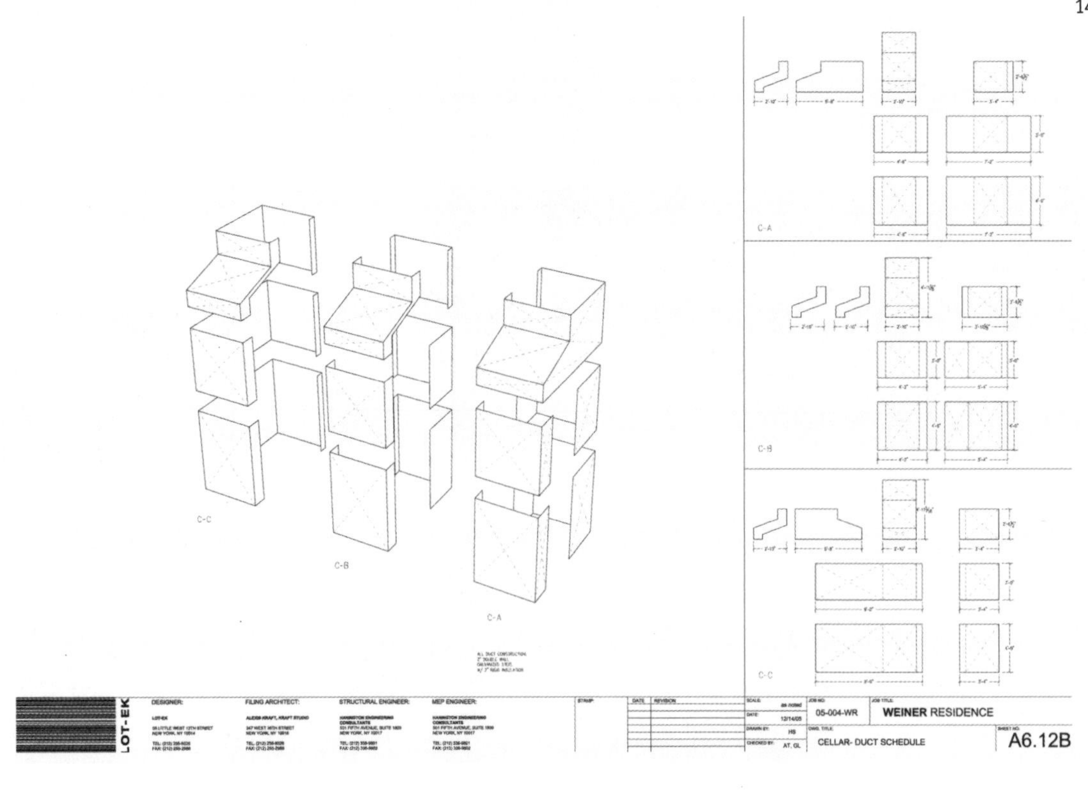

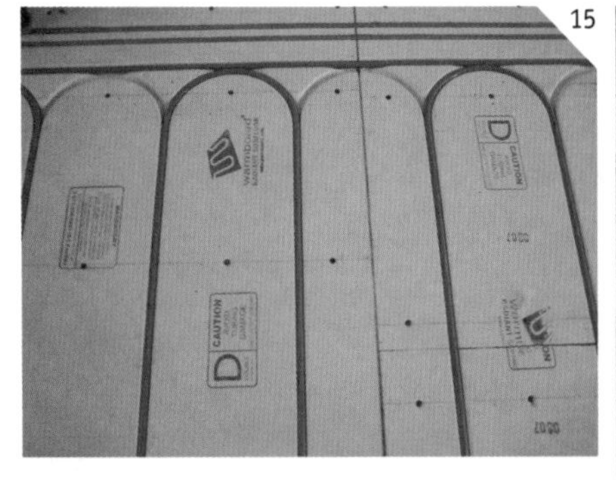

14 / Design development drawing of the duct: The architects had to learn how to work with a 2-D material (a metal sheet) to give it the necessary strength to perform as a structural panel. The panels are folded to create creases that operate as reinforcement. The sheets are combined through 'crimping', folding the edges of two adjacent panels together.

15 / Among the house's many green features is a highly efficient premanufactured radiant floor-heating system manufactured by Warmboard. The plywood panels come scored ready for the insertion of the hot-water hose. They are laminated with aluminium on the top surface to spread the heat.

16 / Rear façade under construction: The contract was design only but LOT-EK kept a constant presence on site.

17 / The rear wall is prefabricated and was erected on site over the course of two days. The system is normally used in industrial buildings and has a higher insulating value than conventional glass. It is translucent but still lets a high level of light into the interior. A band of clear glass at head height on each floor allows for clear views onto the back yard.

18 / A truck section is craned into place.

19

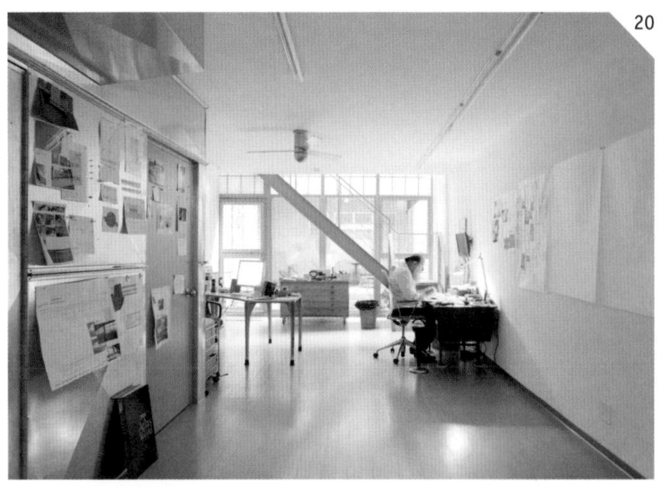

20

21

22

19 / The house features a green roof and photovoltaic panels. Alice Weiner was insistent that the house should be as sustainable and eco-friendly as possible. As well as the high R-value curtain wall, the energy-saving underfloor heating and the solar panels, cross ventilation is encouraged – there is no air-conditioning. The windows are operable, the internal spaces are open and the shaft at the rear of the property creates optimum air movement.

20 / Lawrence Weiner's studio.

21 / Alice Weiner's archive workspace.

22 / The ceiling and floor on each level are in contrasting colours that enliven the 'simple' interiors. Throughout the house they are pale and gentle, but bright orange and lime green were used in the penthouse.

La Llotja de Lleida

Mecanoo

Location: Lleida, Spain
Principal use: Theatre and conference centre
Client: Centre de Negocis i de Convencions SA, Lleida
Competition client: Municipality of Lleida
Site area: 16,500 m² (177,604⅓ ft²)

Interior area: 29,800 m² (320,764¼ ft²)
Total build area: 37,500 m² (403,646¼ ft²)
Design period: June 2005 – May 2006
Construction period: February 2007 – January 2010
Budget: €35,000,000

Mecanoo, named after the creative and innovative British construction toys (Meccano), was established in 1984 and today is headed by one of its original founders, Francine Houben. There are not many internationally recognized women architects but with extensive experience gained over more than 25 years, and designs that blend pragmatism with material sensuality, she is known worldwide for a series of warm and tangible projects that range from houses, schools, theatres, libraries, hotels and museums to complete neighbourhoods.

'Architecture must appeal to all the senses and is never a purely intellectual, conceptual or visual game alone,' says Houben. '[It] is about combining all of the individual elements in a single concept. What counts in the last resort is the arrangement of form and emotion.'

Each project that Mecanoo undertakes is unique and relates to its urban, social and cultural context. It's these considerations that drove the design of the Llotja de Lleida.

The commission was awarded as a result of an international competition with the brief to supply a theatre and conference centre with two congress halls, an exhibition space, two multipurpose foyers and parking, to be set in a piazza. An office building was also included in the mandate. Houben speaks poetically about her introduction to Lleida (after Barcelona the second most important city in Catalonia) prior to starting on the design of her competition entry. It was a visit that would form the basis of her concept. She talks of the site, a former fruit market situated 8 metres (26 feet) above the nearby Segre River, overlooked by the imposing thirteenth-century Seu Vella Cathedral, and of the distant views of the giant grain silos that define the flat landscape. She also describes the atmosphere of the city, and the strong weather contrasts between summer and winter when fierce sun is replaced by lashing rain and fog. She started to form ideas. The silos reminded her of ocean liners and she fantasized that the site was a 'beach', a relaxed and open space for Lleida's inhabitants to enjoy, dominated by a 'shelter' with cantilevers that would act as protection against the inclement weather conditions. She realized that by placing a foyer on a higher level than the view towards the spectacular cathedral, the outlook could be made a key feature, while situating the offices opposite, in a separate tiered structure, made it possible to create an open-air forum.

Back in the Netherlands she developed the concept in close collaboration with the local architect, Labb arquitectura, who visited Mecanoo's office frequently in the early stages of design. The practice acted as a consultant on Lleida's culture and context as well as on Spanish building regulations, and was later responsible for detailing Mecanoo's design intent drawings, took legal responsibility for the contract and supervised the construction.

The competition-winning design bears a close resemblance to the structure that was built, with only minor adjustments being made during the development phase. On being awarded the commission, the architects worked to a very tight schedule. The design had to be finalized and all the tender documents delivered in a period of nine months, and the building handed over in a little more than three years. The building was kept compact as a response to the multifunctional programme. The complex is composed of three parts connected by underground parking: the two-storey Mercolleida office building, the Llotja Square with parking beneath and the theatre itself, which has one underground and three above-ground levels. The unconventional volume with its dramatic overhangs defines the construction. The enormous steel projections are connected to the second-floor façade by steel columns that form a Vierendeel beam that runs around the perimeter of the building, unifying the cantilevers and minimizing deformation on their outer edge. A very rigid reinforced-concrete box was needed for the main structure in order to control the horizontal forces exerted on the upper-floor slabs.

The 80 x 80-metre (262 x 262-foot) monolith, clad in natural stone, rises from the ground and spreads outwards giving form to the idea of 'shadow and shelter'. The processional entry route ascends via a giant staircase and ramp to the second-floor foyer, which offers the possibility of entering the auditoria dramatically from the top. A roof-top terrace provides views over the city and is protected by a lush vegetation-covered pergola. Giant sculptural light shafts bring daylight down into the multifunctional room which is separated from the congress room by a glass wall, lending legibility to the building's arrangement. The ground floor provides space for a restaurant overlooking the riverfront parade. In order to undertake such an ambitious construction both externally and in terms of the circulation and programming of the theatre and conference centre, Mecanoo collaborated with Labb arquitectura to find ways to economically realize its concepts for the piazza, the landscaping and the interior design, so that the majority of the budget could be devoted to the main structure.

Although writing in general about Houben's work, Aaron Betsky, Professor in Architecture and Design at the University of Cincinnati, could just as well have been describing La Llotja when he stated in the introduction to Images Group Publishing's monograph *Mecanoo*: 'She makes buildings whose organization is rational and that fit into their site, but that present themselves as strong, yet fluid forms. These are neither abstract, technocratic assemblies, nor are they isolated bravura monuments. Instead they are coherent and sensuous objects that Houben presents in sweeping cartoon-like imagery full of strong colour.'

1 / The theatre rises monolith-like from its surroundings. The structure cantilevers out over the square below, offering protection from the sun or rain.

1

2

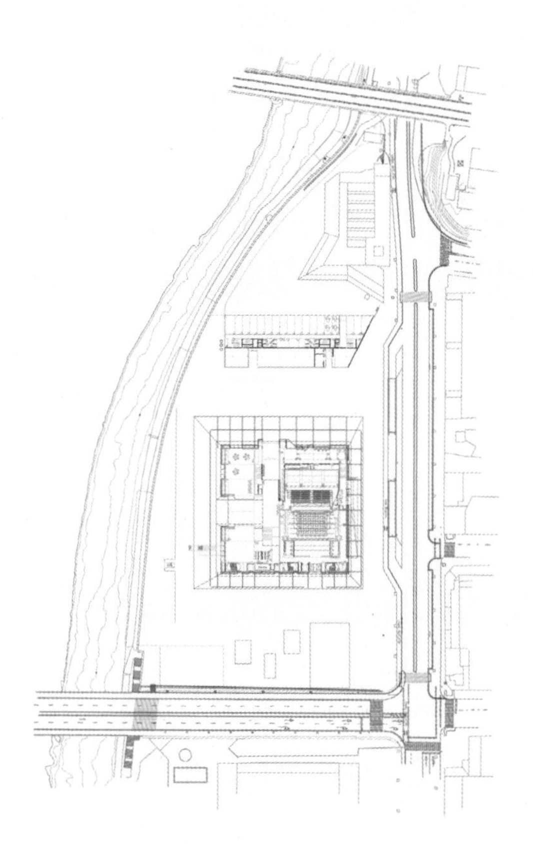

3

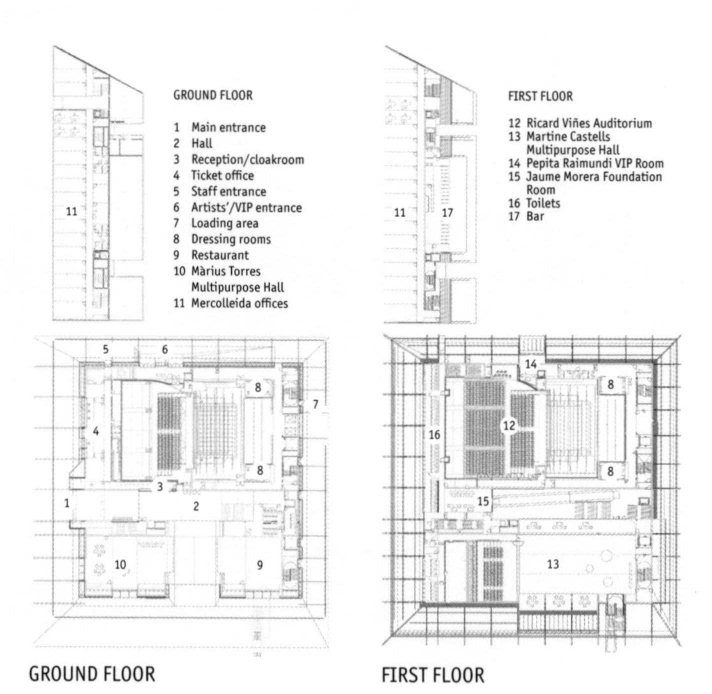

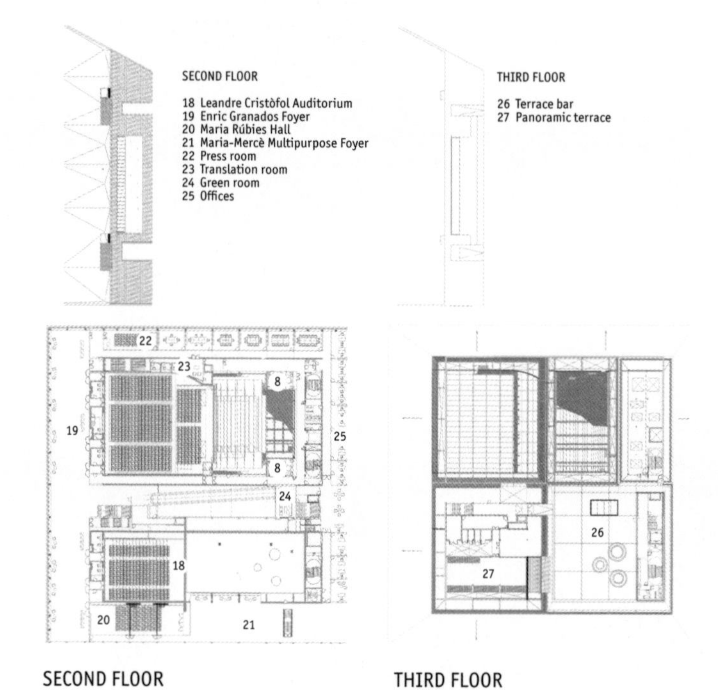

2 / The site is bordered by the Segre River and by the high-speed rail line into Lleida.

3 / Ground- to third-floor plans.

4 / Section.

5 / Mecanoo uses conventional methods to develop a schematic design from sketches and rudimentary models to renderings and computer drawings. The concept is based on the idea of shadow and shelter.

6 / Houben saw the site as a beach along the river with views to the cathedral.

7 / Early sketch of the circulation: The idea for a processional ramp rising to the second-floor foyer was present from the beginning.

8 / Sketches working through ideas for both the interior and exterior of the building.

4

5

6

7

8

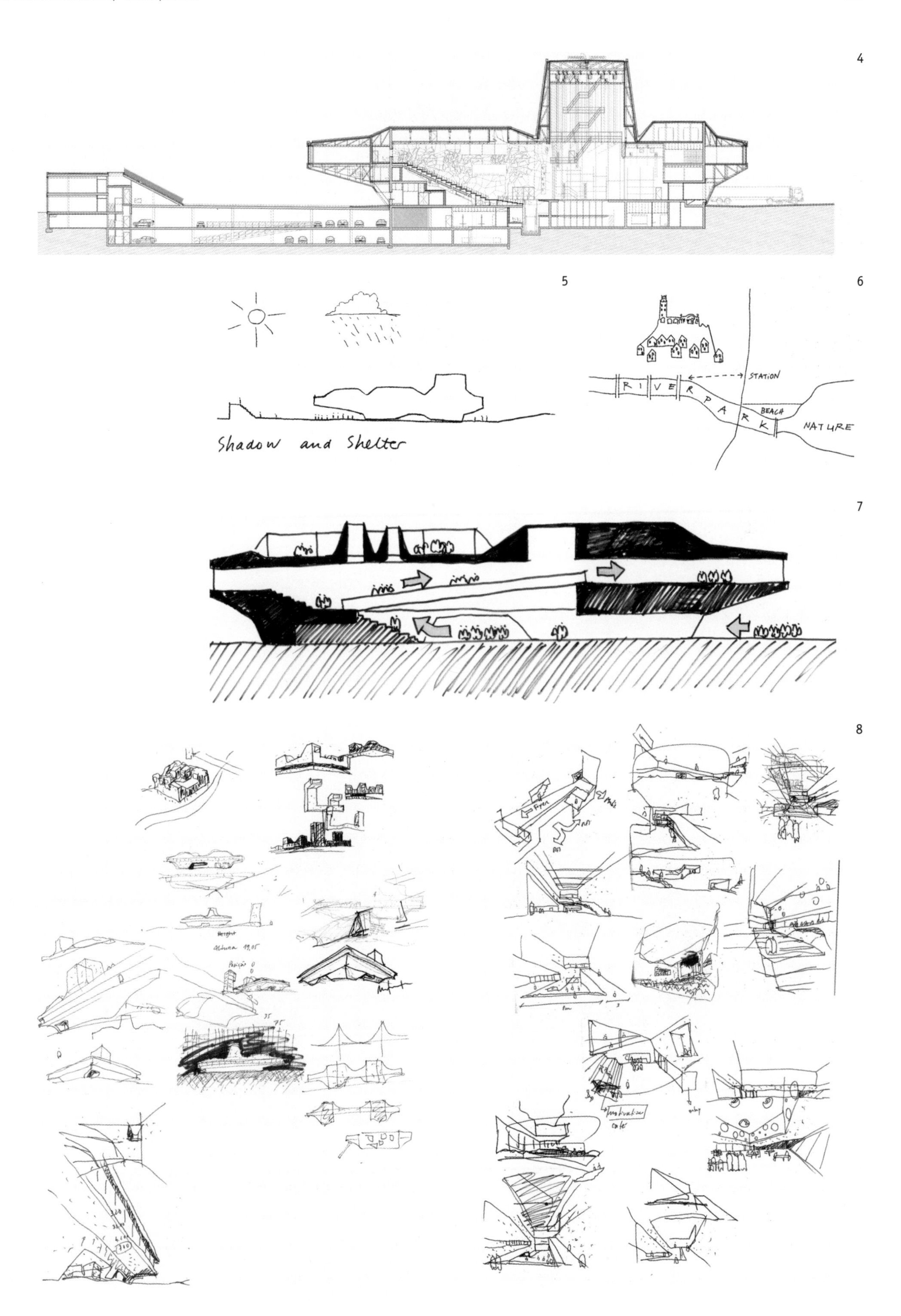

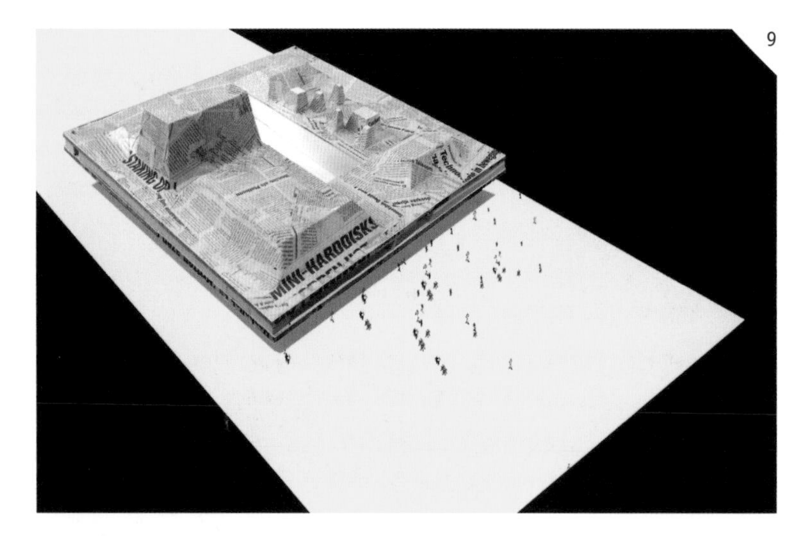

9

10

9 / Competition model made from newspaper.

10 / Presentation renderings: The brief was detailed but the client allowed the architects complete freedom to build up the aesthetic concept.

11 / A second competition model was made from resin and demonstrated the positioning of the theatre hall (red), the multifunctional hall (yellow) and the chamber hall (blue).

12 / The concept for the interior was developed once the commission was awarded. It is based on the importance of orchards to Lleida, and in particular on the Aqui Fruinem (Here We Eat Fruit) campaign, the logo for which appears on the city's menus. Seeking a unique experience that characterized the region, Houben chose this as her theme both in the choice of colours for the circulation spaces and for the detailing of the main auditorium.

13 / Rendering for the theatre: Houben proposed silhouettes of fruit trees for the vertical lighting on the walls that combines with ceiling spots in the form of foliage.

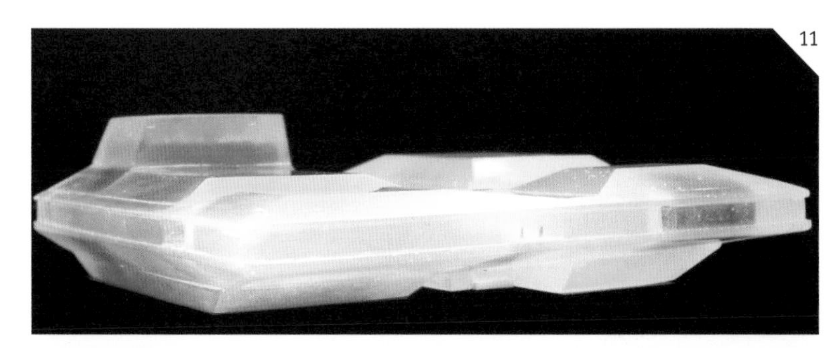
11

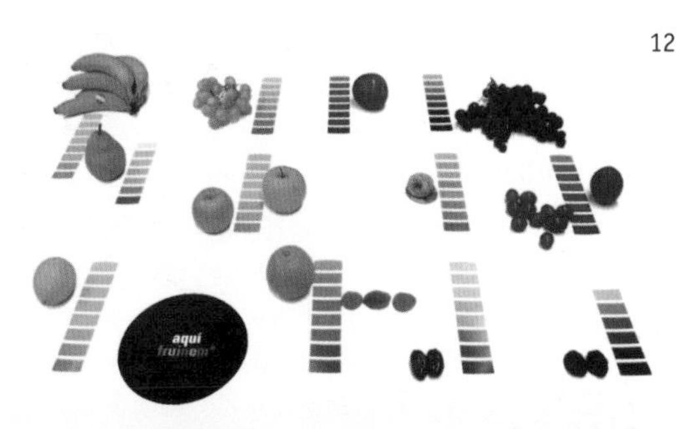

12

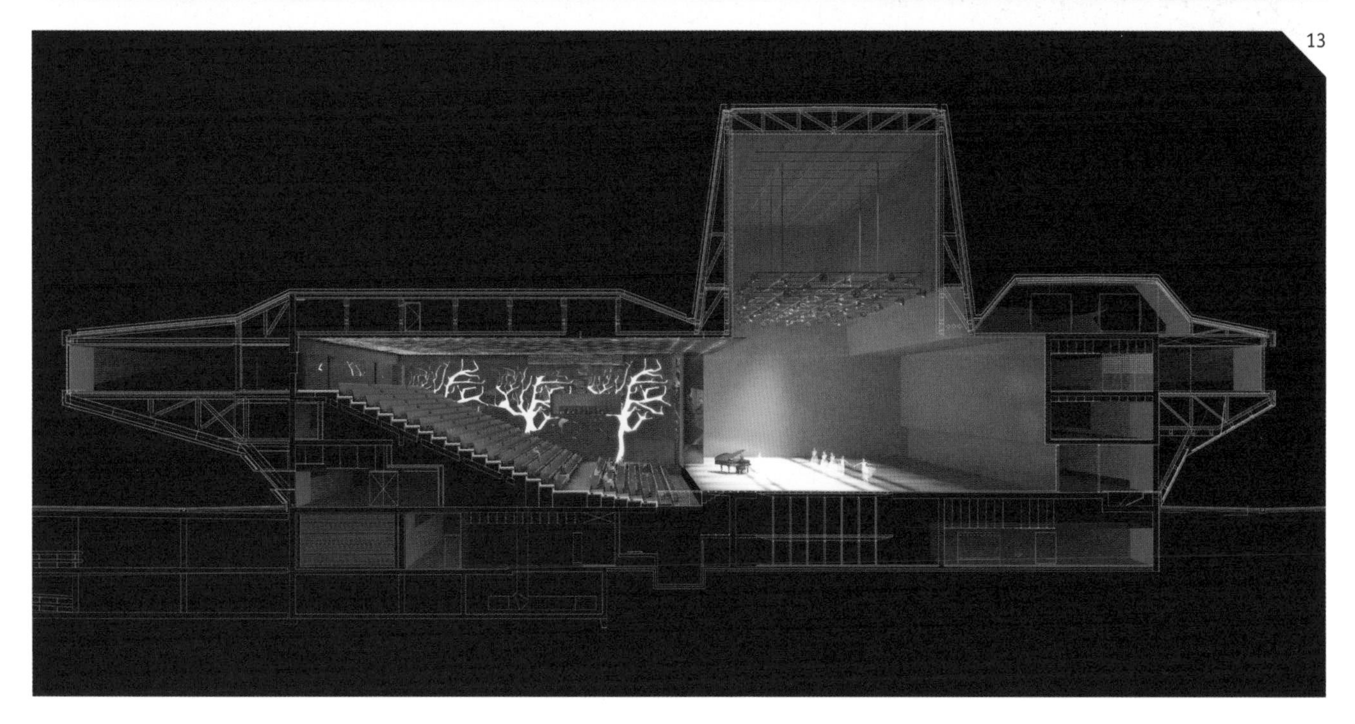
13

14

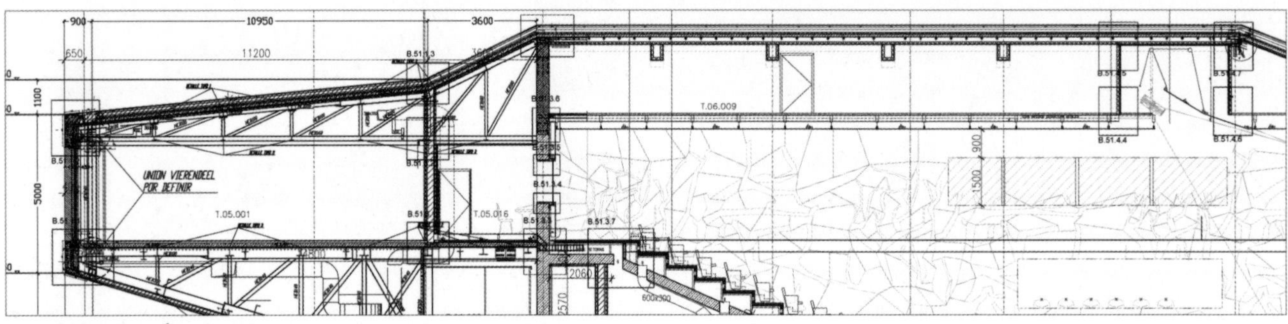

FRAGMENTO DE SECCIÓN 51 1:100

15

16

14 / Design intent drawing: The cantilevers are made from a steel structure that is composed of a lower and an upper beam. The beams are connected to the second-floor façade by steel columns. The columns in turn form part of a Vierendeel beam structure that unifies all the cantilevers around the edge of the building.

15 / Presentation section showing the cantilever and underground parking.

16 / Computer model assessing the stresses within the building.

17

18

19

17 / The rigid 60 x 65 m (197 x 213 ft) concrete box is formed from massive post-stressed floor slabs in spans of up to 18 m (59 ft). The interior is stiffened by the 'backbones' of longitudinal and transverse walls that span the box according to the spatial and functional organization of the building.

18 / Construction of the cantilever: A horizontal belt consisting of a 3 m (10 ft) wide and 40 cm (15¾ in) high horizontal post-stressed concrete beam attached to the box at the second upper-floor level guarantees the distribution of horizontal forces and minimizes deformation of the outer edge of the cantilevers. It is connected from one side of the structure to the other by tension cables that run into the 'backbone' walls of the interior of the box.

19 / Mecanoo had suggested using prefabricated concrete for the cantilevers and the technical equipment tower. This building technique is used less frequently in Spain and more steel structures were introduced to optimize construction time and adapt to local building strategies.

20 / The stone cladding was technically difficult to achieve as it had to 'hang' from the cantilevers. Labb arquitectura investigated different systems with the contractor on site who made mock-ups to define the best substructure, the optimum fixation methods and the proportion of the stone plates.

21 / The stones are fixed by brushed stainless-steel hooks that secure the plates. For safety reasons six were used.

22 / Series of construction images.

23 / Integrated LED lighting on the underside of the ramp allows for a changing colour scheme in the entrance hall. The local lighting contractor had initially been asked for a coloured fluorescent lighting system, but by the time the lights were ready for installation LED technology was much more advanced. Labb studied alternatives with the contractor who produced prototypes (right).

24 / Mecanoo worked with specialist consultants from schematic design onwards, including one of the world's two best-known specialists in acoustics for auditoria and concert halls.

25 / Sculptural light wells on the roof bring daylight into the multifunctional foyer below.

24

25

New Youth Centre in Rivas Vaciamadrid

Mi5 Arquitectos

Location: Madrid, Spain
Principal use: Youth centre
Client: Rivas Vaciamadrid Council
Site area: 1,834 m^2 (19,741 ft^2)
Interior area: 1,834 m^2 (19,741 ft^2)
Total build area: 2,244 m^2 (24,154 ft^2)
Design period: March 2006 – January 2007
Construction period: March 2008 – October 2009
Budget: €3,236,351

Mi5's statement for the Casa Más Grande (as the youth centre in Rivas has come to be known) reads like a manifesto: 'From the beginning, the project was conceived as the possibility of making the "underground" visible, a construction devised as a radical manifestation of the youthful spirit of Madrid's outskirts in general, and of Rivas' youth groups in particular. The project aspires to become an explicit teen communication vehicle by appropriating their language and voices as the ingredients. In this way, the project's team embraces all Rivas' youth groups by means of an open participation process, in which the future users of the centre, along with technicians and politicians, will contribute their decisions, their concerns, their fantasies and their aesthetics to create a contemporary social monument.'

The commission was the result of an open competition. The client, Rivas Town Council, has strong political leanings to the left and was very concerned that the project should be democratic. The mandate was undefined in terms of programme but stipulated that all the parties concerned, in particular the teenagers who would be using the building, should play an active role in the design process. Information on the site, a 16 x 16-metre (52 x 52-foot) lot in a park near the main highway from Madrid to Valencia, was provided by the council, as was the budget and detailed demographic information on the local youth population. The district is a new town with socialist ideals, which grew incrementally around a small village on the outskirts of the capital but had no distinguishing features.

The competition jury included a representative of the mayor and two members of the youth council. An architect and structural expert were present to assess the appropriateness of a design to its surroundings as well as the suitability of the architectural concept, and a sociologist was engaged to evaluate the impact a scheme would have on the user community. Mi5 has built up a reputation in Spain for avant-garde pro-Modernist social housing and public buildings. Its profile is one of 'architecture + social fantasy' and the architects have talked about their work as 'the erection of identities of collective recognition, exploiting fantasy as a powerful, dynamic motor of social processes'. However, as the presentations had to be made anonymously, the jury's decision was made solely on the merit of the architects' pitch. Mi5's initial idea was for an iconic building that would be a natural part of its environment, with a large terrace overlooking the surrounding countryside. What particularly appealed to the jury, however, was the possible participation protocol the architects put forward. This took the form of a 'game' in which small transparent boxes with different volumes could be moved around in a larger plastic cube to define different programmes and develop a working brief.

Once the commission had been awarded, Manuel Collado Arpia and Nacho Martín Asunción, Mi5's principals, took six months to develop their design in constant dialogue with all the parties concerned. 'Playing' the game with the youngsters it became apparent that they had clear priorities. Foremost were dance, music and gymnastics rooms, followed by IT facilities, and recreational and information points including a terrace with an open-air cinema and chill-out zones. Of less importance were youth council offices, a library, lecture rooms and workshop/study spaces. The teenagers also wanted to break down the rigorous height- and size-controlled volumes set out in the first briefing into large soaring spaces and explosive shapes that would better represent their age and vitality. Their eccentric, fresh imaginations and aesthetic values were encouraged by images of graffiti art, comics and MTV video clips that were brought into the brainstorming sessions to act as inspiration.

At the beginning of a project Mi5 like to spend a lot of time discussing possibilities, and researching context and cultural references. They delay committing themselves to drawing until the concept is strong enough to create very specific 3-D computer modelling, digital photomontages and physical models (they produce very few sketches). These are then assessed and amended in an ongoing process of trial and error until the design is formalized and ready to be converted into construction documents. Arpia says, 'Sometimes we advance and other times we move backwards ... We like to keep the radicality, freshness and communicative power of the original idea as essential and straightforward as a logo [while rejecting] completely the idea of the genial sketch that becomes a model and then like a mannequin receives the evening gown.'

The dynamic youth centre erupts out of its drab plot in an explosion of jagged walls, ceilings and windows. To add to the effect the architects used strong, primary, pop colours that they refer to as having the 'bang' effect. Bright cerise and orange announce the exterior of the building and continue into the interior where they are occasionally softened by the use of cooler hues, such as moss green, sun-kissed yellow and a paler pink. The centre's expressive form and vibrant palette unite to mimic the energetic spirit of Rivas' youth culture, creating a structure that has been described as 'a comic-strip space in 3D'.

The experience of collaborating in such stimulating and informal workshops was a first for the young population of Rivas and for Mi5, but for both it has been mutually beneficial. The teenagers, whose opinions would not normally have been sought, were given the opportunity to contribute to the sociocultural progress of their neighbourhood, while the architects have produced a unique and striking design that challenges the pragmatic sense and function of a public building.

1 / La Casa Más Grande (The Biggest House) erupts from the ground in an explosion of colour and dynamic forms that represent the vitality and spirit of the youth of Rivas.

1

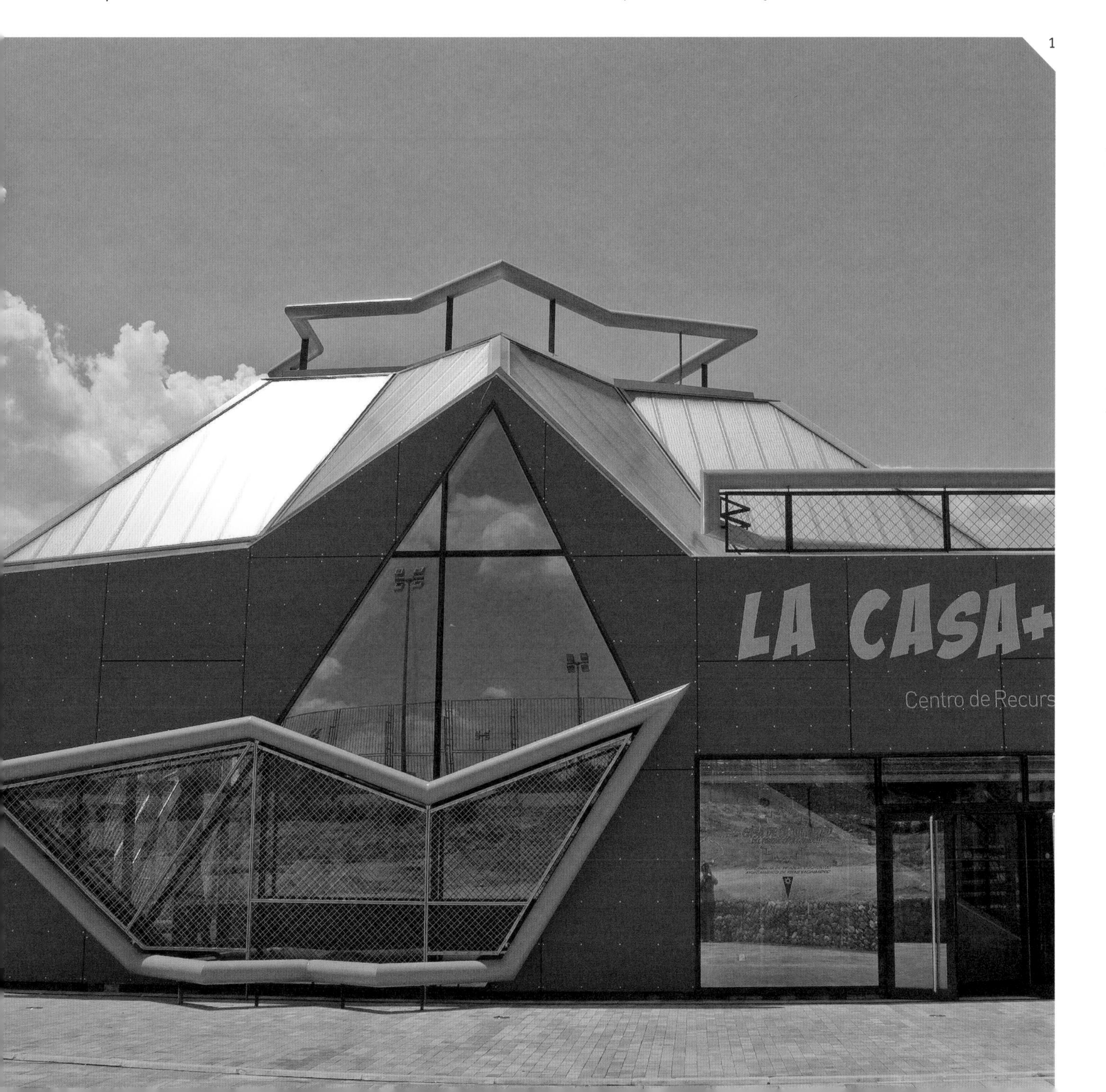

2

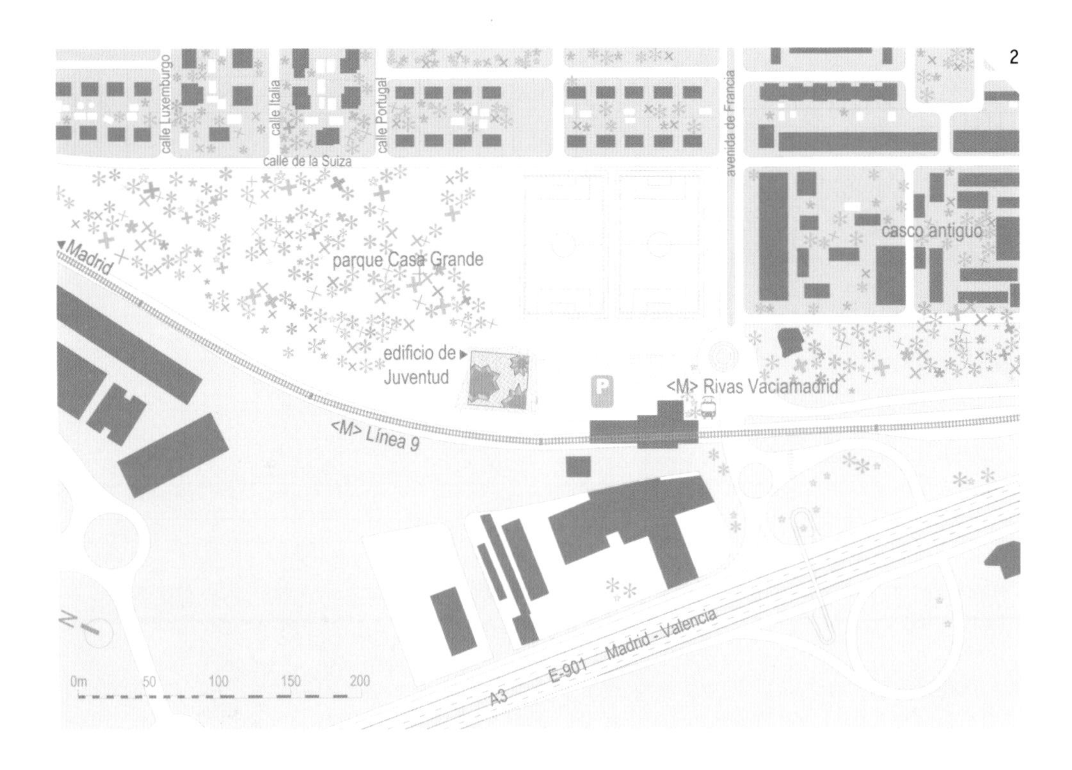

calle Luxemburgo
calle Italia
calle Portugal
calle de la Suiza
avenida de Francia
casco antiguo
Madrid
parque Casa Grande
edificio de Juventud
<M> Rivas Vaciamadrid
<M> Línea 9
A3
E-901
Madrid - Valencia
0m
50
100
150
200

3

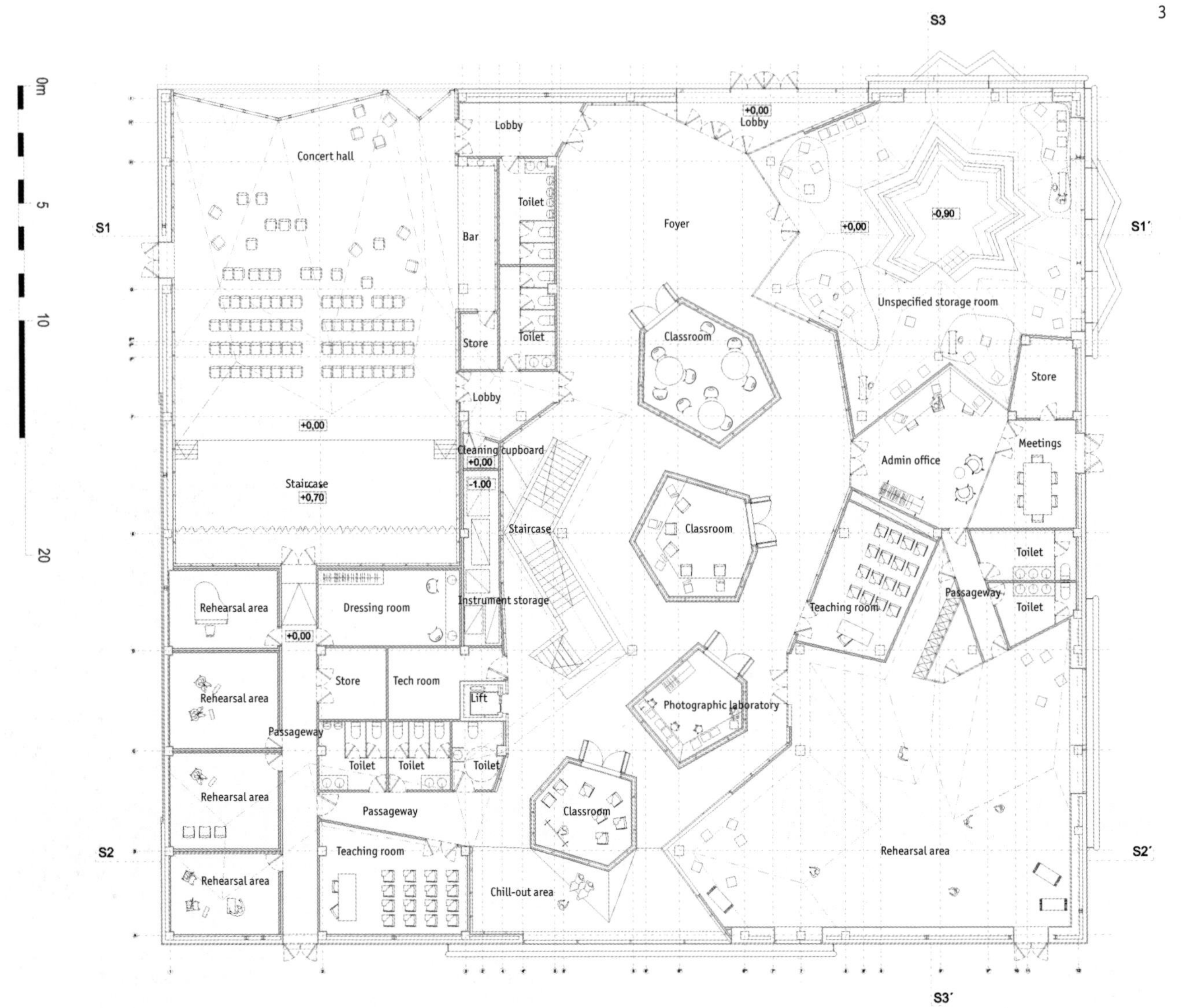

S3
0m
5
10
20
S1
S1´
Lobby
+0,00
Lobby
Concert hall
Toilet
Bar
Foyer
+0,00
-0,90
Unspecified storage room
Store
Toilet
Classroom
Store
Lobby
+0,00
Meetings
Admin office
Cleaning cupboard
+0,00
-1.00
Staircase
+0,70
Staircase
Classroom
Toilet
Passageway
Toilet
Rehearsal area
Dressing room
Instrument storage
Teaching room
+0,00
Store
Tech room
Lift
Rehearsal area
Passageway
Photographic laboratory
Toilet
Toilet
Toilet
Rehearsal area
Passageway
Classroom
S2
Teaching room
Rehearsal area
S2´
Rehearsal area
Chill-out area
S3´

4

Non-walkable roof
Non-walkable roof
Walkable roof
Walkable roof
Unspecified storage room
Admin Office
Gymnasium

Seccion 1-1´

5

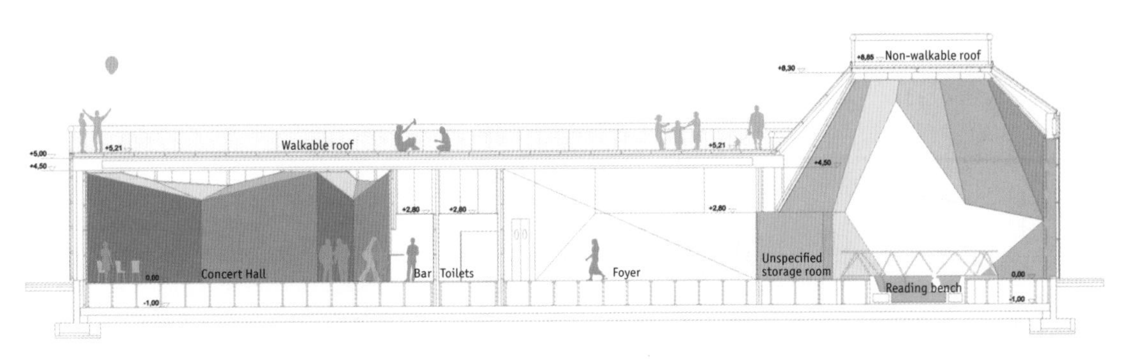

0m 5 10 20

6

2 / Site plan.

3 / Ground-floor plan.

4 / Section 1-1.

5 / Section 2-2.

6 / Brainstorming session.

5VALIDACIÓN

7
Casa Grande
Partycipa!
Arquitectos

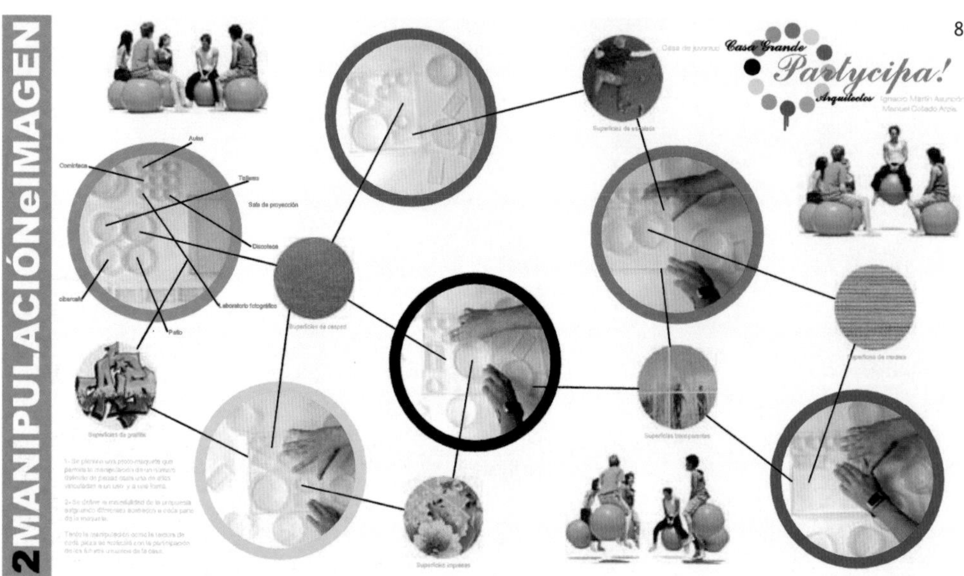
2MANIPULACIÓNeIMAGEN
8
Casa Grande
Partycipa!
Arquitectos

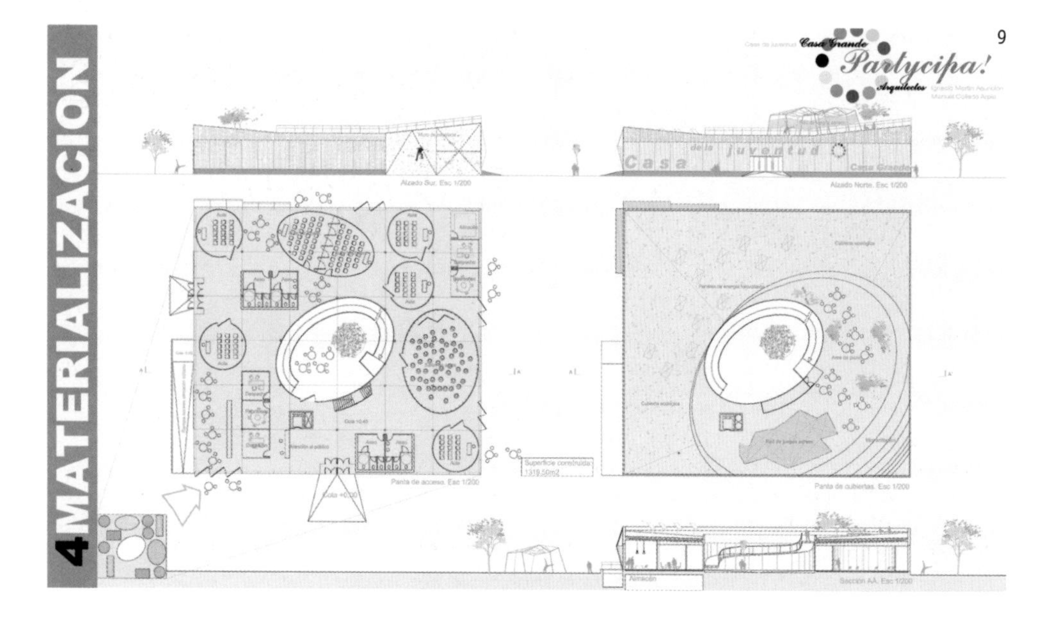
4MATERIALIZACION
9
Casa Grande
Partycipa!
Arquitectos
Casa de la juventud

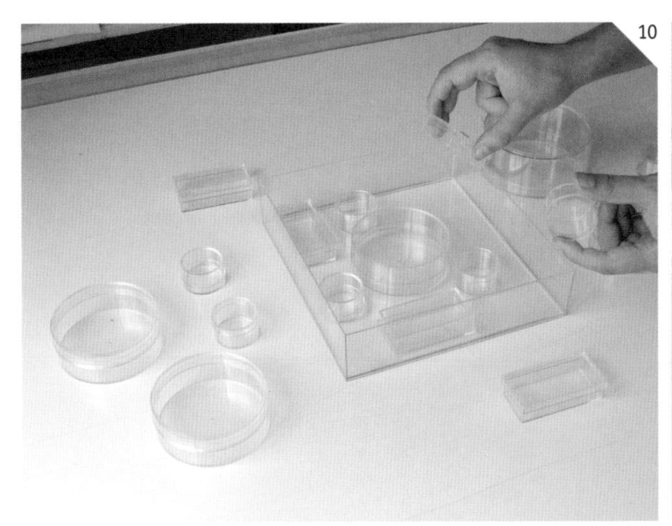

10

11

12

7 / Competition presentation: The original concept was for an iconic building that would be part of its surroundings, with a large terrace overlooking the park in which it would be situated.

8 / The jury was impressed by the game, or puzzle, the architects devised to encourage the involved parties, from politicians and sociologists to the teenagers themselves, to participate in the design process. Moving shapes that represented the different programme elements around a transparent box would be an easily understandable, and fun, way to determine their best location within the building.

9 / Mi5's original suggestion for the layout of the youth centre was presented with ground and roof-top plans, elevations and a section.

10 / Close-up of the game: Once the final programme was set the architects and user community prioritized the different facilities and the sizes they should be relative to one another.

11 / Model used in Phase 2 of the development.

12 / Renderings of the exterior and roof terrace from Phase 2 of the development: The form of the building is closer to the one that was built, but the materiality has not been finalized. An early idea was for the façade to be dark purple with a shimmering effect.

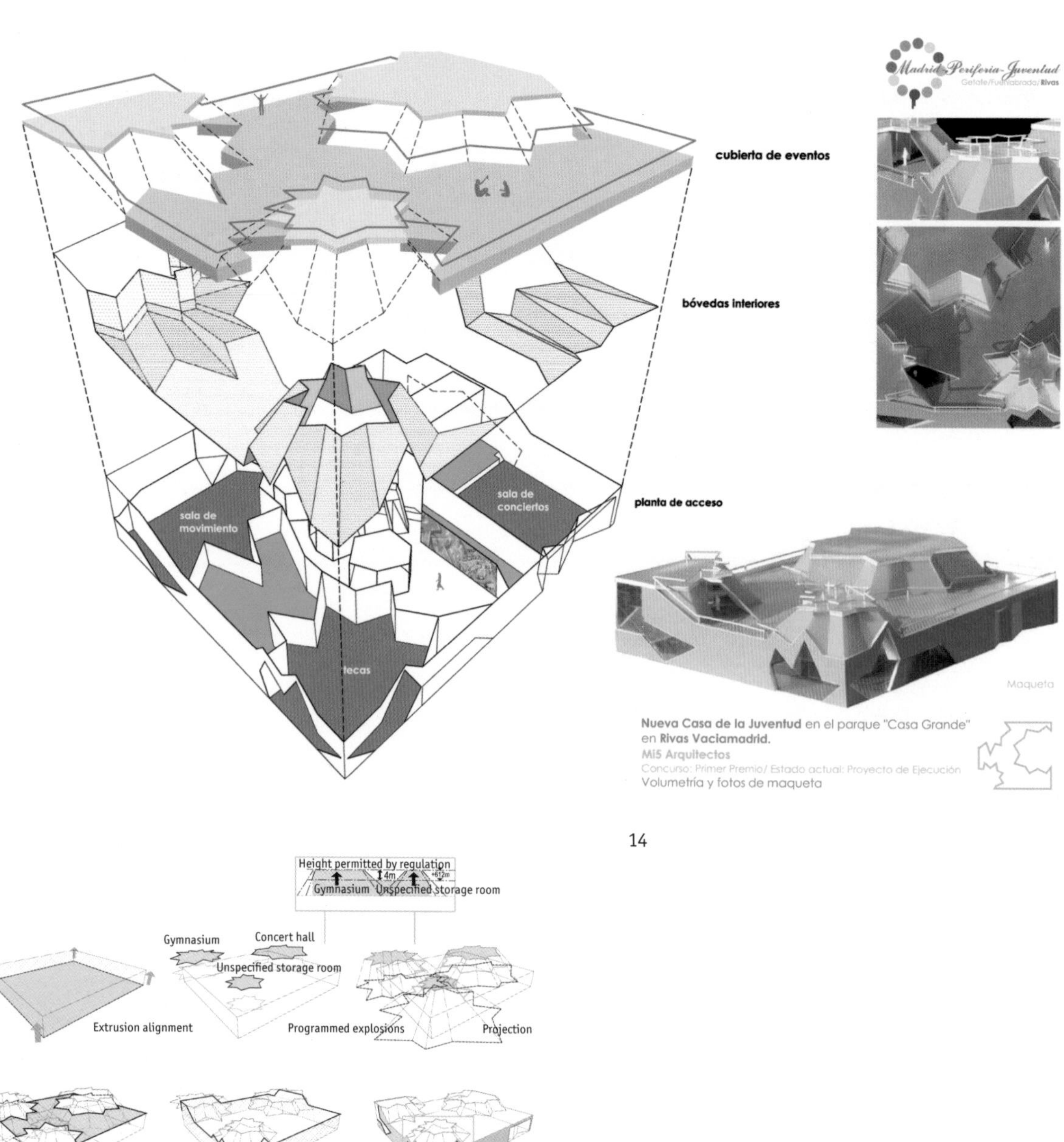

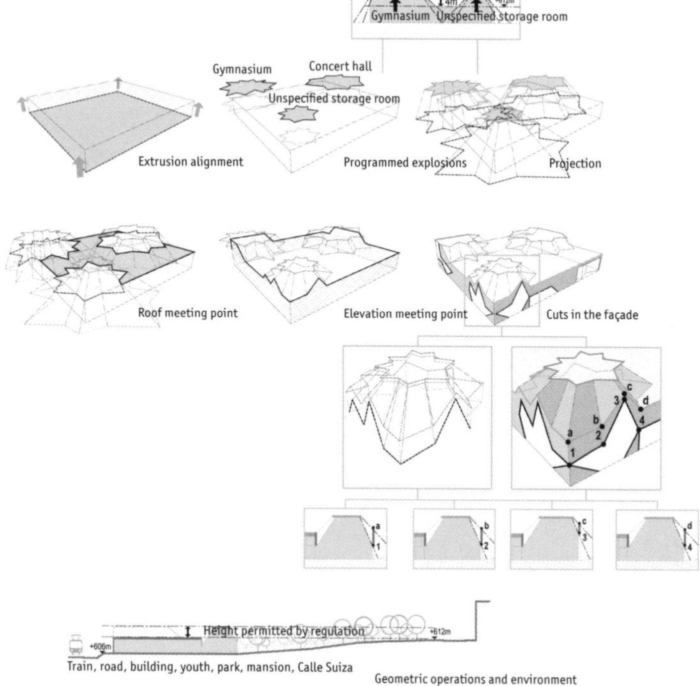

13 / Phase 3 presentation showing the final axonometric and model.

14 / Generation sequence from the Phase 3 presentation.

15 / A cartoon was devised to communicate the style and atmosphere of the project.

16 / Construction drawing of (from bottom to top) the foundation, façade, skylight and roof: The contract included construction and detailed documentation. The architects were responsible for hiring the mechanical and structural engineers (with whom they collaborated from the beginning of the project) and selected the contractor.

15

TENGO COLEGAS QUE HAN PARTICIPADO EN EL PROYECTO
HEY HO... LETS GO
PUES VENGA

16

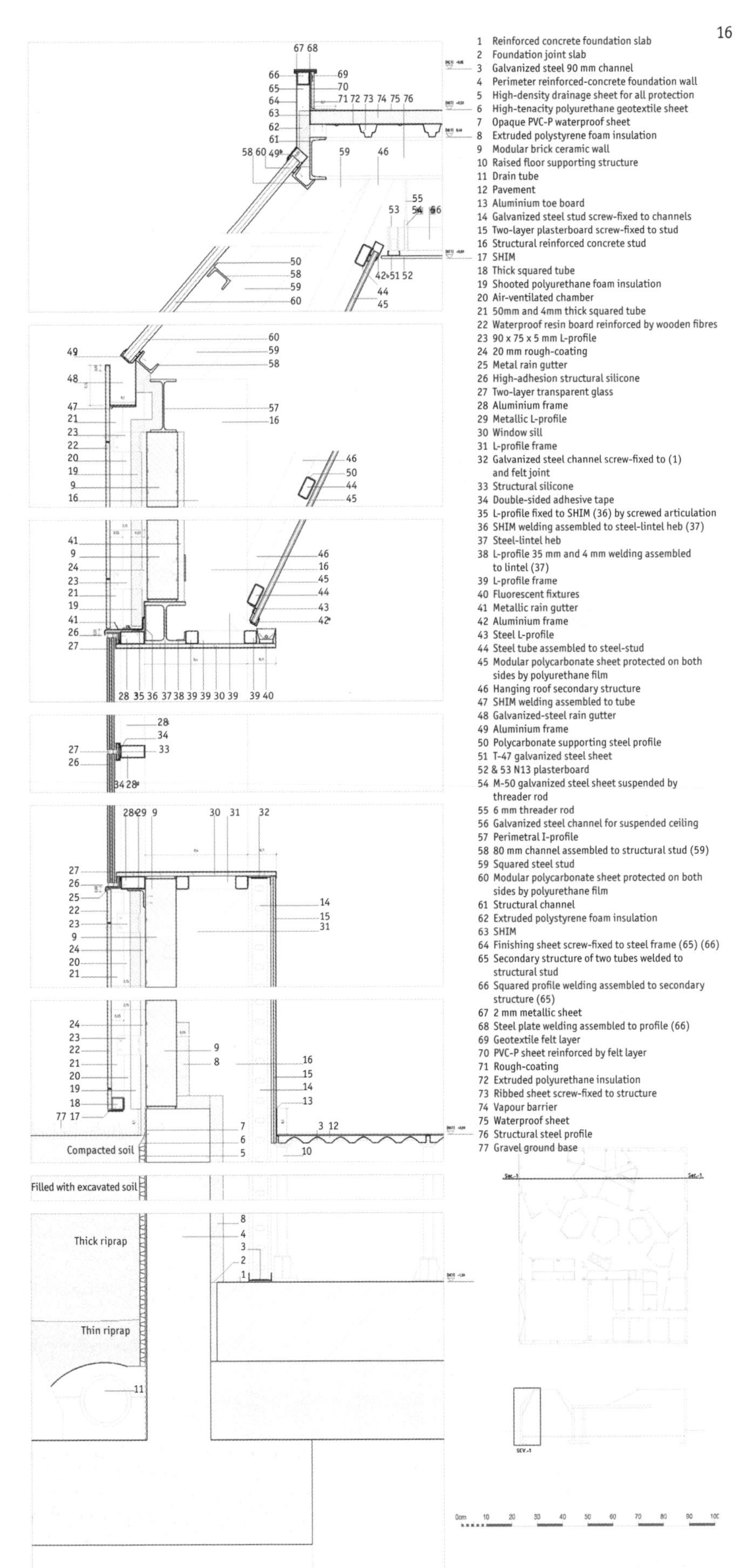

1 Reinforced concrete foundation slab
2 Foundation joint slab
3 Galvanized steel 90 mm channel
4 Perimeter reinforced-concrete foundation wall
5 High-density drainage sheet for all protection
6 High-tenacity polyurethane geotextile sheet
7 Opaque PVC-P waterproof sheet
8 Extruded polystyrene foam insulation
9 Modular brick ceramic wall
10 Raised floor supporting structure
11 Drain tube
12 Pavement
13 Aluminium toe board
14 Galvanized steel stud screw-fixed to channels
15 Two-layer plasterboard screw-fixed to stud
16 Structural reinforced concrete stud
17 SHIM
18 Thick squared tube
19 Shooted polyurethane foam insulation
20 Air-ventilated chamber
21 50mm and 4mm thick squared tube
22 Waterproof resin board reinforced by wooden fibres
23 90 x 75 x 5 mm L-profile
24 20 mm rough-coating
25 Metal rain gutter
26 High-adhesion structural silicone
27 Two-layer transparent glass
28 Aluminium frame
29 Metallic L-profile
30 Window sill
31 L-profile frame
32 Galvanized steel channel screw-fixed to (1) and felt joint
33 Structural silicone
34 Double-sided adhesive tape
35 L-profile fixed to SHIM (36) by screwed articulation
36 SHIM welding assembled to steel-lintel heb (37)
37 Steel-lintel heb
38 L-profile 35 mm and 4 mm welding assembled to lintel (37)
39 L-profile frame
40 Fluorescent fixtures
41 Metallic rain gutter
42 Aluminium frame
43 Steel L-profile
44 Steel tube assembled to steel-stud
45 Modular polycarbonate sheet protected on both sides by polyurethane film
46 Hanging roof secondary structure
47 SHIM welding assembled to tube
48 Galvanized-steel rain gutter
49 Aluminium frame
50 Polycarbonate supporting steel profile
51 T-47 galvanized steel sheet
52 & 53 N13 plasterboard
54 M-50 galvanized steel sheet suspended by threader rod
55 6 mm threader rod
56 Galvanized steel channel for suspended ceiling
57 Perimetral I-profile
58 80 mm channel assembled to structural stud (59)
59 Squared steel stud
60 Modular polycarbonate sheet protected on both sides by polyurethane film
61 Structural channel
62 Extruded polystyrene foam insulation
63 SHIM
64 Finishing sheet screw-fixed to steel frame (65) (66)
65 Secondary structure of two tubes welded to structural stud
66 Squared profile welding assembled to secondary structure (65)
67 2 mm metallic sheet
68 Steel plate welding assembled to profile (66)
69 Geotextile felt layer
70 PVC-P sheet reinforced by felt layer
71 Rough-coating
72 Extruded polyurethane insulation
73 Ribbed sheet screw-fixed to structure
74 Vapour barrier
75 Waterproof sheet
76 Structural steel profile
77 Gravel ground base

17

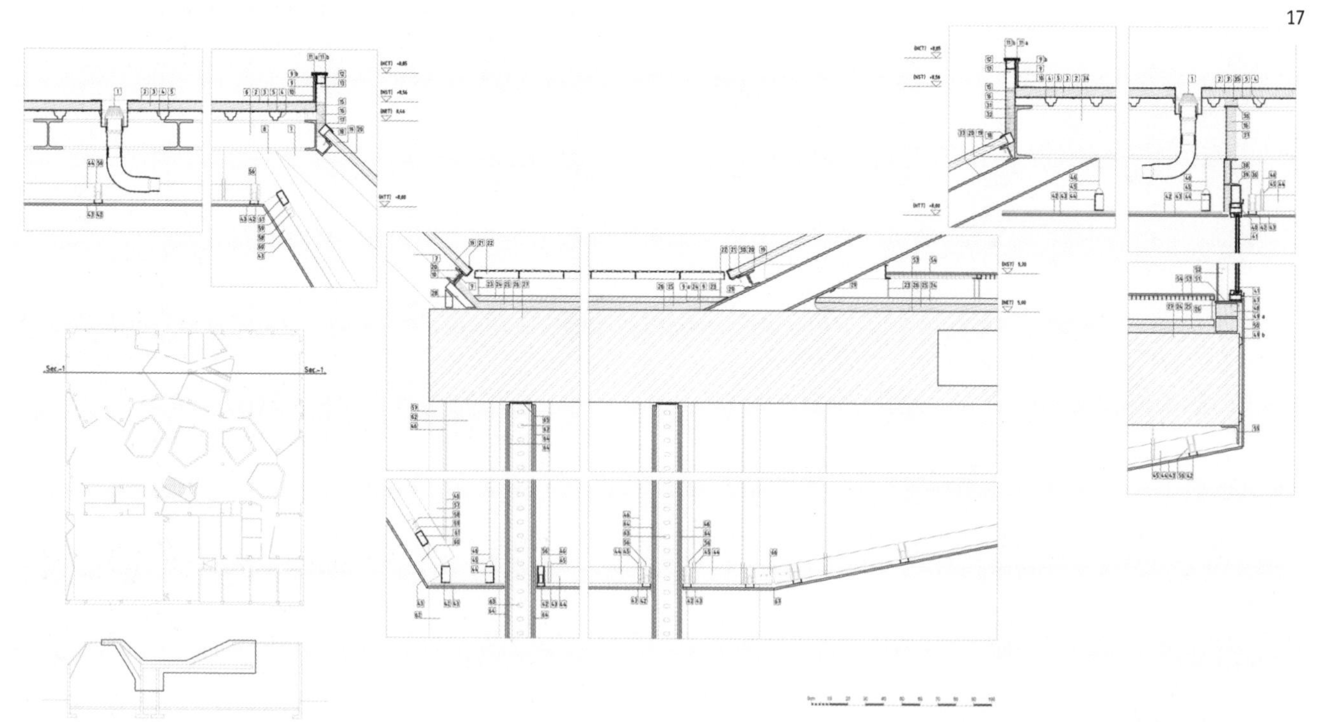

1 Drain
2 Waterproof sheet
3 Extruded polystyrene foam insulation
4 ACL-56S profile screw-fixed to structure
5 Vapour barrier
6 HEB 160 steel beam
7 Squared structural steel tube
8 Secondary structure steel stud
9 PVC-P sheet reinforced by felt layer
9a Geotextile sheet
9b Geotextile felt layer
10 Rough coat
11a 2 mm metal sheet
11b Steel plate welding assembled to tube (12)
12 40 mm steel tube welding assembled to secondary structure (13)
13 Secondary structure consisting of two squared 40 mm profiles
15 2.5 mm metal sheet
16 Polyurethane foam
17 Structural steel channel
18 Aluminium tubular frame
19 Modular polycarbonate sheet protected on both sides by polyethylene film
20 Structural steel channel welding assembled to stud
21 Aluminium tubular frame
22 Aluminium grating
23 Aluminium leveller
24 30 mm mortar cement
25 Shooted polyurethane foam insuation
26 Vapour barrier
27 Slab
28 Double hollow bricks
29 Gutter
30 L-profile
31 Shooted polyurethane foam insulation
32 Structural steel channel
33 200 mm squared steel profile
34 HEB 280 steel beam
35 Insulation
36 Metal SHIM
37 Steel plate
38 IPE 140 beam
39 Aluminium tubular frame
40 Double-tube aluminium frame
41 Two-layer transparent glass
42 T-47 galvanized steel profile
43 N13 plasterboard
44 Galvanized steel channel for suspended ceiling
45 M-50 galvanized steel sheet suspended by threader rod
46 6 mm threader rod
47 Aluminium frame
48 Modular brick ceramic wall
49 Galvanized steel profile
50 N13 plasterboard
51 5 mm SHIM
52 Handrail consisting of T60 studs
53 'PCP' galvanized steel pavement
54 Rubber grain-synthetic grass pavement
55 Structural L-profile
56 0.6 mm galvanized steel SHIM
57 Structural L-profile for suspended ceiling support
58 Galvanized steel stud
59 & 60 Galvanized steel channel
61 Tubular rectangle profile metallic welding assembled to secondary suspended ceiling structure
62 Reinforced concrete stud
63 90 mm galvanized steel stud
64 Two-layer plasterboard screw-fixed to stud
65 90 mm galvanized steel stud
66 Galvanized steel SHIM
67 Adhesive tape

18

19

17 / Construction drawing of (left to right), skylight, slab and terrace: The architects wanted the middle foyer to be free of columns and the main concrete slab of the terrace had to have extra reinforcement to make this possible.

18 / Construction: The structure consists of concrete and steel pillars with a reinforced precast concrete slab. The skylights have a steel frame and polycarbonate cover, and the façade is clad with Trespa panels.

19 / Construction: Mi5 make very detailed drawings to instruct the contractor and control the build. Their buildings are often very complex, and the architects need to keep a constant presence on site to troubleshoot while in the field.

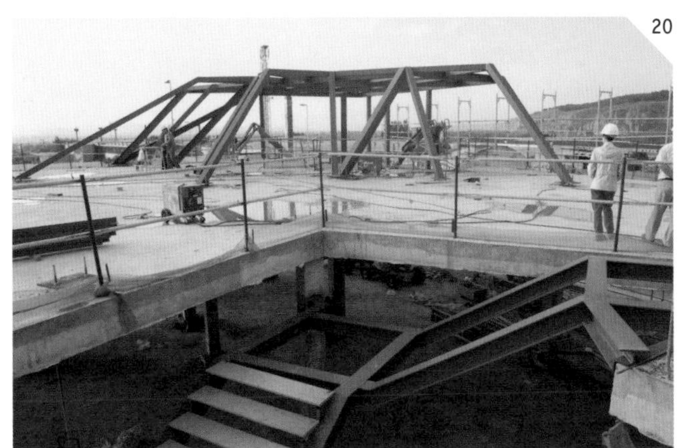

20

21

22

23

20 / Construction: The architects held meetings with local planners to negotiate an increase in the height of the building, to allow for a more panoramic view from the terrace.

21 / The single-storey building features faceted interiors in clashing colours, evoking the explosion of activities on offer.

22 / The main staircase masks the only column in the middle foyer.

23 / The movement room is used for gymnastics and dance. From the first discussions with the teenagers it was clear that this space was one of their main priorities.

Mapungubwe Interpretation Centre

Peter Rich Architects with Michael Ramage and John Ochsendorf

Location: Mapungubwe National Park, Limpopo Province, South Africa
Principal use: Heritage centre
Client: South African National Parks (SANParks)
Site area: 2 hectares (5 acres)

Interior area: 1,650 m^2 (17,760½ ft^2)
Total build area: 2,780 m^2 (29,923½ ft^2)
Design period: January 2007 – August 2007
Construction period: October 2007 – August 2010
Budget: ZAR 14,000,000

Johannesburg architect Peter Rich, Honorary Fellow of the American Institute of Architects (AIA) is the leading proponent of a contemporary African architecture that fuses Modernism and tradition born from a deep understanding of African indigenous architecture. Edward Allen, a Fellow of the AIA, wrote: 'His work astonished me. It was so fresh, so open to local and regional influences, so very, very good without being at all fashionable. I saw in his work the sensibilities of an academically-trained architect being employed with great imagination and skill to create highly attractive community facilities for underprivileged populations in South Africa. The architectural quality was stunning and the flexibility of his mind in incorporating native themes, forms, and materials was admirable. Here, I said to myself, is an architect's architect who is also an architect of the people.'

The Mapungubwe National Park is located on the borders of Botswana and Zimbabwe in a landscape formed by violent geological events that have given rise to the deep valleys and mesas (flat-topped hills with vertical cliff faces) that define the area. The famous golden rhino statue – today the symbol of Africa's precolonial greatness – was found on one such rocky outcrop. The Mapungubwe Hill is of major archaeological importance and has UNESCO World Heritage status. Evidence from graves indicates that civilized societies that enjoyed trading links with Egypt, Persia, India, Malaysia and China inhabited the area between the ninth and twelfth centuries. Their descendants still exist, and tribal elders visit Mapungubwe to pay homage to their ancestors and worship at the sacred site.

The Interpretation Centre, which will house archaeological artefacts including the golden rhino, is the outcome of a national competition organized by SANParks. The brief called for a museum, an educational facility, a new headquarters and a day visitor centre in which the tribal elders could gather. The buildings had to tell the story of this unique area through communicating contemporary interpretations of its complex and diverse history. The location of the centre was artfully chosen to protect Mapungubwe Hill, which had already suffered years of tourist exploitation. The site ascends the southern slope of a sister mesa a kilometre away; the view from the summit of the hill reveals the ancient archaeological remains, with the confluence of the Limpopo and Shashe rivers in the distance to the north.

The inspiration for Rich's competition design was drawn from the immediate context of the landscape and the forces of nature. The composition of the buildings he proposed was held together by a subliminal mathematical geometry based on the architectural order of equilateral triangles found in traditional Venda and Shangaan tribe dwellings. The visitor experience was structured as a pilgrimage route from the entrance, through a group of domed forms layered up the hillside (echoing the shape of the vegetation and the texture of the rocky terrain as well as calling to mind native South African route markers) and the mesa profile outlined against the sky. The concept had its genesis in the idea of the cave, denoting not only shelter and refuge but also evoking sacred ritual practices.

During the period that Rich was brainstorming for the competition he was introduced to British-based South African architect Issy Benjamin whose latest work at Pines Calyx, outside Dover, UK, consisted of twin tile-vault domes. This kind of structure originated in the Mediterranean, was used extensively in Catalonia and was made famous by Gaudí in Spain and the Guastavino Company in the USA before it was virtually forgotten because of the widespread use of reinforced concrete. Following natural forces, tile vaulting can achieve large spans with minimal structure. The simplicity of its construction means it can be built by a low-skilled workforce using locally sourced material, which made the methodology ideal for Mapungubwe's poverty relief project and for Rich's concept. The vaults would have a cave-like quality while remaining light and elegant. Dressed in stones found on site, they could be read as an extension of the land.

Benjamin introduced Rich to engineers John Ochsendorf from MIT and Cambridge University's Michael Ramage (who were researching the use of tile vaulting in the USA, in such buildings as Grand Central Station) as well as James Bellamy, a young New Zealander who had trained with Spanish vault-builders. Together Ramage, Ochsendorf and Rich designed vaults for the competition entry following Rich's vision for the centre. A programme to educate unemployed members of the local community in how to construct the domes, and in the fabrication of the pressed-earth tiles from which they would be made, was also set up.

Beating off competition from nearly 300 schemes, shortlisted from 67 different countries, the Mapungubwe Interpretation Centre won the World Building of the Year in 2009. The judges, chaired by Rafael Viñoly and including internationally renowned architects Kengo Kuma, Farshid Moussavi and Matthias Sauerbruch, praised the project for the way it related to the landscape, and its hand-crafted intelligence. They also commended the use of local materials and the careful handling of sustainability issues.

Peter Rich maintains that he designs not for an architectural audience but for ordinary people. One such person commented that the centre looked as if it had grown out of the earth. Rich concludes: 'It doesn't have form like a building in a building sense, but looks as if it has always been there and although it's modern it feels like it's ancient. Like a ruin it captures people's imagination.'

1 / The centre's vaults and cairns ascend the southern slope of a mesa overlooking the sacred site of Mapungubwe Hill. Covered in sandstone iodized with age and gathered from the site, they look as if they have sprung from the earth.

1

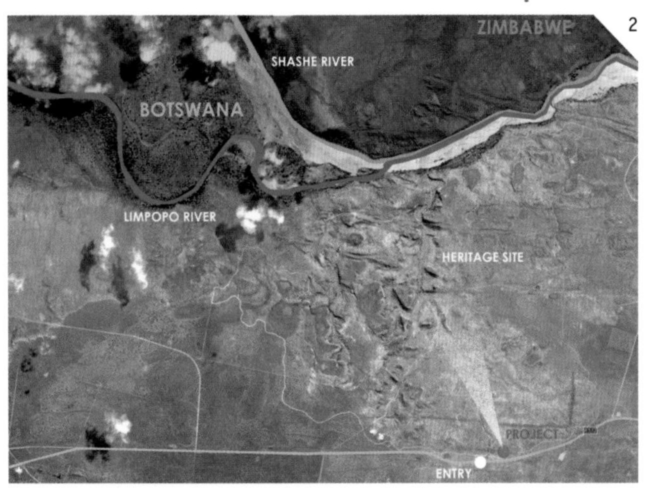
ZIMBABWE
SHASHE RIVER
BOTSWANA
LIMPOPO RIVER
HERITAGE SITE
PROJECT
ENTRY

2

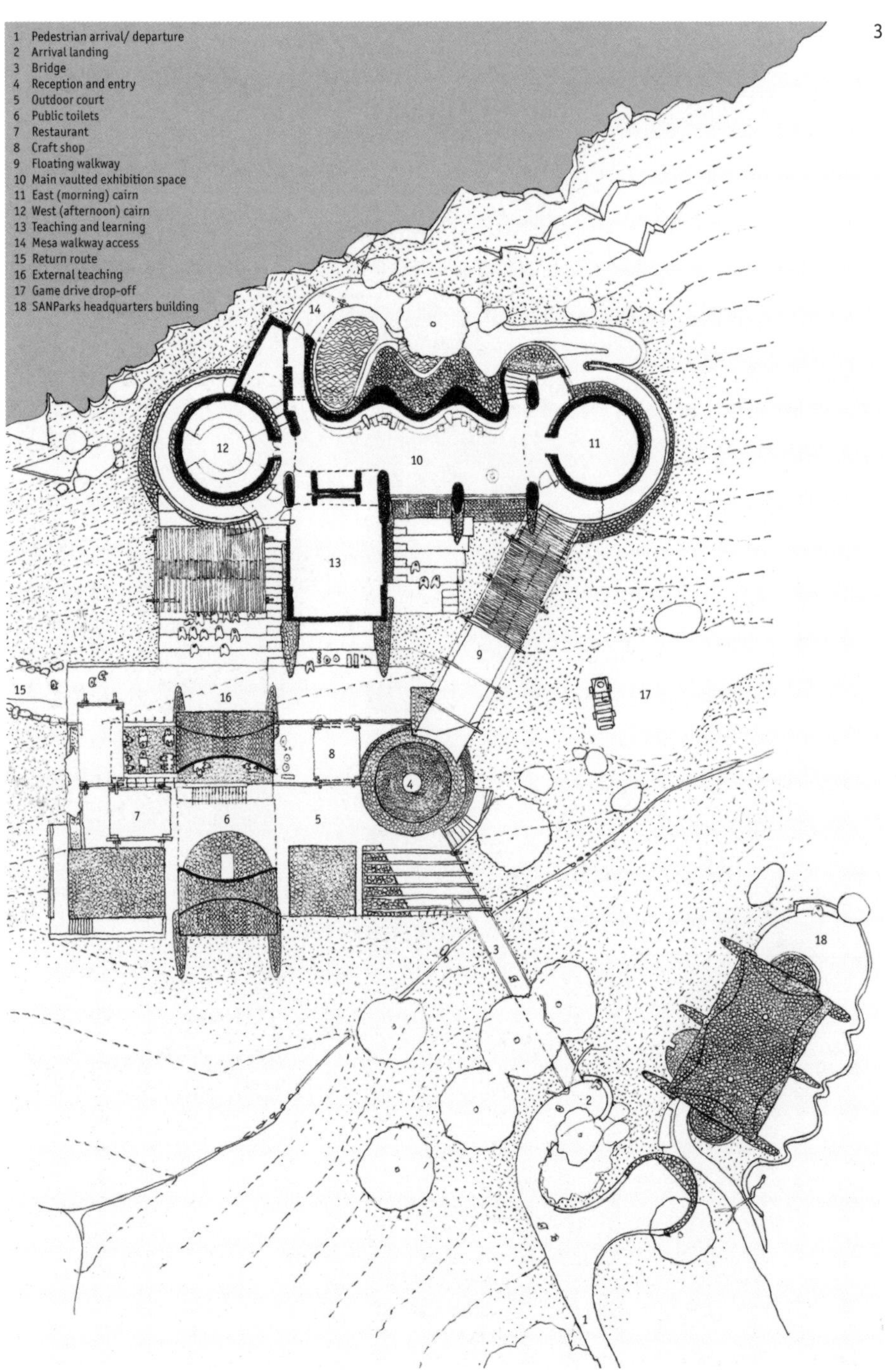
1 Pedestrian arrival/ departure
2 Arrival landing
3 Bridge
4 Reception and entry
5 Outdoor court
6 Public toilets
7 Restaurant
8 Craft shop
9 Floating walkway
10 Main vaulted exhibition space
11 East (morning) cairn
12 West (afternoon) cairn
13 Teaching and learning
14 Mesa walkway access
15 Return route
16 External teaching
17 Game drive drop-off
18 SANParks headquarters building

3

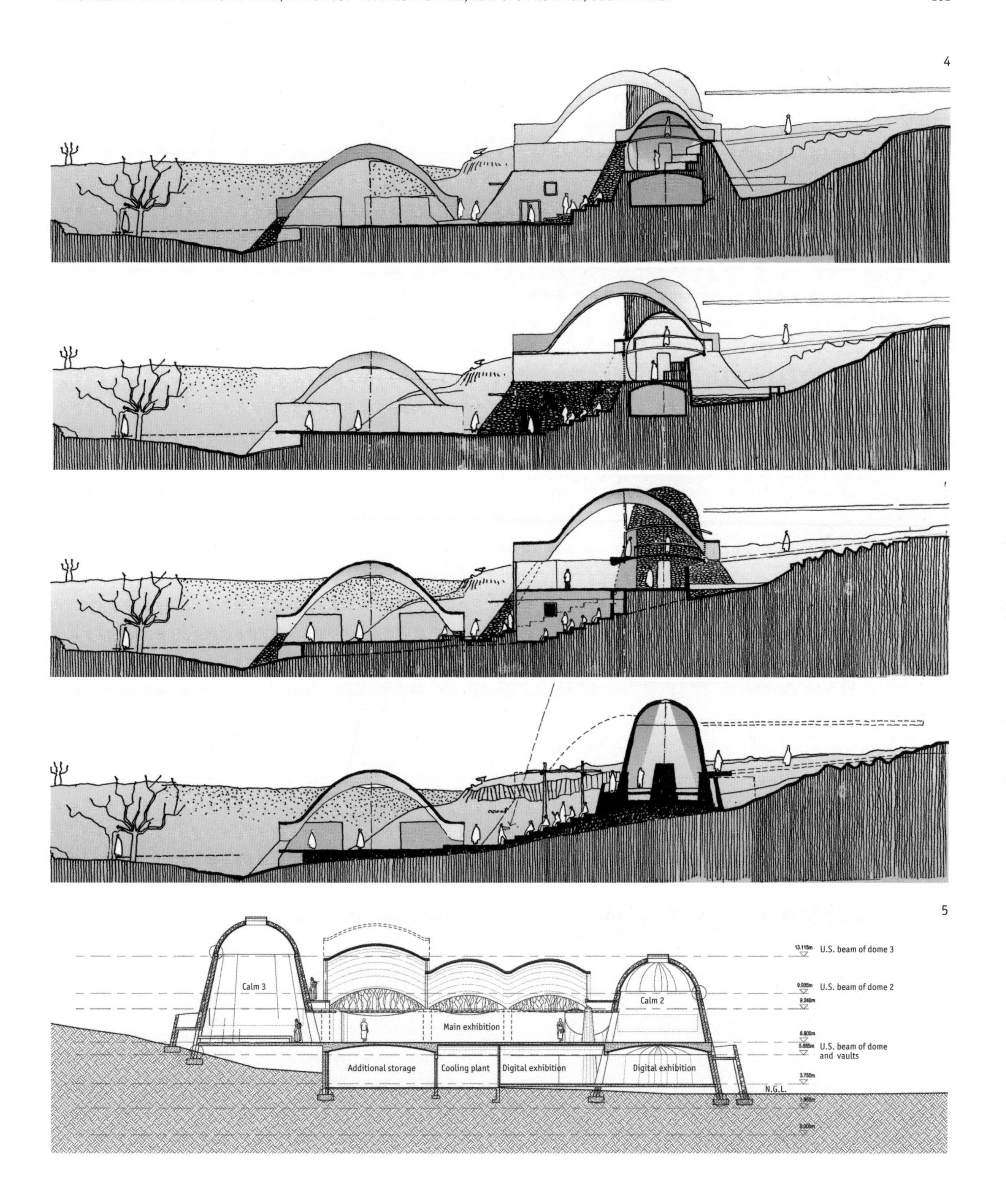

2 / Location map.

3 / The complex includes the main exhibition space, restaurant, shop and educational facilities as well as SANParks' new headquarters housed in a separate building. The visitor centre for tribal elders is situated 700 m (765 yd) to the east on an extension of the same mesa. The changing spatial sequence is based on a physical and cultural narrative translated into an exhibition experience.

4 / Cross-sections.

5 / Longitudinal section.

6

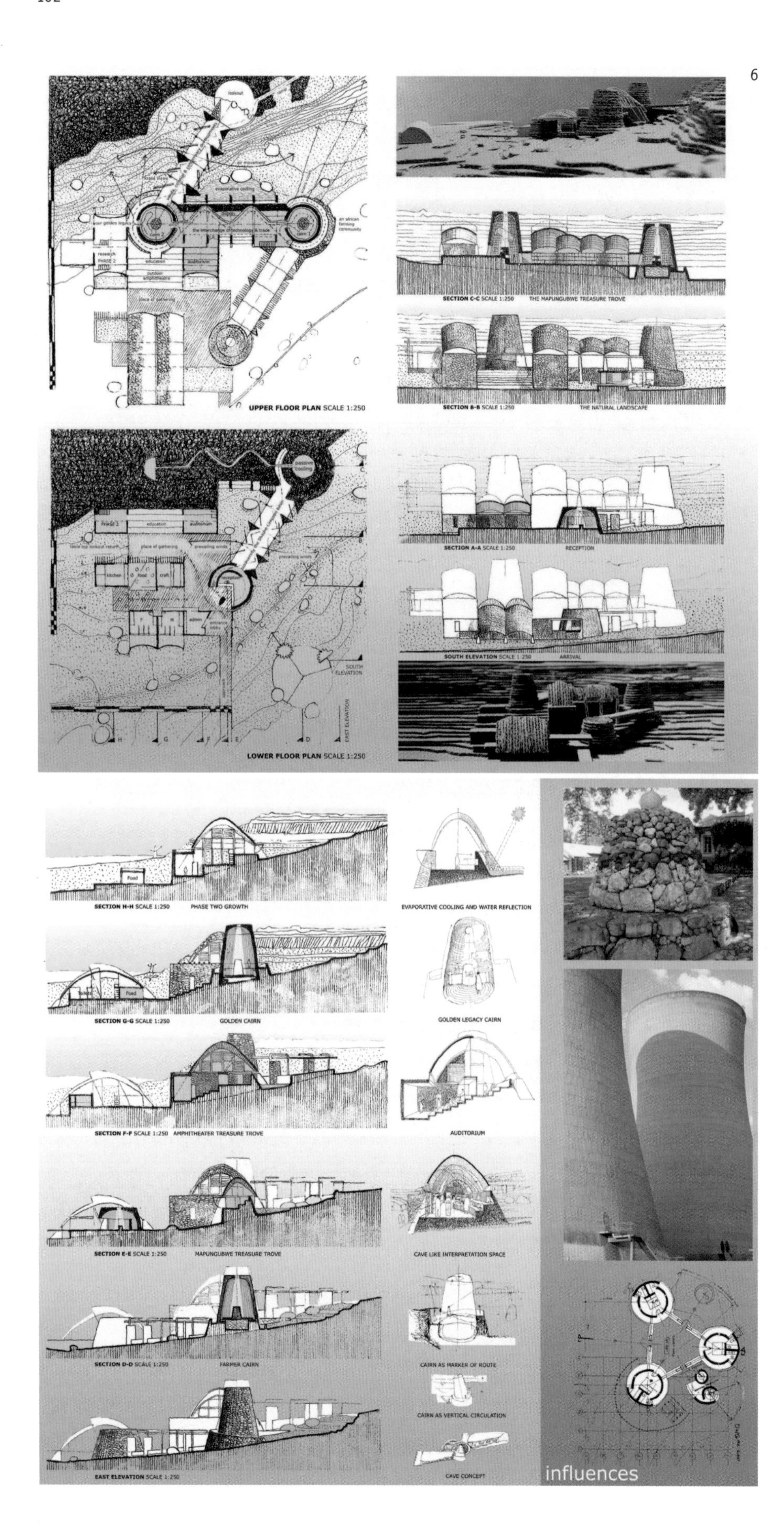
UPPER FLOOR PLAN SCALE 1:250
SECTION C-C SCALE 1:250 THE MAPUNGUBWE TREASURE TROVE
SECTION B-B SCALE 1:250 THE NATURAL LANDSCAPE
LOWER FLOOR PLAN SCALE 1:250
SECTION A-A SCALE 1:250 RECEPTION
SOUTH ELEVATION SCALE 1:250 ARRIVAL
SECTION H-H SCALE 1:250 PHASE TWO GROWTH
EVAPORATIVE COOLING AND WATER REFLECTION
SECTION G-G SCALE 1:250 GOLDEN CAIRN
GOLDEN LEGACY CAIRN
SECTION F-F SCALE 1:250 AMPHITHEATER TREASURE TROVE
AUDITORIUM
SECTION E-E SCALE 1:250 MAPUNGUBWE TREASURE TROVE
CAVE LIKE INTERPRETATION SPACE
SECTION D-D SCALE 1:250 FARMER CAIRN
CAIRN AS MARKER OF ROUTE
CAIRN AS VERTICAL CIRCULATION
EAST ELEVATION SCALE 1:250
CAVE CONCEPT
influences

7

8

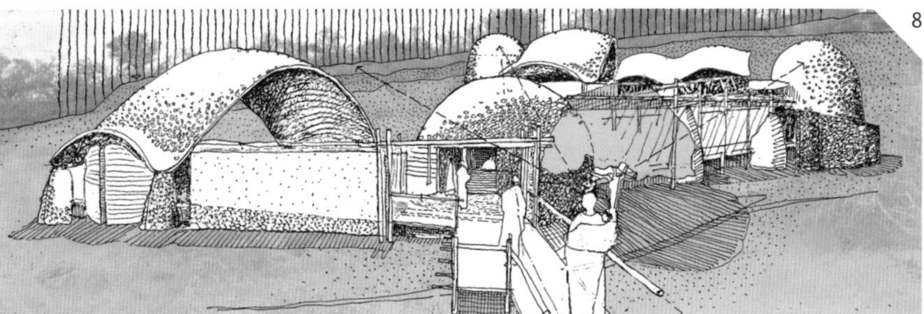

9

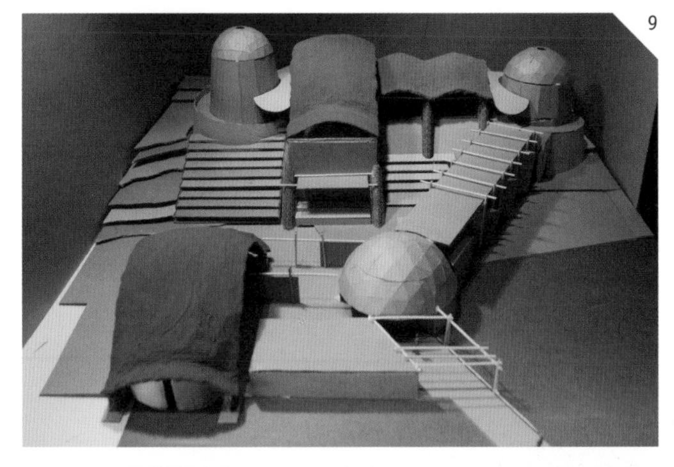

10

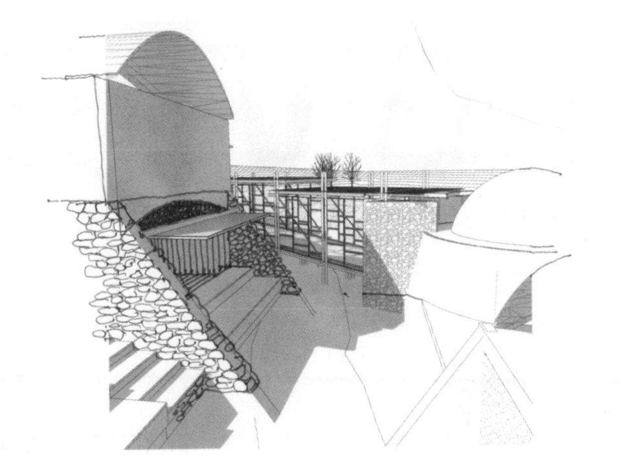

11

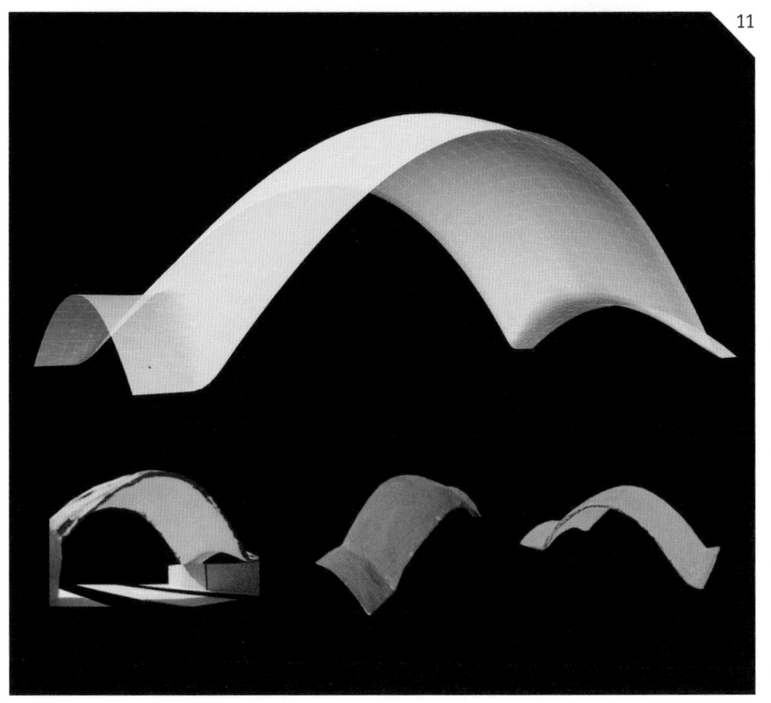

12

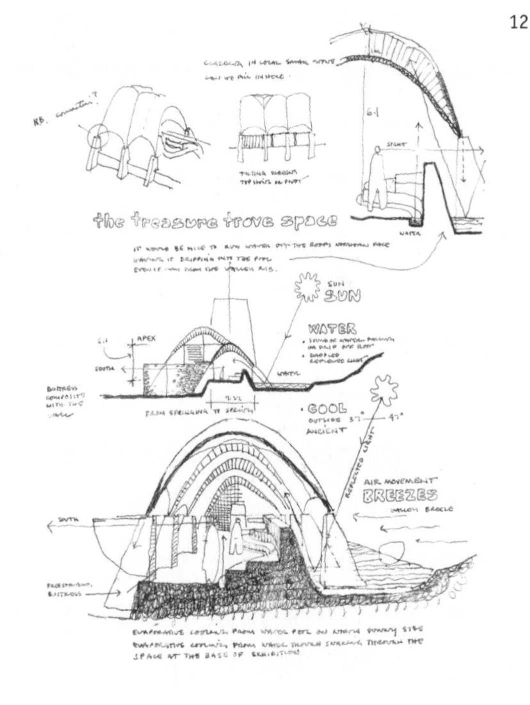

6 / The presentation to the client was made using hand-drawings and sketches. The concept was a brave deviation from the thatch-and-gum-pole constructions with which SANParks was familiar.

7 / Sketch of the restaurant area.

8 / Arrival: The idea of using tile vaulting was present from the start. SANParks unanimously accepted the competition design but a conserv-ative lobby became nervous when the construction documentation was submitted. Rich had to emphasize the wisdom of his design by presenting costings for alternative techniques so that the client could appreciate that concrete, for example, would be unsuitable for the context and more expensive.

9 / A 1:150 model was made to help convey the design concept to the client.

10 / The practice uses the hand as a thinking tool. 3-D drawings are often manually produced (illustrated here) and computer drawings are sketched over to give them character.

11 / Computer model and cardboard models examining stress loads.

12 / Sketch drawing investigating the use of natural cooling: Provision for passive cooling was made dependent on the level of control the exhibition displays needed. At the time of going to print it was undecided whether original artefacts or replicas would be housed in the centre.

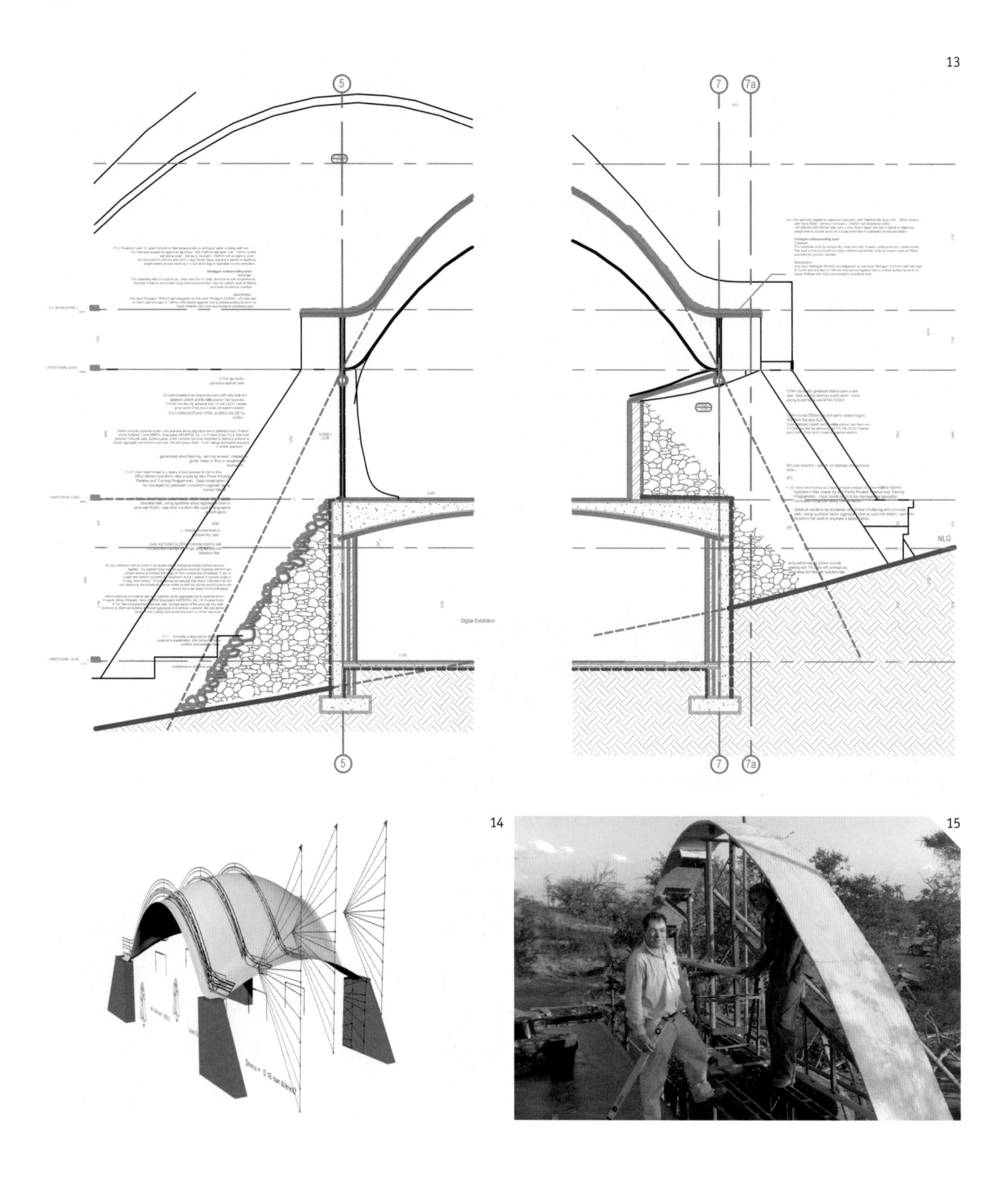

13 / Rich produced construction drawings that were also used for tender. The specifications were very detailed as many of the techniques were rarely practised. He was responsible for site supervision, handover to the client and defects assessment.

14 / Structural analysis: Michael Ramage was the project engineer and secured indemnity insurance for the vaults through Cambridge University. Tile vaulting is based on the mathematical and geometric order found in nature and uses the same economy of means. It has no steel reinforcement and relies purely on the form for strength and stability.

15 / The vaults need little formwork and are light for their span, allowing for minimum foundations and buttressing.

16 / Tiles are laid in rapid-setting gypsum mortar in a herringbone pattern that allows the mason to stand on the lower parts of the structure in order to build the higher ones. Two or more layers of overlapping tiles are used.

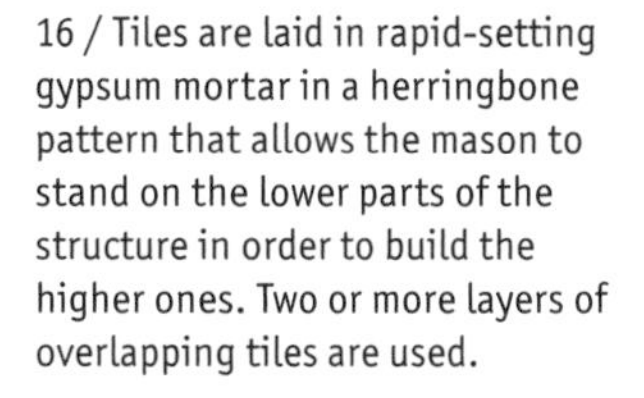

17 / Local unemployed people instructed by Bellamy (seen here on the left) were engaged to make the stablilized earth tiles as part of SANParks' poverty relief programme.

18 / The 18 mm- (3/4 in-) thick tiles were made from local soil. 5 per cent of cement was added to a wet/dry mix which was hand-pressed in a Hydraform steel manufactured press using a wooden pallet cot.

19 / The tiles were left to cure.

20
21
22
23
24
25

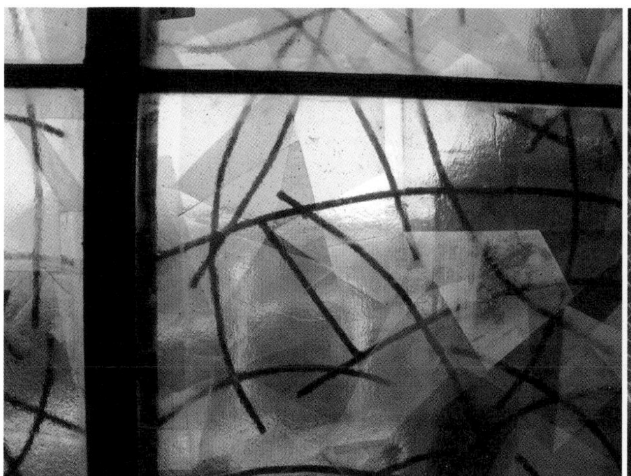

26

27

28

20 / Stones were embedded in mortar over floating screed and waterproofing layers. In order for them to work with the forces of the vault and not be deadweights they had to touch one another.

21 / Heavy rains post-construction showed there was water ingress causing the edge tiles to fall off. A drip detail was introduced.

22 / The base of the columns is concrete to accord with national building regulations. It was poured in situ. Also because of building regulations, the buttresses and supporting walls had to be clad with quarried stone brought from off site.

23 / The visitor centre is a thatched pergola structure. The use of breeze blocks allows for natural ventilation. They are based on vernacular mud bricks but constructed in concrete using a custom mould.

24 / The domical language is contrasted by walkways that create a zigzagging ramped circulation through the complex. Visitors have a choice of route: ramp or stair, internal or external, to ascend to the upper parts of the vaults.

25 / The reception is marked by the first of the hollow cairns lit by an oculus tracking the sun. The hollow domes are reminiscent of native South African route-markers. The cairns are situated at points where the triangular geometry changes direction.

26 / Daylight penetrates the main exhibition area through openings at the edge of the vaulting and is filtered by patterned glass, evoking the colours of the landscape.

27 / Ponds cool the air that naturally ventilates the building.

28 / The strength of the sun is tempered by horizontally slatted natural timber that evokes traditional shade structures, and by rusted steel screens denoting the branches of indigenous trees.

Step Up on Fifth

Pugh + Scarpa Architects (now Brooks + Scarpa Architects)

Location: Santa Monica, California, USA
Principal use: Multi-unit residential accommodation for homeless people with mental disabilities
Client: Step Up on Second
Site area: 696.7 m² (7,500 ft²)

Interior area: 1,123.8 m² (12,097 ft²)
Total build area: 2,935.7 m² (31,600 ft²)
Design period: October 2004 – February 2007
Construction period: February 2007 – August 2009
Budget: $11,400,000

Step Up on Fifth, a mixed-use scheme that provides 46 affordable studio apartments for the mentally disabled homeless population of Santa Monica, pushes the envelope technologically and environmentally, and impacts on both the community and the city. As such, it is a perfect example of Pugh + Scarpa's (now Brooks + Scarpa) work. In 2004, Lisa Iwamoto, Associate Professor of Architecture at the University of California, Berkeley, commented on Lawrence Scarpa's architecture: 'It is environmentally sustainable, but it is not about "sustainable design". It employs new materials, digital practices and technologies, but it is not defined by nor moulded by technologies. It is socially and community conscious, but it is not created as a politically correct statement. Rather, it is deeply rooted in conditions of the everyday and works with our perception and preconceptions to allow us to see things in new ways.'

The client comprised Step Up on Second, a service provider for citizens in need, and the Community of Friends, a developer of affordable housing and supportive centres, with the city of Santa Monica providing a significant second source of funding. It was the city that recommended Pugh + Scarpa, having worked with them in 2002 on Colorado Court, the first LEED-certified multifamily housing project in the USA.

The site was a tight, 15.2 x 45.7-metre (50 x 150-foot) infill plot with three façades, one to the street and the others facing south and west. The architect was given a rudimentary brief to provide a functional and sustainable design consisting of as many units as possible, plus communal spaces that would be sympathetic to the particular needs of the mentally challenged tenants. In addition, the city wanted the building to contribute to the urban environment with pedestrian-oriented use at street level.

Following research into the specific demands of designing for such a specialist user group, and analysis focused on the placement of building components to take advantage of abundant natural ventilation and light, and control heat gain and loss, several design options were presented using three-dimensional hand-drawings, renderings and plans. Scarpa maintains that he is never short of ideas and likes to include clients in his thought processes. The design was developed collaboratively through ongoing dialogue between Scarpa and Step Up's leadership.

Ideas that were rejected included building to the maximum 26-metre (85-foot) height allowed, as anything over (15.2 metres (50 feet) would have meant going from a residential to a high-rise type construction, using concrete and complex mechanical systems with a concomitant cost implication. Also rejected for financial reasons was Scarpa's first notion for the street level. As the Step Up organization employs its population in a catering business for local events, his initial suggestion was for a kitchen to support this enterprise. On open view at street level, this would have provided visual engagement between the general public and the building's tenants. In addition, the materiality for the façade was deliberated. Although there were to be no housing units on the ground floor, there was still accommodation off the street. To offer privacy to the tenants, a form of screening was proposed. Scarpa researched the possibility of using Trex©, a reclaimed wood and recycled plastic composite, in an undulating form but this was found deficient in controlling light, solar gain and ventilation.

Most frustrating was that two designs had to be put forward, one with parking and one without. Santa Monica's building codes dictate that 0.5 parking spaces be provided for every tenant of a newly constructed residential building; ironic in a compact, environmentally responsible building, compounded further by the fact that most of Step Up's tenants would not be allowed to drive. The team was hoping for an exemption, but this would have needed time-consuming bureaucracy and great expense, and could have jeopardized the build. Eventually the scheme with parking (reduced to 0.25 spaces per resident) was adopted, taking up a third of the total project cost.

The concept that was brought through tender and detailed design documentation changed little. The construction is Type V, a wooden frame over a reinforced concrete ground floor and basement, rated to maintain its structural integrity in case of fire for one hour. The architect worked closely with the engineer on the complex wooden framework and on the development of a shear wall layout; to support vertical loads and to prevent deformation of the frame. Care was taken to make sure that all the walls were earthquake-proof. The studio apartments are held to the outside of the plan to the east, north and west, with community rooms on alternate floors completing an E-shaped plan. Two private internal courtyards provide residents with secure and welcoming surroundings. On the ground floor there is a computer room and an area dedicated to exhibiting artworks created by some of the organization's 18,000 members. Water-jet-anodized aluminium panels shield the street façade. The material is also used as a strategic arrangement of screens on west- and south-facing walls, offering privacy and shading from the sun. Passive solar design strategies make the building 50 per cent more efficient than a conventionally designed structure.

In conclusion, Scarpa says: 'We would argue that a building that is an energy hog that everyone loves is more sustainable than a building that uses no energy but nobody likes. Our goal was to create a beautiful, low-maintenance high-quality building ... that is also environmentally friendly.'

1 / Step Up on Fifth provides homes, support services and rehabilitation for homeless, mentally disabled people in downtown Santa Monica.

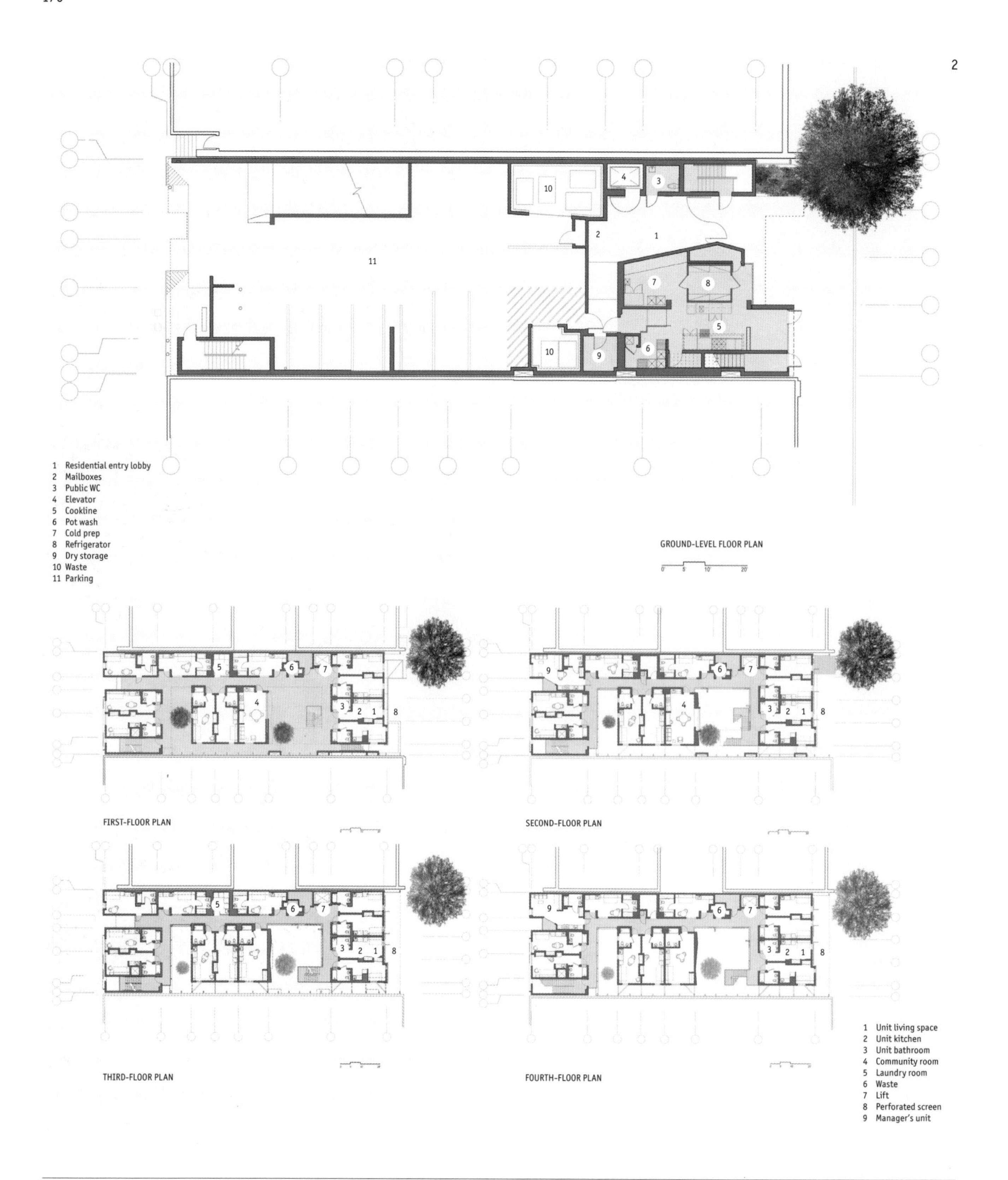

2 / Ground- to fourth-floor plans: Each of the 46 units is less than 23.2 m² (250 ft²). The density of Step Up is 258 dwelling units per acre, which exceeds the average density of Manhattan by more than 10 per cent.

3 / East, west and south elevations.

4 / Section A: The car parking is accessed via car lifts and a ramp from ground to basement-level 1. The limited site did not allow for a second ramp to basement level 2.

5 / The site was an infill plot between housing and a car body-shop. The shop had built windows on the property line that were venting fumes onto the lot. Instead of making the owner brick them in, Scarpa built ventilation shafts for the windows that redirected the shop's ventilation system back over its own roof.

6 / Early sketches developed different variations on a similar concept.

7 / A computer model showing Scarpa's idea to use Trex© in flowing forms on the street façade.

8 / Presentations to the client were ongoing, using 3-D drawings, renderings and plans.

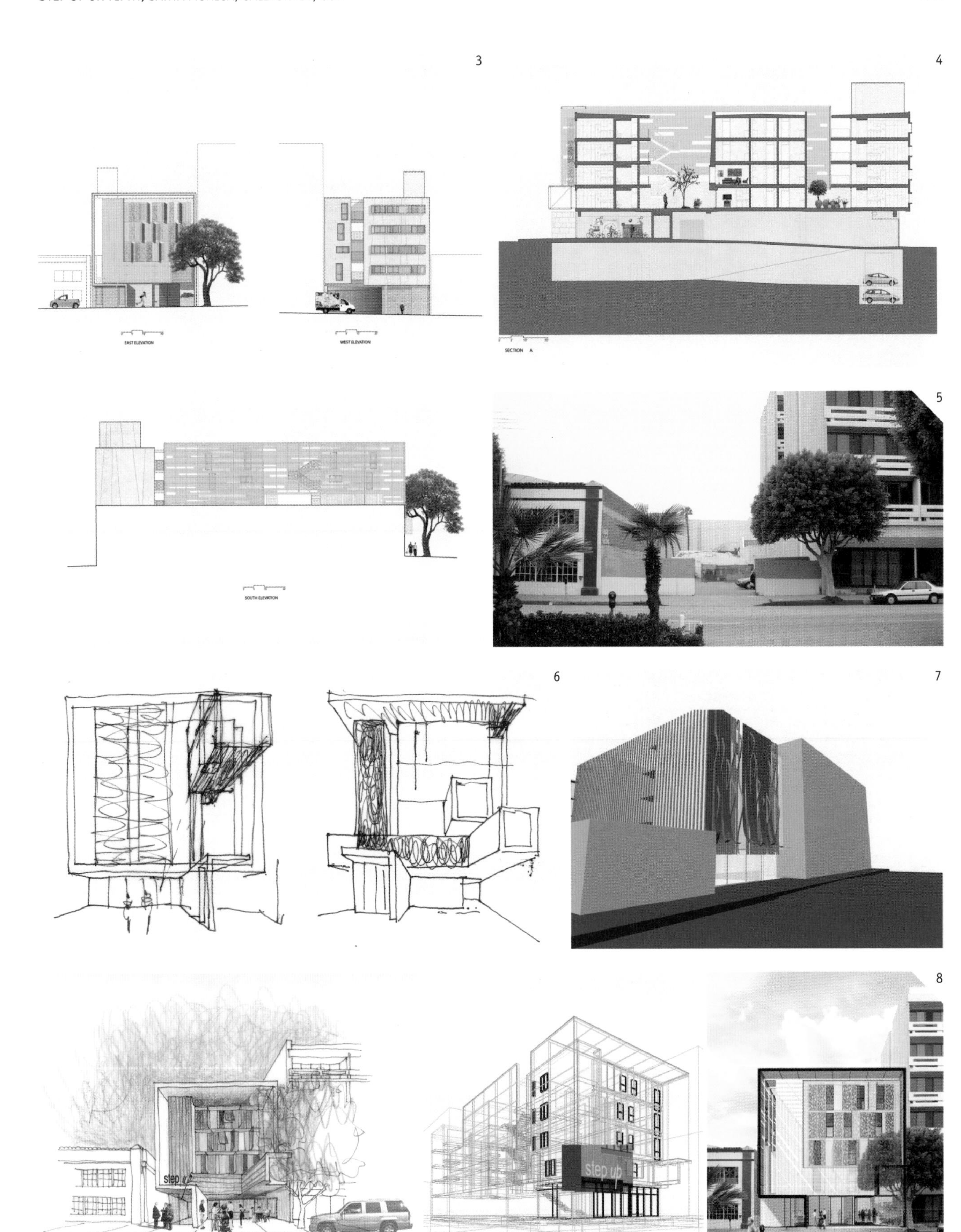
EAST ELEVATION
WEST ELEVATION
SECTION A
SOUTH ELEVATION
step up

3

4

5

6

7

8

9

10

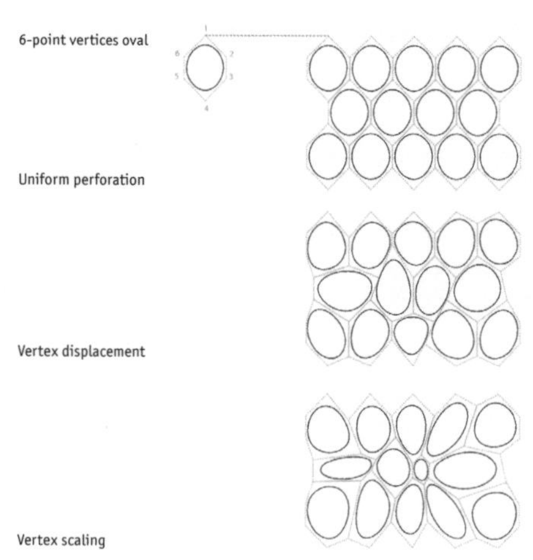

11

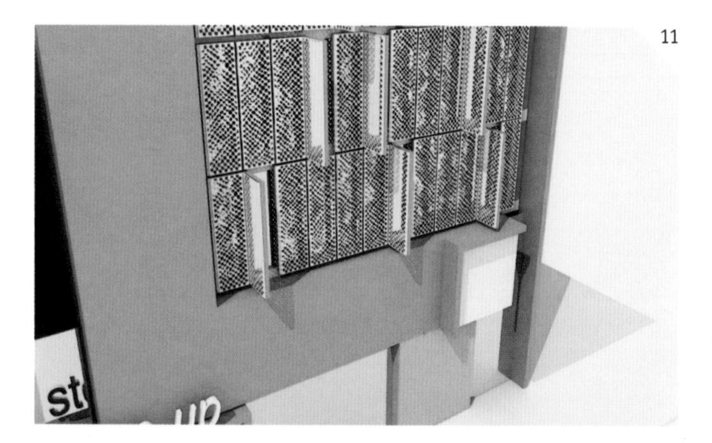

12

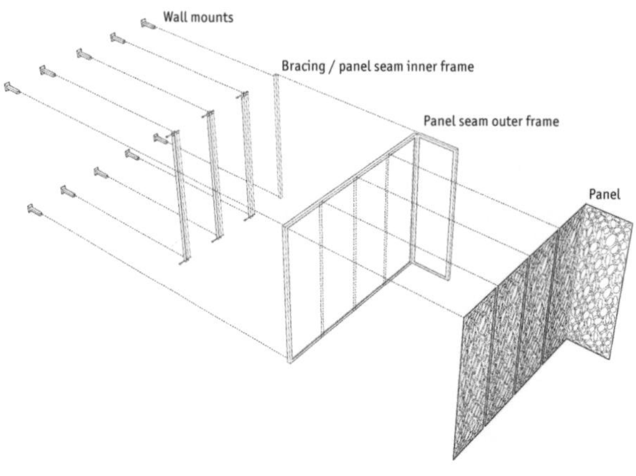

13

9 / Models were used in tandem with computer modelling for in-house design development. Physical models are produced for presentation only if specifically requested.

10 / Many iterations for the patterning of the screen were made to find the most efficient use of the aluminium and to gauge the best balance between privacy and solar control; variation A is shown here. The perforations are morphed using a software program to first displace and then scale the vertices, giving an irregular design.

11 / Maquette: Five full-scale prototypes of possible screen designs were made, as were test models.

12 / Diagram showing how the screens are attached to the wall.

13 / The building's exterior metal screens function as a light filter and shading device, but also create visual and acoustic privacy in a dense urban environment. They were designed to Scarpa's fabrication drawings and were water-jet-cut off site.

14 / Construction drawing for the screens on the west and east elevations with screen attachment detail: The architect worked closely with the engineer on the complex wooden framework and on the shear wall layout. Shear walls were used extensively to support vertical loads and prevent deformation of the frame.

14

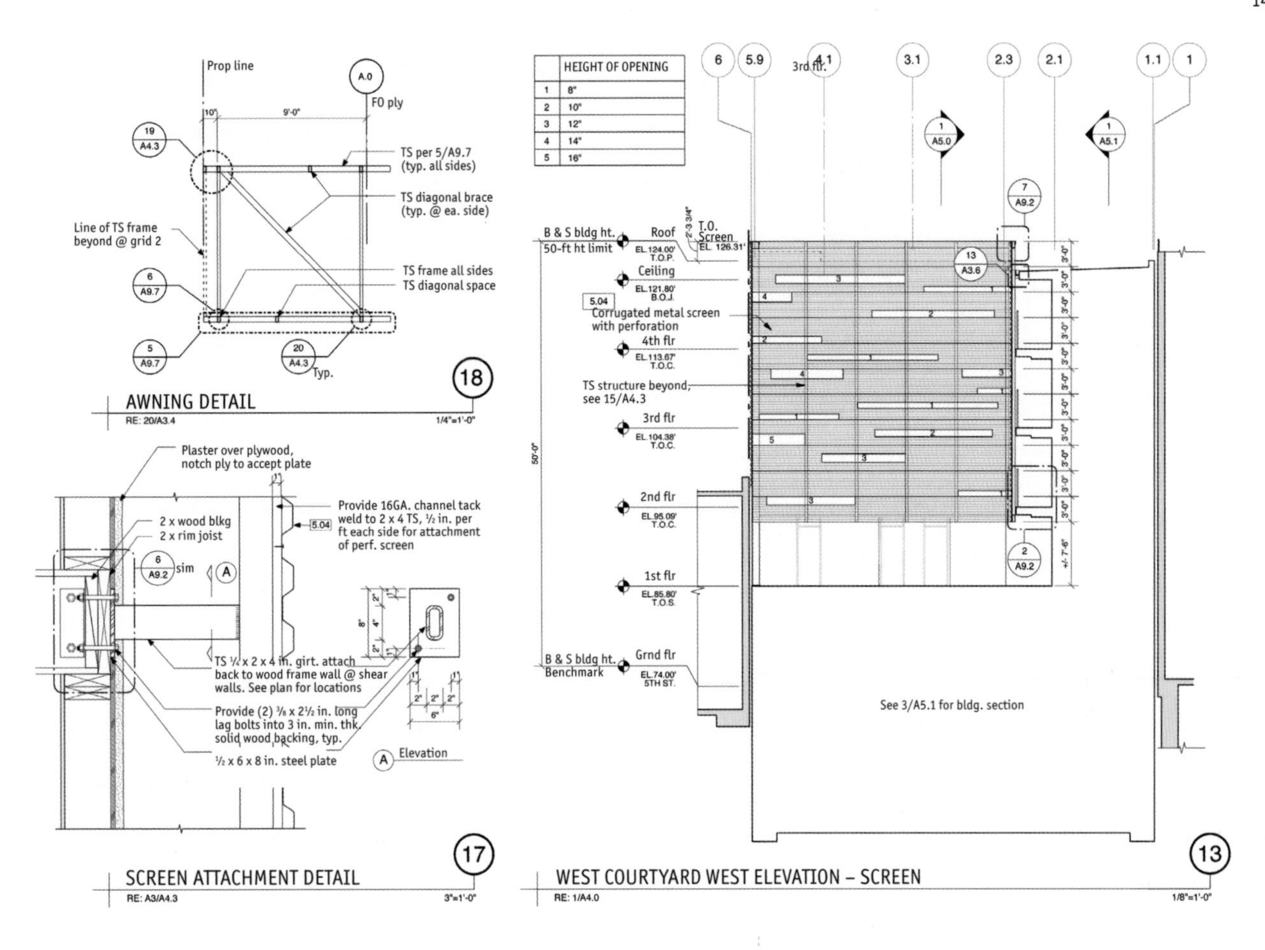
Prop line
FO ply
TS per 5/A9.7 (typ. all sides)
TS diagonal brace (typ. @ ea. side)
Line of TS frame beyond @ grid 2
TS frame all sides
TS diagonal space
Typ.
AWNING DETAIL
RE: 20/A3.4
1/4"=1'-0"
Plaster over plywood, notch ply to accept plate
Provide 16GA. channel tack weld to 2 x 4 TS, ½ in. per ft each side for attachment of perf. screen
2 x wood blkg
2 x rim joist
sim
TS ¼ x 2 x 4 in. girt. attach back to wood frame wall @ shear walls. See plan for locations
Provide (2) ⅜ x 2½ in. long lag bolts into 3 in. min. thk. solid wood backing, typ.
½ x 6 x 8 in. steel plate
Elevation
SCREEN ATTACHMENT DETAIL
RE: A3/A4.3
3"=1'-0"
HEIGHT OF OPENING
1 8"
2 10"
3 12"
4 14"
5 16"
B & S bldg ht.
50-ft ht limit
Roof
T.O. Screen
Ceiling
Corrugated metal screen with perforation
4th flr
TS structure beyond, see 15/A4.3
3rd flr
2nd flr
1st flr
B & S bldg ht. Benchmark
Grnd flr
See 3/A5.1 for bldg. section
WEST COURTYARD WEST ELEVATION – SCREEN
RE: 1/A4.0
1/8"=1'-0"

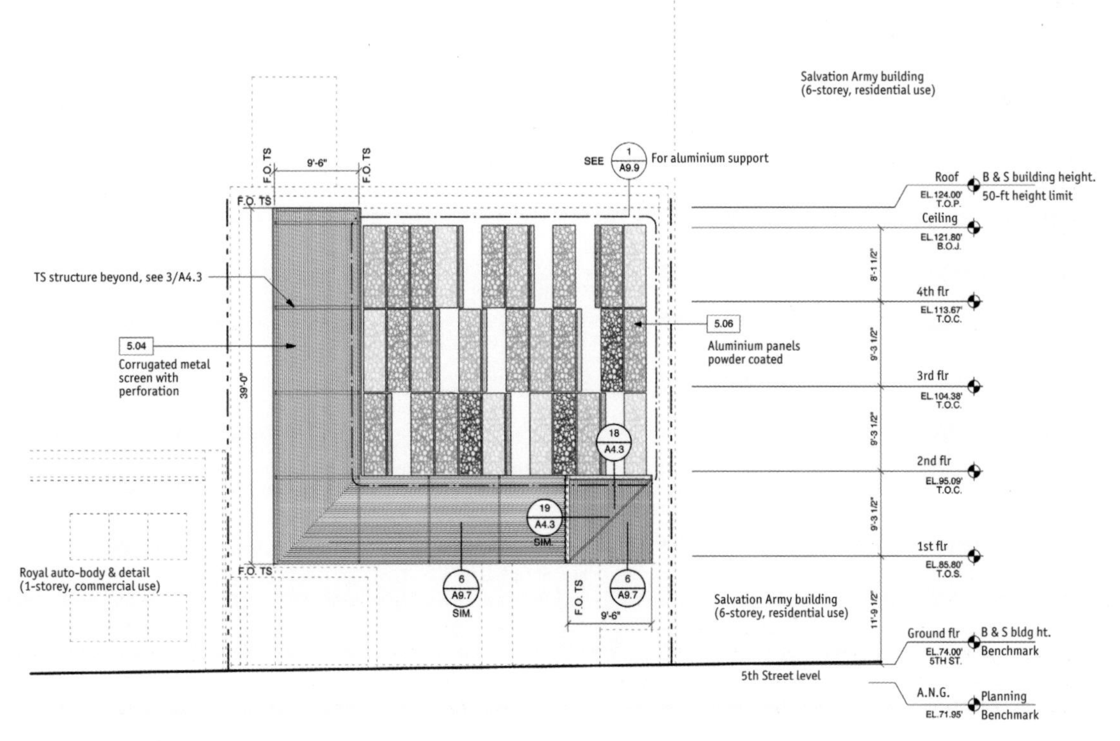
Salvation Army building (6-storey, residential use)
SEE
For aluminium support
F.O. TS
9'-6"
TS structure beyond, see 3/A4.3
5.04
Corrugated metal screen with perforation
5.06
Aluminium panels powder coated
Roof
B & S building height. 50-ft height limit
Ceiling
4th flr
3rd flr
2nd flr
1st flr
Royal auto-body & detail (1-storey, commercial use)
Salvation Army building (6-storey, residential use)
Ground flr
B & S bldg ht. Benchmark
5th Street level
A.N.G.
Planning Benchmark

1

EAST ELEVATION – SCREEN

15

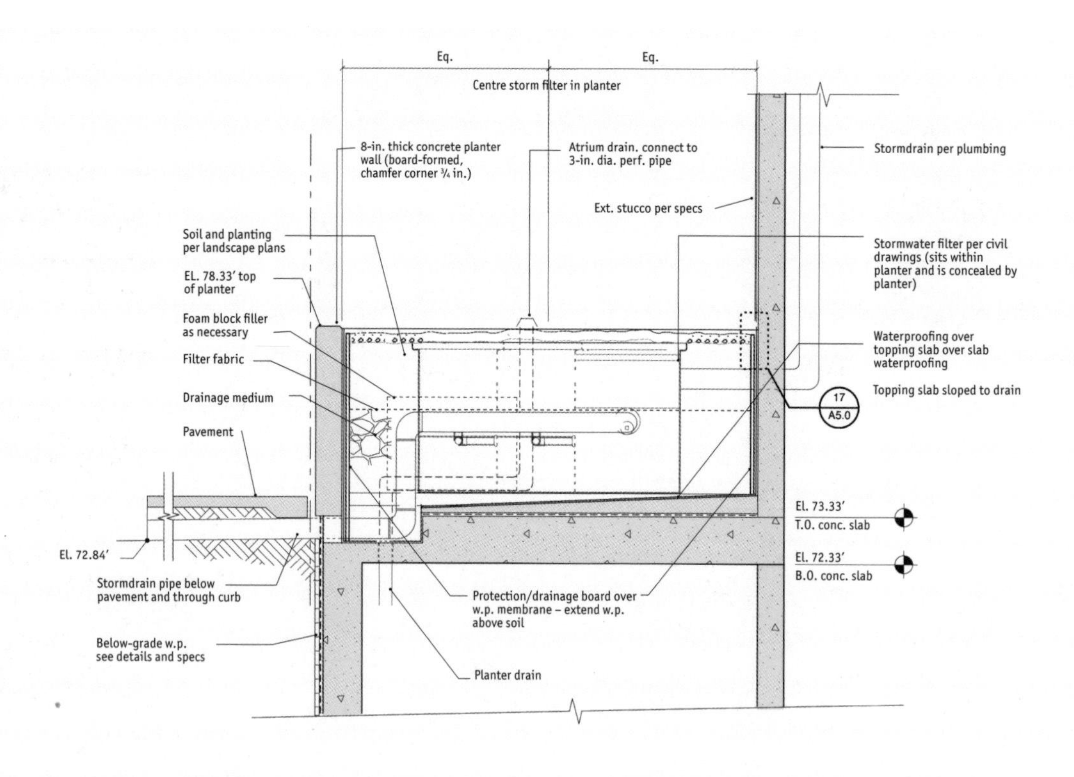

16

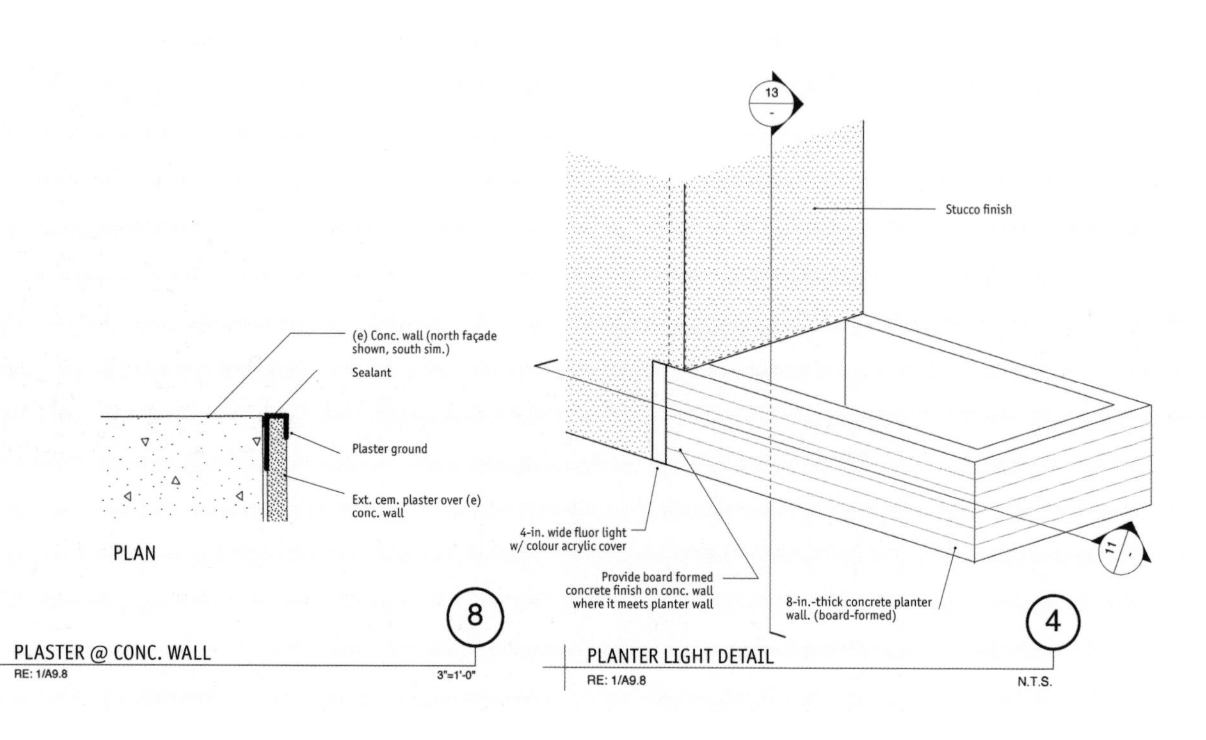

15 / Detail drawing of external concrete planter: 100 per cent of precipitation is captured by planters on site and collected in a subsurface infiltration system. It is returned to the groundwater only after being cleaned of pollutants.

16 / Planter light detail: The planter intersects a concrete and a stucco wall. At the small overlapping enclosure at this junction the drawing shows provision for an exterior light. An oversight by the contractor meant that the gap was not made and the detail had to be redesigned without the light to save money and time. Lack of shop drawings meant this was not an isolated incident, and the architect had to be continuously present on site to correct errors and make adjustments in the field.

17 / Series of construction shots showing the timber frame, shear walls (which were eventually covered in stucco) and the addition of the screens. The construction process was managed to be as resource-efficient as possible. The architects provided the contractor with a waste management plan that resulted in over 70 per cent of the construction waste being recycled.

18 / Local planning dictates that multistorey buildings have to be set back from the street to avoid casting long shadows on the surrounding structures. To maximize the floor space and thus create as many units as possible, the architects shifted planes and punched holes in the design instead of employing a conventional staggered set-back strategy. The building averaged the required 24.4 m (80 ft) of set-backs across its entire surface. The highly perforated south wall is only 1.5 m (5 ft) from its neighbouring structure.

19 / The courtyards are arranged to induce airflow and provide maximum natural light. Other passive strategies include: locating and orienting the building to control solar cooling loads and exposure to prevailing winds; shaping the building and designing windows to make use of natural ventilation; shading south-facing windows and minimizing west-facing glazing.

20 / Interior of one of the units: Each studio has its own bathroom and kitchenette. Although the studios have limited floor area, 3-m (10-ft) -high ceilings, ceiling fans, and large windows with lots of natural light and abundant cross-ventilation make them feel bright and spacious. To maximize the space, Murphy beds double as sofas during the day.

Bodegas Protos

Rogers Stirk Harbour + Partners (RSHP)

Location: Peñafiel, Valladolid, Spain
Principal use: Winery
Client: Bodegas Protos
Site area: 7,500 m² (80,729¼ ft²)
Interior area: 18,980 m² (204,298¾ ft²)

Total build area: 23,090 m² (248,538½ ft²)
Design period: June 2003 – October 2006
Construction period: October 2006 – September 2008
Budget: £15,000,000

Richard Rogers is the latest in a long line of world-acclaimed architects who have turned their hand to the design of wineries, thanks to an industry that has come to recognize the potential marketing gains signature buildings can bring by raising the profile of a brand.

Peñafiel, a small village near Valladolid in Castille, northern Spain, has been home to Bodegas Protos since 1927 when a consortium of 250 wine growers formed a cooperative to maximize production. Peñafiel is dominated by its medieval castle that sits on top of a rocky outcrop and surveys the surrounding countryside. Taking advantage of the thermal properties of the caves beneath the castle, the winery was originally housed in a subterranean system of more than 2 kilometres (1¼ miles) of tunnels and galleries used for ageing the wine, but in recent years it could no longer respond to the increasing demand for Protos wines. RSHP (formerly Richard Rogers Partnership) was commissioned to extend and modernize the facilities.

The modern *bodegas* is connected to the old via an underground link and was built as a contemporary reinterpretation of traditional winery construction. Graham Stirk, one of RSHP's five senior directors and project director for this building, is quick to point out that its design reflects the core concerns of the company – legibility, flexibility, energy efficiency and teamwork – and has its origins in the Reliance Controls electronics factory completed by Rogers and Norman Foster in 1969. Going against current trends, the architecture of the factory unified blue- and white-collar workers, emphasizing the importance of team dynamics and operational efficiency.

Although Bodegas Protos wanted a structure that would raise the profile of the cooperative and had commissioned RSHP for this reason, it primarily wanted a wine-making – rather than a visitor – facility and was wary of making too bold a statement.

Stirk's research examined neighbouring *bodegas*, which he discovered were typified by kitsch Spanish-style façades behind which huge energy-guzzling air-conditioned lightweight sheds were hidden; all at surface level.

Respecting the three necessary stages of wine production – fermentation, maturation/storage and bottling – his response showed deference to both the original Bodegas Protos and the Reliance Controls building. Designing in section, he pushed all the functions that needed steady-state control (no daylight and a constant temperature) below ground and the vats and office areas were placed at two different levels above ground. The idea was that both front-of-house and back-of-house should be located under one roof in a democratic, adaptable and easily readable space. Proposing one unified interior reduced the wall area needed and thus allowed more of the restricted budget to be used on better quality materials. From the beginning the triangular site governed the plan, with each of the angles forming a key entrance: public and service delivery access at either side of the thick end of the wedge, and the grapes arriving at the apex.

Unusually, because of the strength of the design concept, the project was moved from Rogers' London office to Spain at a very early stage of development and there was close cooperation between the architect, client, co-architect, agro-industrial consultants and engineers throughout the process. Protos was heavily involved in making decisions about function, but did not contradict aesthetic judgements unless there were financial implications. Presentations were kept simple using explanatory diagrams, models and discussion. Each stage of the thought process was explained to the client, with rejected ideas shown alongside the chosen options.

The principle of the design was retained, although it went through a series of iterations that examined materiality, design details and the construction of the roof. Timber was chosen in preference to steel for the vaults, to meet the £100-per-square-foot budget. The concrete structural elements were precast and the timber frame manufactured off site, which kept the costs low and meant quality control was tighter. Local stone was sourced for the rampart walls that conceal ventilation and servicing requirements. The modular form of the five interlinked barrel vaults supported by parabolic arches breaks down the overall mass and scale to create an edifice that is sympathetic to the surrounding buildings and the countryside. In moving from the notion of semicircular arches to parabolic arches, the engineers were able to halve the amount of material needed to bridge the five 5.5-metre (18-foot) spans, which yielded further significant savings. Removing the need for columns also kept the ground-floor space open and flexible.

The use of traditional earthy materials belies the sophistication of the roof structure as well as the technical processes involved in wine-making, but contextually they complement the Castilian countryside and the vernacular architecture of Peñafiel. In conclusion Stirk maintains: 'With the winery, I don't think it's about the materiality but more about the context. I think if we had built something in colourful and shiny steel it wouldn't have worked.' He continues, 'It would have appeared immensely insubstantial and that's not something we would want to represent in an industry that has been happening over thousands of years. It's all about emphasis.'

1 / Bodegas Protos is defined by its parabolic roof shells supported on laminated-timber arches. Glazed façades on either side offer openness and transparency, making visible what is usually hidden in the anonymous and soulless production facilities that typify the wine-making industry.

1

1 Public entrance
2 Accessible deck over fermentation tanks
3 Covered bay – grapes in
4 Void over sunken garden
5 Tunnel link to existing winery
6 Production/fermentation tanks
7 Loading bay – wine out
8 Offices
9 Plant
10 Bottle room
11 Barrel room
12 Tasting suite
13 Sunken garden

2

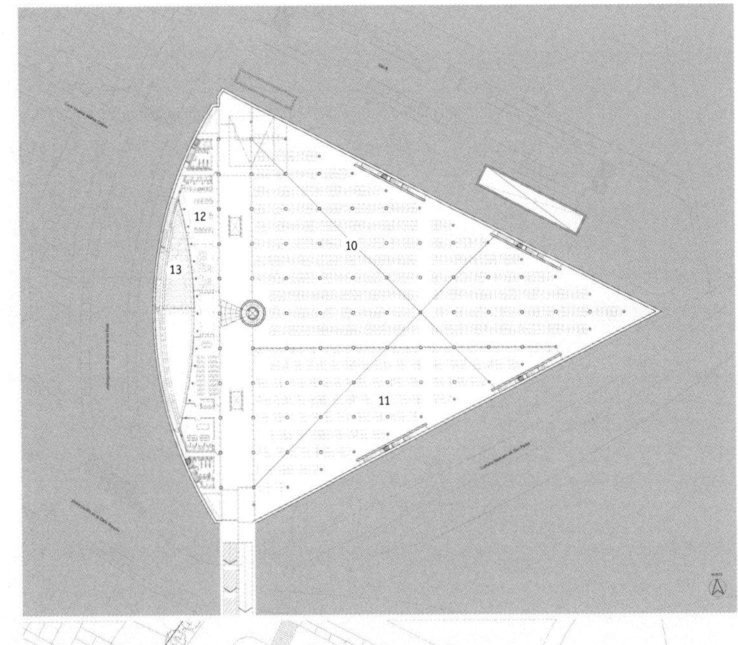

CELLAR/MEZZANINE-LEVEL PLAN

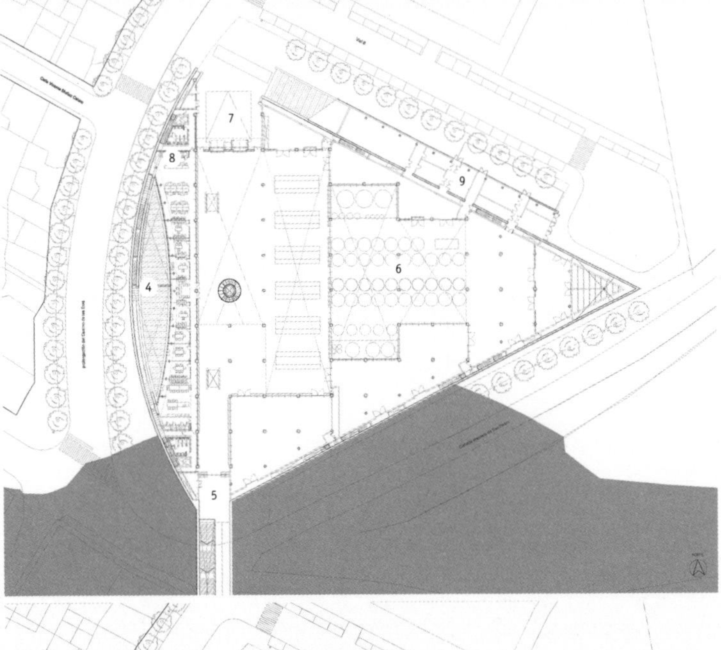

PRODUCTION-LEVEL PLAN

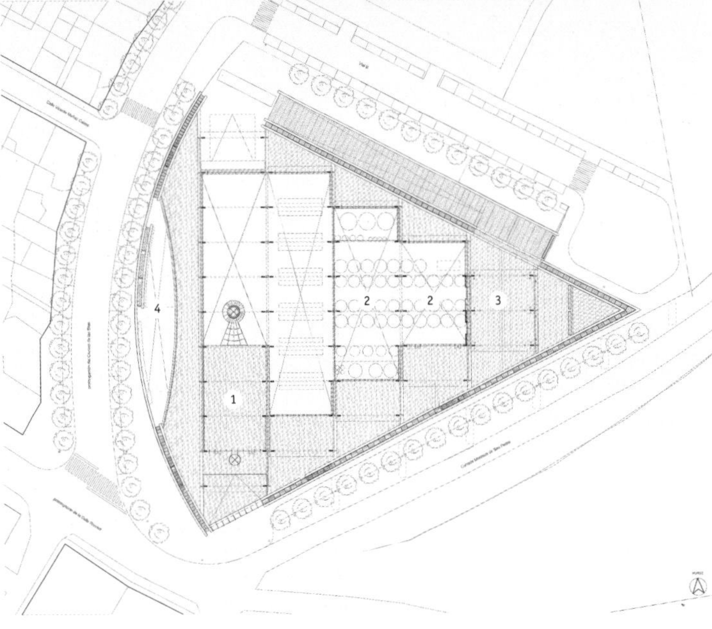

ENTRY/GRAPE-DELIVERY-LEVEL PLAN

3

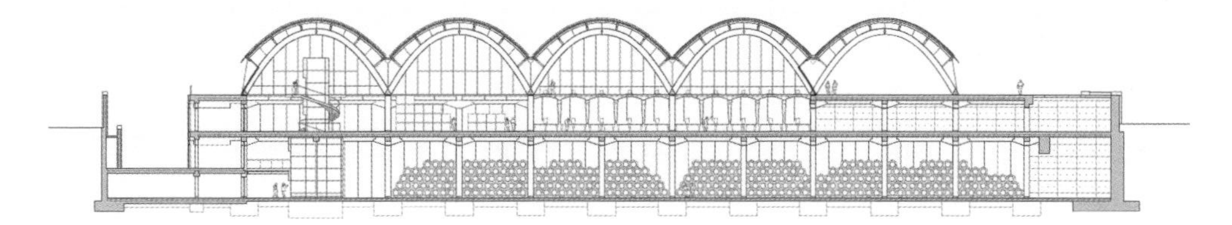

4

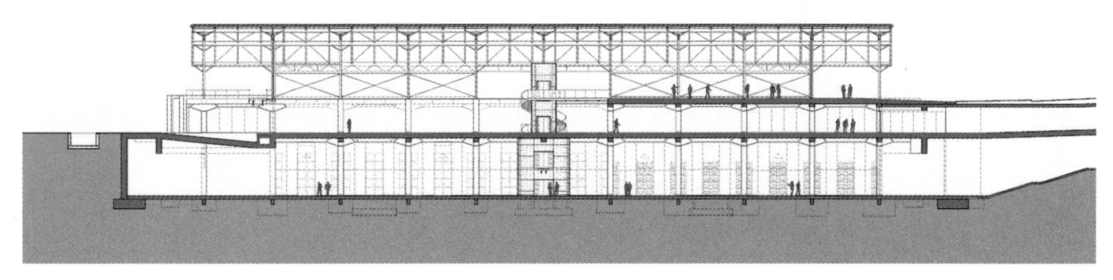

5

6

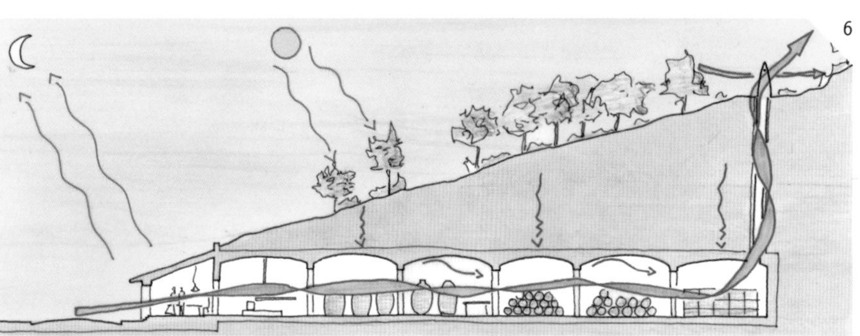

7

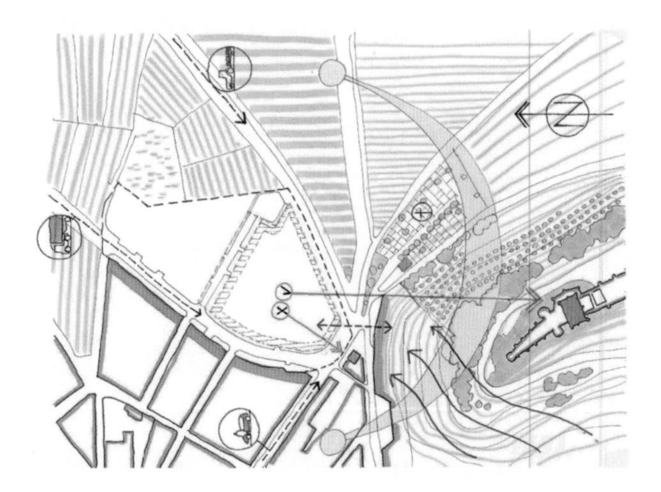

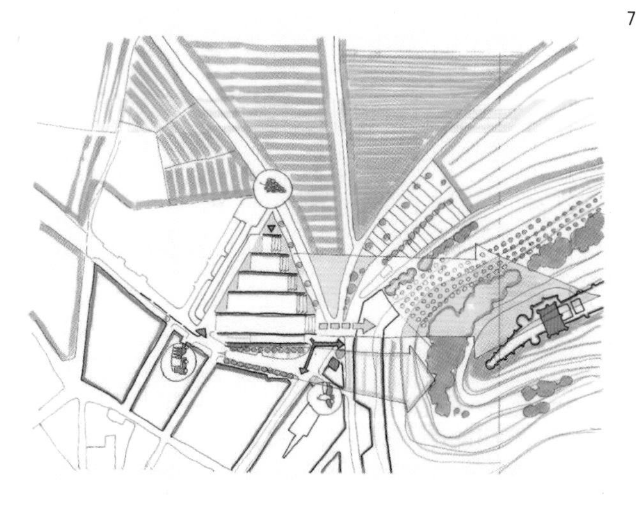

2 / Entry-, production- and cellar-/ mezzanine-level plans.

3 / East–west section.

4 / North–south section.

5 / The original Bodegas Protos is situated underground in the caves beneath the castle. Stone cairns are used for ventilation.

6 / Hand-drawn sketch showing the natural thermal advantages of placing the original facility below ground.

7 / RSHP always produces analysis drawings that illustrate what's present and its response to the situation. These are often not made at the same time but are always presented simultaneously as this illustrates a summary of ideas and directions that have been explored.

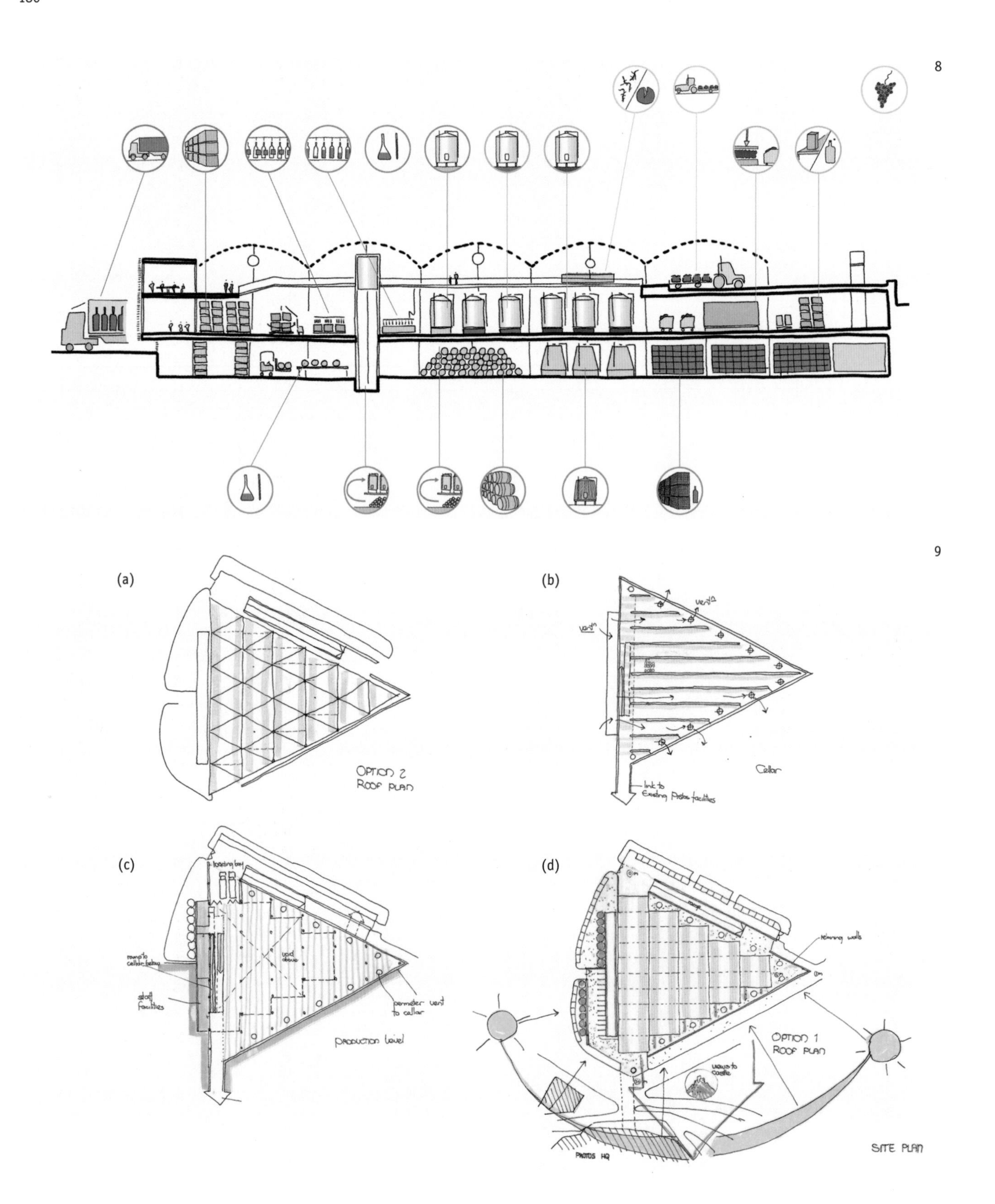

8 / A pictogram was shown to the client in one of the first meetings. Symbols represent the different processes of wine-making and were used to demonstrate how they could work in section across the building.

9 / Early sketches made in the first few weeks: they were used in-house to look at the possibility of (a) creating one simple big roof and (b) a system of vaults like the existing tunnels under the hill; and also to look at (c) the flexibility in the production level and (d) the organization towards the castle and direction of the sun as well as a roof variant. They show how function is considered before a working plan is fully delineated.

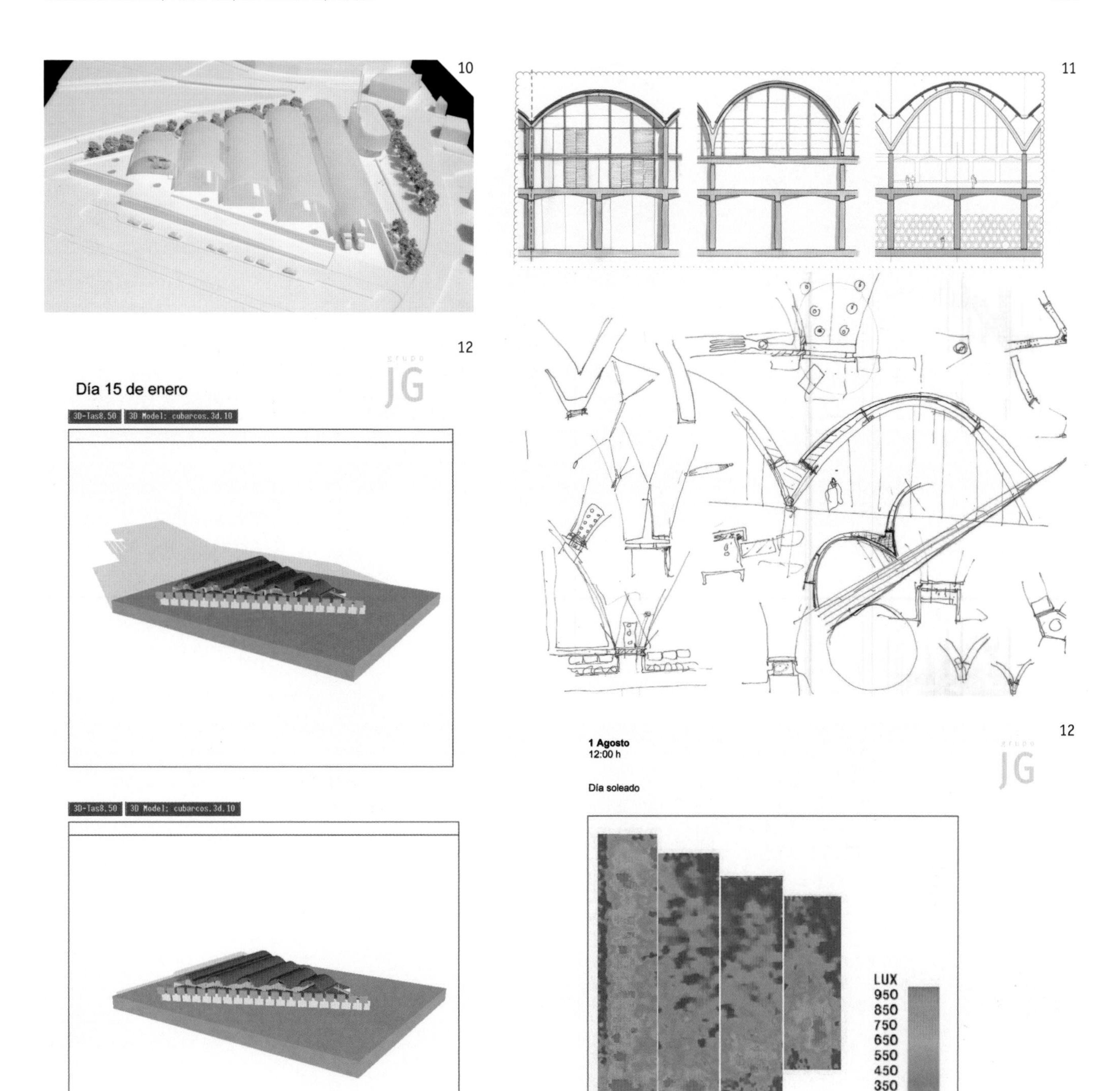

10 / Early presentation model showing an initial idea to have the front-of-house located in a separate building: RSHP has its own modelling workshop and produces maquettes that increase in refinement throughout the design process.

11 / Series of drawings showing the evolution of the roofing system from an arch supported by columns to barrel vaults separated from the supporting arches: Detaching the roof from the structure meant there were no obstructions and allowed vats to be moved easily in the large open space beneath. Details were discussed at the same time, here how the junction of the arches could work and be made waterproof.

12 / Daylight studies investigating solar implications: Specified lux levels had to be maintained. To determine the need for shading, engineers studied solar paths at different times of the day. A balance was sought between the amount of light allowed into the production level (as much as possible so that it could be generally naturally lit) and solar gain through the windows that would result in a build-up of heat.

13

14

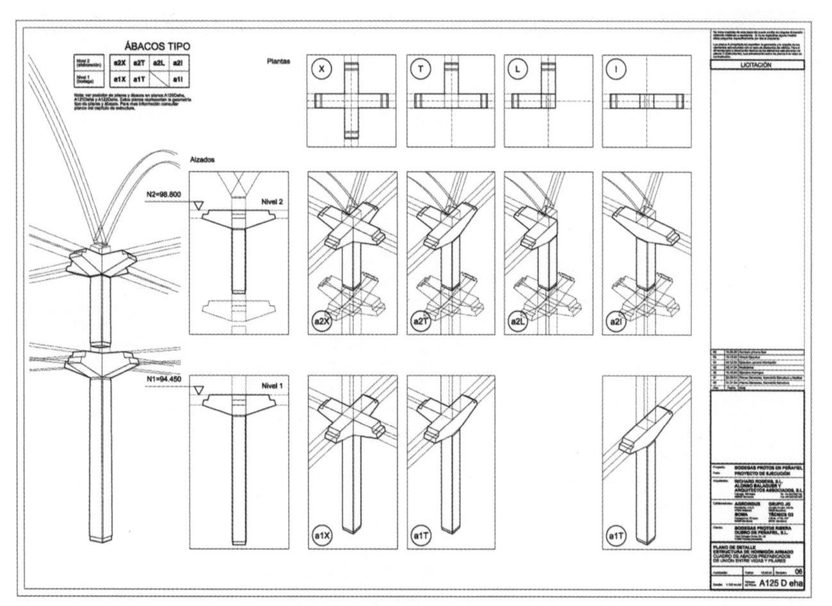

15

16

17

18

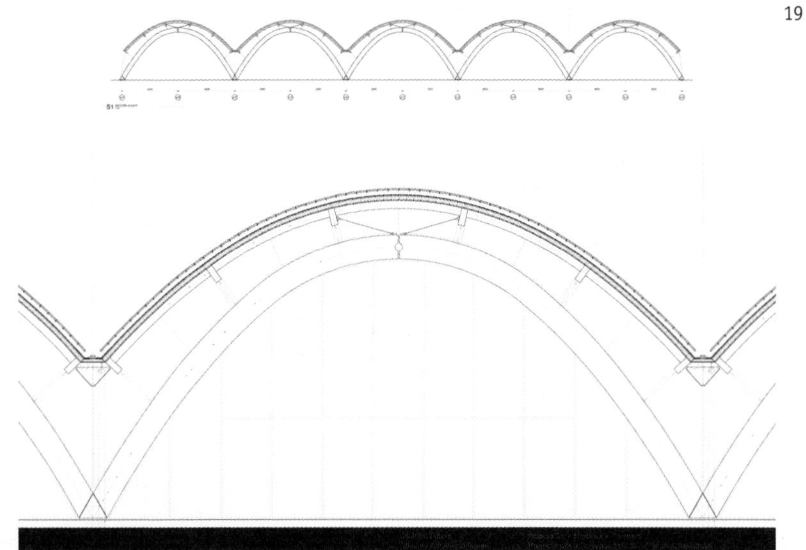

19

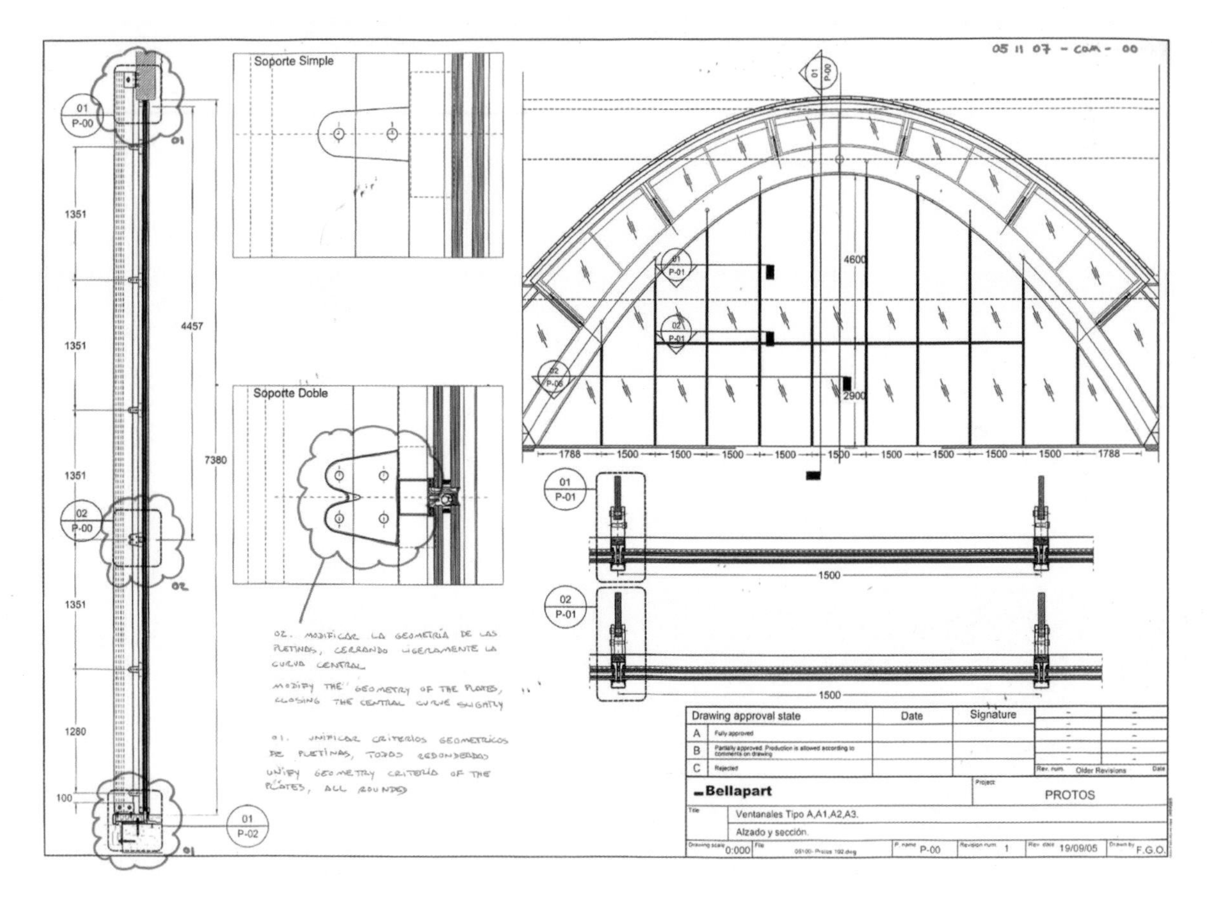

20

13 / Presentation perspective drawing of the final design.

14 / A massive 12-m (39-ft) hole is dug.

15 / Detail design drawing of the precast concrete structural elements and how they fit together.

16 / The concrete elements (and prefabricated timber) were key in the design and construction process, and off-site manufacture meant quality control was tighter. RSHP worked closely with industry on the specifications, design, production and logistics of these parts.

17 / The elements on site: The structure was erected Meccano-style. It was designed to be self-supporting in intermediate phases to create a growing skeleton. This resulted in a faster construction programme.

18 / The cellar with some of the services in place. The concrete slab was laid afterwards.

19 / Model and detail drawing used to discuss how the barrel vault is secured to the parabolic arches by means of props, allowing separation between the two elements.

20 / The juncture between the timber and the glazing was complicated, and took two years to resolve in collaboration with the glazing contractor. RSHP believe that once they have defined basic principles it is best to work closely with the producers. Their detailed design drawings are generic and are adapted in dialogue with the manufacturers.

21

1 Ceramic piece type Terreal Maestral Model 300 x 1480 x 40 mm. Colour red

2 Stainless steel Terreal anchor piece for type pieces

3 Waterproofing EPDM rubber sheet on geotextile timber battens

4 Laminated pine batten type with autoclave treatment to the curvature of the covering. 100 x 132 mm section with rounded top edges

5 Mechanical fixing of battens to the sandwich panel. Screw head embedded in the batten using mechanical slot

6 Mechanical fixing of battens to the roof structure (rafters). Screw head embedded in the batten using mechanical slot

7 Waterproofing EPDM rubber sheet on geotextile of the sandwich-type panel covers

8 Freestanding sandwich panel made of layers of spruce 27 mm, polystyrene 100 mm and spruce 27 mm

9 Hidden diagonal gutter formed by section U-shaped aluminium of 190 x 140 x 140 mm exteriors

10 End piece setting gutter east-west perimeters made from sections of stainless steel

11 Gargoyle east-west perimeter made from stainless steel tube 80 mm in diameter

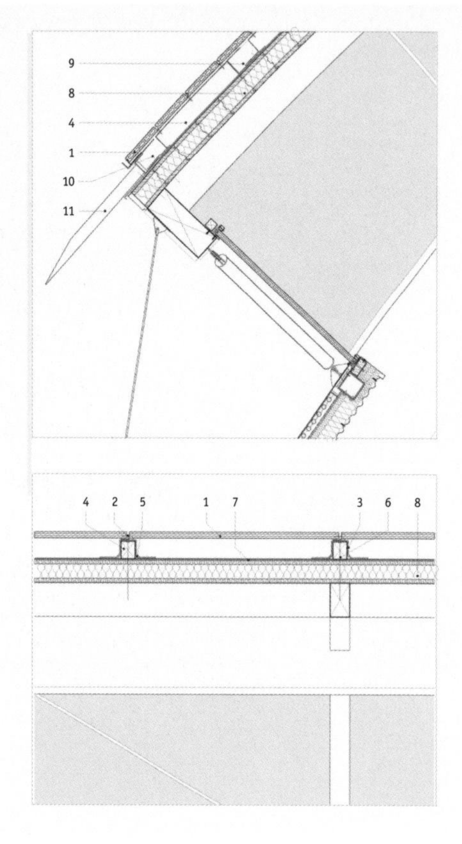

22

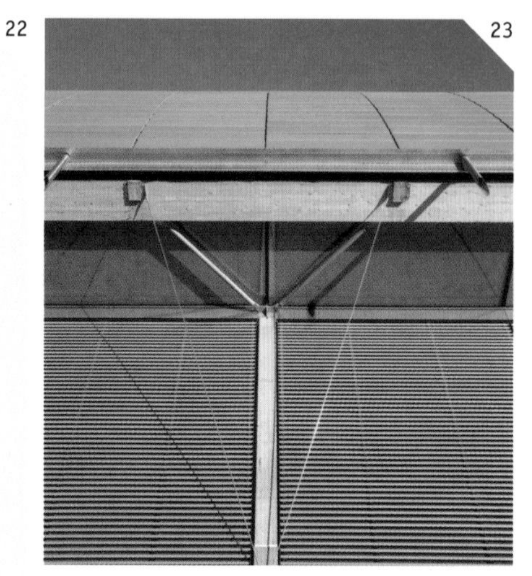

23

24

21 / The timber frame was prefabricated off site. The roof came in c. 1,000 sections that were then bolted together. The timber for the parabolic arches was originally to be manufactured as one piece, but was eventually split into two for transport purposes.

22 / Shop drawing showing how the layers of the roof are built up: The terracotta tiling sits on a waterproof membrane. An air chamber dissipates heat build-up via direct sun radiation to the roof. Gargoyles for drainage are placed in this gap.

23 / Wire-like cables that reach the ground stop the vaults moving sideways and avoid the need for diagonal supports. They tie the roof down in every direction and tether it to the floor.

24 / Tiling on site.

25 / On the southern side the roof overhangs the façade, shading the interior from the fierce sun.

26 / The winery sits beneath the medieval castle (now home to a wine museum) that dominates Peñafiel. The roof structure, topped by terracotta tiles, was designed to be seen from above and mimics the vernacular architecture. The barrel vaults increase in size to fit the triangular site.

27 / Grapes are unloaded directly into vats that are moved above the fermentation tanks below. The tanks are visible through the deck-and-rail system of the ground floor.

28 / A sunken elliptical courtyard is enclosed by offices and visitor areas, and frames a view of the castle above. It also allows light into the basement.

Maggie's London

Rogers Stirk Harbour + Partners (RSHP)

Location: London, UK
Principal use: Cancer support centre
Client: Maggie's
Site area: 1,983 m² (21,344¾ ft²)
Interior area: 370 m² (3,982½ ft²)
Total build area: 615 m² (6,619¾ ft²)
Design period: September 2001 – August 2005
Construction period: August 2006 – April 2008
Budget: £2,100,000

Maggie's London, by Rogers Stirk Harbour + Partners won the Stirling Prize in 2009. At the time the judges spoke of the unique strength of the design: 'How is it possible that a building can generate an immediate and pervasive sense of welcome, warmth, serenity – and even love – in the context of a frantic Hammersmith thoroughfare, and in the shadow of a dauntingly huge NHS hospital?'

Maggie's Centres are the brainchild of Maggie Keswick (wife of the architectural theorist Charles Jencks) who died of cancer in 1995. Her experience of having to undergo chemotherapy in sterile and alienating hospital treatment rooms led to her spending the last 18 months of her life drawing up plans for a cancer support centre. She believed that architecture and environment can affect the way you feel and her concept was for a bright and life-embracing oasis of well-being for patients, built in close proximity to a large hospital but screened from its clinical character. Charles Jencks has since honoured his wife's legacy in a nationwide string of buildings by a lengthening list of high-profile architects: Frank Gehry, Zaha Hadid, Rem Koolhaas, Piers Gough and Richard Rogers to name a few. The projected provision of facilities, offering emotional, psychological and practical support to cancer sufferers, numbers 13.

The client approached Rogers with a mandate that was unique and particular. Apart from the programming it asked for a space that would be both uplifting and protective, in which people could find the strength to live with hope and joy in the face of their diagnosis. The project was assigned to partner Ivan Harbour who, used to the generative power of constraint, was at first intimidated by the openness of the brief and how to recreate atmosphere and emotion in built form. Also, the restrictive corner site in the grounds of Charing Cross Hospital was hostile. Not only did the hospital's institutional buildings loom over it, but it abutted the noisy and polluted streetscape of Fulham Palace Road. He realized that the structure had to be artistic and sculptural to allow its small dimensions to stand out in the overpowering context, and that, in addition, it needed to be sheltered from its unfriendly surroundings.

Harbour's first sketches played with the idea of keeping the environment at bay by way of a spiral that, like a snail's shell, led people into the heart of the building and safeguarded them from the outside world. Through a series of further sketches and models he investigated how the envelope could also form the roof in an all-protective structure. He describes the breakthrough for the concept being the moment when he decided to separate the two.

The design was developed collaboratively with the client, who took up residence in RSHP's offices and was instrumental in all decisions. The practice approaches every project in the same manner, whether it's the 370 square metres (3,982 square feet) of Maggie's or the 1.2 million square metres (13 million square feet) of Terminal 4, Barajas Airport, Madrid (2005). The company is non-hierarchical and weekly forums are held during which all are welcome to express their opinions and put forward ideas; a collegiate approach, it maintains, is a valuable creative force. Engineers and consultants are brought in from the schematic design stage, so they become part of the team and design process and are involved beyond the technical aspects of construction. Plans are kept simple. Maggie's, the Pompidou Centre, Lloyd's of London and the Bordeaux Law Courts all share straightforward rectangular layouts but their beauty and complexity lie in the third dimension.

The centre is conceived as a series of four 'tables', the legs of which embrace the sitting rooms, consulting rooms, library and bathrooms. The kitchen, a double-height space at the centre of the building, is framed by the edges of the tables. The upper-level spaces – sitting rooms and offices – are placed on the table tops, where each is split into an internal space and an outside terrace. The whole is capped by a 'floating roof' that oversails the outer walls and acts as the enclosure to the heart of the building. Small courtyards are formed between the building and its walls.

Light fills the building through the glazed walls at first-floor level and through openings in the roof. Despite being on a busy main road, the centre is quiet inside, thanks to the protection of the wall and birch trees which wrap around it. RSHP worked with the client on all aspects of the interiors, not only the layout but also on the FF&E (furniture, fixtures and equipment). Harbour's intention was that Maggie's should feel like a home – but even better – and he insisted on sourcing design classics (rugs by Paolo Lenti and furniture by Alvar Aalto) and ensuring that the materials used, the birch-faced ply and fair-faced concrete, were of the utmost quality to evoke a comfortable, inviting, calm and relaxed atmosphere.

In his book *The Architecture of Hope*, Charles Jencks poses the question, 'Is there an architecture that helps you to live?' The burnt orange of the centre immediately announces its warmth and energy. The domestically proportioned interiors are flooded with light, and the materials used are natural and homely: Rogers writes, 'When the scale is that small the smallest things matter – even the way the firewood is piled in the courtyards. Wood has character: if you pile it nicely it will give you a feeling of hearth and home.' No one is arguing that walking through the doors of Maggie's Centre, London, offers a miraculous cure, but by uniting soul and body the sanctuary helps patients to learn to live with cancer.

1 / Maggie's London offers an oasis of calm within its busy setting. With no visible means of support, the roof appears to hover over the protecting walls.

1

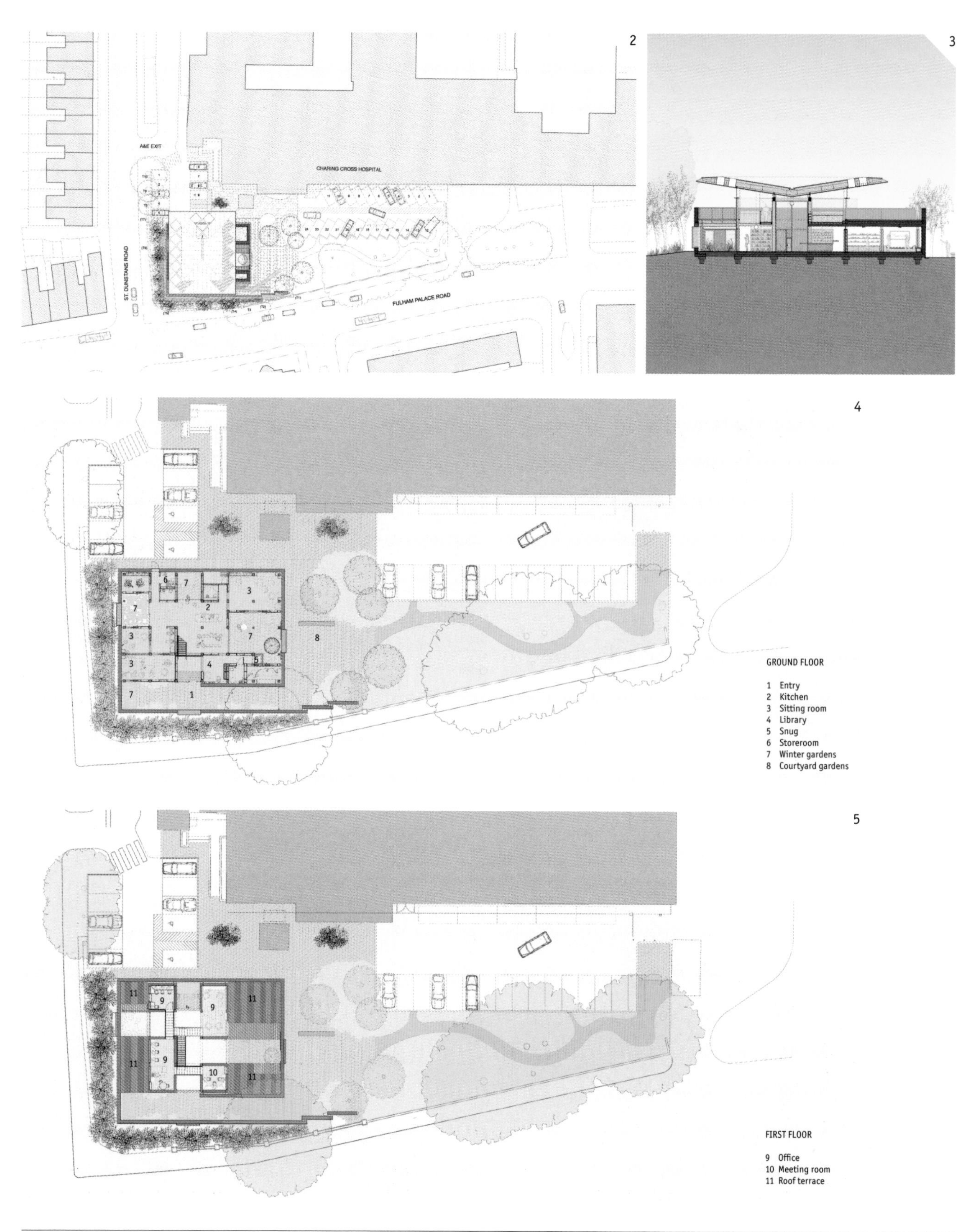

2 / Site plan.

3 / Section: The main load of the roof rests on the central concrete portal frame, and then cantilevers out and is propped at the window line to minimize vibration.

4 / Ground-floor plan: RSHP went contrary to a conventional urban formula by not placing the entrance on the street front. The decision was pragmatic, and protected the users from the sight of a funeral parlour across the road.

5 / First-floor plan.

6

7

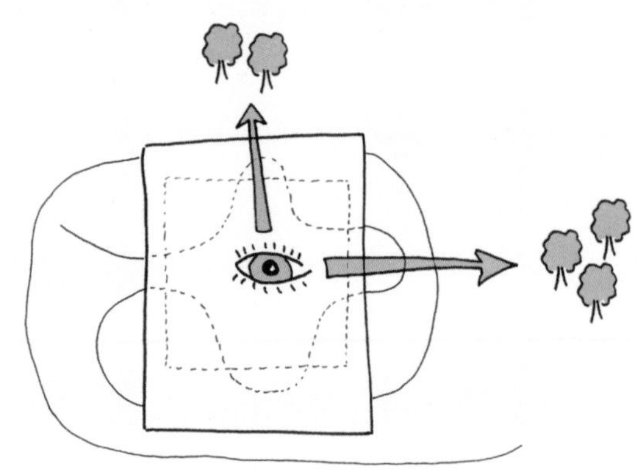

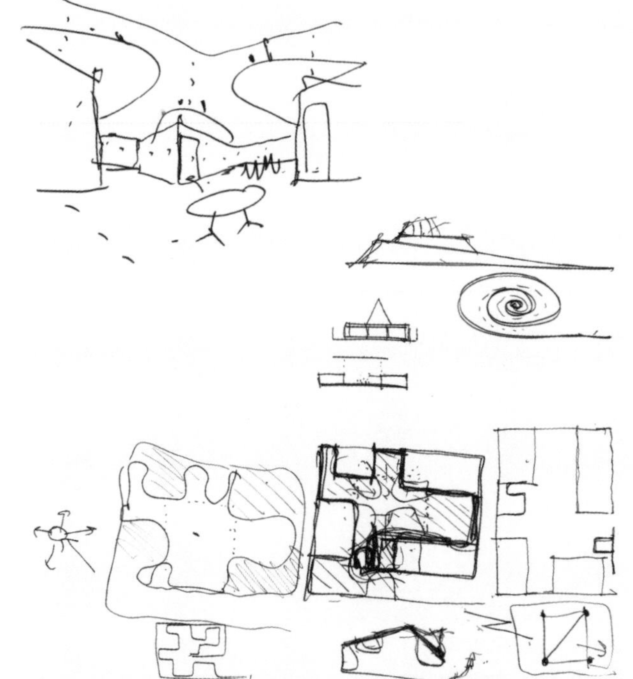

8

9

10

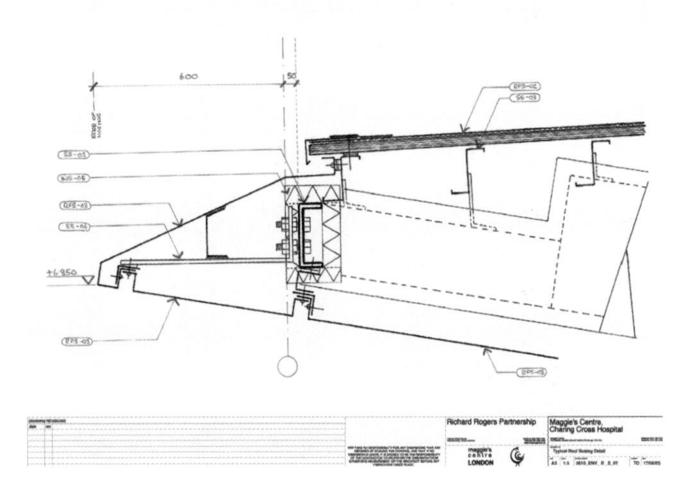

6 / The concept was developed from the idea of a protective spiral that would lead the users into the centre, the heart, of the building.

7 / The relationship with the client was informal. The design concepts were discussed as they evolved using sketches and models. Larger, formal presentations would not have conveyed the passion for the project. Harbour maintains that the design process does not stop until a building is complete.

8 / 3-D rendering used for planning: No objections were raised.

9 / RSHP has its own model shop. A series of models was made throughout the process and used as design aids; the final one (illustrated here) for presentation.

10 / Typical roof-nosing detail: Tender drawings were hand-drawn. They were fully detailed to ensure that estimates for each of the packages were as accurate as possible. This ensured that sufficient funds could be raised before the project went on site. It is vital that the budget is maintained when working for a charity.

11

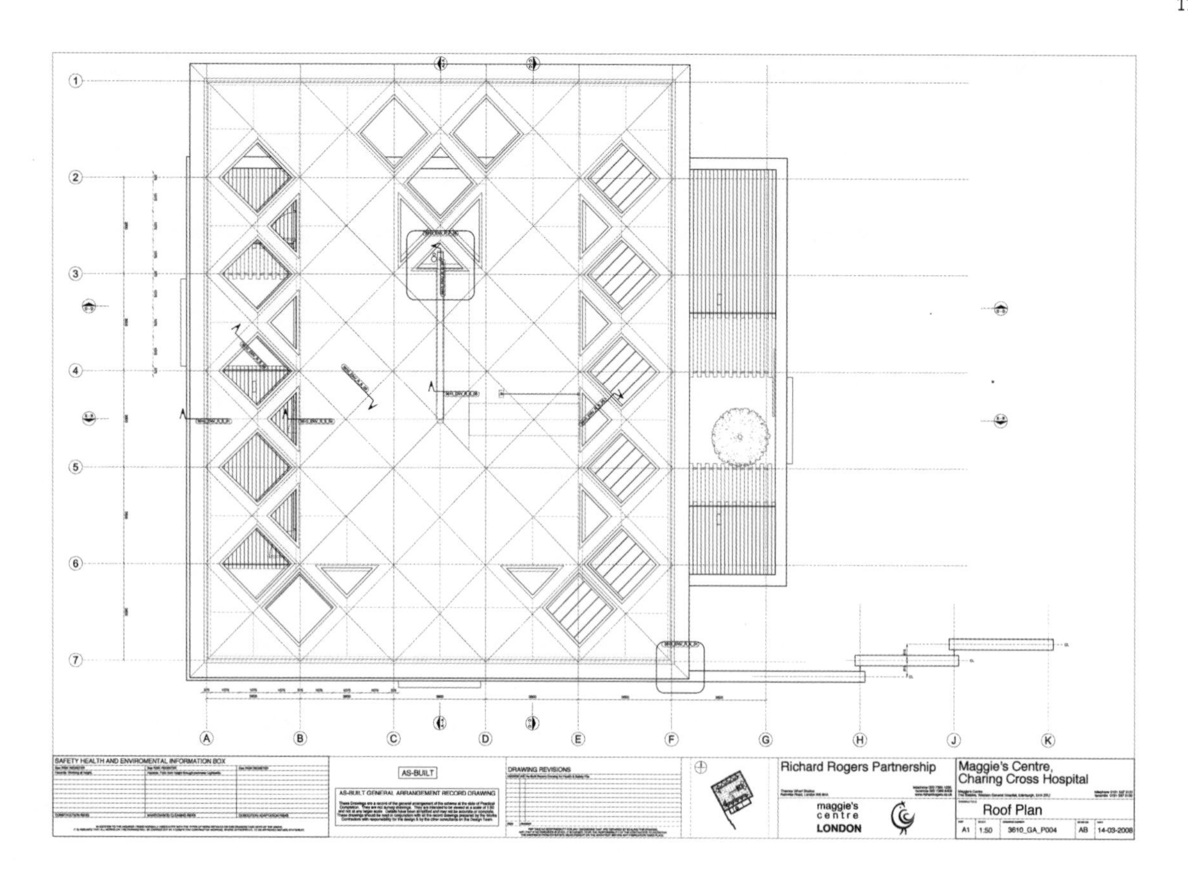

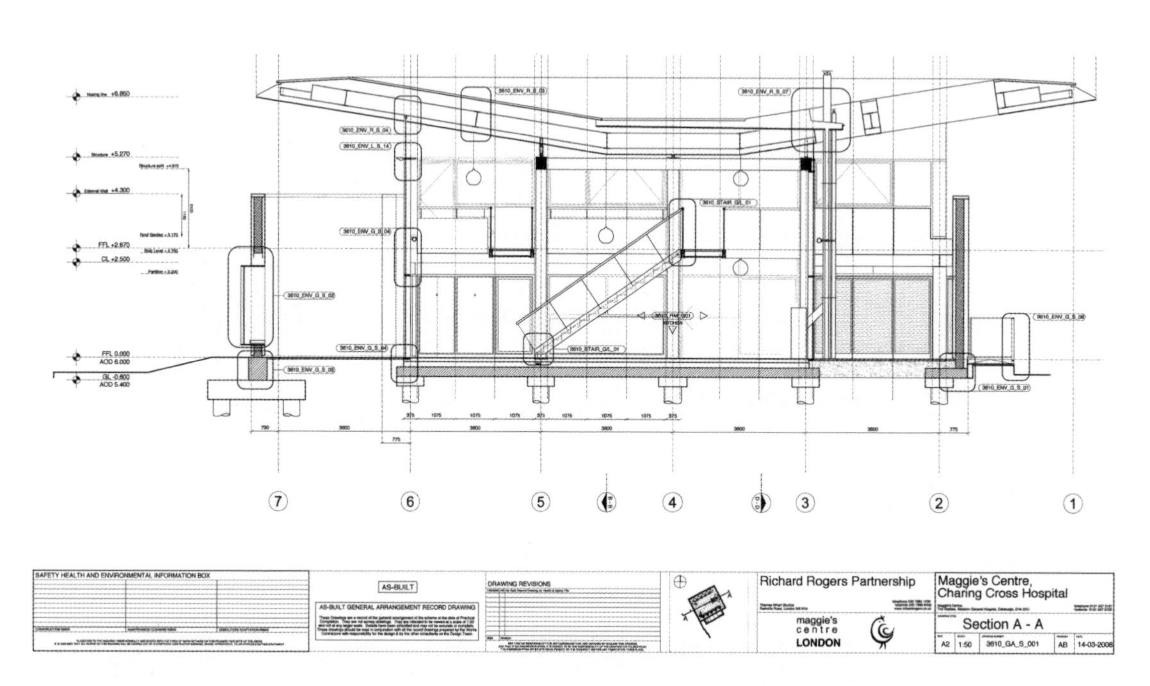

11 / GA documents of the roof and Section A-A: In section the roof is a wide V-shape while in plan it is based on a simple diagonal rectangular grid of steel panels. As it is angled upwards the rectangles become diamond-shaped. Tolerances between the ceiling and the steel roof structure were addressed through the design of the ceiling brackets.

12 / Shop drawing of the soffit cladding and typical skylight with solar shades: The roof contractor was SAS International who worked closely with the architect.

13 / The primary steel for the roof, prefabricated off-site, was lifted and bolted into place in sections to form a diagrid structure.

14 / Once the secondary steel had been fitted, the waterproof membrane and soffit panel were erected.

12

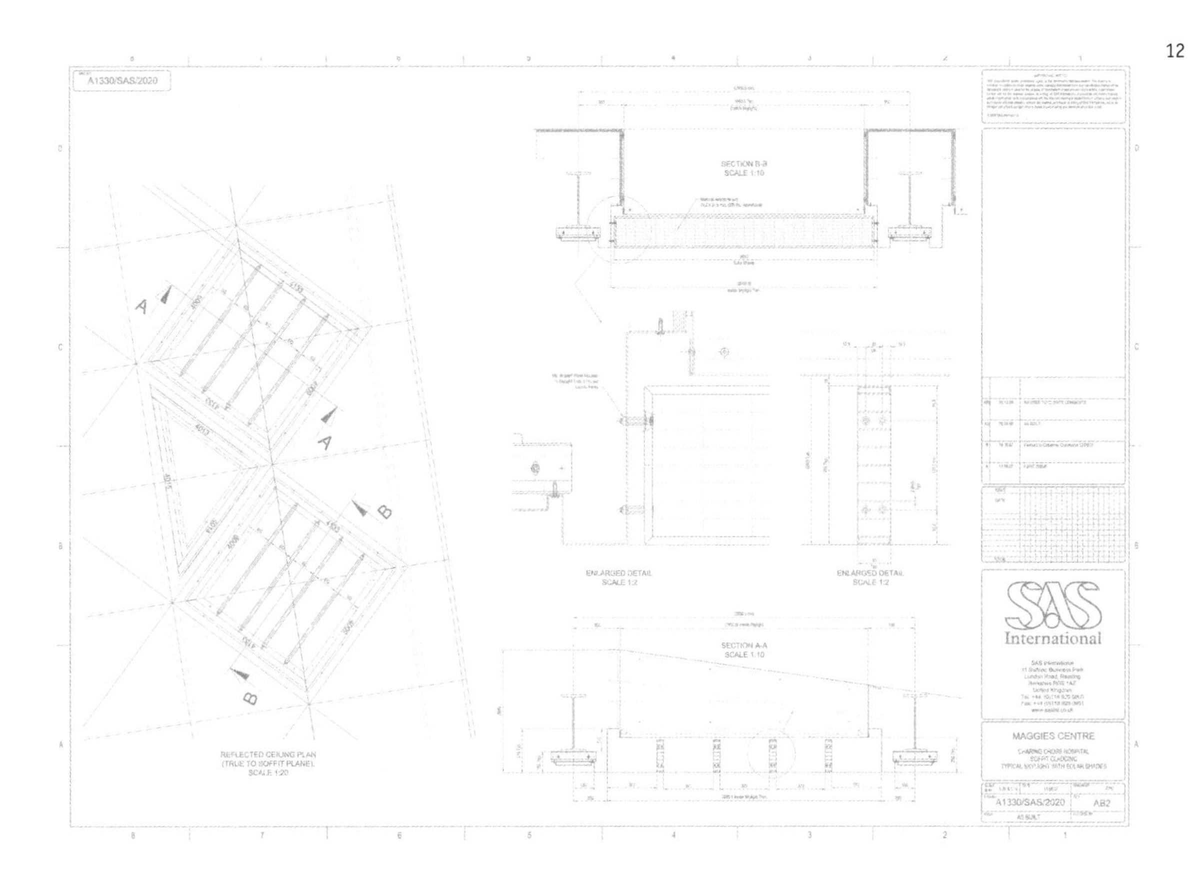
A1330/SAS/2020
SECTION B-B
SCALE 1:10
REFLECTED CEILING PLAN
(TRUE TO SOFFIT PLANE)
SCALE 1:20
ENLARGED DETAIL
SCALE 1:2
ENLARGED DETAIL
SCALE 1:2
SECTION A-A
SCALE 1:10
SAS
International
MAGGIES CENTRE
A1330/SAS/2020
AB2
AS BUILT

13

14

15

16

15 / The main concrete structural frame consists of fair-faced concrete columns supporting four separate first-floor slabs, or 'tables', the legs of which create the main spaces of the ground floor. At the centre, six of the columns extend upwards to the second storey to create the portal frame that supports the roof.

16 / Polished concrete screed was then poured, which allowed for the prefabricated joinery modules to be installed together with the steel link bridges, the staircase and glazing to the curtain wall.

17 / RSHP worked closely with the joinery contractor to create the internal divisions. Details were drawn by the architect, and reinterpreted in shop drawings, and mock-ups were built and discussed.

18 / The central kitchen is the heart of the building. Polished concrete was chosen for the floor because it is hard-wearing, but also for its honesty.

19 / Dan Pearson was engaged to design the landscape and worked with RSHP to integrate the gardens with the building. The strategy unites the existing hospital and the centre, while creating a therapeutic environment around, and within, the building. The entrance is approached from the hospital grounds.

20 / The three key external garden areas – the northern, eastern and southern winter gardens – are treated as extensions of the interior. The courtyards and roof terraces allow cross ventilation.

21 / The key feature is the roof, which oversails the outer walls. It is punctuated by unglazed roof-lights that allow natural light, wind and rain into the terraces below. A clear, glazed storey is used where the roof meets the building, to enhance the impression of a floating structure.

22 / The centre has a variety of flexible spaces to allow users to either interact and be sociable or find moments for solitude and reflection. The interiors (some of which can be divided by sliding partitions) provide changing scales of space. Furnishings and finishes were selected to be neutral, clean and non-institutional.

17

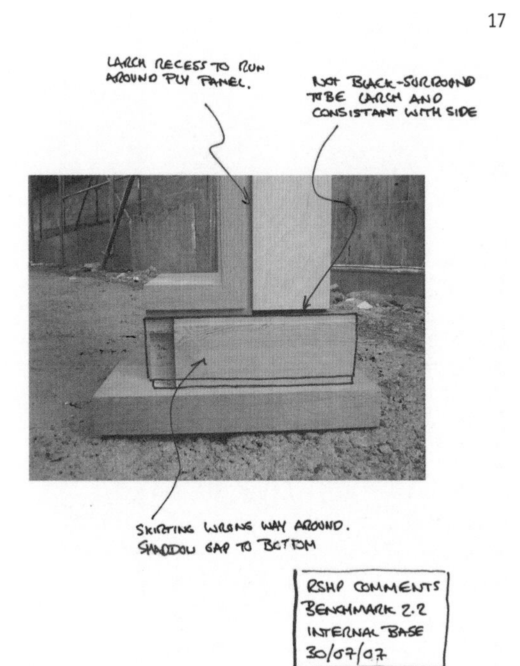

18

19

20

21

22

Design Museum Holon (DMH)

Ron Arad Associates

Location: Holon, Israel
Principal use: Design museum
Client: Municipality of Holon
Site area: 4,100 m^2 (44,132 ft^2)
Interior area: 2,700 m^2 (29,063 ft^2)
Total build area: 3,200 m^2 (34,445 ft^2)
Design period: January 2005 – May 2006
Construction period: September 2006 – January 2010
Budget: €11,000,000

Ron Arad's experimentation with form, process and material has put him at the forefront of contemporary design for the past three decades. Since founding his product design/architecture practice, Ron Arad Associates (RAA), he has produced a steady stream of interiors and small-scale architectural projects, but the Design Museum Holon is his first complete building. It also happens to be the first museum in Israel dedicated to design. In creating what is in effect two distinct buildings – an intricate yet extravagant sculpture of twisting Möbius-like Cor-ten steel bands that wrap around, protect and support two simple, orthogonal gallery spaces – Arad has produced a tour de force. He has successfully fulfilled the brief, which demanded both an iconic edifice that could 'appear on a postage stamp' and a logical international platform for design collections and presentations.

Holon is an important industrial centre and, over recent years, it has been designated a new cultural and educational hub for central Israel. Although much of its architecture is unremarkable, consisting of high-rise concrete blocks, it is home to the Mediatheque, the country's largest media and material library, and one of the nation's two prime polytechnics geared towards product design and engineering, as well as an important national children's museum. The site for the design museum occupies a semi-rectangular lot, surrounded on the northern and eastern sides by the city's main traffic arteries, on the west by the Mediatheque and on the south by a vacant area set aside for housing. Its restricted nature was one of the key influences on the design as was Arad's aim to visually protect the museum's visitors from the banality of the neighbouring buildings while not entirely turning his back on the city.

When Arad was initially approached by the municipality of Holon he turned down the commission as the administrators had yet to define a programme for the museum. The brief called for an icon that would cater to a large selection of user groups, and stipulated that the design should incorporate strong links to both industry and, because of the proximity of the children's museum, to a young demographic. There was no clear instruction as to how the building would function. Arad accepted the commission only when the client returned with the proposition that he should develop the brief. Asa Bruno, the project architect, describes the opportunity as rare and precious: 'A lot of developers and authorities would really benefit from including the architect in that process simply because function and building don't then become disparate factors.' In collaboration with Daniel Charny, a designer/curator with a keen interest in design thinking, a detailed outline for the building was deliberated through a reappraisal of other European design museums, and research into local interests and design activity. Bruno was then entrusted with the task of making sure that enough of the programme made it into the building concept.

RAA is a very democratic office, with each member of the small, 17-strong practice qualified and educated to take on any role from cost analysis, meeting the client and working on design development to three-dimensional modelling, construction drawings, detailing and surveying. Teams are set up for each project and ideas are discussed at every stage. Arad works with a Painter XI on a Wacom tablet. Within seconds what he has sketched appears on the screens of his team and can be manipulated and translated into 3-D drawings. Computer modelling is used from day one and only later taken into 2-D floor plans, sections and construction drawings.

Arad prefers to present only one concept to the client. In the case of Holon, the practice worked for three months before showing its initial idea – a vertical differentiation of two main galleries divided at a splayed angle to create an intimate courtyard between them. Already in place was the 4.8-metre (16-foot) ramp, which would act not only as access to both halls, but also as a curatorial tool and exhibition space in its own right. A further three months was taken to develop the bands. Initially, the design was for a rounded shell-like structure with an uninterrupted surface that would have been complex and costly to create. To preserve the overall curviness while at the same time creating a system of parts that would lend itself to a degree of repetition and thus, economy, the volume was divided into five individual bands, each 'performing' a relatively restrained meander through the air but together playing out the whole form with drama.

The contract was traditional, and RAA produced a full set of construction documents that was then handed to the main contractor. However, a local architect, who was responsible for planning and procurement strategies, managed the build. The difficulty was finding a resident contractor capable of creating a concrete substructure to support and interface with the complex Cor-ten steelwork, which was cut and assembled by Marzorati-Ronchetti, a family-run company of metalworkers based in Cantu, Italy, with whom Arad has worked for many years.

Because the museum was a local authority project, the budget was minimal. The finished building is a careful balance between ambition and invention and the practicalities of delivery. Asked what lesson he had learnt from the experience, Bruno says: 'Ron's attitude, that you cannot curb an idea at the early stages of design development, has been instrumental to the success of the building. Letting your vision fly, within reason – Holon has taught us that you can retain a dream and achieve a lot on very humble resources.'

1 / The five Cor-ten Steel bands give the building its dramatic iconic form and are also the structure that holds the exhibition spaces up in the air.

1

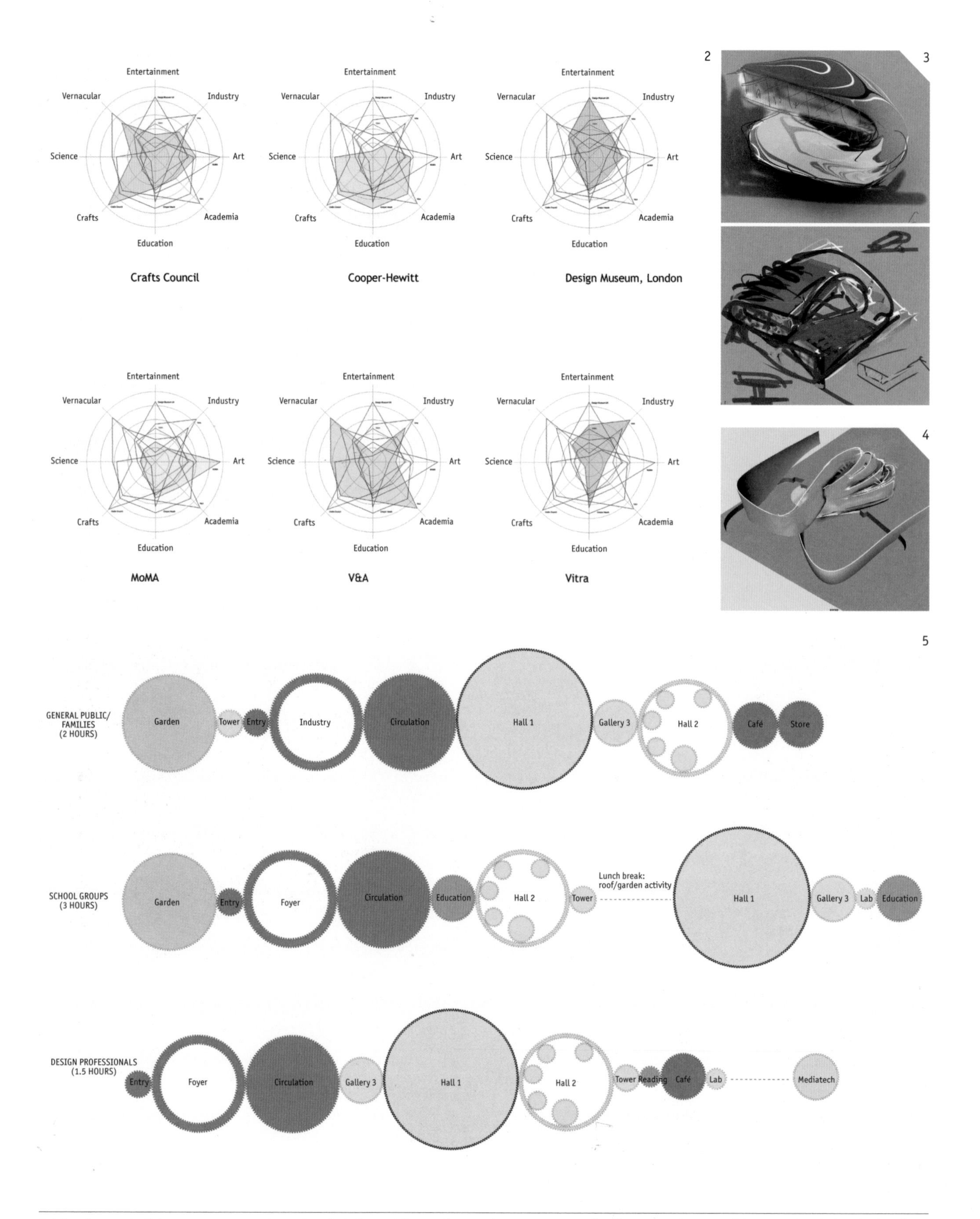

2 / Development of the programme: Comparative aim diagrams map the emphasis of design museum collections throughout the world. Superimposed in red is the intention for Holon with a bias towards entertainment (general public) and industry.

3 / Arad sketches using a Wacom tablet. The initial form was for a shell-like structure with a homogeneous and uninterrupted surface containing the two main galleries with a protected courtyard between.

4 / Concept sketch developing the idea for the bands.

5 / Schematic diagram showing the facilities that various user-groups are likely to use.

6

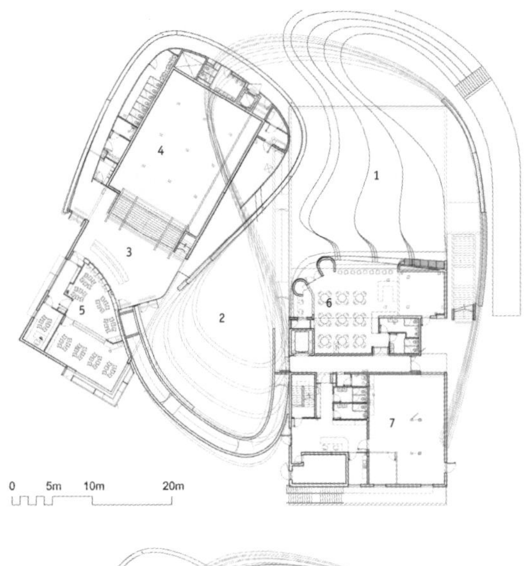

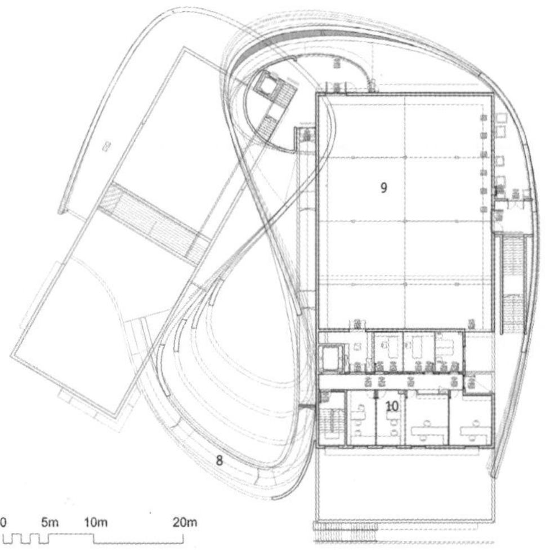

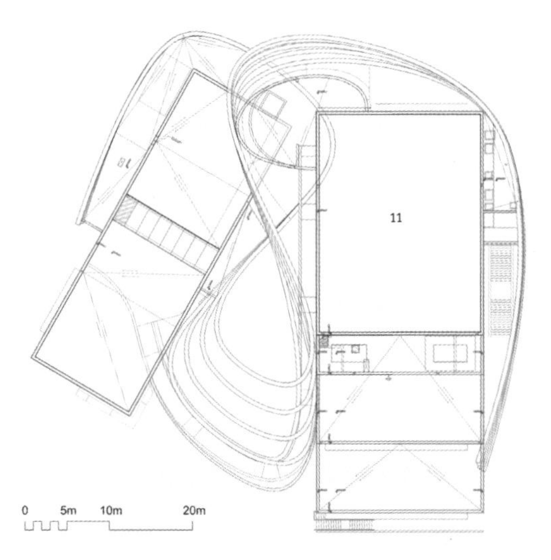

7

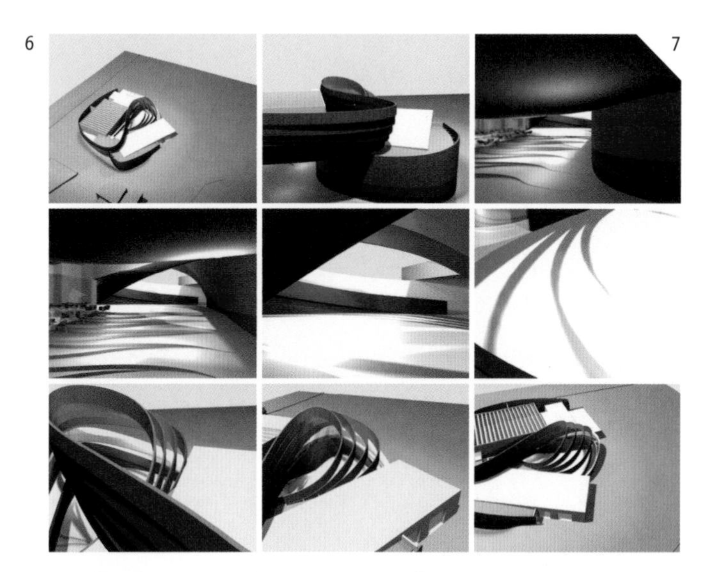

8

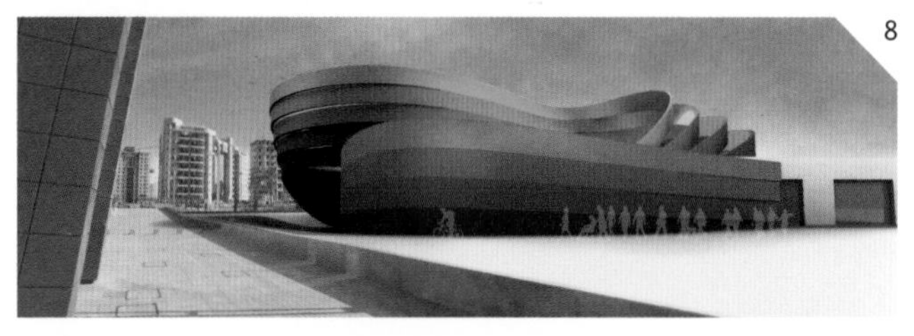

9

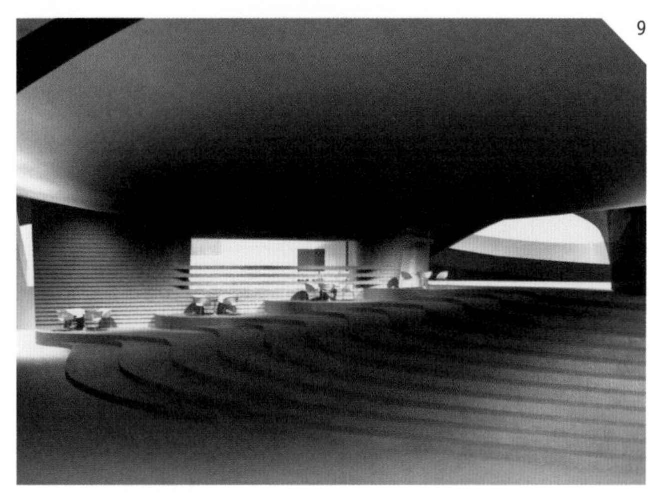

1 Outdoor (covered) performance and gathering space
2 Internal courtyard
3 Main entrance foyer
4 Gallery 2
5 Education wing and resident designer's lab
6 Café and shop
7 Curator's workroom and staff facilities
8 Circulation ramp
9 Gallery 1 (main)
10 Administrative offices
11 Naturally lit roof

6 / Plans for ground-floor, first-floor and roof level.

7 / Early concept renderings used to convey the design to the municipality of Holon.

8 / This example clearly shows the notion of a variation in the colour of the bands. The client demanded that this be replicated in the final design, and RAA spent two years finding a way to achieve the effect.

9 / Approach to the courtyard: Subconsciously a transition is made from outside to in by walking under the suspended gallery. Once the courtyard is accessed, the city can no longer be seen. The building draws in then envelops the visitor.

10

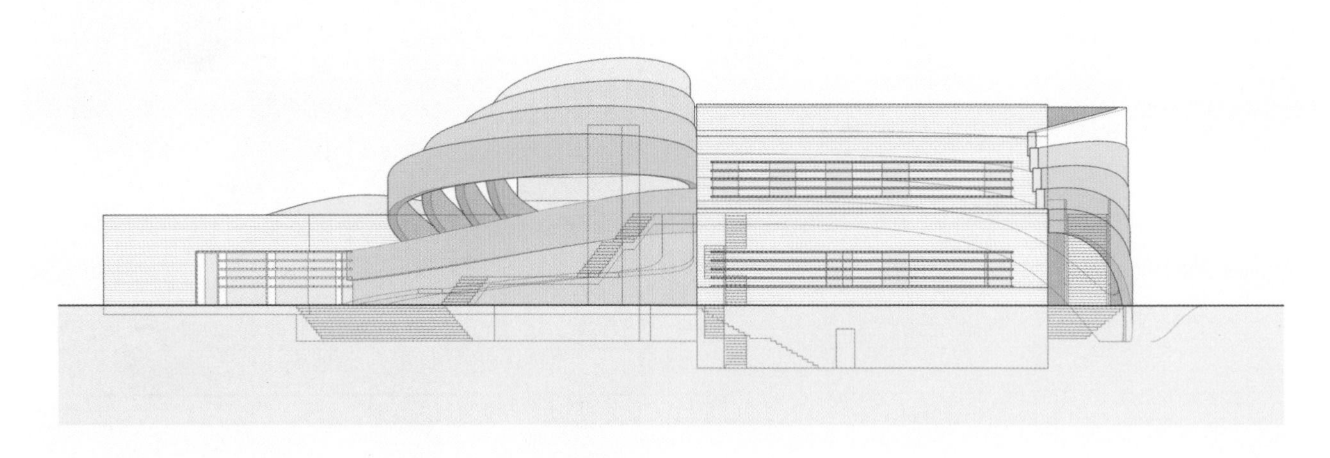

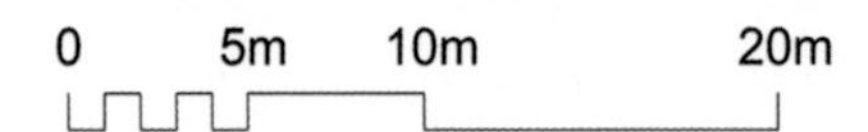

11

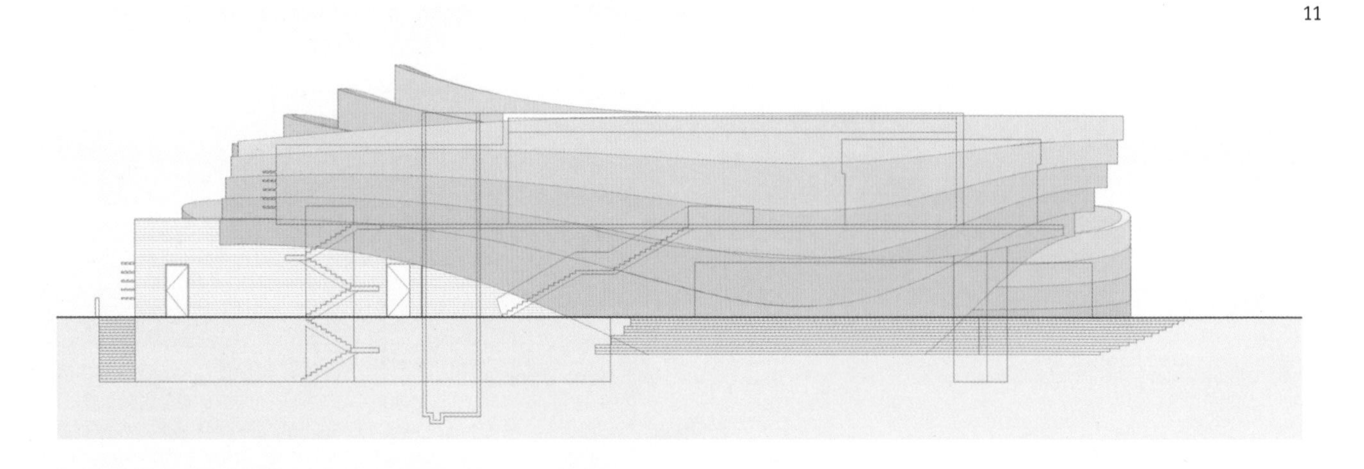

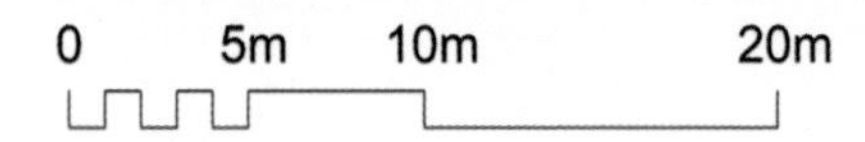

10 / South elevation.

11 / East elevation.

12 / Setting out of bands 1 and 5: The complex geometry of the bands would have been impossible before CAD. However, even if all computers had failed on the day of construction each band had been meticulously drawn in plan and elevation.

13 / Preliminary structural sketches.

14 / 3-D structural key: The main 500m^2 (2,153 ft^2) gallery is naturally lit and the second, 200m^2 (2,153 ft^2)exhibition space is a 'black box', allowing for curatorial flexibility. Back-of-house facilities include a curators' workroom.

12

13

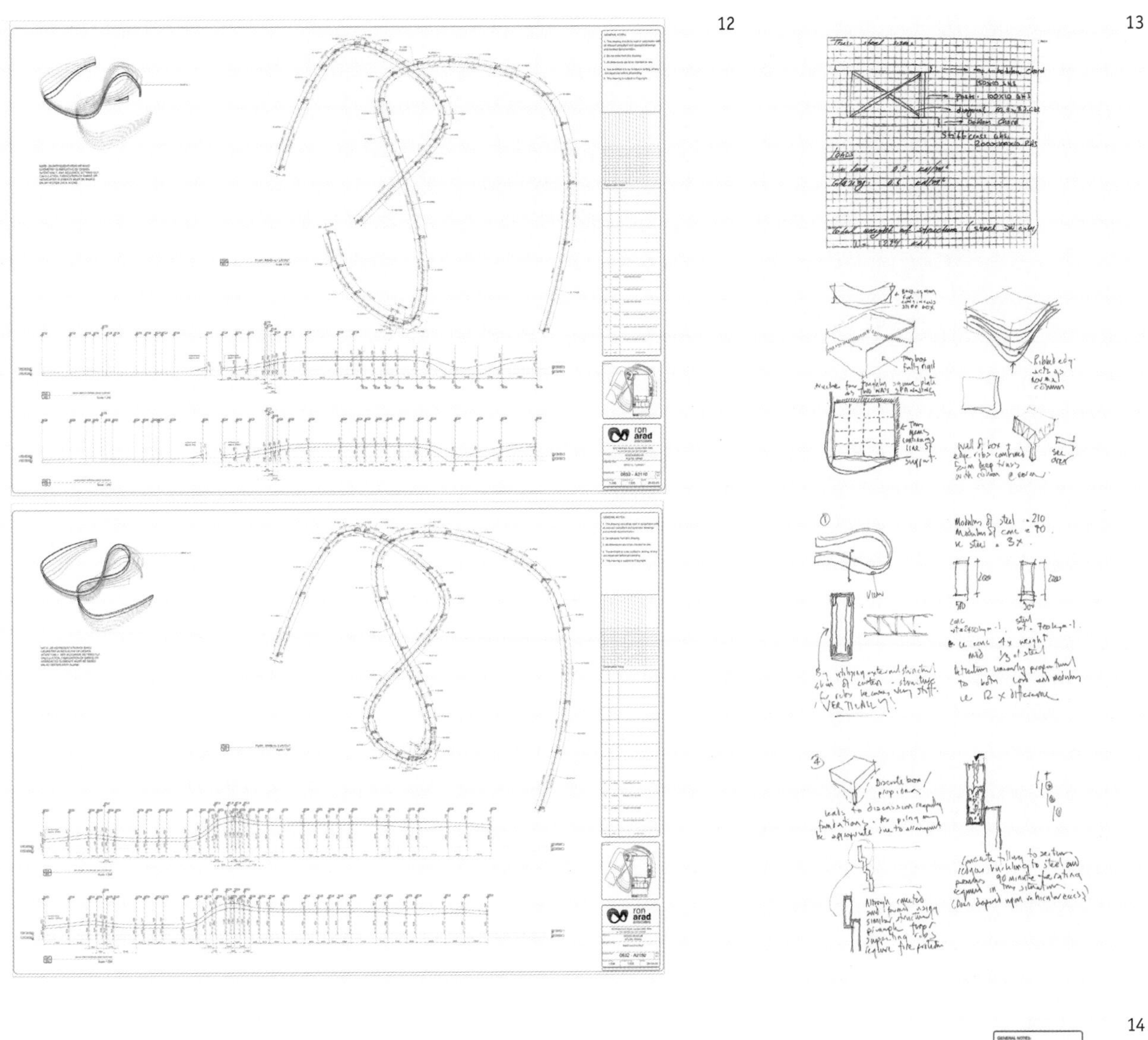

14

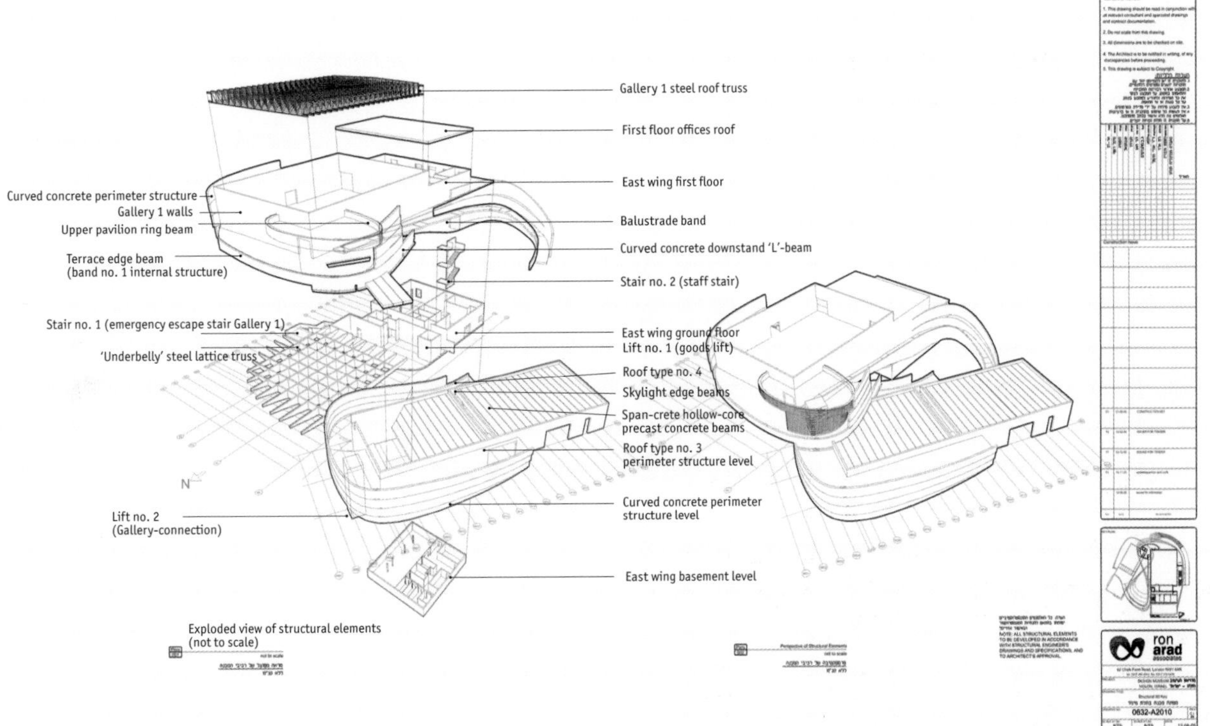
Gallery 1 steel roof truss
First floor offices roof
East wing first floor
Balustrade band
Curved concrete downstand 'L'-beam
Stair no. 2 (staff stair)
Curved concrete perimeter structure
Gallery 1 walls
Upper pavilion ring beam
Terrace edge beam
(band no. 1 internal structure)
Stair no. 1 (emergency escape stair Gallery 1)
'Underbelly' steel lattice truss
East wing ground floor
Lift no. 1 (goods lift)
Roof type no. 4
Skylight edge beams
Span-crete hollow-core
precast concrete beams
Roof type no. 3
perimeter structure level
N
Lift no. 2
(Gallery-connection)
Curved concrete perimeter
structure level
East wing basement level
Exploded view of structural elements
(not to scale)
ron
arad
0632-A2010

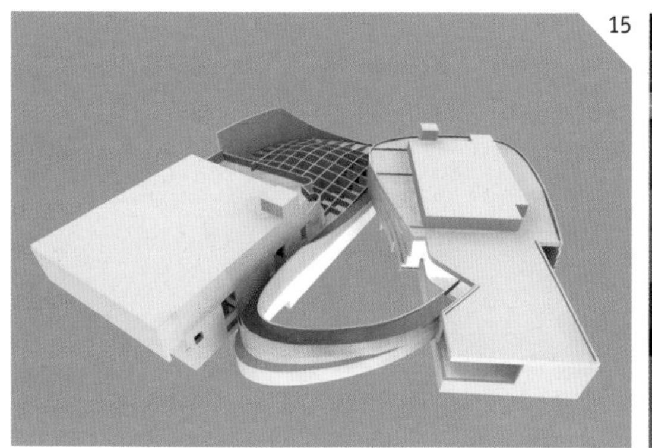

15

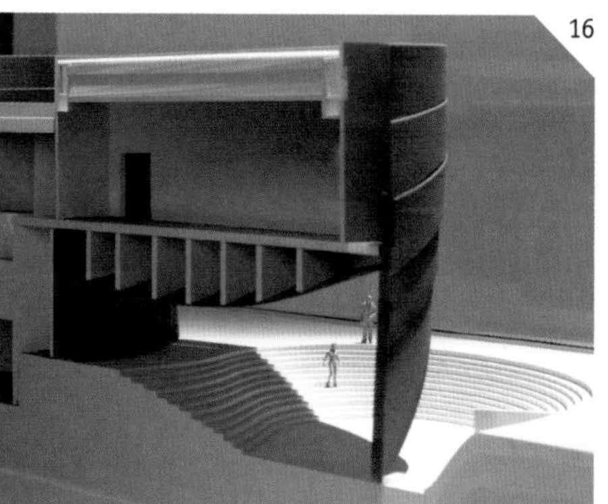

16

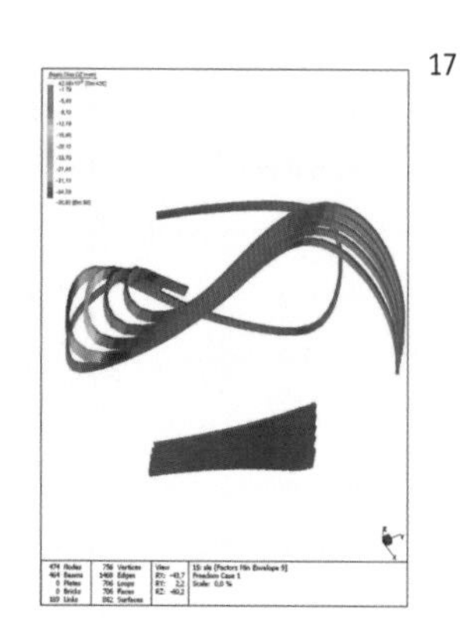

17

18

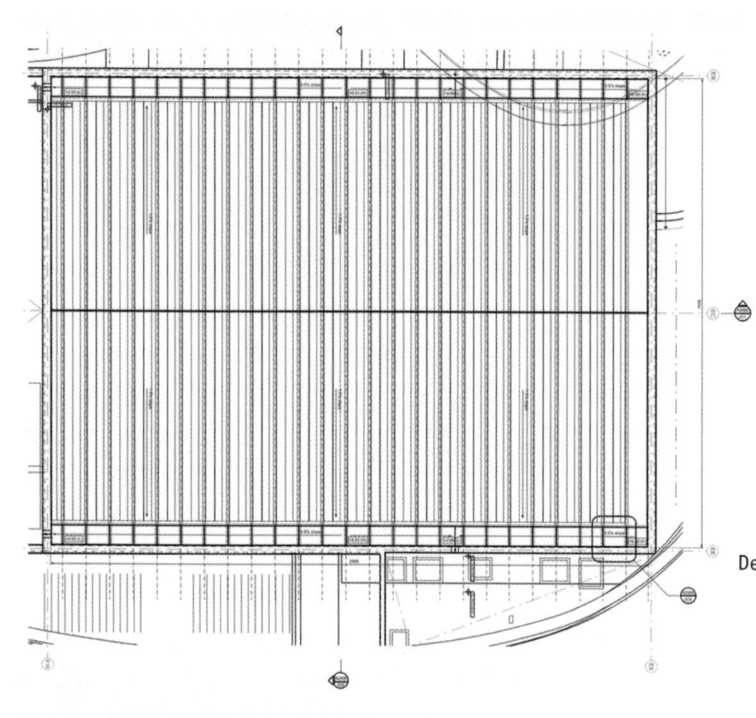

Plan of roof type #1 (Gallery 1), scale 1:50

Note: All spot-heights of roof 1 are taken from top of main flat steel truss at +1053.50 cm

1 2 3 4 5 6 7 8 9 10 11 12 13 14 15

Detail section of 'X' beam element, scale 1:50

16 17 18 19 20 21 22 23 24

Perspective of 'X' beam components, scale 1:5

1 50 x 50 mm steel RHS as roof base frame (to structural engineer's specifications)
2 Sprinkler head
3 120 x 60 x 5 mm steel RHS as truss compression member (to structural engineer's specifications)
4 40 x 40 x 3.2 mm steel RHS as truss horizontal reinforcement member (to structural engineer's specifications)
5 Side reinforcement frame
6 40 x 40 x 3.2 mm steel RHS as truss vertical reinforcement member (to structural engineer's specifications)
7 Fixing bracket
8 25 mm thick marine ply support flanges for light baffle element
9 Powder-coated aluminium 'T' profile as plasterboard terminator edge detail
10 50 x 25 mm horizontal flange reinforcement battens
11 Sprinkler 1 in. diameter local supply pipe
12 Two layers of 6 mm thick bendable plasterboard, skimmed and paint finished, as light baffle surface
13 120 x 60 x 5 mm steel RHS as truss tension member (to structural engineer's specifications)
14 Sprinkler 2 in. diameter distribution pipe
15 Light track for gallery display spotlights

16 25 mm thick marine ply support flanges for light baffle element
17 50 x 25 mm horizontal flange reinforcement battens
18 Two layers of 6mm thick bendable plasterboard, skimmed and paint finished, as light baffle surface
19 Fixing bracket
20 120 x 60 x 5 mm steel RHS as truss members (to structural engineer's specifications)
21 Powder-coated aluminium 'T' profile as plasterboard terminator edge detail
22 Sprinkler head
23 Sprinkler 2 in. diameter distribution pipe
24 Light track for gallery display spotlights

15 / Preliminary structural model: The floor is made of a grid of curved trusses clad in flexible materials that are able to resist movements caused by people and shock-loading of objects in the gallery above. It is not of a uniform thickness, and is sculpted into the inverted dune-like mass (the underbelly) that forms the entrance.

16 / Model: The aim for the museum as a whole and particularly the galleries was to be column-free. The main hall is 20 x 25 x 6 m (65½ x 82 x 19¾ ft) and is suspended in the air. In collaboration with the engineer the mass of the floor was increased and rests on two stacks of bands on either side, like a bridge.

17 / Final structural analysis.

18 / Construction drawing for roof type 1: The light modulators/reflectors in the main gallery form a third layer beneath acoustic glass and a product, ControLite, produced by the Dan kibbutz and normally used in agriculture. Effectively this is extruded polycarbonate with electronically controlled elements inside that enable the space to be lightened and darkened quickly and cheaply.

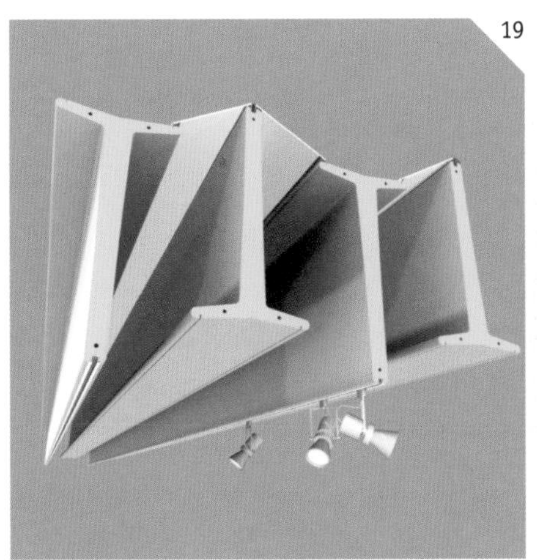

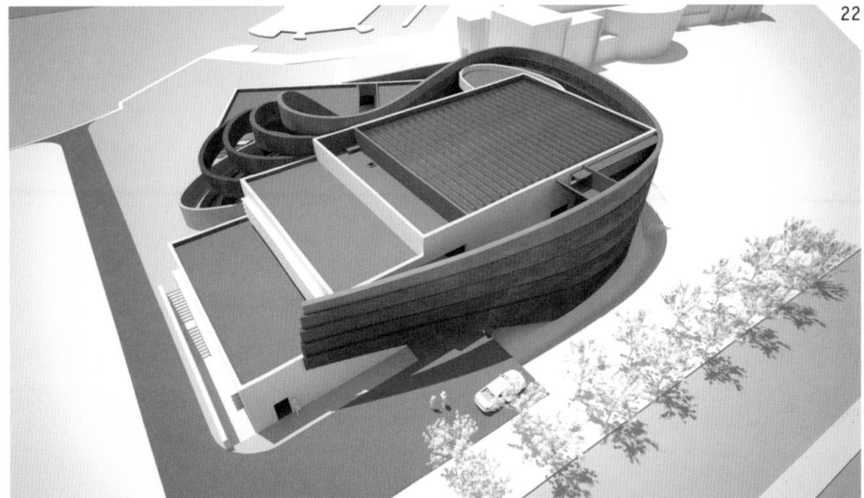

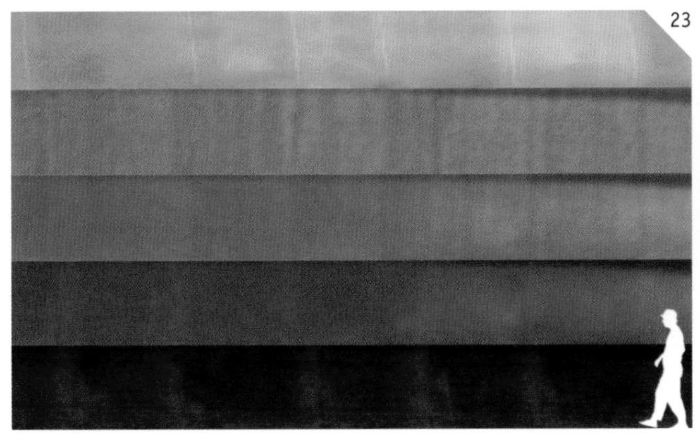

19 / Lighting experiments: Initially the T-shaped beams of the ceiling in the main gallery were to be precast in concrete, with alternate beams flipped upside down. However, the direction of pouring and settling structural concrete is crucial to the performance of the beam. The alternative to flipping the beams would have been to increase their mass, thus losing the desired slender aesthetic. They were finally constructed as composites of steel trusses wrapped in fibreglass.

20 / Gallery 1 assembly.

21 / The gradation of treated patinas and the subsequent weathering of the steel over the lifetime of the museum echo the familiar geological striations of the Israeli desert. This was the effect Arad desired and it is present in all the final renderings.

22 / Final rendering of the museum.

23 / Cor-ten band finishes.

24 / A system to arrest the oxidization of the Cor-ten was sought. A hot-wire technique in which a solid metal wire is fed at high temperature and high velocity through a heated nozzle was ineffective. It produced too uniform a finish and over time the metal flaked off the Cor-ten.

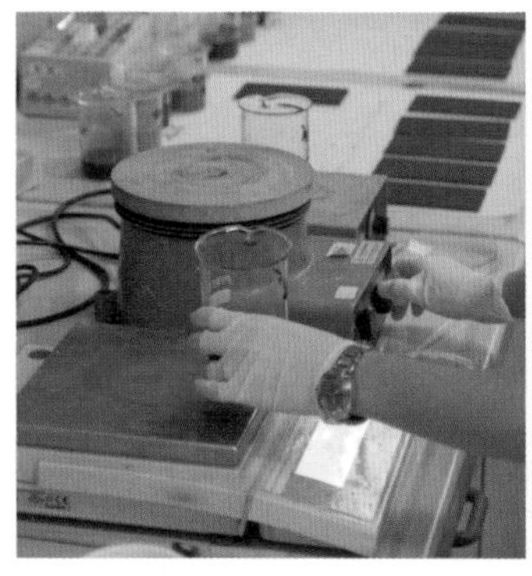

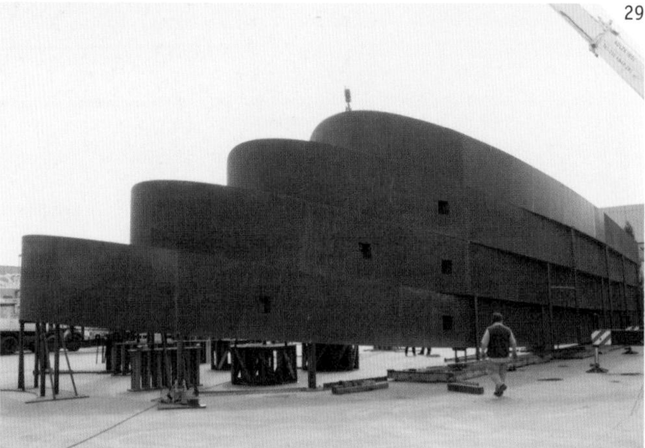

25 / In collaboration with Dr Gasparini of the Milan Polytechnic Institute of Oil and Grease, the final finish was obtained through a sequence of pretreating the steel with sandblasting, acid cleaning and accelerated patination, followed by the impregnation of the metal with a mixture of carrier-oils and pigments.

26 / Prototype construction: Each band is 50 cm (19¾ in) wide, contains equidistant reinforcement ribs, and is made in the same way as its neighbour. Using CAD/CAM systems during manufacturing, a flat sheet of metal was curved in one plane only. By bending the metal in a bi-planar manner (the ribbons never twist) time and money were saved.

27 / The armature formwork was created in Italy by Marzorati-Ronchetti to ensure the accuracy of the concrete, which needed to match exactly the form of the steelwork.

28 / Complete concrete skeleton.

29 / Cor-ten bands off site before assembly.

30 / Underbelly assembly on site: Traditional render could not be used because of the weight loading from the gallery above. A flexible resin-based product, Villaboard, was coated in a polymer-based render that had to be applied in one go. Twenty-two people completed the task in one day.

31

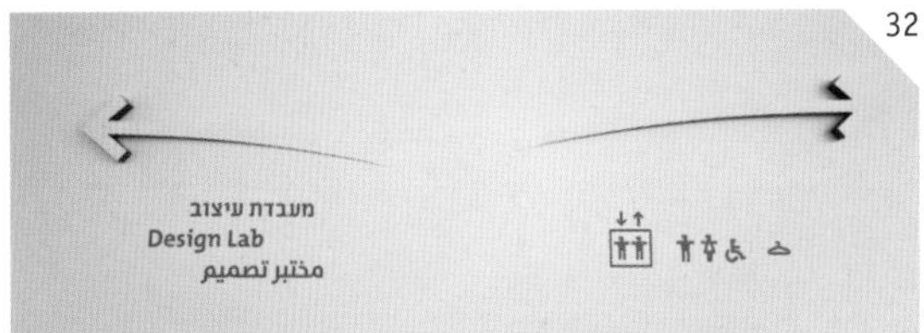

32

33

34

31 / Assembly: At some points the steelwork follows, and is attached to, the concrete inner core. This allows the concrete to act as a structural anchor when the bands start to fly.

32 / The signage is in Hebrew, Arabic and English and was stencilled onto the walls. The three-dimensional directional arrows act as sculptural pieces.

33 / Entrance is gained through a ‘cave’. The ceiling has been formed from the underside of the main gallery. The visitor passes from the glaring heat, through a moment of cooling before gaining the courtyard where the sun is mediated by the bands. The design enables partial shading of the museum. Almost half the building is designed to be without air-conditioning.

34 / Detail of the flying bands.

Long Studio

Saunders Architecture

Location: Fogo Island, Newfoundland, Canada
Principal use: Artists' studio
Client: Shorefast Foundation and the Fogo Island Arts Corporation
Site area: 2,000 m² (21,527¾ ft²)
Interior area: 120 m² (1,291¾ ft²)

Total build area: 211 m² (2,271 ft²)
Design period: June 2008 – June 2009
Construction period: June 2009 – June 2011
Budget: N/A. The Long Studio acted as a test trial for the costing and building techniques of the subsequent studios.

The rocky outcrop of Fogo Island lies an hour's ferry ride from the coast of Newfoundland, itself one of the most isolated parts of the world. Symptomatic of rural communities in remote areas, its population of 2,700 is in serious decline, previous generations having earnt their living from the now over-exploited sea. It's an unlikely venue for an international centre of artistic production, but that's what it is hoping to become – thanks to one of its inhabitants who left the island at the age of 16, to return over 30 years later after earning a fortune in the dot-com boom. Wanting to give something back to the people and culture to which she feels inextricably linked, Zita Cobb devised a plan to help the community. In 2006 she created the non-profit Shorefast Foundation with a mission to foster social entrepreneurship, and personally invested $6 million of the capital required to develop the Fogo Island Arts Corporation.

The arts residency programme is a sustainable business initiative that will boost the fragile economy and go hand in hand with the waning cod-fishing industry, and also fit in with Fogo Island's culture, history and ecology. Although pioneering, Cobb's vision is not without precedent. In 1967 the island became associated with the Fogo Process, an experiment that used media technology to encourage its inhabitants to participate through film in recording, and coming to terms with, the social depression that isolation and the slow demise of their traditional livelihood were causing. Similarly, Cobb's plan is to rejuvenate the island through the arts, by attracting acclaimed artists who in turn will act as magnets for select and wealthy visitors, bringing tourist dollars and creating much-needed jobs. Rather than opting for one iconic building, Cobb recognized the importance of creating a master plan of small studios located on various sites around Fogo's shores so that the resident artists could intermingle with, and become part of, the daily lives of the islanders.

To support her personal and passionate endeavour Cobb sought an architect who would understand the island's heritage. Although she considered practices in Canada, Europe and the USA, she found what she was looking for in a young Canadian architect based in Norway. Todd Saunders was brought up in Newfoundland and spent a lot of his childhood on Fogo Island. He admits that when Cobb contacted him he did not have the experience for such an ambitious project, but describes how she recognized his enthusiasm: 'She knew that I wouldn't back off from the challenge. As the culture meant so much to me I would never give up.'

The brief evolved during discussions with the client but in essence asked for six artists' studios, six artists' residences (later abandoned in favour of renovating existing houses on the island) and a five-star 29-room boutique hotel containing a small conference centre, a spa, an art-house cinema and an art gallery. The Long Studio is the first of the facilities to be completed.

Each of the studios was conceived to be aesthetically and programmatically different and is specifically suited to its location on the island. Saunders and Cobb chose the sites together, and once these had been decided design possibilities were discussed over the course of several meetings before drawing began.

The idea for the Long Studio was based on the seasons when it will be in operation. The form went through a series of minor iterations but the initial concept was retained. The long linear structure consists of three spaces. An open but covered area representing spring marks the entrance. The central portion is left open to be enjoyed during the long summer days, and the end is fully enclosed to protect the user from autumn's harsh weather. A connection to the exterior is maintained through a strategically framed view of the surroundings and the bare interior is flooded with daylight from a skylight on the roof. Utilities and storage are hidden behind a 1-metre (3¼-foot) wall to avoid any visual distraction.

Saunders experimented with traditional building methods and materials, and worked with local carpenters to reinterpret the vernacular into a contemporary idiom that both contrasts with and complements the harsh yet fragile beauty of the natural landscape. He likes to work with wood for its malleable and forgiving properties and its suitability for the regions in which he builds. The frame of the Long Studio is made from laminated LBL beams and rises from a floor slab, which is anchored to the ground at one end by a small concrete foundation and supported on wooden stilts at the other. It is clad in local spruce on the exterior and interior, and in western red cedar on the gently sloping roof, ensuring that the environment will leave its marks on the building by weathering the structure over time. Orientated towards the pounding Atlantic Ocean, the oblique form appears to hover above the shoreline and offers the resident artist the feeling of being totally isolated and unbound.

Once all the studios are up and running, and the hotel opens its doors in March 2012, the initiative hopes to draw 3,000 people annually. The residency and a programme of workshops and art projects based on locally inspired site-specific themes will offer visitors, in Cobb's words, 'a less crowded, less packaged opportunity to breathe and learn', while the local people will benefit from a renewed sense of confidence and pride. Cobb continues: 'We hope to attract all those who are curious, well-travelled and interested in meaningful cultural experiences, as well as the richness that comes from time spent in the sublime, powerful physical world that we are lucky to have on our island.'

1 / The Long Studio is situated on an isolated promontory with a ten-minute walk to the nearest track. Its geometric form appears to erupt from the volcanic rock of the shoreline.

1

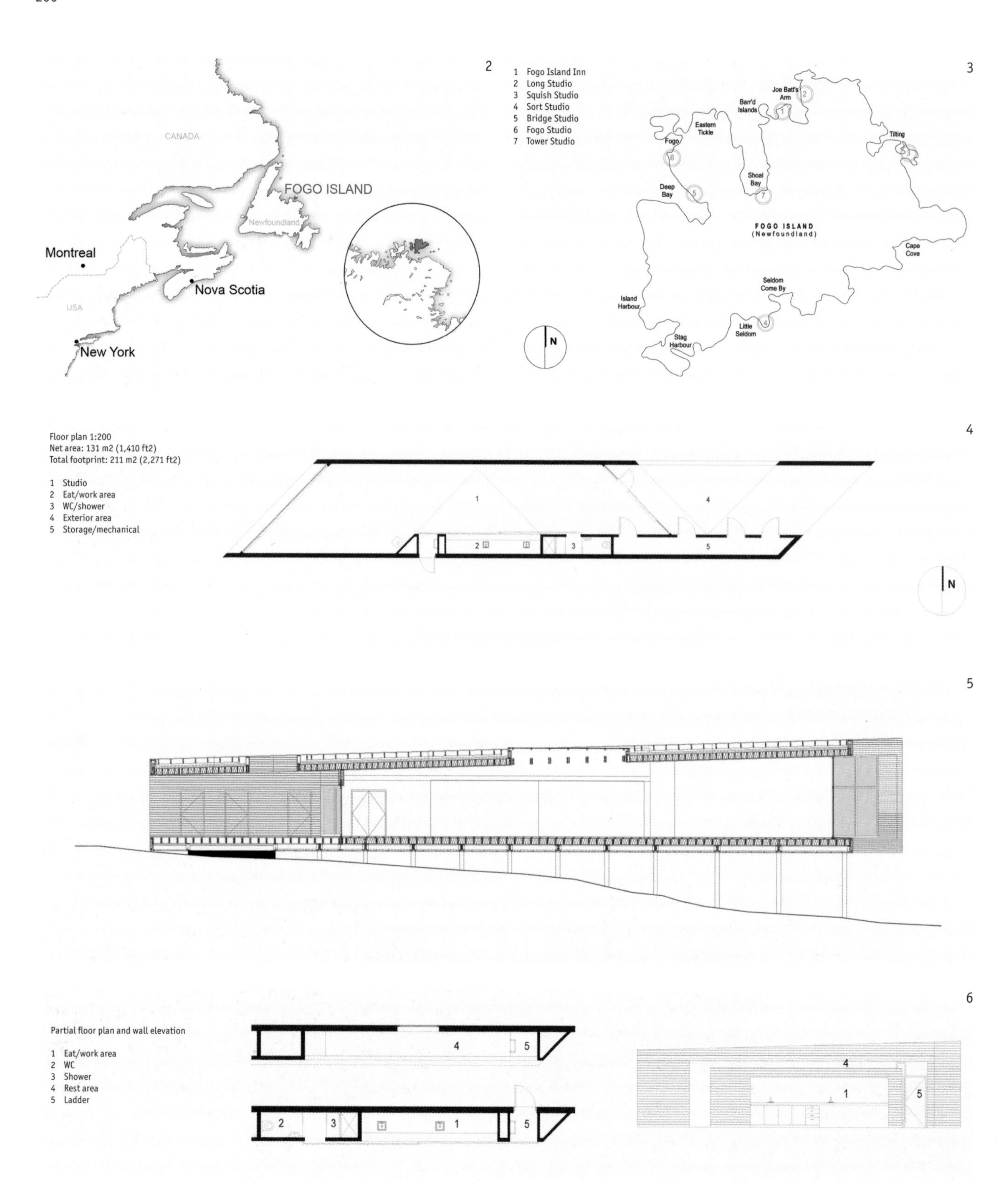

2 / Location map showing Fogo Island.

3 / Location map showing the sites for the six studios and the Fogo Island Inn.

4 / Floor plan.

5 / Section.

6 / Partial floor plan and wall elevation.

7 / Rendering of the Bridge Studio placed in its setting: The studios all draw inspiration from the vernacular architecture of clapboard and pile construction.

8 / Renderings of the Short (centre), Squish (bottom left) and Tower (bottom right) studios: The Fogo Studio was being designed at the time of going to print.

7

8

9

10

11

9 / Rendering of the Fogo Island Inn.

10 / Local residences were renovated to provide accommodation for the artists and their families. The original idea was for living and working spaces to be contained in the studios. Saunders pointed out that this would be intrusive for the families and not provide the artists with the seclusion they needed. The houses are located within ten minutes' walk of the studios.

11 / Presentation renderings: Saunders worked collaboratively with the client in face-to-face meetings or using WebEx. Early discussions centred on metaphors for how the buildings should feel, after which he was given complete creative freedom to interpret the themes. Variation in the form and materiality for the Long Studio were shown. The idea for three spaces was present from the beginning.

12

13

14

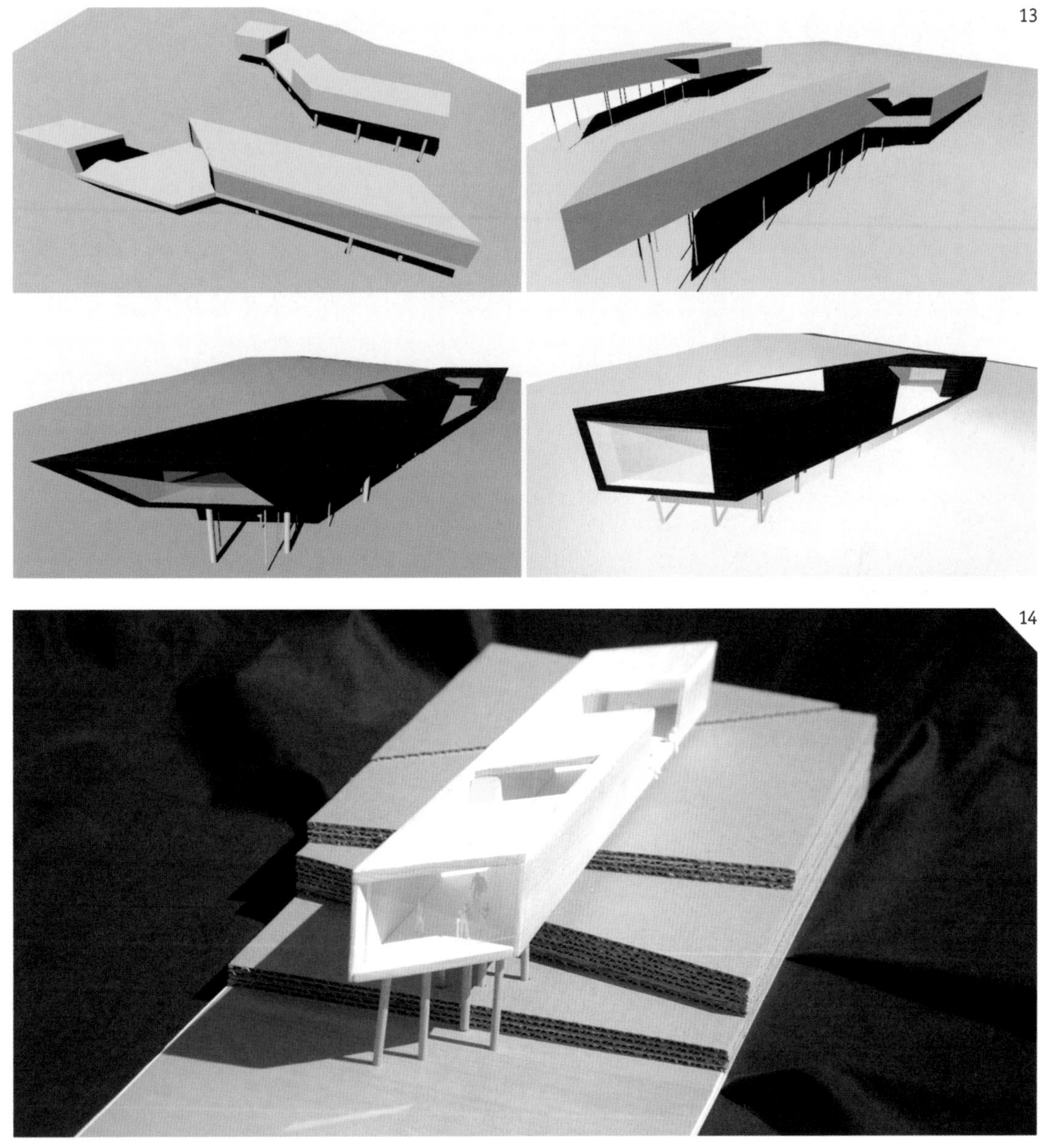

12 / An early notion gathered the studios together in clusters. The idea was rejected as it contradicted the concept of retreat.

13 / Saunders does not sketch but develops a design straight away on the computer using Rhino. 3-D drawings progress in a linear fashion, each iteration evolving from the last.

14 / A model was made midway through the design process and shown to the client. Simplifications were suggested by the architect and the design was redrawn on the computer.

15

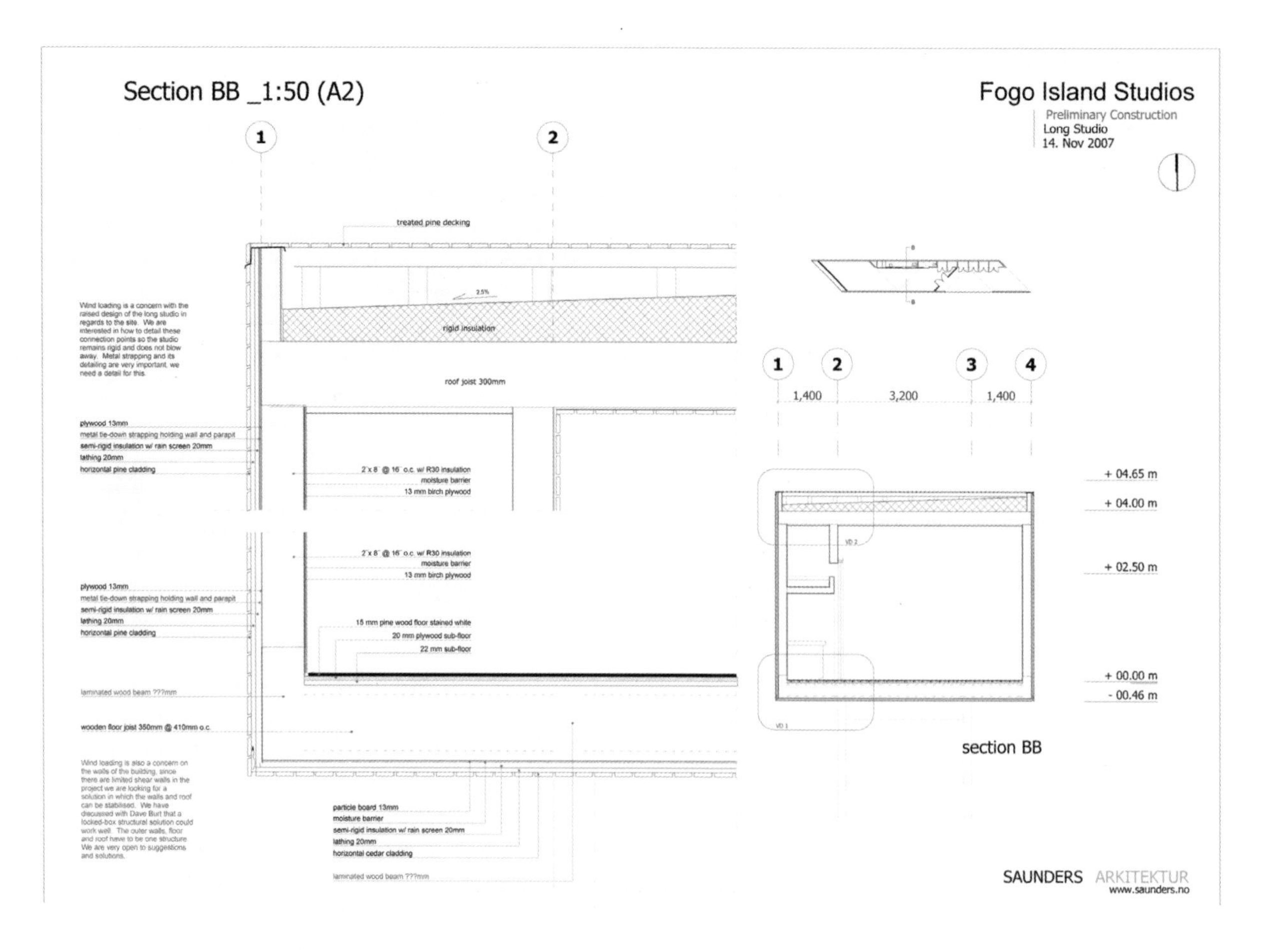
Section BB _1:50 (A2)
Fogo Island Studios
Preliminary Construction
Long Studio
14. Nov 2007
treated pine decking
rigid insulation
roof joist 300mm
plywood 13mm
metal tie-down strapping holding wall and parapit
semi-rigid insulation w/ rain screen 20mm
lathing 20mm
horizontal pine cladding
15 mm pine wood floor stained white
20 mm plywood sub-floor
22 mm sub-floor
particle board 13mm
moisture barrier
semi-rigid insulation w/ rain screen 20mm
lathing 20mm
horizontal cedar cladding
1,400
3,200
1,400
+ 04.65 m
+ 04.00 m
+ 02.50 m
+ 00.00 m
- 00.46 m
section BB
SAUNDERS ARKITEKTUR
www.saunders.no

16

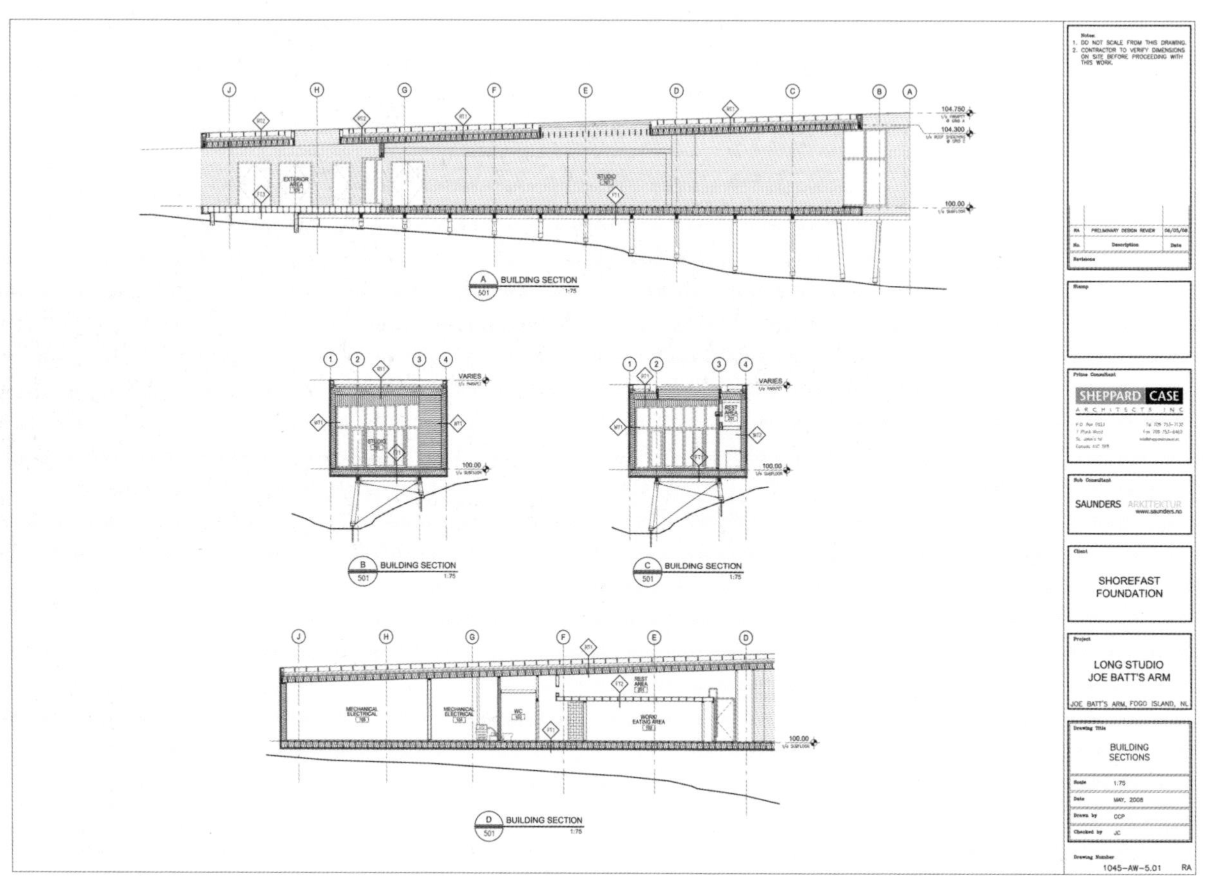
BUILDING SECTION
SHEPPARD CASE
SAUNDERS ARKITEKTUR
SHOREFAST FOUNDATION
LONG STUDIO
JOE BATT'S ARM
BUILDING SECTIONS
1045-AW-5.01

17

Wall section 1:50

RT1
Spruce decking
Wood joists
Wood sleepers
Roof membraine
Protection board
Rigid insulation
Plywood
Wood joists
Batt insulation
Vapour barrier
Birch veneer plywood
Spruce cladding

WT1
Horizontal spruce cladding
Wood strapping
Rigid insulation
Air barrier
Plywood sheathing
Wood studs/insulation
Vapour barrier
Gypsum board
Birch veneer plywood
Horizontal spruce cladding

FT1
Spruce plank floor
Wood sleepers
Concrete topping
Membrane
Plywood
Wood I-joists
Batt insulation
Plywood
Rigid insulation
Plywood
Spruce cladding

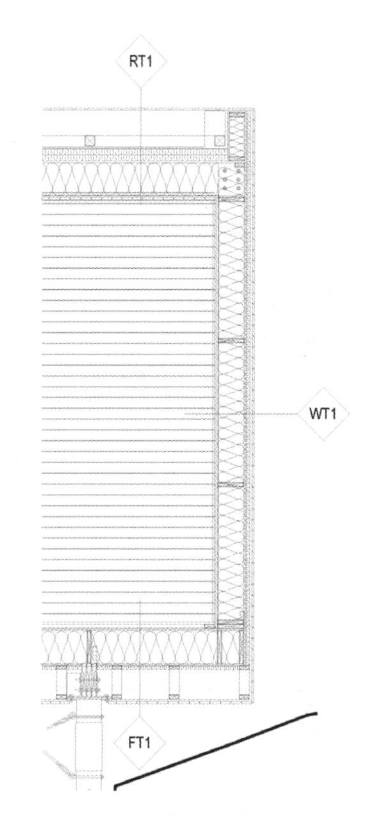

18

15 / Construction intent drawing: The architect wanted the structure to look like a sculpture and detailed the wall, floor and roof planes to meet seamlessly. The process is labour-intensive and expensive, but as the carpenters were employed by the client, time and cost were not so closely linked.

16 / Saunders worked with a local structural engineer to produce preliminary construction drawings. These were converted by the local architect, Sheppard Case, to comply with Canadian standards (illustrated here).

17 / Wall section.

18 / Saunders enjoyed a close collaboration with the lead carpenter, who used his mobile to take and e-mail digital photographs of the build every few days so that all details of construction could be discussed. The studio is placed on pillars at the sea end.

19

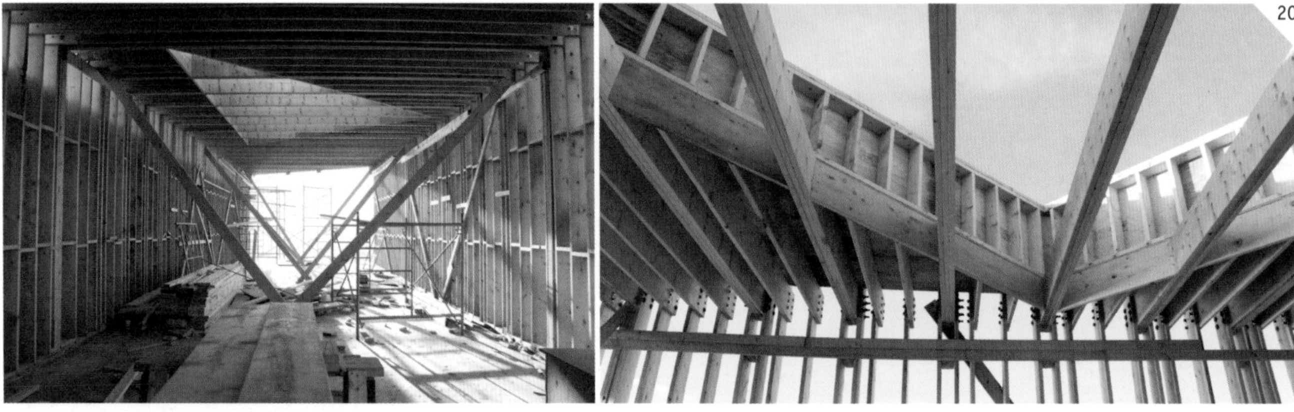

20

21

22

23

24

19 / The frame is made from laminated LBL beams. The entrance area has a small concrete foundation for anchoring the structure to the landscape.

20 / The structure gently increases in height. Every 60 cm (23⅝ in) each partition, slightly taller than the previous one, is bolted to the horizontal frame. Because of the severe weather conditions the building was intentionally over-engineered for insurance purposes.

21 / The frame is clad in local spruce on both the interior and exterior. Western red cedar is used on the gently sloping roof – to mitigate the problem of rainwater lying on the roof a softer more tolerant wood than spruce was needed.

22 / The studio is not connected to mains electricity or plumbing. It is powered by solar panels and served by rainwater collected from the roof. Toilets are composting. The services are concealed in rooms in the 1 m (3¼ ft) east–west direction wall, and accessed through external doors (visible in the building section, image 5).

23 / Internally the long linear form maximizes wall space. The kitchen and bathroom are hidden behind sliding doors to avoid visual distraction.

24 / The entrance is open to the elements, but covered.

Centre Pompidou-Metz (CPM)

Shigeru Ban Architects with Jean de Gastines and Philip Gumuchdjian

Location: Metz, France
Principal use: Arts centre
Client: Communauté d'Agglomération de Metz Métropole (CA2M)
Site area: 12,000 m² (129,166¾ ft²)
Interior area: 8,118 m² (87,425 ft²)
Total build area: 11,330 m² (121,955 ft²)
Design period: October 2003 – November 2006
Construction period: January 2007 – April 2010
Budget: €51,000,000

The Pompidou in Paris is the first major French arts centre to be committed to cultural decentralization. Metz lies at the crossroads of three frontiers and at the heart of Europe. Since Roman times it has been an undisputed site of interchange and today, with its high-speed train links, it is a popular tourist destination. Both the mayor and the Metz Métropole share an enlightened attitude when it comes to promoting new art and architecture; a progressive outlook that saw the city beat off competition for the centre from towns that included Calais, Boulogne and Amiens. Creating an institution that manifested the polydisciplinary ideology of the Pompidou was a daunting task. It was essential that the CPM should have a clear identity of its own and be housed in a building as iconic as Richard Rogers' and Renzo Piano's 1977 design. In 2003 an international competition was launched that attracted over 150 architects including Herzog & de Meuron, FOA (Foreign Office Architects), Dominique Perrault and Nox Architects.

The commission was awarded to Shigeru Ban, internationally recognized for his innovative work with paper, particularly recycled cardboard tubes used to house disaster victims quickly and efficiently. His team comprised Frenchman Jean de Gastines and Londoner Philip Gumuchdjian who had worked with Rogers on the refurbishment of the Centre Pompidou in 1998. Gumuchdjian describes the collaboration as being 'almost perfect': 'For me the complementary aspect of it is that I have a strong contextual, urban, side to my work while Shigeru has an incredible architectural and structural inventiveness. Our team was able to produce a proposal that was both innovative and contextual but that also empathetically met the Pompidou's insistence on flexibility.'

The brief was for an internationally recognized arts centre but also a venue where the public could congregate and socialize. The programme included a forum that would be used to greet visitors, three identically sized exhibition galleries, and a 'Grand Nef' or central atrium large enough to accommodate oversized artworks and installations, together with a lecture hall, bookshop, restaurant, offices and a studio space for performing arts. The site was once an extensive freight yard. The eventual master plan for the area is for a 'town within a town' with the museum (the only built element at the time of going to print) situated on a triangular 'island' at the end of the plot, cut off from the city and the suburbs by the railway tracks and roads that flank it.

The concept that was developed arose from the architects' respective expertise. The difficulty lay in retaining the Pompidou's philosophy while not mimicking it, so the client was presented with an innovative structure that retained the principles that had made the Paris landmark so successful. The capital's museum is based on the notion of a democratic permeability of space that proposes a piazza, as well as a building that is visually open to the public. In Metz, pushing the construction as far into its corner site as possible presented the opportunity of creating a park and civic space that could act as a much-needed link between the old city on one side of the railway tracks and the 'new town' on the other. The architects perceived a pastoral context for the CPM, with a trellised timber pavilion at the centre's heart, contrasting with the Paris Pompidou, which forms the fourth side of an urban and 'mineral' square. Ban's initial consideration was to avoid the recent phenomenon dominating art museum design, which he calls the Bilbao effect – a sculptural architecture that draws in the tourists but spoils its functionality by disregarding the optimum conditions for displaying and viewing art. His solution was to articulate the programme into straightforward volumes with a clear circulation among them that would architecturally leave a deep impression on visitors.

The concept was simple; its realization was not. The galleries are based on 15-metre (49-foot) wide modules that create three square tubes with long, 90-metre (295¼-foot) deep rectangular volumes inside. Picture windows frame views of the two defining buildings in the city – the cathedral and the central station – uniting the isolated museum with its historical context. The tiered and shifted galleries are stacked around a hexagonal steel tower that contains the stairs and lifts, with the space beneath creating the Grand Nef exhibition space. Two further volumes, one round and one square, house the restaurant and auditorium respectively. The ensemble is unified into a cohesive whole by a billowing roof of translucent

Teflon and fibreglass supported on vertiginous timber latticework that touches the ground in six places.

The Centre Pompidou-Metz may be a feat of engineering but it's a testament to all the parties concerned that the original design reached fruition. Building a museum of this nature was hugely political; it involved not just the client and user (who themselves had conflicting objectives both financially and programmatically) but also the French government. The CPM also has wider implications culturally, socially and diplomatically that had to be negotiated every step of the way. Although the concept of the design was maintained, the process of building was complex. Ban had to find an alternative team of timber engineers to construct his geometrically complicated vortex of wood, which meant that although the centre came in on budget it was two years late on delivery.

The architects describe the project as 'providing a new type of public institution'. As visitors approach the museum they see a bright, luminous building that appears both strong yet light and invites them to shelter under its protective roof. 'We wanted the architecture to convey a sense of well-being, openness and multicultural mix in a building that has a direct, sensory relationship with its surroundings,' says Ban.

1 / The CPM sits like a wooden pagoda in the surrounding parkland. Influenced by the large eaves common in traditional Japanese architecture the roof's overhang harbours and protects visitors and creates open areas for the public to enjoy while shielding the glazed façades from the sun.

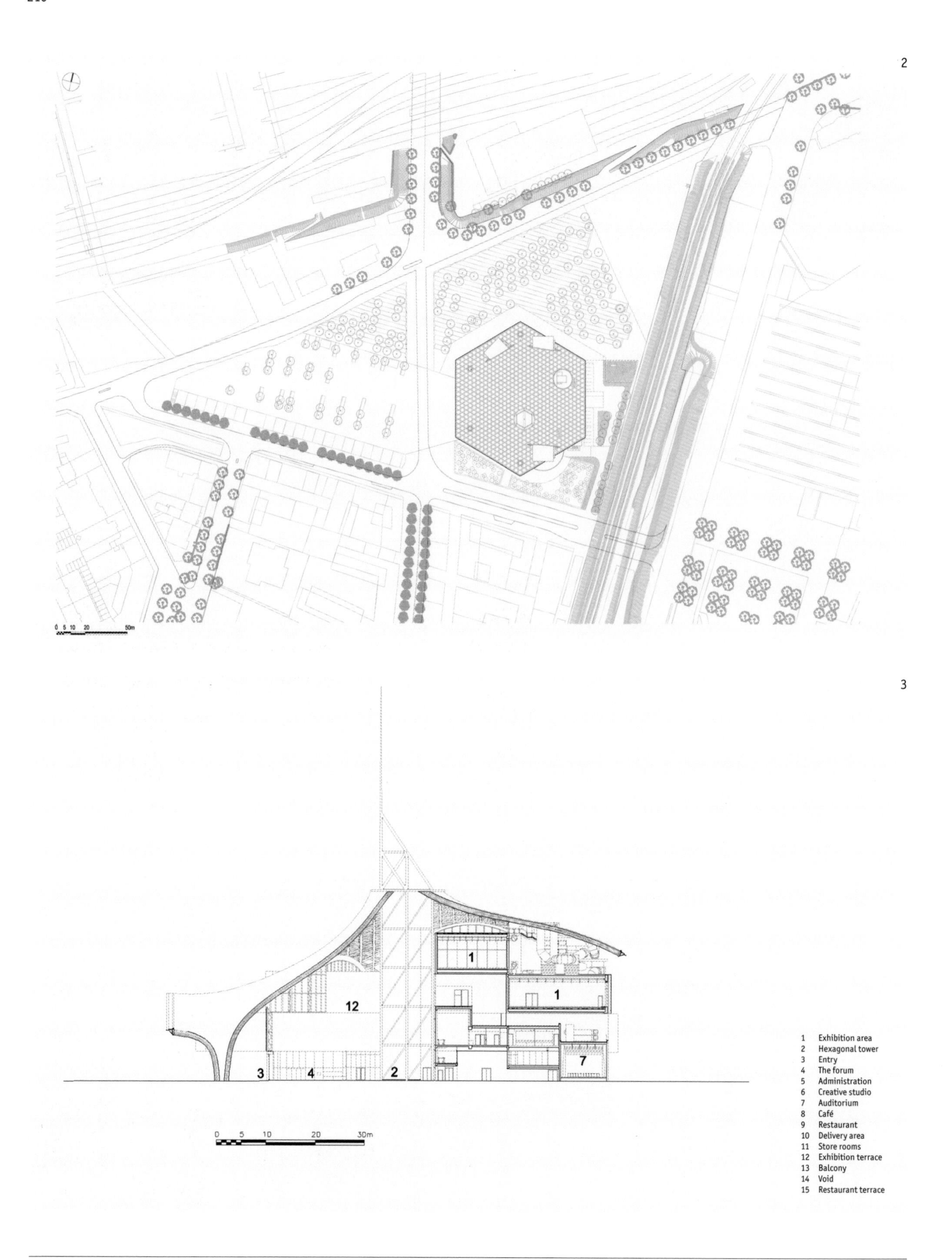

2 / Site map: The centre is pushed to the corner of its triangular site, around which the park acts as a link between the city of Metz and the new town which will be developed as part of the overall master plan.

3 / Section.

4 / Ground- to roof-level plans.

4

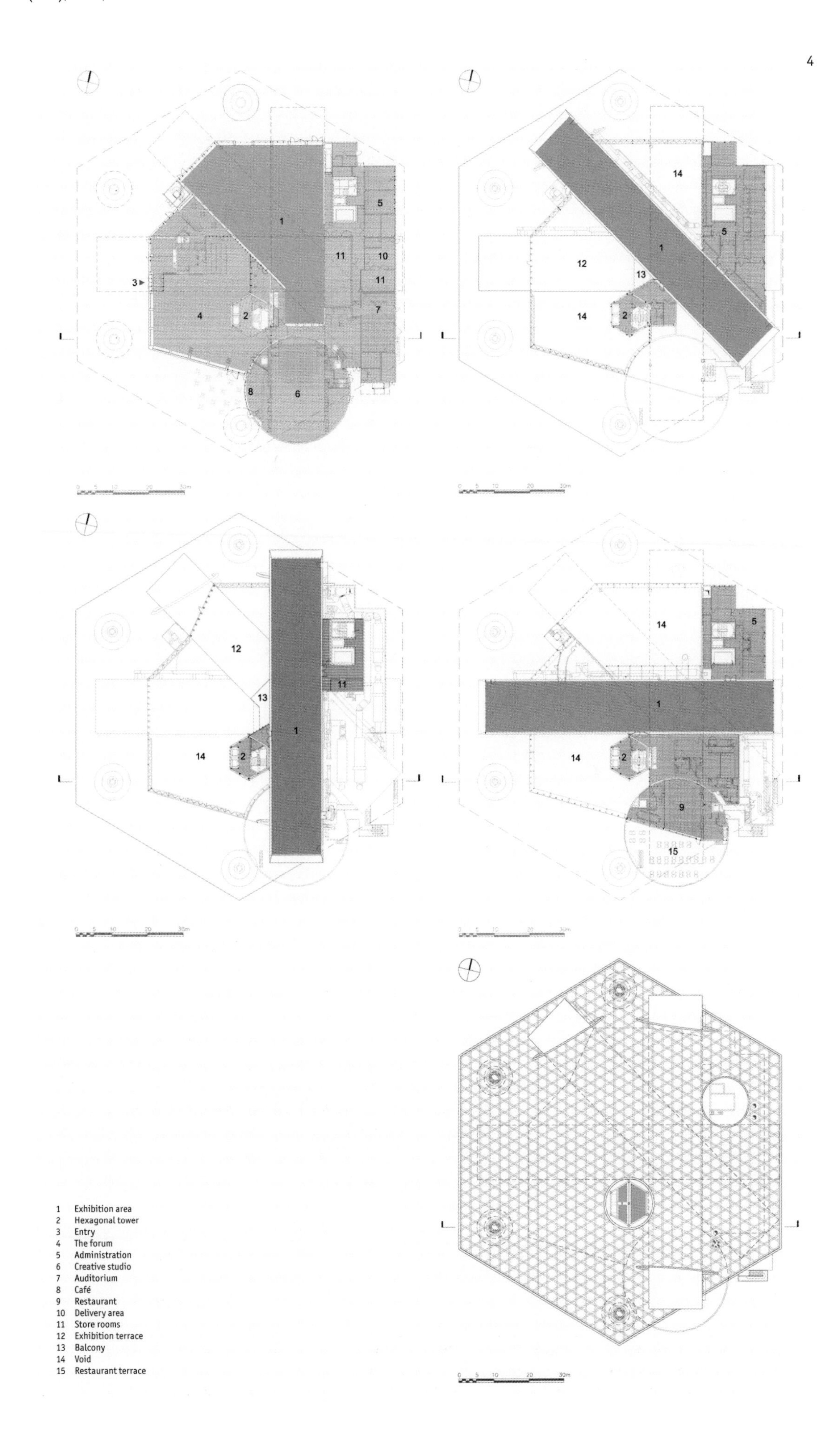

1 Exhibition area
2 Hexagonal tower
3 Entry
4 The forum
5 Administration
6 Creative studio
7 Auditorium
8 Café
9 Restaurant
10 Delivery area
11 Store rooms
12 Exhibition terrace
13 Balcony
14 Void
15 Restaurant terrace

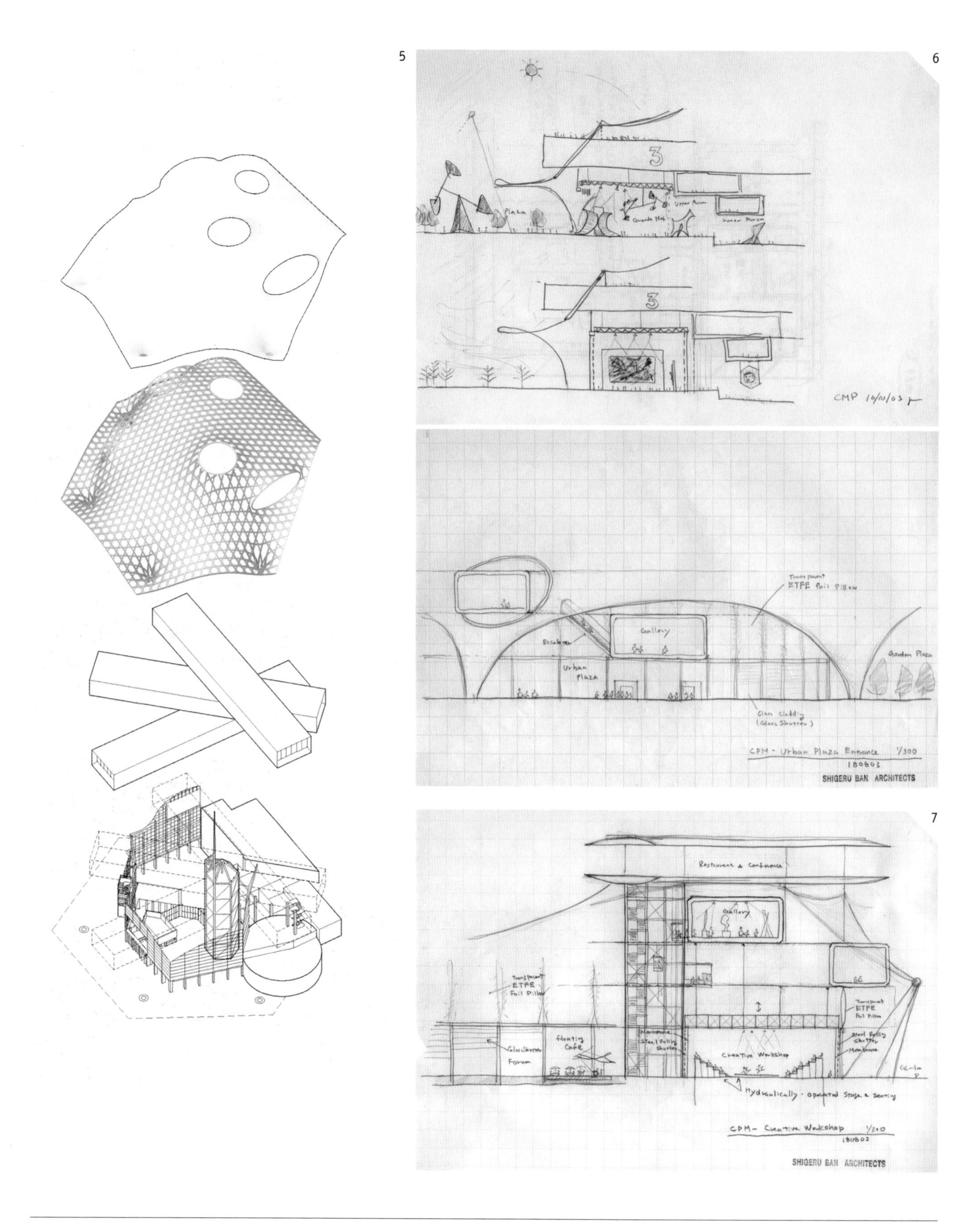

5 / Axonometric.

6 / Ban's early sketches: The concept grew from consideration of the essential qualities of the Pompidou Centre and how those could be integrated into a proposal for the CPM without mimicking the original design. The sketches here investigate visible permeability and how the entrance and public space of the forum could engage with the external environment.

7 / Inspired by the soaring interior of Metz' cathedral, early notions centred around the idea of creating a towering secular space topped by an impressive roof under which all the activities could take place.

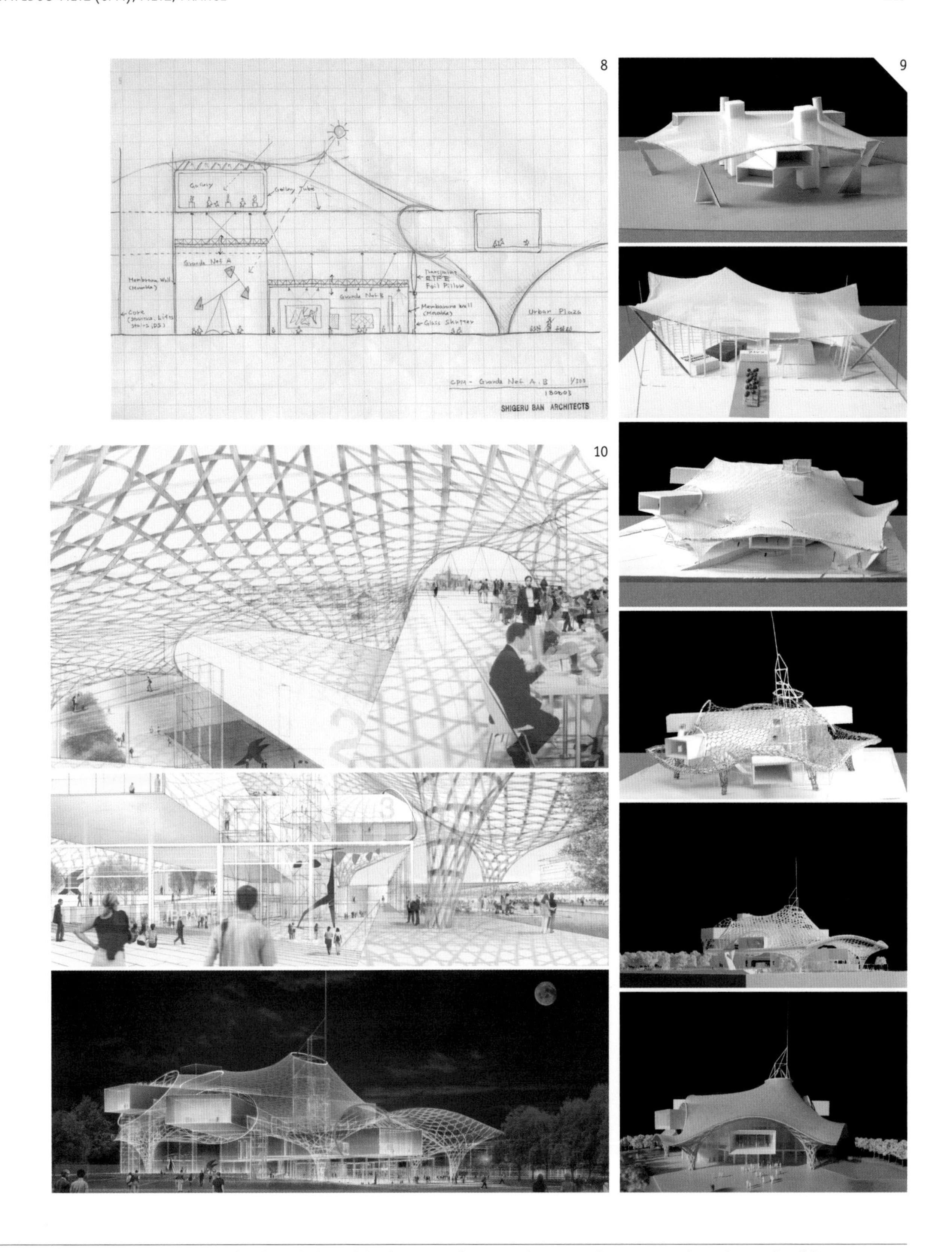

8 / Ban simplified the programme into simple volumes united by the protective roofscape through which the galleries, each aligned along a different axis, would penetrate.

9 / A sequential series of models was created over a period of eight weeks and used to work out the way the galleries could sit under the roof and punch through it. The models were also used to develop the idea of the tower generating a dramatic silhouette and to determine how the structure might meet the ground. An early idea was that it should rest on concrete pillars. Rapid prototyping was needed to form the complex shape of the roof.

10 / Presentation was made on four A1 (33.1 x 23.4 in) panels and included renderings. The competition was anonymous with each team being given the name of a famous artist. The architects (Miró) worked with the structural engineer Arup and specialist consultants to develop the proposal. The presentation showed every detail from heating and ventilation to how the structure could be detailed to meet building regulations. Gumuchdjian was instrumental in the schematic design but did not work on its development.

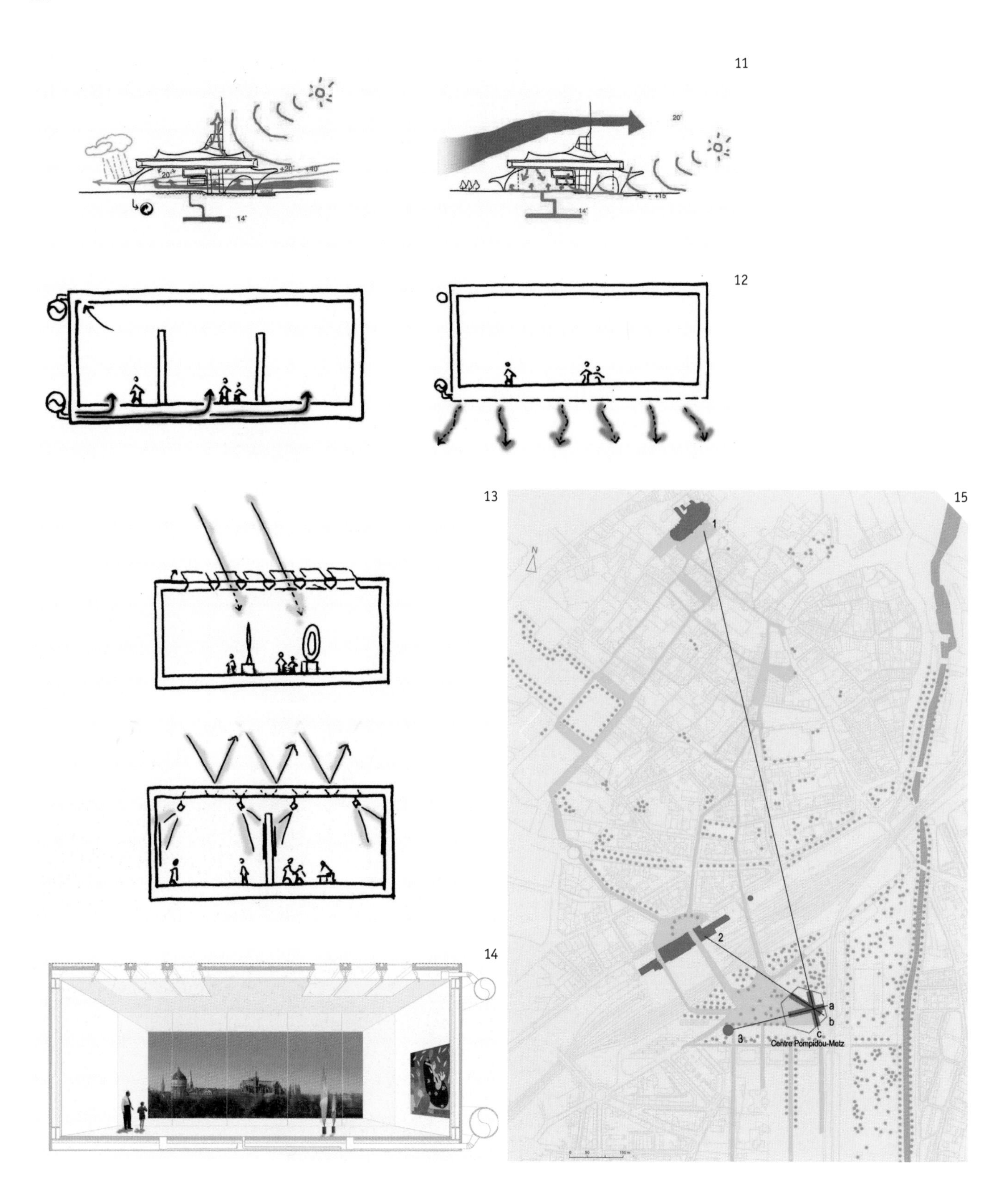

11 / Presentation: To insulate the whole building would have been prohibitively expensive. The main volume works passively with natural elements. Summer (left) and winter (right).

12 / Presentation: The temperature and humidity of the galleries has to be carefully controlled. The exhaust air that comes from them exits into the centre making it cooler in summer and warmer in winter.

13 / Presentation: The galleries can be lit naturally from above or turned into black boxes.

14 / Presentation: An important element of the concept is the view through the galleries' picture windows, which visually links the centre to the city of Metz.

15 / Presentation diagram showing the centre in its urban context and demonstrating how the site could be made to feel part of the main city. Routes are in yellow and sight lines in black.

16

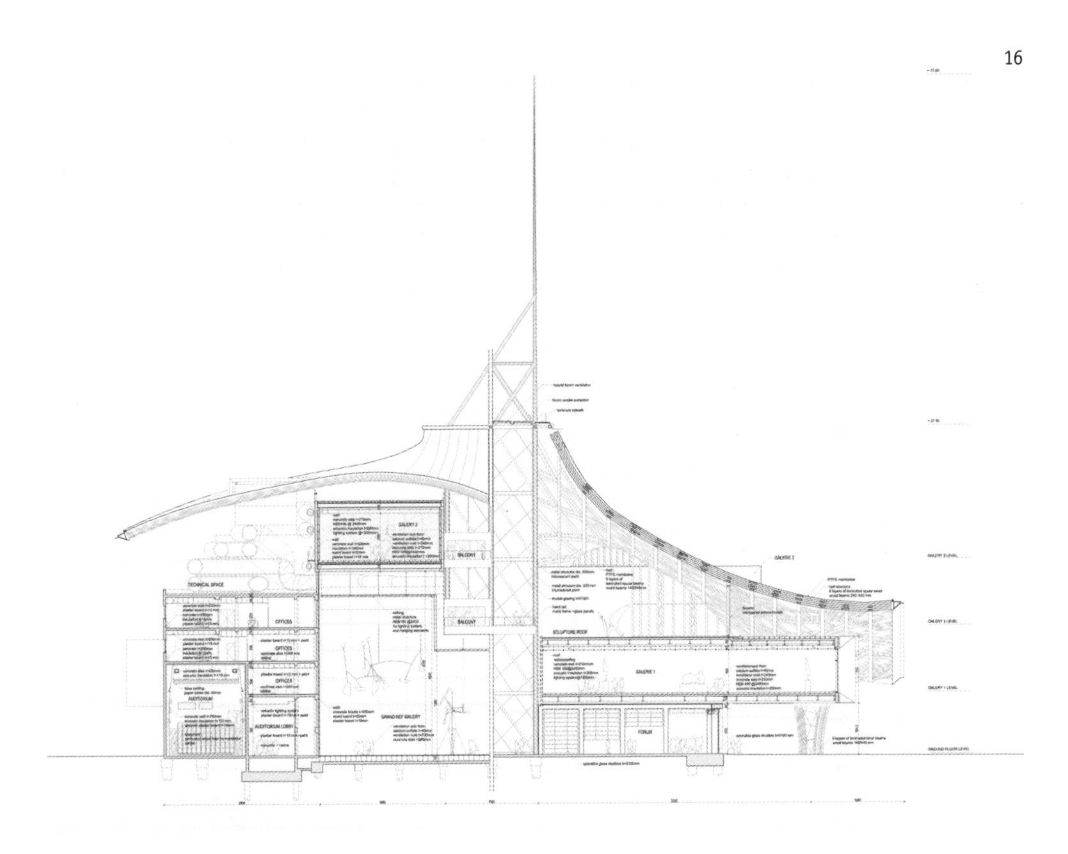

17

18

19

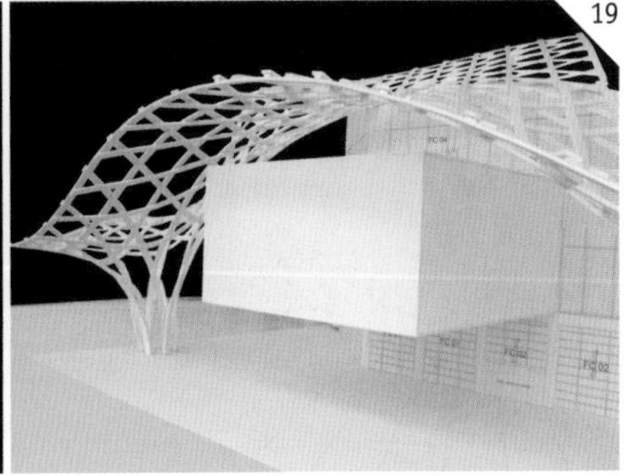

16 / Design intent drawing: Jean de Gastines heads Shigeru Ban's European office and was the architect charged with delivering the building. A full set of construction and detailed drawings was made.

17 / Once a timber specialist who was capable of producing the structure on budget and without using steel reinforcement had been sourced, the build was relatively smooth. Ban and de Gastines maintained a presence on site to control the French contractors and ensure corners were not cut or the design concept diluted.

18 / The roof was inspired in part by the patterns of hexagons and equilateral triangles found in woven Chinese hats and baskets. The hexagon is also the symbol of France.

19 / Studies and model for working out the patterning of the timber latticework.

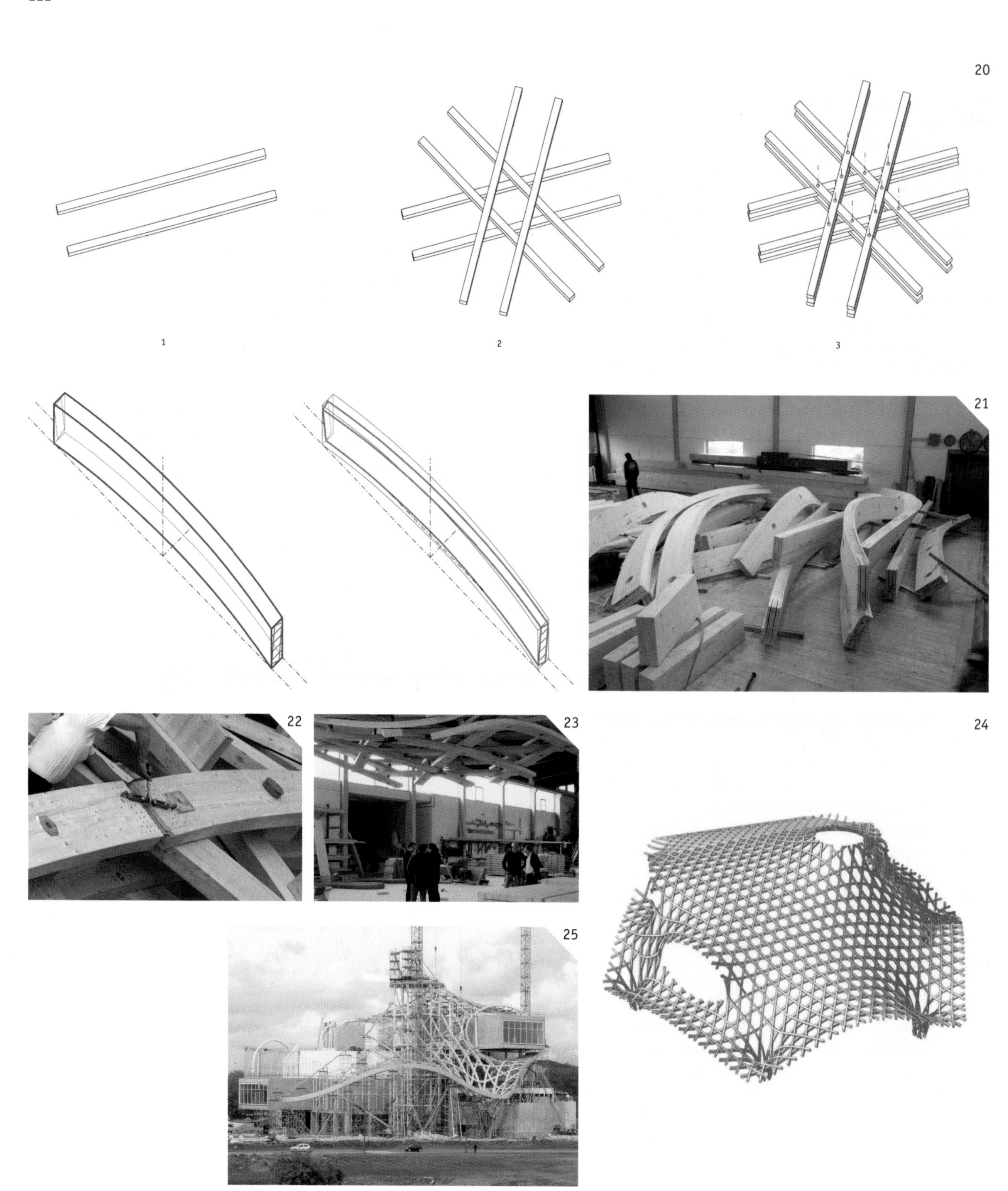

20 / The construction is a three-way, double-layered woven hexagonal timber lattice structure. The glue-laminated planks measure 49 x 14 cm x 15 m (19¼ x 5½ in x 49 ft) and are overlaid in three directions. A second layer, separated from the first by wooden blocks, is added to strengthen the assemblage. By using hexagons and triangles only four wooden elements ever overlap. The intersections do not use mechanical joints.

21 / The planks were prefabricated in Germany. Each has a single custom curve along its length and is CNC-milled to form a second twist.

22 / The timber is joined using steel plates at the ends of the planks, which are bolted together.

23 / Full-scale prototype of the wood timbering.

24 / Computer model of the timber latticework.

25 / The hexagonal tower supports the top of the structure with a tubular steel band. The grid-shell was built outwards from this point to the edge beams. Steel bands were also used to form the openings through which the galleries protrude.

26

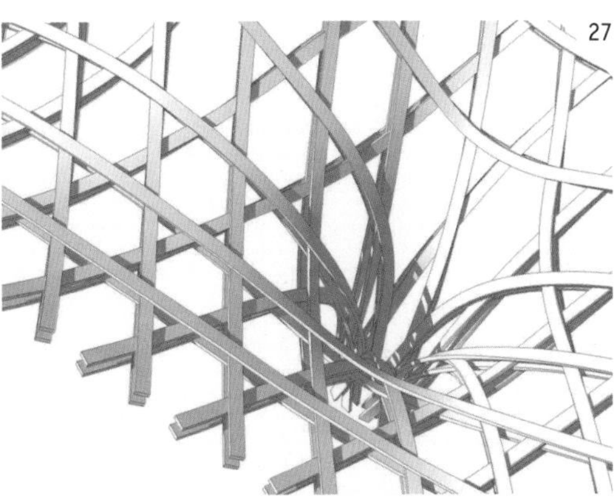

27

28

29

30

26 / The latticework descends into six three-dimensional columns set back from the edge of the structure. Steel bands hold the fibreglass and Teflon (PTFE) fabric in place.

27 / Computer model of the column geometry.

28 / The timberwork is covered by a waterproof membrane. It is secured by T-section steel elements. A gap between the layers allows for air movement and prevents condensation.

29 / In the spirit of the original Pompidou Centre, the galleries are unexpressed. Gumuchdjian describes them as 'extruded factories for exhibiting art'. Their neutrality offers curators the flexibility to mount a variety of exhibitions. An optical illusion makes Metz' Gothic cathedral appear to change size as visitors approach the window.

30 / The doors of the entrance space can be raised to bring the outside 'piazza' into the public space of the interior.

Brick Weave House

Studio Gang Architects

Location: Chicago, Illinois, USA
Principal use: Family residence
Client: David Hernandez and Tereasa Surratt
Site area: 344.2 m^2 (3,705 ft^2)
Interior area: 302 m^2 (3,250 ft^2)
Total build area: 223 m^2 (2,400 ft^2)
Design period: January 2005 – October 2006
Construction period: October 2006 – November 2008
Budget: $450,000

Jeanne Gang founded her architectural practice in 1997. Emphasizing the importance of research in the earlier stages of the design process, she describes her 35-strong studio as a laboratory that tests ideas on every scale from cities to the properties of materials. This methodology has led to an impressive worldwide portfolio in which place and a purpose-specific approach are evident. The mixed-use Aqua Tower in Chicago (2010), for example, uses sensuous and undulating balconies to create a community on its façade, and the 120,774-square-metre (1.3 million-square-foot) residential development in Hyderabad, India (2008), transforms the traditional Indian courtyard house into a modern and sustainable type for a growing local demographic.

At 223 square metres (2,400 square feet), the two-bedroom Brick Weave House was on the drawing board at the same time as the 82-storey Chicago skyscraper. Although on a much more intimate scale, it is no less striking in the way it uses materials and form expressively and innovatively to make that which is solid appear light and permeable. The clients, David Hernandez and Tereasa Surratt, are advertising executives with a keen visual eye, a passion for design and a quirky take on lifestyle that demanded that their collection of vintage cars and motorcycles be displayed as art pieces. Despite the restricted budget, Gang was attracted to the commission as the couple offered her complete artistic freedom.

In the late 1990s, Hernandez had purchased the property (a wood-frame stable dating from the 1880s that had been haphazardly added to over the years), drawn by its location, the extra-long site and the double-height space. A few years later he made a superficial attempt at renovation, but realized that a radical intervention was needed to make the house a home. Hernandez' and Surratt's initial response was to try to restore the original building but Gang's forensic engineering investigation revealed that neglect, water infiltration and fire damage meant that not enough of the original structure remained, and any attempt at refurbishment would be meaningless. However, in order to avoid zoning regulations that would have meant a set-back from the street, and to maintain a green approach to her design, she also ruled out the prospect of demolition in favour of strategically cutting away damage and weaving in a new construction to preserve as much of the footprint as possible.

Communication with the clients was informal and centred around conversations about how they liked to live, in order to develop the brief. It emerged that – as well as wanting their cars and motorcycles to be part of their living environment – they liked to entertain but had no interest in a showcase kitchen. Presentations were made in the form of physical models that allowed a better understanding of the layout and volumes as well as plans, sections, elevations and renderings.

Gang proposed several options for the plan. Her general design approach is self-challenging. She normally has a strong concept in mind but likes to come up with alternatives and discuss these with the client. In the case of the Brick Weave House the most radical programming was selected: the existing layout was reversed by creating two floors of living space in the former towering stable block, at that point used to display the cars. In turn, the lower part of the structure was made into a fully insulated but seldom-used garage that formed more of a 'sculpture gallery' and opened directly onto the dining area.

In the proposed sequence a hallway, which doubles as the kitchen, leads from a dining area at the front of the house and opens out into the two-storey living room at the rear. From here stairs lead to a loft and guest room, and a second short flight of steps connects these spaces to the master bedroom. In elevation the full extent of the site was retained. Although the front and side walls had to be removed, Gang worked on a way to create a more diaphanous and lighter façade abutting directly onto the street that still preserved privacy. Initially, she considered punching large apertures through newly constructed walls but quickly decided on a screen. By subtracting a 74.3-square-metre (800-square-foot) portion of the house's front she made room for a garden secreted behind a single-width masonry veil braced by steel columns and beams that extended outwards from the roof.

The architect collaborated with specialist consultants from the schematic design onwards. The structural engineer wanted to add a stiffer steel support but this would have restricted the brick screen's movement. The masons insisted the stiffer support would cause cracking in the joints as they expanded and contracted. A second engineer who specialized in designing hardware for masonry was employed to resolve the problem. He called for small steel trusses in the masonry joints and specified custom-made clips that extend from the brick mortar back up between the Norman brick into slotted connections welded to the steel columns. Because of the ambitious nature of the design, an expert in preservation and masonry construction was brought in to carry out a peer review of the engineers' work and sanction Gang's detailing.

The façade of the Brick Weave House is uncompromising in relation to the eclectic vernacular, late-nineteenth- and early-twentieth-century workers' cottages and townhouses on the suburban West Town block where it is situated. However, this did not pose planning problems as Gang was building on the previous foundation and preserving as much (30 per cent) of the original structure as possible. Both the interiors (which allow for the clients' individuality), and the sculptural exterior (which throws patterns of light into the house during the day and acts as a lantern at night), express a unique emotional warmth unusual in what is essentially a Modernist design.

1 / The Brick Weave House shines like a beacon on its limited site in the middle of a block of eclectic but unremarkable turn-of-the-20th-century urban housing.

1

2

4

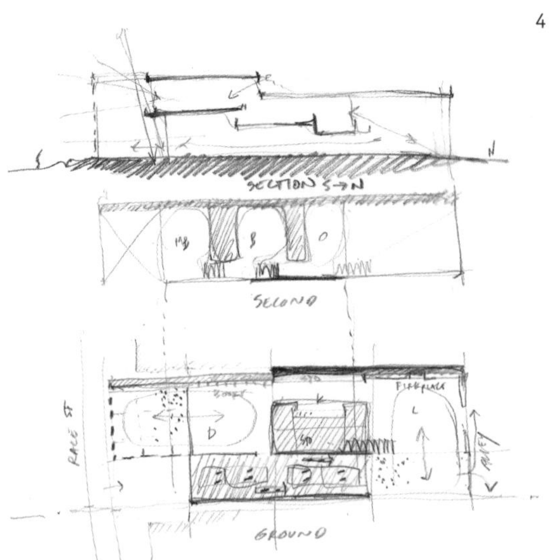

3

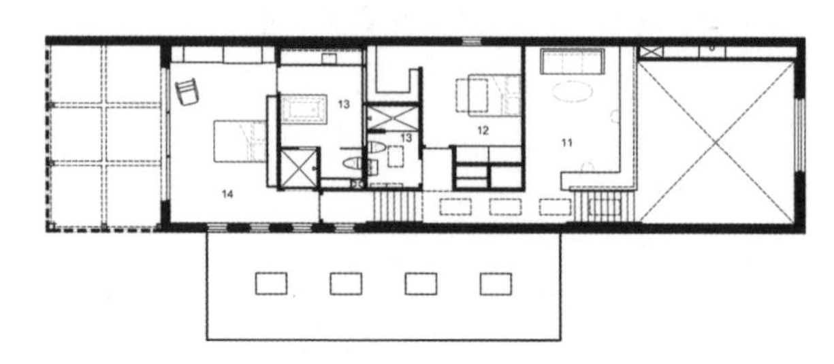

1 Garden
2 Dining room
3 Kitchen
4 Library
5 Living room
6 WC
7 Laundry room
8 Storage room
9 Mechanical
10 Garage
11 Family room
12 Study/bedroom
13 Bathroom
14 Bedroom

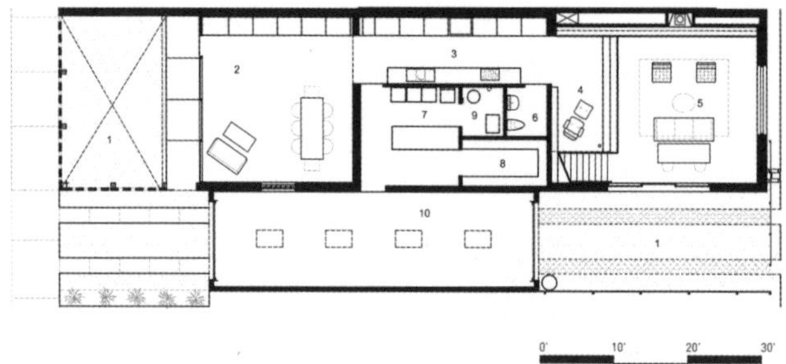

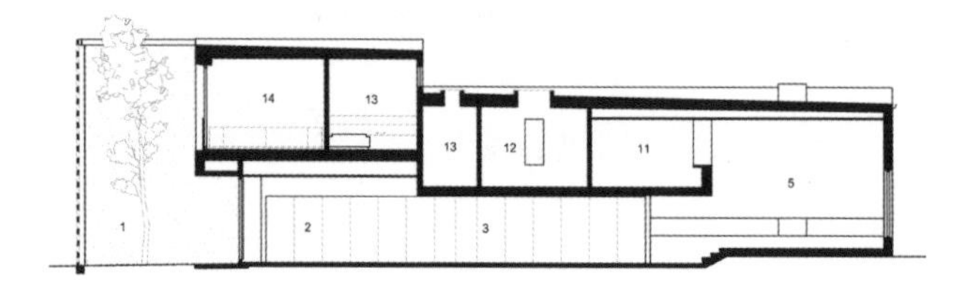

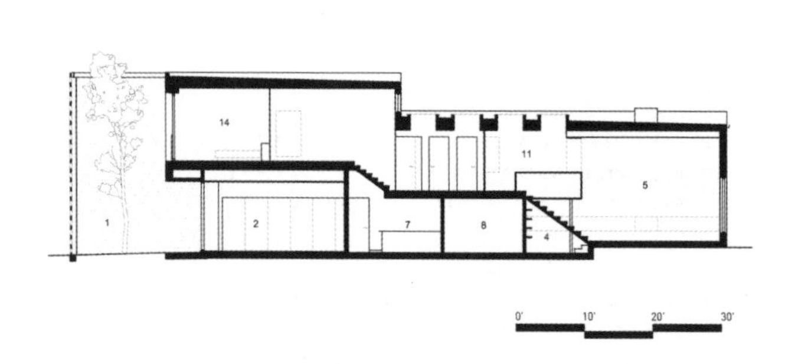

5

6

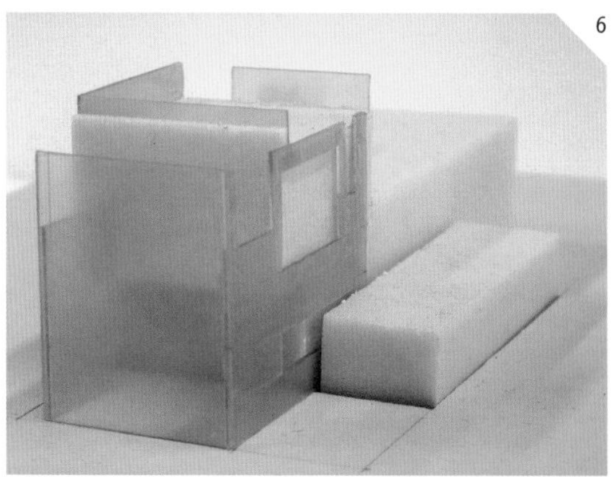

7

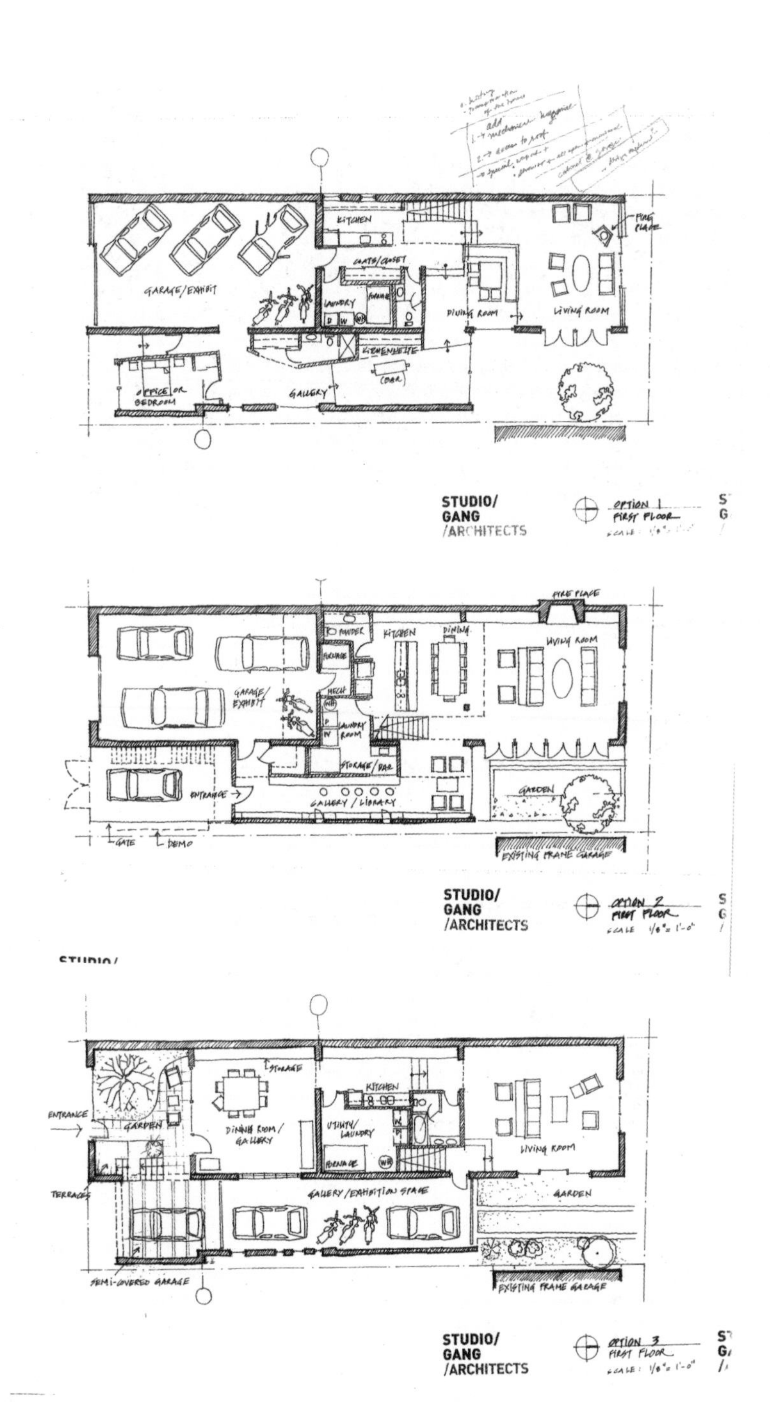

2 / The original building.

3 / Floor plans and sections: The site is long and linear. Gang manipulated ceiling heights and floor levels to create an interior landscape that matched the clients' brief for a small kitchen, entertainment space, integrated storage, rooms upstairs that could be used as spare bedrooms when needed and the all-important display area for the vintage car and motorcycle collection.

4 / Gang uses sketches extensively to communicate with her team face to face. The studio makes a point of instructing its interns on the art of hand-drawing as this is rarely taught in college.

5 / Gang believes there is a real art in getting a team to work together to progress a project. All the people involved discuss every aspect of a design, from concept to detailing, so if team members change everyone remains fully informed. Reinforcing the initial concept with each design decision and during construction is important so that the original goal is not lost.

6 / Before the brick screen concept had been developed many foam models were made to explore the way light could enter the building.

7 / Three alternative plan concepts were shown to the clients, all very different from one another.

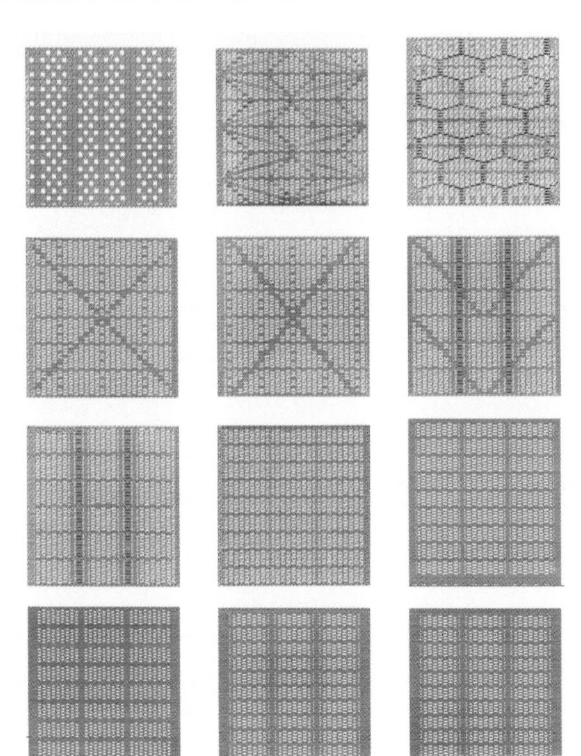

8 / Gang likes to use a large physical model to present to clients so that they can fully understand the spatial proportions of a building. Plans, sections and elevations were also used.

9 / Renderings were shown to illustrate how the building would appear aesthetically. The office worked with Autodesk/AutoCAD.

10 / The office also employs computer modelling to create design options and analyze geometric shapes. Here it illustrates how the screen sits in relation to the front façade of the house, and how it is attached.

11 / The patterning of the screen was conceived to match structural requirements and to maximize light and visibility while retaining privacy. Various iterations were investigated.

12 / Building section: The contract was a formal AIA design contract. Studio Gang was the architect of record, with the engineers working under it. The clients acted as the general contractor as they had knowledge of the building industry. The architect was responsible for the tender and construction documents and advised on selection of the sub-contractors, especially where the masonry was concerned.

13 / Detailed drawing: The screen is only one wythe thick, approximately 85 m (28 ft) tall and has no roof. To resist lateral (wind) loads, steel columns and beams tie it back to the rest of the house. The brick has to be attached to the steel columns to minimize horizontal movement but must be allowed to expand and contract in a vertical direction. Small steel trusses lie horizontally in the masonry joints, as well as custom-made clips that extend out and fit into slots in the columns to allow for the motion. Following the peer review the horizontally reinforced mortar joints were increased by 6 mm (¼ in) to provide additional coverage for the steel inside.

12

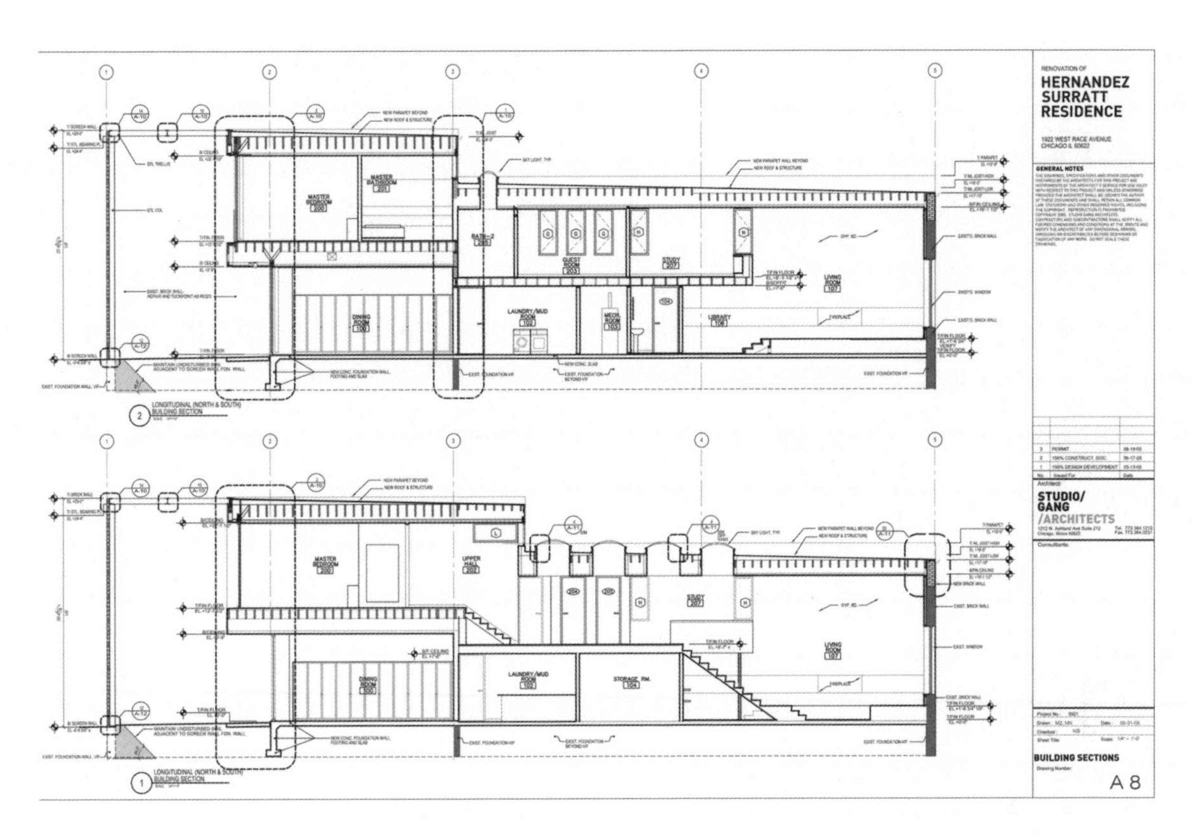
RENOVATION OF
HERNANDEZ SURRATT RESIDENCE
1922 WEST RACE AVENUE
CHICAGO IL 60622
GENERAL NOTES
MASTER BEDROOM 200
MASTER BATHROOM 201
BATH - 2 205
GUEST ROOM 203
STUDY 207
LIVING ROOM 107
DINING ROOM 100
LAUNDRY/MUD ROOM 102
LIBRARY 106
UPPER HALL 202
STORAGE RM. 104
LONGITUDINAL (NORTH & SOUTH) BUILDING SECTION
STUDIO/ GANG /ARCHITECTS
BUILDING SECTIONS
A8

13

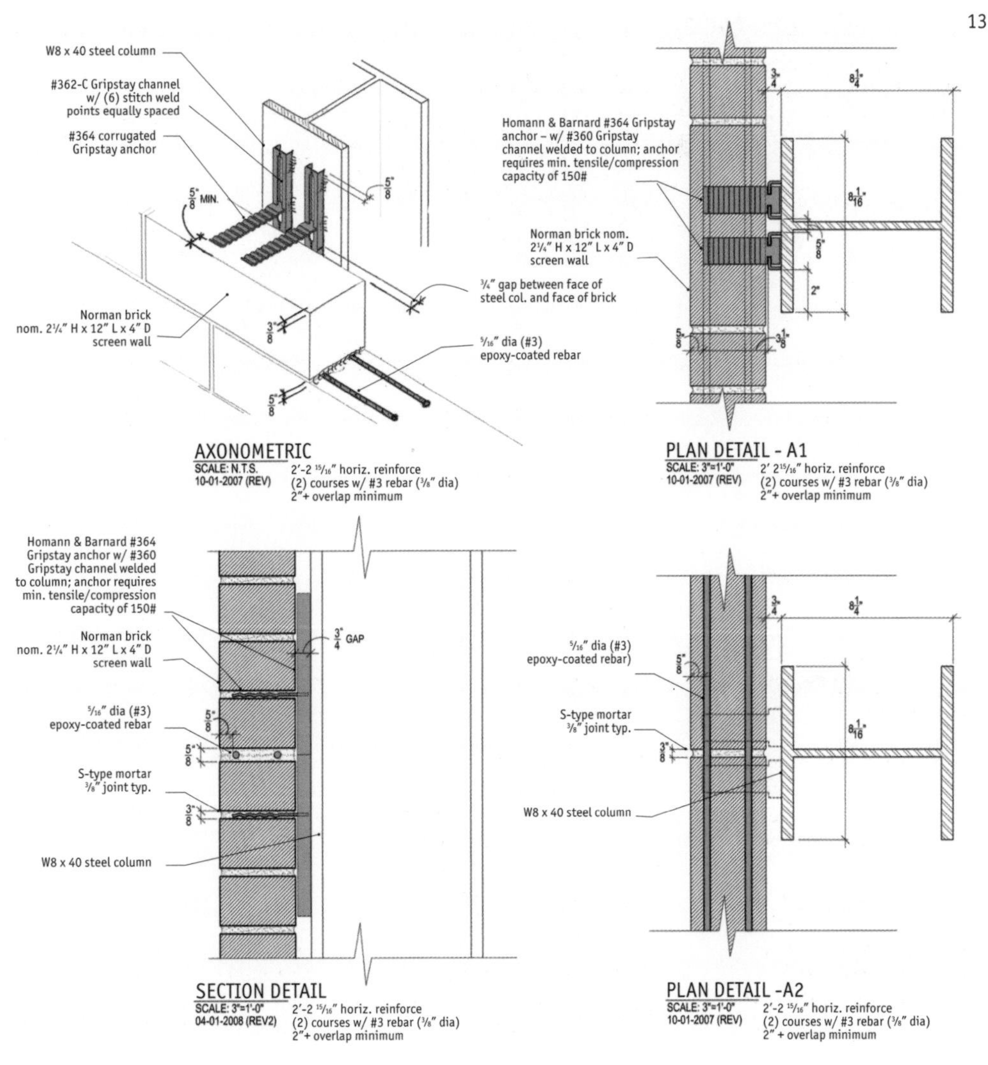
W8 x 40 steel column
#362-C Gripstay channel w/ (6) stitch weld points equally spaced
#364 corrugated Gripstay anchor
5/8" MIN.
Norman brick nom. 2¼" H x 12" L x 4" D screen wall
¾" gap between face of steel col. and face of brick
5/16" dia (#3) epoxy-coated rebar
AXONOMETRIC
SCALE: N.T.S.
10-01-2007 (REV)
2'-2 15/16" horiz. reinforce (2) courses w/ #3 rebar (3/8" dia) 2"+ overlap minimum
Homann & Barnard #364 Gripstay anchor – w/ #360 Gripstay channel welded to column; anchor requires min. tensile/compression capacity of 150#
Norman brick nom. 2¼" H x 12" L x 4" D screen wall
8¼"
8 1/16"
2"
PLAN DETAIL - A1
SCALE: 3"=1'-0"
10-01-2007 (REV)
2' 2 15/16" horiz. reinforce (2) courses w/ #3 rebar (3/8" dia) 2"+ overlap minimum
Homann & Barnard #364 Gripstay anchor w/ #360 Gripstay channel welded to column; anchor requires min. tensile/compression capacity of 150#
Norman brick nom. 2¼" H x 12" L x 4" D screen wall
5/16" dia (#3) epoxy-coated rebar
S-type mortar 3/8" joint typ.
W8 x 40 steel column
¾" GAP
SECTION DETAIL
SCALE: 3"=1'-0"
04-01-2008 (REV2)
2'-2 15/16" horiz. reinforce (2) courses w/ #3 rebar (3/8" dia) 2"+ overlap minimum
5/16" dia (#3) epoxy-coated rebar)
S-type mortar 3/8" joint typ.
W8 x 40 steel column
PLAN DETAIL -A2
SCALE: 3"=1'-0"
10-01-2007 (REV)
2'-2 15/16" horiz. reinforce (2) courses w/ #3 rebar (3/8" dia) 2" + overlap minimum

14 / During demolition it was discovered that charred joists supporting one of the roofs that was to be preserved had been covered over. The roof had to be sacrificed but this gave the architect the opportunity to build higher and let the design breathe.

15 / Solid Norman bricks were chosen to build the screen wall. Cored brick was used elsewhere.

16 / Close-up shot of the clips.

17 / The kitchen doubles as a corridor that leads from the dining room to the library.

18 / The dining room opens directly onto the garage, which is primarily used as a display area for the clients' cars such as the prized yellow 1968 Camaro Rally Sport.

19 / The open plan and operable windows allow air to move from the front to back of the house. Careful insulation and natural ventilation mean the building requires less energy than most. Skylights and clerestories illuminate the upper floors.

17

18

19

Index

Page numbers in *italics* refer to picture captions

Project credits

Villa Welpeloo
Client: T. J. Knol and I. E. C. Blans
Architect: 2012Architecten
www.2012architecten.nl
Project Team: Jan Jongert, Jeroen Bergsma (project architects); John Bosma, Frank Feder (full-time staff); Tanja Lina, Wojtek Witek, Caroline Karamann (interns); Iris de Kievith, Petra Jutten (interiors); Jos de Krieger (3-D model)
Main Contractor: Den Boer Bouwen en Installeren
Contractor – Primary Construction: J. Kerkhofs
Installation Consultant: Technisch Adviesburo Sanes (E. E. Pinas)
Construction Consultant: Bouwkundig Adviewsburo bv (N. Plukkel)
Ground Survey: Fugro Ingenieursbureau bv
Foundation Consultant: Mos Grondmechanica bv
Construction Specifications Consultant: Bureau Parmentier
Window Frame Installation: Staalbouw ter Huurne
Fittings: Bert Elshof Installatietechniel bv
Lighting: Elektro Dalenoort bv
Ventilation: Jakon Air
Platonised Cable Reel Wood: Plato International bv
Textile Machinery: Louwers & Co bv
Cable Reel Wood: Twentse Kabel Fabriek
Reclaimed Construction Wood: Komu
Finishing in the Sanitary Areas: Smile Plastics UK
Custom-made Cabinets in Kitchen and Bathroom: Houtwerk BV
Designer Lighting: En-Fer Atelier
Designer Wood and Glass Detailing: Studio Letterman

YTL Residence
Client: Private family
Architect: Agence JouinManku
www.patrickjouin.com
Project Team: Patrick Jouin, Sanjit Manku (partners-in-charge); Yann Brossier (architect); Richard Perron (designer)
Local Architect: YTL Design Group
Project Team: Baldip Singh (lead architect); Lee Hang Meng (civil and structural engineer); Fiona Lim Kah Yee (project manager); Regina Myra Sampil Superio (project interior designer)
Landscape Designer: Officina del Paesaggio, Sophie Agata Ambroise
Teak spiral staircase: YTL Joinery – Ng Har and Hee Chan Fook
Marble counter: Milano Marble Design – Francesco del Bubba and Alessandro Bogazzi with Luciano Massari

The YAS Marina Hotel
Client: Aldar Properties PJSC, Abu Dhabi
Architect: Asymptote Architecture – Hani Rashid + Lise Anne Couture
www.asymptote.net
Project Team: Hani Rashid, Lise Anne Couture (partners-in-charge); Mick McConnell, Andrew Drummond (project directors); Theo Sarantoglou Lalis, Constantin Doehler, Matthew Utley (project managers); Danny Abalos, Keehyun Ahn, Sebastian Andia, Bernardo Crespo, Greg Derrico, Reed Finlay, William Garcia, Armand Graham, Moritz Greiling, Justine Groves, John Guida, Kurt Hanzlik, Robert Hendrick, Tyson Hosmer, Robert Ivanov, Jeremiah Joseph, Feby Kuriakose, David Lessard, Sophie Luger, Brooks McDaniel, Jonathan Podborsek, Klaus Ransmayr, Ben Ritter, Greg Spaw, Ariane Stracke, Linda Stromgren, Kyle Stover, Tae-Hyung Park, Martin Zangerl, Christoph Ziegler (designers); Manca Ahlin, Phuttipan Askawool, Ali Baker, Christoph Boeckeler, Julie Bogdanowicz, Remi Chevrillon, Claudia Friesz, Hiroe Fujimoto, Daniel Angulo Garcia, Daniel Gillen, Avital Gourary, Richard Heger, Katharina Hieger, Julia Hoins, Ji Young Kim, Siyoung Kim, Jonathan Kleinhample, Adam Koogler, Rolando Lineros, Brendan Maloney, Mirai Morita, Tom Raymont, Friedrich Rohde, Sander Schuur, Greg Spaw, Jeff Walker, Robert Wehinger, Michael Whalen, Ann Wright, Margaret Yoo (assistants); Chris Delusky (commercial director)
Local Architects: Dewan Architects & Engineers; Tilke & Partners W.L.L.
Structural Engineers: Dewan Architects & Engineers; ARUP
Grid-shell Engineers: Schlaich Bergermann und Partner; Waagner-Buro
Grid-shell Building Information Modelling (BIM) Consultant: Gehry Technologies
Grid-shell Lighting Consultant: ARUP Lighting (Rogier van der Heide, Brian Stacy, Richard Fisher)
Grid-shell Wind Engineers: Wacker-Ingenieure
Grid-shell Node Housing Consultant: Billings Jackson Design
Façade Consultant: Front Inc; TAW & Partner
Link Bridge Engineers: ARUP Bridge; Centraal Staal
MEP Engineer: Red Engineering Middle East
Interior Design Consultants: Jestico + Whiles; Richardson Sadeki; De8 Architetti
Lighting Consultants: LAPD Lighting Design; Bartenbach LichtLabor GmbH; Red Engineering Middle East; ARUP Lighting
Landscape Design: Cracknell Landscape Architects
Audio, Visual and IT Consultants: Cyber-Consult
Traffic Consultant: WSP Middle East Ltd
Water Feature and Pool Consultant: Belhasa Projects, LLC
Fire Safety: Wagner Fire Safety Management Consultants
Signage and Wayfinding Strategy: GS Fitch
Vertical Transportation: VDA
Security: Oliver Group
Kitchen and Laundry: Tricon Foodservice Consultants PLC
Food and Beverage: Future Food

Nordwesthaus
Client: Hafen Rohner GmbH & Co. KG
Architect: Baumschlager Eberle Lochau
www.baumschlager-eberle.com
Project Architect: Christoph von Oefele
Project Management: Baumschlager Eberle Lochau
Building Technology: GMI Ing. Peter Messner GmbH AT
Structural Engineer: Madr + Flatz AT
Façade: Glas Marte GmbH AT
Superstructure: Oberhauser-Schedler Bau AT
Lighting: Baumschlager Eberle Lochau (concept) in cooperation with Zumtobel Lighting GmbH AT (technical lighting consultant) and Ledon Lighting GmbH AT (installation)

Ozeaneum – German Oceanographic Museum
Client: Deutsches Meeresmuseum Stralsund
Competition and Schematic Design: Behnisch & Partner - Günter Behnisch, Manfred Sabatke
Architect: Behnisch Architekten – Stefan Behnisch, Martin Haas, David Cook (partners-in-charge)
www.behnisch.com
Project Team: Peter Schlaier, Elke Reichel (project management); Jakob Fürniß, Sebastian Wockenfuß, Antonella Sgobba, Florian Kneer, Berthold Jungblut, Katja Knaus, Jörg Knaus, Michael Kern, David Mrugala
Project Consultancy: Stadterneuerungsgesellschaft mbH
Construction Administration: ARGE Schnittger PG/AIU Stralsund GmbH
Structural Engineer: Schweitzer GmbH Beratende Ingenieure
Energy Consultant: Transsolar Energietechnik
Exhibition Design: Atelier Lohrer (exhibition); argea fassbender heppert (aquarium and kinderland); Leitfaden-Design (exhibition illustrations and graphics)
Signage: OCKERTUNDPARTNER
Landscape Design: Prof. Nagel, Schonhoff & Partner
Fire Codes: TÜV Nord Systems GmbH
Aquarium Engineering: Ingenieurbüro Joecks
Mechanical Engineering: SCHREIBER Ingenieure Gebäudetechnik GmbH
Plumbing Engineering: Ingenieurbüro Thomas Engelbrecht
Heating Engineering: INROS Lackner AG
Building Physics: Ingenieurbüro Horstmann + Berger
Electrical and Lighting: Ingenieurbüro Walter Bamberger
Elevator Consultant: AIU Stralsund GmbH
Building Management Systems: Ingenieurbüro Uwe Trepping
Façade Consultancy: EURO-Fassadentechnik GmbH
Waterproofing: Umweltplan GmbH
CA Consultancy: Ingenieurbüro für Bauleitung Arndt
Surveyor: Krawutschle . Meißner . Schönemann

Etrium
Client: HIBA Grundbesitz GmbH & Co. KG
Architect: Benthem Crouwel Architekten GmbH
www.benthemcrouwel.nl
Project Team: Markus Sporer, Sascha Rullkötter, Cornelius Wens
General Contractor: Friedrich Wassermann GmbH
Structural Engineer: Martin Gerdes – Beratender Ingenieur
Technical Engineer: Zeiler + Partner
Building Physics: ISRW Dr. -Ing Klapdor GmbH
Fire Protection: Heister + Ronkartz
Simulations: ifes GmbH
User at time of going to press: Econcern GmbH

The Neues Museum Berlin
Client: Stiftung Preußischer Kulturbesitz represented by Bundesamt für Bauwesen und Raumordnung
User: Staatliche Museen zu Berlin
Architect: David Chipperfield Architects in collaboration with Julian Harrap Architects
www.davidchipperfield.co.uk; www.julianharraparchitects.co.uk
Consultant/Site Supervision (restoration): Pro Denkmal GmbH
Landscape Architect: Levin Monsigny Landschaftsarchitekten
Exhibition Design: architetto Michele de Lucchi SrL
Structural Engineer: Ingenieurgruppe Bauen
Services Engineer: Jaeger, Mornhinweg + Partner Ingenieurgesellschaft (heating, ventilation and sanitation)
Services Engineer: Kunst und Museumsschutz Beratungs und Planungs GmbH (electrical and security)
Building Physics: Ingenieurbüro Axel C. Rahn GmbH
Site Supervision: Lubic & Woehrlin GmbH
Lighting Consultant: Kardorff Ingenieure Lichtplanung
Quantity Surveyor: Nanna Fütterer for David Chipperfield Architects
Project Management: Ernst & Young Real Estate GmbH

The Hotel Cha Am
Client: KS Resort and Spa Co. Ltd
Architect: Duangrit Bunnag Architect Limited (DBALP)
www.dbalp.com
Project Team: Duangrit Bunnag (design director); Saranya Srisakulchairak (architect group head); Kahitha Boonyatasaneekul (architect); Prinpond Boonkham (interiors); Thiti Tritrakarn (landscape architect)
Contractor: Square Tech Co. Ltd.
Structural Engineer: EMS Consultant Co. Ltd.
System Engineer: Fusion Consultant Co. Ltd.
Construction Management: Arun Chaseri Consulting Engineers Co. Ltd.

House at No. 85 Swain's Lane
Client: Richard Elliott
Architect: Eldridge Smerin
www.eldridgesmerin.com
Project Team: Nick Eldridge, Piers Smerin, George Dawes, Amalia Skoufoglou, Alison Poole
Main Contractor, in situ concrete: Harris Calnan
Structural Engineer: Elliott Wood Partnership
Services Engineer: Mendick Waring
Concrete Consultant: David Bennett
Quantity Surveyor: AB Associates
Lighting Designer: ILS
Home Entertainment/Security: SMC Integration
Glass: Ide Contracting
Glass Sliding Doors: Fineline Aluminium
Glass Floors: Compass Glass
Sliding Glass Rooflight: Glazing Vision
Grass Roof System: Bauder
Stone Cladding and Flooring: G. Miccoli & Son
Steel Mesh: Potter and Soar
Metal Cladding/Flashings: Dutton Engineering; Brent Fabrications.
Doors/Specialist Joinery: Opus Magnum; 3D Joinery
Kitchen Supplier: Bulthaup
Bathroom Fixtures: Alternative Plans
Blinds: Levolux
Multi-Room HiFi/AV System: Meridian

Moses Mabhida Stadium
Client: Municipality of Durban (eThekwini Municipality) Strategic Projects Unit (SPU)
Architect: gmp - von Gerkan, Marg und Partners Architects, Berlin, Germany, in cooperation with Ibhola Lethu Consortium, South Africa
www.gmp-architekten.de
Project Team: Volkwin Marg and Hubert Nienhoff with Holger Betz (design); Holger Betz, Burkhard Pick, Elisabeth Menne (project leaders); Christian Blank, Alberto Franco Flores, Rüdiger von Helmolt, Jochen Köhn, Martin Krebes, Helge Lezius, Florian Schwarthoff, Kristian Uthe-Spencker (staff – design); Barbara Düring, Robert Essen, Alberto Franco Flores, Chris Hättasch, Martin Paul, Michèle Rüegg, Susan Türke (staff – execution).
Ibhola Lethu Consortium (ILC): Theunissen Jankowitz Architects, Ambro Afrique Architects, Osmond Lange Architects, NSM Designs, Mthulusi Msimang Architects South Africa
Structural Concept and Roof Design: schlaich bergermann und partner – Knut Göppert with Markus Balz
Structural Engineering: BKS (pty) Ltd
Project Management: Ibhola Lethu Project Management JV
General Contractor: Group Five WBHO + Pandev JV

Ecomusée du Pays de Rennes
Client: Rennes Métropole
Program: Préprogram
Architect: Guinée*Potin
www.guineepotin.fr
Project Team: Hervé Potin, Anne-Flore Guinée (partners-in-charge); Solen Nico (project manager); Céline Monvoisin, Adélaide Fiche, Jérôme Le Denmat
Engineering: Isateg Atlantique Bureau d'Études, Nantes (engineering department) – Isabelle Lainel (construction manager), Sebastien Briand (MPE engineer), Alain Mallier (electrical engineer), Christophe Breard (structural engineer)
Engineering Supervisor: DEKRA (Hervé Pateau)
Outside developments and waterways: Lehagre
Building Shell: Bouchard
Wooden Frame and Waterproofing: Cruard
Exterior Woodwork: Le Blanc
Iron and Metalwork: Loca Métal
Interior Woodwork and Fittings: Heude Bâtiment
Partition Walls: Armor Rénovation
False Ceilings and Tiling: Sarl Louis Brel
Concrete Screed: Cote Béton
Flooring: Malle
Paintwork: Tiriault
Heating, Ventilation and Sanitation: Hamon
Electricity: Satel
Lift: ABH
Wrought-ironwork: SAS Cin'équip
Furnishing: Formes Nouvelles
Signage: Élite Enseignes

The Dovecote Studio
Client: Aldeburgh Music
Architect: Haworth Tompkins
www.haworthtompkins.com
Main Contractor: Elliston Steady and Hawes (building) Ltd
Structural Engineer: Price and Myers LLP
Environmental Engineer: Ernest Griffiths
CDM Coordinator: PFB Construction Management Services Ltd

UK Pavilion, Shanghai World Expo
Client: Foreign and Commonwealth Office
Architect: Heatherwick Studio
www.heatherwick.com
Project Team: Thomas Heatherwick, Katerina Dionysopoulou (project architect), Robert Wilson, Peter Ayres, Stuart Wood, Ingrid Hu, Jaroslav Hulin, Chiara Ferrari, Ramona Becker
Executive Architect: Architectural Design & Research Institute of Tongji University
Supporting Architect: RHWL
Project Manager: Mace Group
Structural Engineer: Adams Kara Taylor
Environmental Engineer: Atelier Ten
Fire and Risk Engineering: Safe Consulting
Quantity Surveyor: Davis Langdon & Seah
Walkway Exhibition Design: Troika
Content Advisory Team: Mark Jones, John Sorrell, David Adjaye
Content Advisor: Philip Dodd
Content Coordinator: Adriana Paice

Loblolly House
Client: Stephen Kieran
Architects: KieranTimberlake Architects
www.kierantimberlake.com
Project Team: Stephen Kieran, James Timberlake, David Riz, Marilia Rodrigues, Johnathan Ferrari, Alex Gauzza, Jeff Goldstein, Shawn Protz, George Ristow, Mark Rhoads
Fabrication and Assembly: Bensonwood Homes
Construction: Arena Program Management
Structural Engineer: CVM Structural Engineers
MEP Engineer: Bruce Brooks & Associates
Civil Engineer: Lane Engineering
Geotechnical Engineer: John D. Hynes & Associates
Interiors: Marguerite Rodgers
Landscape Design: Barbara Seymour Landscapes

Weiner Townhouse
Client: Lawrence and Alice Weiner
Architect: LOT-EK
www.lot-ek.com
Project Team: Ada Tolla + Giuseppe Lignano (principals); Haruka Saito (project architect)
Structural and MEP Engineer: Hanington Engineering
Sustainability Consultant: Buro Happold
Lighting Design: L'Observatoire International
Contractor/Construction Manager: Cross Architecture
Truck Bay Windows: Truck Body East

La Llotja de Lleida
Client: Centre de Negocis i de Convencions SA, Lleida
Architect: Mecanoo architecten in cooperation with Labb arquitectura
www.mecanoo.nl
Technical Architect: J/T Ardèvols i Associats SL, Barcelona
Main Contractor/Builder: UTE Dragados + Obrum
Project Manager: Eptisa SA, Direcció Integrada, Barcelona
Structural Engineer: ABT bv, Delft (competition); BOMA, Barcelona
Acoustics: Peutz bv, Zoetermeer (competition); Arau Acústica, Barcelona
Electrical and Mechanical Engineer: Deerns Raadgevende Ingenieurs bv (competition), Rijswijk; Einesa, Lleida
Building Cost Consultant: Besalt Bouwkostenadvies, Nieuwegein (competition); J/T Ardèvols i Associats SL, Barcelona
Security and Fire Safety Consultant: Einesa Ingenieria SL, Leida
Principal Collaborators: Suris, Soclesa, Samaca, Eurogramco, Scenic Light, Chemtrol, Bujvar Cnes, Schindler, Tecnotec, Variopark, Comercial Helvetia, Aris, Impersegre, Nou Estil, Dynamobel

New Youth Centre
Client: Rivas Vaciamadrid Council
Architect: Mi5 Arquitectos
www.mi5arquitectos.com
Project Team: Manuel Collado, Nacho Martín (project architects); Eider Holgado, Richar Barajas, Diego Barajas
Structural Engineer: Juan Travesí
Main Contractor: Dragados
Installation Engineer: Juan Travesí
Structural Engineer: Tomás Dalda
Building Engineer: MariCarmen Nombela

Mapungubwe Interpretation Centre
Client: SANParks (South African National Parks)
Architect: Peter Rich Architects
www.peterricharchitects.co.za
Project Team: Peter Rich (principal architect); Heinrich Kammeyer (project architect); Desrae Dunn, Heinrich Kammeyer, Abdullah Abbas (contract documentation); Jennifer Ban Den Busche (administration)
Timbrel Design and Construction Engineers: Michael Ramage and John Ochsendorf
Timbrel Construction Training and Implementation Engineering Agent: James Bellamy
Soil Cement Consultant: Dr Anne Fitchett in collaboration with Hydraform and Matt Hodges (MIT)
Civil and Structural Engineering: Henry Fagan Architects
Quantity Surveying: DHCT Management Consulting
Main Contractor: Ousna Bouers

Step Up on Fifth
Client: Step Up on Second
Architect: Brooks + Scarpa Architects (formerly Pugh + Scarpa Architects)
www.brooksscarpa.com
Project Team: Lawrence Scarpa (design architect), Angela Brooks (principal-in-charge), Brad Buter, Silke Clemens, Ching Luk, Matt Majack, Luid Gomez, Omar Barcena, Dan Safarik, Gwynne Pugh
Main Contractor: Ruiz Brothers
Consultants: Laschober + Sovich (food services), Helios International, Inc. (environmental)
Structural Engineer: John Martin & Associates
MPE Engineering: Alan Locke (IBE Consulting Engineers)
Metal Fabrication: Ramsey Daham
Landscape Architect: Landscape Scenarios

Bodegas Protos
Client: Bodegas Protos
Architect: Rogers Stirk Harbour + Partners (RSHP)
www.richardrogers.co.uk
Project Team: Raquel Borrás, Maxine Campbell, Mike Fairbrass, Silvia Fukuoka, Russell Gilchrist, Lennart Grut, Jan Güell, Juan Laguna, Ronald Lammerts Van Beuren, Tim Mason, Jack Newton, Tamiko Onozawa, Susana Ribes, Richard Rogers, Graham Stirk, Patricia Vázquez, Martin White, Neil Wormsley, Andrew Yek
Co-architect: Alonso Balaguer i Arquitectos Asociados
Project Manager: CEM Management
Main Contractor: Fomento de Construccionnes y Contratas
Structural Engineer: Arup; BOMA; Agroindus
Services Engineer: BDSP Partnership; Grupo JG; Agroindus
Quantity Surveyor: Tècnics G3; Agroindus; José María Garrido
Lighting Consultants: Biosca & Botey
Mechanical Services Sub-contractor: Internacional Tecair
Electrical Services Sub-contractor: Crespo y Blasco
Syphonic Drainage System Manufacturer and Sub-contractor: Fullflow
Precast Concrete: Prefabricados Pujol
In-situ Concrete: Ferrallas y Armados Tecozam (reinforcement manufacturer and sub-contractor)
Formwork: Doka (manufacturer and sub-contractor)
Concrete Sub-contractor: Valentín de Lucas
Concrete Rafts Sub-contractor: Rinol Rocland Suesco
Steel Structures Sub-contractor: Talleres CYM
Timber Structure Manufacturer and Sub-contractor: Holtza
Tension Rods: Halfen – Deha
EPDM Rubber Membrane Manufacturer and Sub-contractor: Giscosa Firestone
Terracotta Tiles: Saint Gobain Terreal España (manufacturer); Ferrotec (installation sub-contractor)
Façades Manufacturer and Sub-contractor: Bellapart
Limestone Quarry and Sub-contractor: Marmolera Vallisoletana
Ceramic Floor Tiles: Rosa Gres
Internal Glass Partitions Manufacturer and Sub-contractor: Bellapart
Glass Floors and Glass Balustrades: Cricursa (manufacturer); Etxeglass (installation)
Office Partitions Manufacturer and Sub-contractor: Arlex

Maggie's London
Client: Maggie's Centres
Architect: Rogers Stirk Harbour + Partners (RSHP)
www.richardrogers.co.uk
Project Team: Ivan Harbour (project director), William Wimshurst (project architect); Ed Burgess, John Dawson, James Curtis, Mike Fairbrass, Tom Lacy, Carmel Lewin, Annette Main, Tim Mason, Annie Miller, Liz Oliver, Richard Rogers, Laura Salisbury, Paul Thompson, Martin White, Neil Wormsley
Landscape Architect: Dan Pearson Partners
Lighting Consultant: Speirs and Major Associates
Planning Supervisor: TPS Schal
Fire Consultant: Warrington Fire Consultants
Quantity Surveyor: Turner Townsend
Services Engineer: Arup
Structural Engineer: Arup
Specifications Consultant: Davis Langton Schumann Smith
Main Contractor: ROK
Access Consultant: Vin Goodwin
Approved Inspectors: Butler & Young
Roof Subcontractor: SAS International
Concrete Sub-contractor: Whelan & Grant
Joinery Sub-contractor: Midland Joinery
Concrete Floor: Steyson Granolithic Contractors

Design Museum Holon
Client: The Municipality of Holon
Architect: Ron Arad Architects
www.ronarad.co.uk
Project Team: Ron Arad, Asa Bruno (project architect), James Foster, Tavis Wright
Executive Architect: Waxman Govrin Engineering Ltd (Ms Sharon Ben Shem)
Project Manager: Waxman Govrin Engineering Ltd (Mr Yigal Govrin)
Main Contractor: Asher Green Construction Co.
Structural Engineer: Harmel Engineering
Mechanical Engineer: D. Hahn Consultant Engineers
Electrical Engineer: G. B. Engineering
Quantity Surveyor: Gamzo Engineering Services
Lighting Designer: RTLD
Landscape Architect: TeMA Landscape Architecture
Steel Sub-contractor: Marzorati-Ronchetti (Roberto Travaglia, Umberto D'Aquino)
Graphic/Signage Designer: Adi Stern Graphic Design

Long Studio
Client: Shorefast Foundation and The Fogo Island Arts Corporation
Architect: Saunders Architects
www.saundersarchitects.com
Project Team: Todd Saunders (principal architect); Ryan Jørgensen, Attila Berés, Colin Hertberger, Cristina Maier, Olivier Bourgeois, Pål Storsveen, Nick Herder (assistants)
Local Architect: Sheppard Case Architects
On-site Supervisor: Dave Torraville
Builders: Arthur Payne, Edward Waterman
Structural Engineer: DBA Consulting Engineers
Mechanical and Electrical Engineer: Core Engineering Inc.

Centre Pompidou-Metz (CPM)
Client: Communauté d'Agglomération de Metz Métropole (CA2M)
Architect: Shigeru Ban Architects with Jean de Gastines Architectes and Gumuchdjian Architects
www.shigerubanarchitects.com; www.jdg-architectes.com; www.gumuchdjian.com
Competition Project Team: Shigeru Ban Architects (Shigeru Ban, Nobutaka Hiraga, Mamiko Oshida, Asako Kimura, Anne Scheou; Toshi Kubota, Hiroshi Maeda (graphic designers)); Jean de Gastines Architectes (Jean de Gastines); Gumuchdjian Architects (Philip Gumuchdjian, Shinya Mori, Ralf Eikelberg)
Design and Site Administration Project Team: Shigeru Ban Architects Europe (Shigeru Ban, Gerardo Perez, Marc Ferrand, Jacques Marie, Fayçal Tiaïba, Elsa Neufville, Vincent Laplante, Alessandro Boldrini, Hiromi Okada, Jeong Hoon Lee, Jae Whan Shin, Jonathan Thornhill, Rahim Danto Barry); Jean de Gastines Architectes (Jean de Gastines).
Structural Engineer – competition: Ove Arup London
Structural Engineer – design and site administration: Ove Arup (Phase I); Terrell, Paris (Phase II)
Structure of the Timber Roof: Hermann Blumer
Construction of the Timber Roof Holzbau Amann; SJB (structural analysis)
General Contractor: Demathieu & Bard
Roof Membrane: Taiyo Europe
MEP: Ove Arup, Gec Ingénierie
Lighting: L'Observatoire 1, Icon
Quantity Surveyor: J. P. Tohier & Associés
Acoustics: Commins Acoustics Workshop
Security Consultant: Cabinet Casso & Cie

Brick Weave House
Client: David Hernandez and Tereasa Surratt
Architect: Studio Gang Architects
www.studiogang.net
Project Team: Jeanne Gang (design principal), Jay Hoffman (project leader), Margaret Cavenagh, Beth Kalin, Miriam Neet, Mauricio Sánchez (designers), Sophia Sebti, Schyler Smith (model makers)
General Contractor: Tom Klein of Highland Home Improvements
Structural Engineer: Michael Hamilton and George J. Podrebarac of Graef, Anhalt, Schloemer & Assoc. Inc.
Structural Peer Review: Edward J. Swierz of Thornton Tomasetti
MEP: Sachin Anand, formerly of CCJM Engineers, Ltd.
Mason: Jakub Zatwarnicki of Build Max Inc.
Steel Fabrication: Grimm Metal Fabricators

Picture credits

Unless listed below all visual material was kindly supplied courtesy of the architects featured and is without a specific credit.

7-T Ltd/Courtesy Rogers Stirk Harbour + Partners (189 top right); Courtesy Adams Kara Taylor (118 bottom right, 120 top); Peter Aaron/ESTO (123, 128 bottom, 129); Iwan Baan (115, 120 middle right and bottom right, 121 top right and bottom); Shigeru Ban/Courtesy Shigeru Ban Architects (218 top, middle and bottom right, 219 top left); James Bellamy/Courtesy Peter Rich Architects (165 bottom left, 166 bottom left); Johannes Bennke for and courtesy of David Chipperfield Architects (66 bottom left, 67 middle and bottom centre, 68 middle right, 70 top); Courtesy Bensonwood Homes (126 top left, bottom right); Courtesy BOMA (145); Didier Boy de la Tour (215, 223 bottom); Marcus Bredt (91, 97 middle right and bottom); Asa Bruno/Courtesy Ron Arad Associates (1, 195, 201 middle left and bottom right, 202 top and bottom right, 203); Asa Bruno and Daniel Charny/Courtesy Ron Arad Associates (196 top left and bottom); Richard Bryant/ARCAID (187, 193 top right, middle and bottom left); Stéphane Chalmeau (99, 104 bottom, 105); David Chipperfield (63 right); Andy Chopping (109 bottom left); Richard Davies (66 middle right); Javier de Paz/Courtesy Mi5 Arquitectos (149, 157 top right and bottom); Courtesy Design to Production (222 bottom right, 223 top right); Lyndon Douglas (81, 88 middle right and bottom, 89); Getty Images/Photographer's Choice Collection/Grant Faint (116 bottom left); Didier Ghislain/Courtesy Shigeru Ban Architects (219 left second, third and fourth down); Jan Guell/Courtesy Rogers Stirk Harbour + Partners (182 top right, left third down and centre third down, 184 top and bottom right); Grupo JG/Courtesy Rogers Stirk Harbour + Partners (181 left middle and bottom and bottom right); Roland Halbe (17, 24 bottom right, 25 top left and bottom right, 49 top left and bottom); Steve Hall/Hedrich Blessing (225, 231); Thomas Heatherwick's sketch (117 top right); Nick Herder/Courtesy of the Shorefast Foundation (211 bottom, 212, 213 top left); Courtesy Holzbau Amman (222 middle right and left third down, 223 top left); Eduard Hueber (35, 40 top, 41); Dean Kaufman (131, 136 bottom centre, 137); Katsuhisa Kida/Fototeca/Courtesy Rogers Stirk Harbour + Partners (185 top left); Katsuhisa Kida/Fototeca 185 (bottom left); Stephan Klonk/Courtesy gmp – von Gerkan, Marg and Partners Architects, Berlin (94 middle); Nikolas Koenig (132 bottom left); Johannes Kramer (68 top); Andrea Kroth (65 bottom left); Eric Laignel/Courtesy Agence JouinManku (25 top right, middle left and bottom left); La fotogràfica (147 bottom); John Edward Linden/ Courtesy Brooks Scarpa (169, 172 bottom left, 175 top right and bottom centre and right); Courtesy Mace (120 bottom centre top image); Macina/Courtesy gmp – von Gerkan, Marg and Partners Architects, Berlin (94 top and bottom); Roman Maerz/Courtesy David Chipperfield Architects (65 middle left, 66 top centre, 68 bottom left); Sanjit Manku/Courtesy Agence JouinManku (23, 24 top right, middle left and bottom left); Daniele Mattioli (119 top centre); Courtesy Will McLean and Pete Silver (222 top and left second down); Courtesy Mecanoo and labb arquitectura (144, 146 top and bottom right); Manos Meisen (51, 58 top left, and bottom, 59); Bjorn Moerman/Courtesy Asymptote (27, 32 middle right and bottom, 33); Moka Studio/Courtesy Behnisch Architeketen (44 middle left); Municipality of Holon/Courtesy Ron Arad Associates (202 middle left); Hubert Nienhoff/Courtesy gmp – von Gerkan, Marg and Partners Architects, Berlin (93 bottom left first sketch); Rik Nys for and courtesy of David Chipperfield Architects (71 bottom right); Obier Oberholzer (159); Courtesy Ostseestaal GmbH (48 top left); Amit Even Paz/Courtesy Ron Arad Associates (202 bottom left); Paul Raftery/VIEW (177, 185 bottom right); Michael Ramage (164 bottom left); Christian Richters (71 bottom left and middle right, 139, 143 middle, 146 bottom left and centre, 147 top); Courtesy SAS International (191 top); Todd Saunders (208 top right); Rainer Schlautmann (184 middle right); Johannes-Maria Schlorke (43, 47 top right, 48 top right, left second and forth down, 49 middle left, centre top, right top and middle); SMB/Zentralarchiv/Courtesy David Chipperfield Architects (63 left); Giacomo Sordi/Courtesy Ron Arad Associates (200 top right); Steve Speller (116 bottom right); Kristian Spencker/Courtesy gmp – von Gerkan, Marg and Partners Architects, Berlin (3, 93 bottom left bottom two sketches); Stiftung Preussischer Kulturbesitz/David Chipperfield Architects, photographer Ute Zscharnt (67 bottom right, 71 top centre and right); Hisao Suzuki (66 middle left); René Synnavåg/Courtesy Saunders Architecture (205, 213 top right and bottom); Neil Thomas/Courtesy Ron Arad Associates (199 top right); Courtesy Troika (121 top left and right second image down); Roberto Travaglia/Courtesy Ron Arad Associates (202 middle right); Wison Tungtanya/ Courtesy DBALP (73, 79 top right, middle and bottom); v-cube/Courtesy Benthem Crouwel Architekten (57 top); Allard van der Hoek (9, 15 middle and bottom); Philip Vile (107, 109 bottom centre and right, 110 top left, 113); Joerg von Bruchhausen (66 bottom right, 70 left, centre and right, second, third and forth rows down); Christoph von Oefele/Courtesy Baumschlager Eberle (38 bottom left, 39, 40 bottom); Morley von Sternberg (193 bottom right); Ute Zscharnt for and courtesy David Chipperfield Architects (61)